THE SEWING BOOK

THE SEWING BOOK

ALISON SMITH

London, New York, Melbourne,
Munich, and Delhi

PROJECT EDITOR
Norma MacMillan

PROJECT DESIGNERS
Viv Brar
Nicola Collings
Mandy Earey
Heather McCarry

PHOTOGRAPHY
Peter Anderson (Tools and Techniques)
Kate Whitaker (Projects)

For Dorling Kindersley

PROJECT EDITOR Ariane Durkin
PROJECT ART EDITOR Caroline de Souza
MANAGING EDITOR Dawn Henderson
MANAGING ART EDITOR Christine Keilty
SENIOR JACKET CREATIVE Nicola Powling
SENIOR PRE-PRODUCTION PRODUCER Jenny Woodcock
SENIOR PRODUCER Mandy Inness
CREATIVE TECHNICAL SUPPORT Sonia Charbonnier

2013 EDITION
JACKET DESIGN Vanessa Hamilton
SPECIAL SALES CREATIVE PROJECT MANAGER Alison Donovan
PRE-PRODUCTION PRODUCER Sarah Isle
PRODUCER Charlotte Oliver

First published in Great Britain in 2009
by Dorling Kindersley Limited
80 Strand, London WC2R 0RL

Penguin Group (UK)

Copyright © 2009, 2013 Dorling Kindersley Limited

2 4 6 8 10 9 7 5 3 1
001 – SD397 – Sept/13

A CIP catalogue record for this book
is available from the British Library.

ISBN 978 1 4093 4243 4

Colour reproduction by MDP, UK

Printed and bound in China
by South China Printing Co. Ltd.

Discover more at
www.dk.com

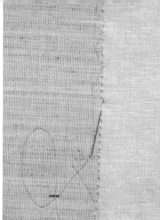

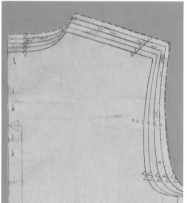

CONTENTS

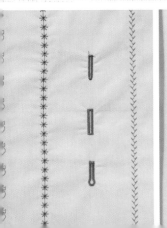

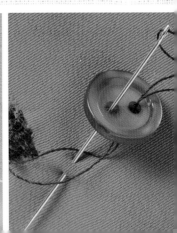

INTRODUCTION

The Sewing Book provides a comprehensive guide to all sewing techniques, whether it be for dressmaking, tailoring, crafts, or soft furnishings. If you are new to sewing, you'll find many tips to help and guide you; if you have been sewing for many years, there will be lots of new ideas to try. I also hope the book will be a valuable reference for all students studying textiles and fashion.

Having sewn since my teenage years and taught dressmaking and fashion for all my adult life, I am truly passionate about sewing. It can be so therapeutic – relaxing and satisfying. The ability to produce a unique item of clothing or something for your home is truly rewarding.

The book is divided into three sections. The first, Tools, covers all the equipment required to sew, including sewing machines; gives an up-to-date guide to fabrics – their properties, care, and how to sew them; and explains how to alter patterns to make clothes that fit you perfectly.

The next section is Techniques, with over 300 different sewing techniques to try, all in a step-by-step photographic format, covering everything from basic stitches and seams through to professional tailoring techniques. Each chapter begins with a visual directory of what the techniques are used for, be it types of pleats or pockets, necklines or sleeves, or buttonhole shapes.

The third section of the book is Projects, where you will find 18 items to make, ranging from quick and easy hats through to Roman blinds and kimonos. All the projects use techniques that appear in the second section of the book.

The final section includes an illustrated directory of fashion and soft furnishing styles, as well as a useful glossary of sewing terms.

Enjoy and happy sewing.

Alison Smith

ABOUT THIS BOOK

For the photographs, we have often used sewing threads of a contrast colour in order for the stitching to be visible. I recommend that you sew with a thread that matches your fabric as closely as possible.

All of the techniques and projects are graded according to difficulty, from * (simple and straightforward) to ***** (more complex and challenging).

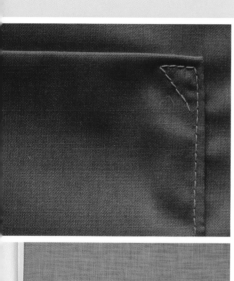

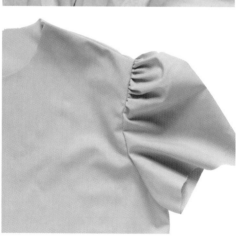

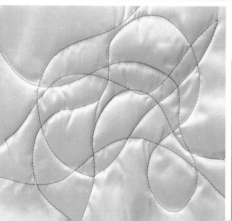

Always cut fabric on the straight grain unless the text instructs otherwise.

Seam allowances throughout are 1.5cm (⅝in) unless otherwise indicated.

On many of the fabric samples in the photographs, neatening of the seams is not shown because this can distract from the technique (seam neatening is only shown when it forms part of the technique). I recommend that you neaten your seams using your preferred technique.

Many of the techniques may vary from those given on your paper pattern, but you might like to try an alternative technique. There are many to choose from.

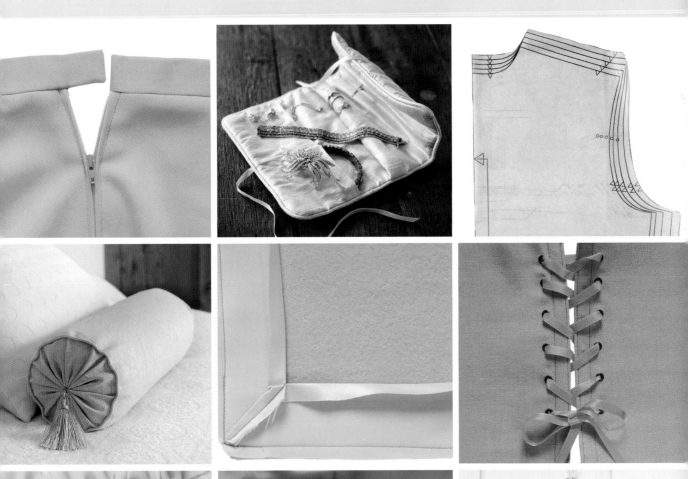

TOOLS

SEWING EQUIPMENT

The minimum equipment for any sewer is a tape measure, at least two pairs of scissors – one pair for cutting fabric and the other for trimming fabrics and threads – pins and needles, possibly a thimble, threads for sewing, a seam ripper, and a container to hold everything. An iron and ironing board will also be needed. There are, however, many other handy gadgets that are invaluable, and for the more enthusiastic sewer, a sewing machine and possibly an overlocker are essential. Whether you are a beginner to sewing or a sewer with many years of experience, some of the following pieces of equipment will no doubt find their way into your work box.

BASIC SEWING KIT

A well-equipped sewing kit will include all of the items shown below and many more, depending on the type of sewing that you do regularly. It is important that a suitable container is used to keep your tools together, so that they will be readily to hand, and to keep them tidy.

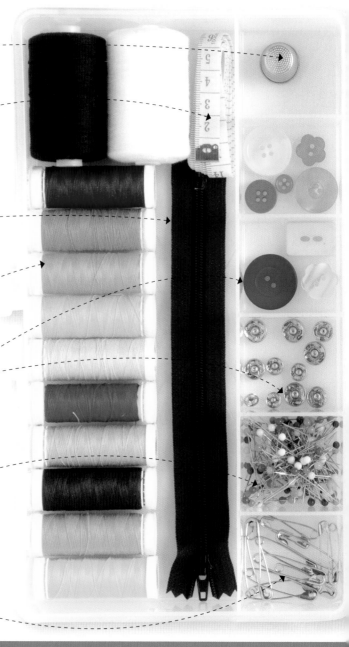

THIMBLE
This is useful to protect the end of your finger when hand sewing. Thimbles are available in various shapes and sizes. **See page 21.**

TAPE MEASURE
Essential, not only to take body measurements, but also to help measure fabric, seams, etc. Choose one that gives both metric and imperial. A tape made of plastic is best as it will not stretch. **See page 18.**

ZIPS
It is always a good idea to keep a couple of zips in your sewing kit. Black, cream, and navy are the most useful colours. **See pages 250–257.**

THREADS
A selection of threads for hand sewing and machine/overlocker sewing in a variety of colours. Some threads are made of polyester, while others are cotton or rayon. **See pages 24–25.**

HABERDASHERY
All the odds and ends a sewer needs, including everything from buttons and snaps to trimmings and elastic. A selection of buttons and snaps in your basic kit is useful for a quick repair. **See pages 26–27.**

PINS
Needed by every sewer to hold the fabric together prior to sewing it permanently. There are different types of pins for different types of work. **See page 23.**

SAFETY PINS
In a variety of sizes and useful for emergency repairs as well as threading elastics. **See page 23.**

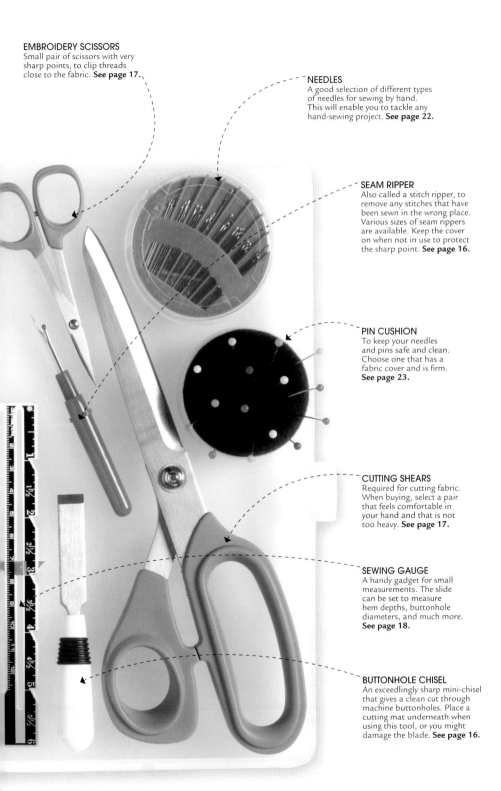

EMBROIDERY SCISSORS
Small pair of scissors with very sharp points, to clip threads close to the fabric. **See page 17.**

NEEDLES
A good selection of different types of needles for sewing by hand. This will enable you to tackle any hand-sewing project. **See page 22.**

SEAM RIPPER
Also called a stitch ripper, to remove any stitches that have been sewn in the wrong place. Various sizes of seam rippers are available. Keep the cover on when not in use to protect the sharp point. **See page 16.**

PIN CUSHION
To keep your needles and pins safe and clean. Choose one that has a fabric cover and is firm. **See page 23.**

CUTTING SHEARS
Required for cutting fabric. When buying, select a pair that feels comfortable in your hand and that is not too heavy. **See page 17.**

SEWING GAUGE
A handy gadget for small measurements. The slide can be set to measure hem depths, buttonhole diameters, and much more. **See page 18.**

BUTTONHOLE CHISEL
An exceedingly sharp mini-chisel that gives a clean cut through machine buttonholes. Place a cutting mat underneath when using this tool, or you might damage the blade. **See page 16.**

BUILD UP YOUR SEWING KIT

CUTTING TOOLS 16–17

BENT-HANDLED SHEARS
CUTTING MAT
PAPER SCISSORS
PINKING SHEARS
ROTARY CUTTER
SNIPS
TRIMMING SCISSORS

MEASURING TOOLS 18

FLEXIBLE RULER
GRIDDED RULER
OTHER TAPE MEASURES

MARKING AIDS 19

CHALK PENCIL
CHALK PROPELLING PENCIL
DRAFTING RULER
TAILOR'S CHALK
TRACING WHEEL AND
CARBON PAPER
WATER/AIR-SOLUBLE PEN

USEFUL EXTRAS 20–21

14-IN-1 MEASURE
AWL
BEESWAX
COLLAR POINT TURNER
DRESSMAKER'S DUMMY
EMERGENCY SEWING KIT
GLUE PEN
LIQUID SEALANT
LOOP TURNER
PATTERN PAPER
PLIERS
TAPE MAKER
TWEEZERS

NEEDLE THREADERS 22

PRESSING AIDS 28–29

CLAPPER
IRON
IRONING BOARD
MINI IRON
PRESSING CLOTH
PRESSING MAT
PRESSING MITTEN
SEAM ROLL
TAILOR'S HAM
VELVET MAT

CUTTING TOOLS

There are many types of cutting tools, but one rule applies to all: buy good-quality products that can be re-sharpened. When choosing cutting shears, make sure that they fit the span of your hand – this means that you can comfortably open the whole of the blade with one action, which is very important to allow clean and accurate cutting lines. Shears and scissors of various types are not the only cutting tools that are required, as everyone will at some time need a seam ripper to remove misplaced stitches or to unpick seams for mending. Rotary cutters that are used in conjunction with a special cutting mat and ruler are invaluable for cutting multiple straight edges.

◀ **SNIPS**
A very useful, small, spring-loaded tool that easily cuts the ends of thread. Not suitable for fabrics.

▼ **ROTARY CUTTER**
Available with different sizes of retractable blades. It must be used in conjunction with a special cutting mat to protect the blade and cutting surface.

▼ **BUTTONHOLE CHISEL**
A smaller version of a carpenter's chisel, to cut cleanly and accurately through buttonholes. As this is so sharp it must be used with a self-healing cutting mat.

▼ **CUTTING MAT**
A self-healing mat to use with the rotary cutter. This mat can also be used under the buttonhole chisel.

◀ **SEAM RIPPER**
A sharp, pointed hook to slide under a stitch, with a small cutting blade at the base to cut the thread. Various sizes of seam ripper are available, to cut through light to heavyweight fabric seams.

◀ **BENT-HANDLED SHEARS**
This type of shear has a blade that can sit flat against the table when cutting out, due to the angle between the blade and handle. Popular for cutting long, straight edges.

PINKING SHEARS ▶
Similar in size to cutting shears but with a blade that cuts with a zigzag pattern. Used for neatening seams and decorative edges.

▼ **CUTTING SHEARS**
The most popular type of shear, used for cutting large pieces of fabric. The length of the blade can vary from 20–30cm (8–12in) in length.

▼ **EMBROIDERY SCISSORS**
A small and very sharp scissor used to get into corners and clip threads close to the fabric.

▲ **TRIMMING SCISSORS**
These scissors have a 10cm (4in) blade and are used to trim away surplus fabric and neaten ends of machining.

◀ **PAPER SCISSORS**
Use these to cut around pattern pieces – cutting paper will dull blades of fabric scissors and shears.

MEASURING TOOLS AND MARKING AIDS

A huge range of tools enables a sewer to measure accurately. Choosing the correct tool for the task in hand is important, so that your measurements are precise. The next step is to mark your work using the appropriate marking technique or tool. Some tools are very specific to one job while others are specific to types of sewing.

Measuring tools

There are many tools available to help you measure everything from the width of a seam or hem, to body dimensions, to the area of a window. One of the most basic yet invaluable measuring tools is the tape measure. Be sure to keep yours in good condition – once it stretches or gets snipped on the edges, it will no longer be accurate and should be replaced.

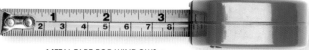

METAL TAPE FOR WINDOWS ▲
A metal tape that can be secured when extended is used to measure windows and soft furnishings.

EXTRA-LONG TAPE ▲
This is usually twice the length of a normal tape measure, at 300cm (10ft) long. Use it when making soft furnishings. It's also useful to help measure the length of bridal trains.

SEWING GAUGE ▲
A handy small tool about 15cm (6in) long, marked in centimetres and inches, with a sliding tab. Use as an accurate measure for small measurements such as hems.

RETRACTABLE TAPE ▶
Very useful to have in your handbag when shopping as you never know when you may need to measure something!

TAPE MEASURE ▲
Available in various colours and widths. Try to choose one that is the same width as standard seam allowance (1.5cm/⅝in), because it will prove exceedingly useful.

FLEXIBLE RULER ▲
A sturdy, bendy piece of plastic, this is perfect to measure armholes or curved shapes. The flexible ruler is also used when altering patterns.

GRIDDED RULER ▶
This type of ruler is larger than a normal ruler and is marked with a centimetre or inch grid. Used in conjunction with the rotary cutter and mat, and also for marking bias strips.

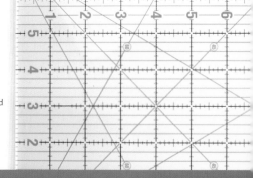

Marking aids

Marking certain parts of your work is essential, to make sure that things like pockets and darts are placed correctly and seamlines are straight as drawn on the pattern. With some marking tools, such as pens and a tracing wheel and carbon paper, it is always a good idea to test on a scrap of fabric first to make sure that the mark made will not be permanent.

▼ CHALK PROPELLING PENCIL
Chalk leads of different colours can be inserted into this propelling pencil, making it a very versatile marking tool. The leads can be sharpened.

DRAFTING RULER ▲
A plastic curved tool, also called a pattern marking ruler, used primarily when drafting or altering patterns.

◄ WATER/AIR-SOLUBLE PEN
This resembles a felt marker pen. Marks made can be removed from the fabric with either a spray of water or by leaving to air-dry. Be careful – if you press over the marks, they may become permanent.

TRACING WHEEL AND CARBON PAPER ▶
These two items are used together to transfer markings from a paper pattern or a design on to fabric. Not suitable for all types of fabric though, as marks may not be able to be removed easily.

▲ TAILOR'S CHALK
Also known as French chalk, this solid piece of chalk in either a square or triangular shape is available in a large variety of colours. The chalk easily brushes off fabric.

▲ CHALK PENCIL
Available in blue, pink, and white. As it can be sharpened like a normal pencil, it will draw accurate lines on fabric.

USEFUL EXTRAS

There are many more accessories that can be purchased to help with your sewing, and knowing which products to choose and for which job can be daunting. The tools shown here can be useful aids, although it depends on the type of sewing that you do – dressmaking, craft work, making soft furnishings, or running repairs – as to whether you would need all of them in your sewing kit.

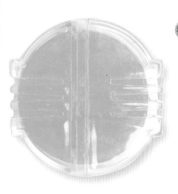

◄ **BEESWAX**
When hand sewing, this will prevent the thread from tangling, and will strengthen it. First draw the thread through the wax, then press the wax into the thread by running your fingers along it.

▲ **AWL**
This sharp tool is used to make holes in fabric for eyelet insertion or for the rounded end of a keyhole buttonhole.

◄ **TAPE MAKER**
Available in 12, 18, and 25mm (½, ¾, and 1in) widths, this tool evenly folds the edges of a fabric strip, which can then be pressed to make binding.

▼ **TWEEZERS**
These can be used for removing stubborn tacking stitches that have become caught in the machine stitching. An essential aid to threading the overlocker.

LOOP TURNER ►
A thin metal rod with a latch at the end. Use to turn narrow fabric tubes or to thread ribbons through a slotted lace.

LIQUID SEALANT ►
Used to seal the cut edge of ribbons and trims to prevent fraying. Also useful to seal the ends of overlock stitching.

▼ **EMERGENCY SEWING KIT**
All the absolute essentials to fix loose buttons or dropped hems while away from your sewing machine. Take it with you when travelling.

GLUE PEN ►
Similar to a glue pen for paper, this will hold fabric or trims temporarily in place until they can be secured with stitches. It will not damage the fabric or make the sewing needle sticky.

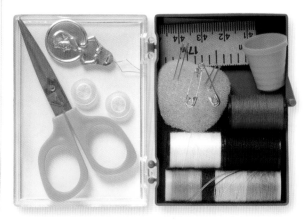

COLLAR POINT TURNER ▶
This is excellent for pushing out those hard-to-reach corners in collars and cuffs.

THIMBLE ▼
An essential item for many sewers, to protect the middle finger from the end of the needle. Choose a thimble that fits your finger comfortably as there are many varieties to choose from.

▲ PLIERS
Specially designed pliers with various heads are used to attach eyelets, metal snaps, and rivets.

◀ 14-IN-1 MEASURE
A strange-looking tool that has 14 different measurements on it. Use to turn hems or edges accurately. Available in both metric and imperial.

DRESSMAKER'S DUMMY ▲
An adjustable form that is useful when fitting garments as it can be adjusted to personal body measurements. Excellent to help in the turning up of hemlines. Available in female, male, and children's shapes and sizes.

PATTERN PAPER ▶
This can be plain or printed with dots and crosses at regular intervals. The paper can be used for drafting patterns, or for altering or tracing patterns.

NEEDLES AND PINS

Using the correct pin or needle for your work is so important, as the wrong choice can damage fabric or leave small holes. Needles are made from steel and pins from steel or occasionally brass. Look after them by keeping pins in a pin cushion and needles in a needle case – if kept together in a small container they could become scratched and blunt.

Needles and threaders

Needles are available for all types of fabrics and projects. A good selection of needles should be to hand at all times, whether it be for emergency mending of tears, or sewing on buttons, or adding trimmings to special-occasion wear. With a special needle threader, inserting the thread through the eye of the needle is simplicity itself.

SHARPS
A general-purpose hand-sewing needle, with a small, round eye. Available in sizes 1 to 12. For most hand sewing use a size 6 to 9.

CREWEL
Also known as an embroidery needle, a long needle with a long, oval eye that is designed to take multiple strands of embroidery thread.

MILLINER'S OR STRAW
A very long, thin needle with a small, round eye. Good for hand sewing and tacking as it doesn't damage fabric. A size 8 or 9 is most popular.

BETWEENS OR QUILTING
Similar to a milliner's needle but very short, with a small, round eye. Perfect for fine hand stitches and favoured by quilters.

BEADING
Long and exceedingly fine, to sew beads and sequins to fabric. As it is prone to bending, keep it wrapped in tissue when not in use.

DARNER'S
A long, thick needle that is designed to be used with wool or thick yarns and to sew through multiple layers.

TAPESTRY
A medium-length, thick needle with a blunt end and a long eye. For use with wool yarn in tapestry. Also for darning in overlock threads.

CHENILLE
This looks like a tapestry needle but it has a sharp point. Use with thick or wool yarns for darning or heavy embroidery.

BODKIN
A strange-looking needle with a blunt end and a large, fat eye. Use to thread elastic or cord. There are larger eyes for thicker yarns.

SELF-THREADING NEEDLE
A needle that has a double eye. The thread is placed in the upper eye through the gap, then pulled into the eye below for sewing.

WIRE NEEDLE THREADER
A handy gadget, especially useful for needles with small eyes. Also helpful in threading sewing-machine needles.

AUTOMATIC NEEDLE THREADER
This threader is operated with a small lever. The needle, eye down, is inserted and the thread is wrapped around.

Pins

There is a wide variety of pins available, in differing lengths and thicknesses, and ranging from plain household pins to those with coloured balls or flower shapes on their ends.

HOUSEHOLD
General-purpose pins of a medium length and thickness. Can be used for all types of sewing.

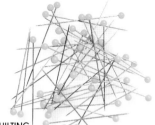

QUILTING
A long pin of medium thickness, designed to hold multiple layers of fabric together.

PEARL-HEADED
Longer than household pins, with a coloured pearl head. They are easy to pick up and use.

LACE OR BRIDAL
A fine, short pin designed to be used with fine fabrics, such as those for bridal gowns, because the pin will not damage the fabric.

FLOWERHEAD
A long pin of medium thickness with a flat, flower-shaped head. It is designed to be pressed over, as the head lays flat on the fabric.

EXTRA FINE
Extra long and extra fine, this pin is favoured by many professional dressmakers, because it is easy to use and doesn't damage finer fabrics.

GLASS-HEADED
Similar to pearl-headed pins but shorter. They have the advantage that they can be pressed over without melting.

DRESSMAKER'S
Similar to a household pin in shape and thickness, but slightly longer. These are the pins for beginners to choose.

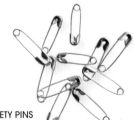

SAFETY PINS
Available in a huge variety of sizes and made either of brass or stainless steel. Used for holding two or more layers together.

STAPLE
A strong pin that looks like a very large staple, used for pinning loose covers to furniture. Take care as staple pins are very sharp.

SPIRAL
Shaped like a spiral with a very sharp point at one end to enable it to be twisted in and out easily. Used to secure loose covers to furniture.

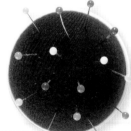

PIN CUSHION
To keep pins clean and sharp. Choose a fabric cover: a foam cushion may blunt pins.

THREADS

There are so many threads available and knowing which ones to choose can be confusing. There are specialist threads designed for special tasks, such as machine embroidery or quilting. Threads also vary in fibre content, from pure cotton to rayon to polyester. Some threads are very fine while others are thick and coarse. Failure to choose the correct thread can spoil your project and lead to problems with the stitch quality of the sewing machine or overlocker.

COTTON THREAD
A 100% cotton thread. Smooth and firm, this is designed to be used with cotton fabrics and is much favoured by quilters.

POLYESTER ALL-PURPOSE THREAD
A good-quality polyester thread that has a very slight "give", making it suitable to sew all types of fabrics and garments, as well as soft furnishings. The most popular type of thread.

SILK THREAD
A sewing thread made from 100% silk. Used for machining delicate silk garments. It is also used for tacking or temporary stitching in areas that are to be pressed, such as jacket collars, because it can be removed without leaving an imprint.

TOP-STITCHING THREAD
A thicker polyester thread used for decorative top-stitching and buttonholes. Also for hand sewing buttons on thicker fabrics and some soft furnishings.

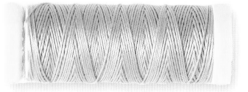

ELASTIC THREAD
A thin, round elastic thread normally used on the bobbin of the sewing machine for stretch effects such as shirring.

OVERLOCKER THREAD
A dull yarn on a larger reel designed to be used on the overlocker. This type of yarn is normally not strong enough to use on the sewing machine.

METALLIC THREAD
A rayon and metal thread for decorative machining and machine embroidery. This thread usually requires a specialist sewing-machine needle.

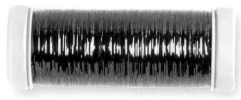

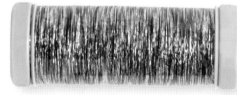

EMBROIDERY THREAD
Often made from a rayon yarn for shine. This is a finer thread designed for machine embroidery. Available on much larger reels for economy.

HABERDASHERY ITEMS

The term haberdashery covers all of the bits and pieces that a sewer tends to need, for example fasteners such as buttons, snaps, hooks and eyes, and Velcro™. But haberdashery also includes elastics, ribbons, trimmings of all types, and boning.

Buttons

Buttons can be made from almost anything – shell, bone, coconut, nylon, plastic, brass, silver. They can be any shape, from geometric to abstract to animal shapes. A button may have a shank or have holes on the surface to enable it to be attached to fabric.

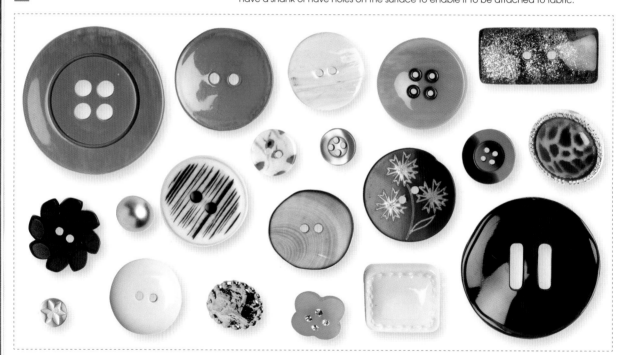

Other fasteners

Hooks and eyes (below left), snaps (below centre), and Velcro™ (below right) all come in a wide variety of forms, differing in size, shape, and colour. Some hooks and eyes are designed to be seen, while snaps and Velcro™ are intended to be hidden fasteners.

Trimmings, decorations, fringes, and braids

Decorative finishing touches – fringes, strips of sequins, ric-rac braids, feathers, pearls, bows, flowers, and beads – can dress up a garment, embellish a bag, or personalize soft furnishings. Some are designed to be inserted into seams while others are surface-mounted.

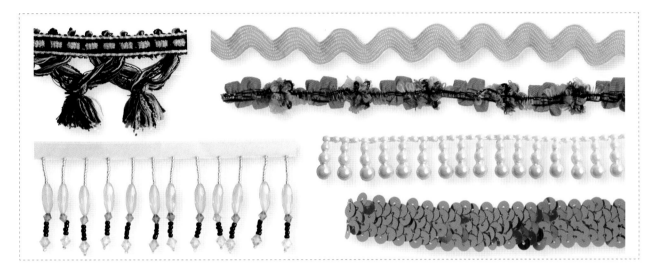

Ribbons

From the narrowest strips to wide swathes, ribbons are made from a variety of yarns, such as nylon, polyester, and cotton. They can be printed or plain and may feature metallic threads or wired edges.

Elastic

Elastic is available in many forms, from very narrow, round cord to wide strips (below left). It may have buttonhole slots in it (below right) or even have a decorative edge.

Boning

You can buy various types of boning in varying widths. Polyester boning (bottom left), used in boned bodices, can be sewn through, while nylon boning (bottom right), also used on boned bodices, has to be inserted into a casing. Specialist metal boning (below left and right), which may be either straight or spiral, is for corsets and bridal wear.

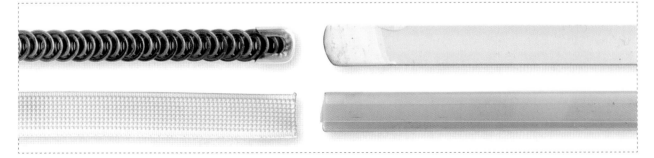

PRESSING AIDS

Successful sewing relies on successful pressing. Without the correct pressing equipment, sewing can look too "home-made", whereas if correctly pressed any sewn item will have a neat, professional finish.

MINI IRON ▶
Useful to get into small corners and gathers. Use in conjunction with the pressing mat.

IRON ▲
A good-quality steam iron is a wonderful asset. Choose a reasonably heavy iron that has steam and a shot of steam facility.

◀ PRESSING MAT
A heat-resistant mat for pressing small items.

◀ TAILOR'S HAM
A ham-shaped pressing cushion that is used to press darts and the shape into curves of collars and shoulders, and in making tailored garments.

▲ SEAM ROLL
This tubular pressing aid is used to press seams open on fabrics that mark, as the iron only touches the seam on top of the roll. Also used for sleeve and trouser seams.

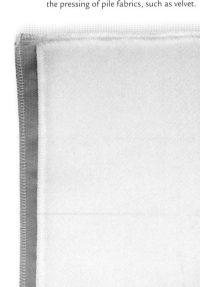

▲ CLAPPER
A wooden aid that pounds creases into a heavy fabric after steaming. The top section is used to help press collar seams and points.

PRESSING CLOTH ▶
Choose a cloth made from silk organza or muslin as you can see through it. The cloth will stop the iron marking fabric and prevent burning delicate fabrics.

▼ VELVET MAT
A pressing mat with a tufted side to aid the pressing of pile fabrics, such as velvet.

▲ IRONING BOARD
Essential to iron on. Make sure the board is height-adjustable.

PRESSING MITTEN ▶
Slips on to your hand to enable more control over where you are pressing.

SEWING MACHINE

A sewing machine will quickly speed up any job, whether it be a quick repair or a huge home-sewing project. Most sewing machines today are aided by computer technology, which enhances stitch quality and ease of use. Always spend time trying out a sewing machine before you buy, to really get a feel for it.

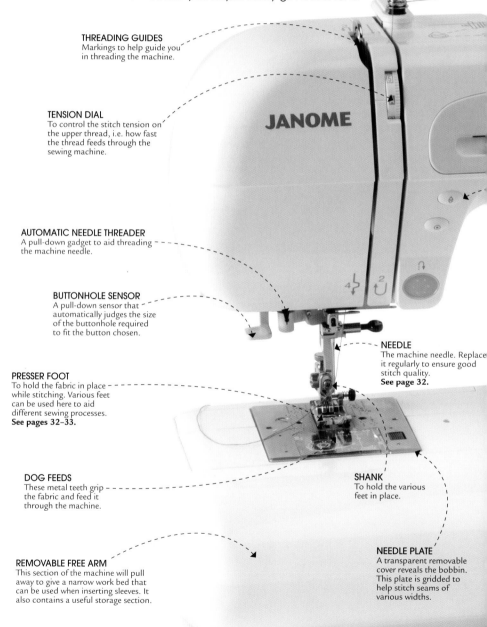

THREADING GUIDES
Markings to help guide you in threading the machine.

TENSION DIAL
To control the stitch tension on the upper thread, i.e. how fast the thread feeds through the sewing machine.

AUTOMATIC NEEDLE THREADER
A pull-down gadget to aid threading the machine needle.

BUTTONHOLE SENSOR
A pull-down sensor that automatically judges the size of the buttonhole required to fit the button chosen.

PRESSER FOOT
To hold the fabric in place while stitching. Various feet can be used here to aid different sewing processes.
See pages 32–33.

DOG FEEDS
These metal teeth grip the fabric and feed it through the machine.

REMOVABLE FREE ARM
This section of the machine will pull away to give a narrow work bed that can be used when inserting sleeves. It also contains a useful storage section.

JANOME

NEEDLE
The machine needle. Replace it regularly to ensure good stitch quality.
See page 32.

SHANK
To hold the various feet in place.

NEEDLE PLATE
A transparent removable cover reveals the bobbin. This plate is gridded to help stitch seams of various widths.

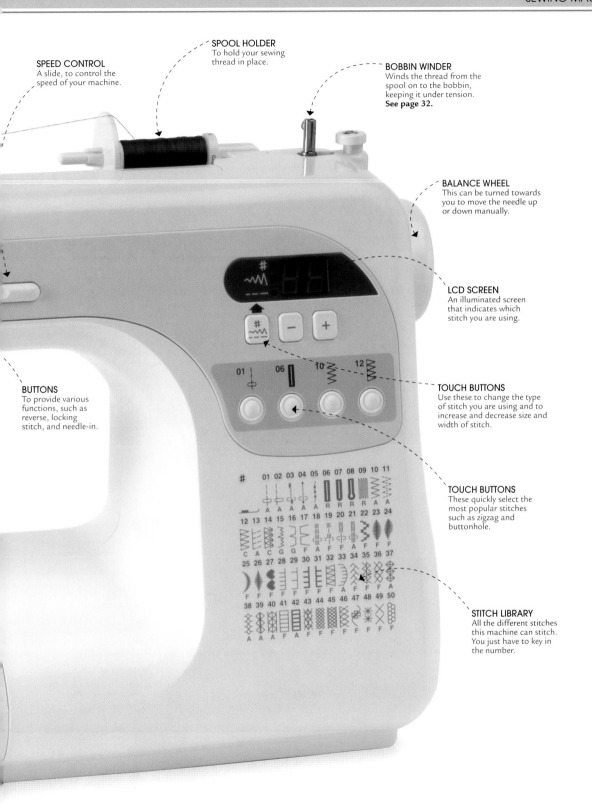

SPEED CONTROL
A slide, to control the speed of your machine.

SPOOL HOLDER
To hold your sewing thread in place.

BOBBIN WINDER
Winds the thread from the spool on to the bobbin, keeping it under tension. **See page 32.**

BALANCE WHEEL
This can be turned towards you to move the needle up or down manually.

LCD SCREEN
An illuminated screen that indicates which stitch you are using.

BUTTONS
To provide various functions, such as reverse, locking stitch, and needle-in.

TOUCH BUTTONS
Use these to change the type of stitch you are using and to increase and decrease size and width of stitch.

TOUCH BUTTONS
These quickly select the most popular stitches such as zigzag and buttonhole.

STITCH LIBRARY
All the different stitches this machine can stitch. You just have to key in the number.

Sewing-machine accessories

Many accessories can be purchased for your sewing machine to make certain sewing processes so much easier. There are different machine needles not only for different fabrics but also for different types of threads. There is also a huge number of sewing-machine feet, and new feet are constantly coming on to the market. Those shown here are some of the most popular.

PLASTIC BOBBIN
The bobbin is for the lower thread. Some machines take plastic bobbins, others metal. Always check which sort of bobbin your machine uses as the incorrect choice can cause stitch problems.

METAL BOBBIN
Also known as a universal bobbin, this is used on many types of sewing machine. Be sure to check that your machine needs a metal bobbin before you buy.

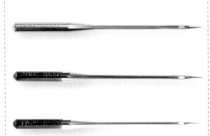

MACHINE NEEDLES
There are different types of sewing machine needle to cope with different fabrics. Machine needles are sized from 60 to 100, a 60 being a very fine needle. There are special needles for machine embroidery and also for metallic threads.

OVEREDGE FOOT
A foot that runs along the raw edge of the fabric and holds it stable while an overedge stitch is worked.

EMBROIDERY FOOT
A clear plastic foot with a groove underneath that allows linear machine embroidery stitches to pass under.

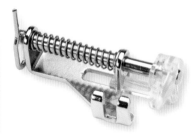

FREE EMBROIDERY OR DARNING FOOT
A foot designed to be used when the dog feeds on the machine are lowered. This enables a free motion stitch to be worked.

BUTTONHOLE FOOT
This extends and the button is placed in the back of the foot. The machine will stitch a buttonhole to fit due to the buttonhole sensor.

BLIND HEM FOOT
Use this foot in conjunction with the blind hem stitch to create a neat hemming stitch.

ROLLED HEM FOOT
This foot rolls the fabric while stitching with a straight stitch or a zigzag stitch.

WALKING FOOT
This strange-looking foot "walks" across the fabric, so that the upper layer of fabric does not push forward. Great for matching checks and stripes and also for difficult fabrics.

ZIP FOOT
This foot fits to either the right or left-hand side of the needle to enable you to stitch close to a zip.

CONCEALED ZIP FOOT
A foot that is used to insert a concealed zip – the foot holds open the coils of the zip, enabling you to stitch behind them.

PIN TUCK FOOT
A foot with grooves underneath to allow multiple pin tucks to be sewn.

PIPING FOOT
A deep groove in this foot allows a piping cord to fit underneath, enabling close stitching to the cord.

RIBBON FOOT
A foot that will feed either one or two ribbons evenly under the machine needle to ensure accurate stitching.

BEADING FOOT, NARROW
This foot has a narrow groove and is used to attach small beads or decorative cords.

BEADING FOOT, WIDE
Beads on a string will fit under the foot, which has a wide groove, and they can then be zigzag stitched over.

ULTRA-GLIDE FOOT
A foot made from Teflon™ that glides over the fabric. Useful for synthetic leathers.

OVERLOCKER

This machine is often used in conjunction with the sewing machine as it gives a very professional finish to your work. The overlocker has two upper threads and two lower threads (the loopers), with a knife that removes the edge of the fabric. Used extensively for neatening the edges of fabric, it can also be used for construction of stretch knits.

OVERLOCKER STITCHES

As the overlocker works, the threads wrap around the edge to give a professional finish. The 3-thread stitch is used primarily for neatening. A 4-thread stitch can also be used for neatening, as well as for construction due to its having the extra thread.

3-THREAD OVERLOCK STITCH

4-THREAD OVERLOCK STITCH

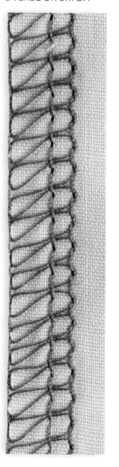

Overlocker accessories

You can purchase additional feet for the overlocker. Some will speed up your sewing by performing tasks such as gathering.

OVERLOCKER NEEDLES
The overlocker uses a ballpoint needle, which creates a large loop in the thread for the loopers to catch and produce a stitch. If a normal sewing machine needle is used it could damage the overlocker.

OVERLOCKER FOOT
The standard foot used for most processes.

GATHERING FOOT
This gadget enables one layer of fabric to be gathered and stitched to a non-gathered layer, all in one application. Especially suitable for net and fine fabrics.

CORDING FOOT
A foot with a coil on the one side through which a thin cord or fishing line is fed. Use in conjunction with a rolled hem setting for decorative effects.

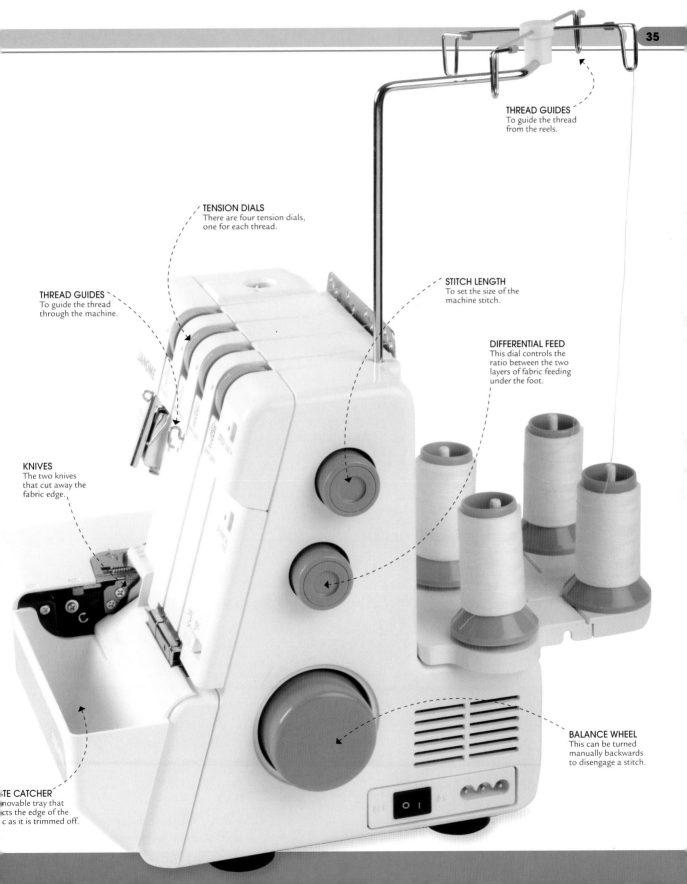

THREAD GUIDES
To guide the thread
from the reels.

TENSION DIALS
There are four tension dials,
one for each thread.

STITCH LENGTH
To set the size of the
machine stitch.

THREAD GUIDES
To guide the thread
through the machine.

DIFFERENTIAL FEED
This dial controls the
ratio between the two
layers of fabric feeding
under the foot.

KNIVES
The two knives
that cut away the
fabric edge.

BALANCE WHEEL
This can be turned
manually backwards
to disengage a stitch.

TE CATCHER
novable tray that
cts the edge of the
c as it is trimmed off.

EMBROIDERY MACHINE

A machine that does not sew but embroiders, th[is] enables you to produce embellished clothing or home wares. Computer-controlled, the machine has plenty of built-in embroidery designs and the[re] are many more designs that can be purchased t[o] use with it. The machine works best with special embroidery threads and bobbin threads.

EMBROIDERY DESIGNS

Here are some examples of the many types of design that can be stitched out, to personalize and embellish clothing and accessories as well as place mats, tablecloths, serviettes, baby blankets, pillows, and many other items.

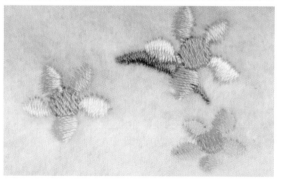

Embroidery machine accessories

Hoops of varying shapes and sizes fit on to the machine carriage to enable the embroidery to be stitched.

A gridded template on the bottom of the embroidery hoop aids placement of the design.

Once the fabric is stretched in the hoop, the ring is pressed down and secured. The fabric must be held taut.

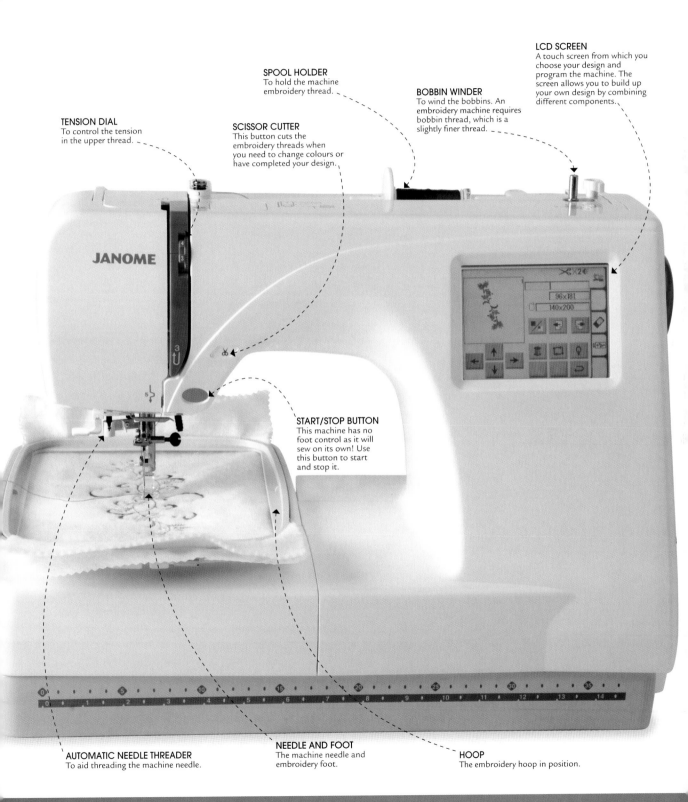

LCD SCREEN
A touch screen from which you choose your design and program the machine. The screen allows you to build up your own design by combining different components.

SPOOL HOLDER
To hold the machine embroidery thread.

BOBBIN WINDER
To wind the bobbins. An embroidery machine requires bobbin thread, which is a slightly finer thread.

TENSION DIAL
To control the tension in the upper thread.

SCISSOR CUTTER
This button cuts the embroidery threads when you need to change colours or have completed your design.

START/STOP BUTTON
This machine has no foot control as it will sew on its own! Use this button to start and stop it.

AUTOMATIC NEEDLE THREADER
To aid threading the machine needle.

NEEDLE AND FOOT
The machine needle and embroidery foot.

HOOP
The embroidery hoop in position.

FABRICS

Fabric is made from fibres. Each fibre is like a small hair. A great number are twisted together to make a yarn, which can then be woven or knitted into fabric. Whether making clothes, soft furnishings, or crafts, it's important to choose the right fabric for your project. When buying, look at the fabric carefully in the store. Feel it, and crease it in your hand. Then ask yourself if it will be suitable. You also need to consider the width of the fabric, the cost, and the care – some have to be dry-cleaned.

TOOLS

Wool fabrics

A natural fibre, wool comes primarily from sheep – Australian merino sheep's wool is considered to be the best. However, we also get wool fibres from goats (mohair and cashmere), rabbits (angora), camels (camel hair), and llamas (alpaca). A wool fibre is either short and fluffy, when it is known as a woollen yarn, or it is long, strong, and smooth, when it is called worsted. The term virgin (or new) wool denotes wool fibres that are being used for the first time. Wool may be reprocessed or reused and is then often mixed with other fibres.

PROPERTIES OF WOOL

- comfortable to wear in all climates as it is available in many weights and weaves
- warm in the winter and cool in the summer, because it will breathe with your body
- absorbs moisture better than other natural fibres – will absorb up to 30 per cent of its weight before it feels wet
- flame-resistant

- relatively crease-resistant
- ideal to tailor as it can be easily shaped with steam
- often blended with other fibres to reduce the cost of fabric
- felts if exposed to excessive heat, moisture, and pressure
- will be bleached by sunlight with prolonged exposure
- can be damaged by moths

CASHMERE
Wool from the Kashmir goat, and the most luxurious of all the wools. A soft yet hard-wearing fabric available in different weights.

Cutting out: as cashmere often has a slight pile, use a nap layout

Seams: plain, neatened with overlocker stitch or pinking shears (a zigzag stitch would curl the edge of the seam)

Thread: a silk thread is ideal, or a polyester all-purpose thread

Needle: machine size 12/14, depending on the thickness of the fabric; sharps for hand sewing

Pressing: steam iron on a steam setting, with a pressing cloth and seam roll

Use for: jackets, coats, men's wear; knitted cashmere yarn for sweaters, cardigans, underwear

CHALLIS
A fine wool fabric, made from a worsted yarn that has an uneven surface texture. Challis is often printed as well as plain.

Cutting out: a nap layout is not required unless the fabric is printed

Seams: plain, neatened with overlocker or zigzag stitch; a run and fell seam can also be used

Thread: polyester all-purpose thread

Needle: machine size 11/12; sharps for hand sewing

Pressing: steam iron on a steam setting, with a pressing cloth; fabric will stretch while warm so handle with care

Use for: dresses, jackets, garments with pleating or draping detail

CREPE
A soft fabric made from a twisted yarn, which is what produces the uneven surface. It is important to preshrink this fabric prior to use by giving it a good steaming, because it will have stretched on the bolt and it is prone to shrinkage.

Cutting out: a nap layout is not required

Seams: plain, neatened with overlocker (a zigzag stitch may curl the edge of the seam)

Thread: polyester all-purpose thread

Needle: machine size 12; sharps or milliner's for hand sewing

Pressing: steam iron on a wool setting; a pressing cloth is not always required

Use for: all types of clothing

≪≪ Needles and pins pp22–23 Threads pp24–25 Pressing aids pp28–29

FLANNEL

A wool with a lightly brushed surface, featuring either a plain or twill weave. Used in the past for underwear.

Cutting out: use a nap layout

Seams: plain, neatened with overlocker or zigzag stitch or Hong Kong finish

Thread: polyester all-purpose thread

Needle: machine size 14; sharps for hand sewing

Pressing: steam iron on a wool setting with a pressing cloth; use a seam roll as the fabric is prone to marking

Use for: coats, jackets, skirts, men's wear

GABARDINE

A hard-wearing suiting fabric with a distinctive weave. Gabardine often has a sheen and is prone to shine. It can be difficult to handle as it is springy and frays badly.

Cutting out: a nap layout is advisable as the fabric has a sheen

Seams: plain, neatened with overlocker or zigzag stitch

Thread: polyester all-purpose thread or 100% cotton thread

Needle: machine size 14; sharps for hand sewing

Pressing: steam iron on a wool setting; use just the toe of the iron and a silk organza pressing cloth as the fabric will mark and may shine

Use for: men's wear, jackets, trousers

MOHAIR

From the wool of the Angora goat. A long, straight, and very strong fibre that produces a hairy cloth or yarn for knitting.

Cutting out: use a nap layout, with the fibres brushing down the pattern pieces in the same direction, from neck to hem

Seams: plain, neatened with overlocker or pinking shears

Thread: polyester all-purpose thread

Needle: machine size 14; sharps for hand sewing

Pressing: steam iron on a wool setting; "stroke" the iron over the wool, moving in the direction of the nap

Use for: jackets, coats, men's wear, soft furnishings; knitted mohair yarns for sweaters

TARTAN

An authentic tartan belongs to a Scottish clan, and each has its own unique design that can only be used by that clan. The fabric is made using a twill weave from worsted yarns.

Cutting out: check the design for even/uneven check as it may need a nap layout or even a single layer layout

Seams: plain, matching the pattern and neatened with overlocker or zigzag stitch

Thread: polyester all-purpose thread

Needle: machine size 14; sharps for hand sewing

Pressing: steam iron on a wool setting; may require a pressing cloth, so test first

Use for: traditionally kilts, but these days also skirts, trousers, jackets, soft furnishings

TWEED, MODERN

A mix of chunky and nobbly wool yarns. Modern tweed is often found in contemporary colour palettes as well as plain, and with interesting fibres in the weft such as metallics and paper. It is much favoured by fashion designers.

Cutting out: use a nap layout

Seams: plain, neatened with overlocker or zigzag stitch; the fabric is prone to fraying

Thread: polyester all-purpose thread

Needle: machine size 14; sharps for hand sewing

Pressing: steam iron on a wool setting; a pressing cloth may not be required

Use for: jackets, coats; also skirts, dresses, soft furnishings

TWEED, TRADITIONAL

A rough fabric with a distinctive warp and weft, usually in different colours, and often forming a small check pattern. Traditional tweed is associated with the English countryside.

Cutting out: a nap layout is not required unless the fabric features a check

Seams: plain, neatened with overlocker or zigzag stitch; can also be neatened with pinking shears

Thread: polyester all-purpose thread or 100% cotton thread

Needle: machine size 14; sharps for hand sewing

Pressing: steam iron on a steam setting; a pressing cloth may not be required

Use for: jackets, coats, skirts, men's wear, soft furnishings

VENETIAN

A wool with a satin weave, making a luxurious, expensive fabric.

Cutting out: use a nap layout

Seams: plain, neatened with overlocker or zigzag stitch

Thread: polyester all-purpose thread or 100% cotton thread

Needle: machine size 14; sharps for hand sewing

Pressing: steam iron on a steam setting with a silk organza cloth to avoid shine; use a seam roll under the seams to prevent them from showing through

Use for: jackets, coats, men's wear

WOOL WORSTED

A light and strong cloth, made from good-quality thin, firm filament fibres. Always steam prior to cutting out as the fabric may shrink slightly after having been stretched around a bolt.

Cutting out: use a nap layout

Seams: plain, neatened with overlocker or zigzag stitch or Hong Kong finish

Thread: polyester all-purpose thread

Needle: machine size 12/14, depending on fabric; milliner's or sharps for hand sewing

Pressing: steam iron on a wool setting, with a pressing cloth; use a seam roll to prevent the seam from showing through

Use for: skirts, jackets, coats, trousers

Cotton fabrics

One of the most versatile and popular of all fabrics, cotton is a natural fibre that comes from the seed pods, or bolls, of the cotton plant. It is thought that cotton fibres have been in use since ancient times. Today, the world's biggest producers of cotton include the United States, India, and countries in the Middle East. Cotton fibres can be filament or staple, with the longest and finest used for top-quality bed linen. Cotton clothing is widely worn in warmer climates as the fabric will keep you cool.

PROPERTIES OF COTTON

- absorbs moisture well and carries heat away from the body
- stronger wet than dry
- does not build up static electricity
- dyes well

- prone to shrinkage unless it has been treated
- will deteriorate from mildew and prolonged exposure to sunlight
- creases easily
- soils easily, but launders well

BRODERIE ANGLAISE
A fine, plain-weave cotton that has been embroidered in such a way as to make small holes. Usually white or a pastel colour.

Cutting out: may need layout to place embroidery at hem edge

Seams: plain, neatened with overlocker or zigzag stitch; a French seam can also be used

Thread: polyester all-purpose thread

Needle: machine size 12/14; sharps for hand sewing

Pressing: steam iron on a cotton setting; a pressing cloth is not required

Use for: baby clothes, summer skirts, blouses

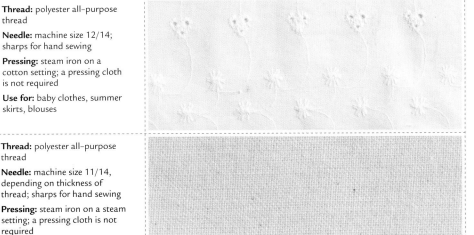

CALICO
A plain weave fabric that is usually unbleached and quite stiff. Available in many different weights, from very fine to extremely heavy.

Cutting out: a nap layout is not required

Seams: plain, neatened with overlocker or zigzag stitch

Thread: polyester all-purpose thread

Needle: machine size 11/14, depending on thickness of thread; sharps for hand sewing

Pressing: steam iron on a steam setting; a pressing cloth is not required

Use for: toiles (test garments), soft furnishings

CHAMBRAY
A light cotton that has a coloured warp thread and white weft thread. Chambray can also be found as a check or a striped fabric.

Cutting out: a nap layout should not be required

Seams: plain, neatened with overlocker or zigzag stitch

Thread: polyester all-purpose thread

Needle: machine size 11; sharps for hand sewing

Pressing: steam iron on a cotton setting; a pressing cloth is not required

Use for: blouses, men's shirts, children's wear

CHINTZ
A floral print or plain cotton fabric with a glazed finish that gives it a sheen. It has a close weave and is often treated to resist dirt.

Cutting out: use a nap layout

Seams: plain, neatened with overlocker or zigzag stitch; a run and fell seam can also be used

Thread: polyester all-purpose thread or 100% cotton thread

Needle: machine size 14; milliner's for hand sewing

Pressing: steam iron on a cotton setting; a pressing cloth may be required due to sheen on fabric

Use for: soft furnishings

CORDUROY

A soft pile fabric with distinctive stripes (known as wales or ribs) woven into it. The name depends on the size of the ribs: baby or pin cord has extremely fine ribs; needle cord has slightly thicker ribs; corduroy has 10–12 ribs per 2.5cm (1in); and elephant or jumbo cord has thick, heavy ribs.

Cutting out: use a nap layout with the pile on the corduroy brushing up the pattern pieces from hem to neck, to give depth of colour

Seams: plain, stitched using a walking foot and neatened with overlocker or zigzag stitch

Thread: polyester all-purpose thread

Needle: machine size 12/16; sharps or milliner's for hand sewing

Pressing: steam iron on a cotton setting; use a seam roll under the seams with a pressing cloth

Use for: trousers, skirts, men's wear

CRINKLE COTTON

Looks like an exaggerated version of seersucker (see page 46), with creases added by a heat process. Crinkle cotton may require careful laundering as it often has to be twisted into shape when wet to put the creases back in.

Cutting out: a nap layout is not required unless the fabric is printed

Seams: plain, neatened with overlocker or zigzag stitch

Thread: polyester all-purpose thread

Needle: machine size 12; milliner's for hand sewing

Pressing: steam iron on a cotton setting; take care not to press out the crinkles

Use for: blouses, dresses, children's wear

DAMASK

A cotton that has been woven on a jacquard loom to produce a fabric usually with a floral pattern in a self colour. May have a sheen to the surface.

Cutting out: use a nap layout

Seams: plain, neatened with overlocker or zigzag stitch

Thread: polyester all-purpose thread or 100% cotton thread

Needle: machine size 14; sharps for hand sewing

Pressing: steam iron on a cotton setting; a pressing cloth may be required if the fabric has a sheen

Use for: home furnishings; coloured jacquards for jackets, skirts

DENIM

Named after Nîmes in France. A hard-wearing twill-weave fabric with a coloured warp and white weft, usually made into jeans. Available in various weights and often mixed with an elastic thread for stretch. Denim is usually blue, but is also available in a variety of other colours.

Cutting out: a nap layout is not required

Seams: run and fell or top-stitched plain

Thread: polyester all-purpose thread with top-stitching thread for detail top-stitching

Needle: machine size 14/16; sharps for hand sewing

Pressing: steam iron on a cotton setting; a pressing cloth should not be required

Use for: jeans, jackets, children's wear

DRILL

A hard-wearing twill or plain-weave fabric with the same colour warp and weft. Drill frays badly on the cut edges.

Cutting out: a nap layout is not required

Seams: run and fell; or plain, neatened with overlocker or zigzag stitch

Thread: polyester all-purpose thread with top-stitching thread for detail top-stitching

Needle: machine size 14; sharps for hand sewing

Pressing: steam iron on a cotton setting; a pressing cloth is not required

Use for: men's wear, casual jackets, trousers

GINGHAM

A fresh, two-colour cotton fabric that features a check of various sizes. A plain weave made by having groups of white and coloured warp and weft threads.

Cutting out: usually an even check, so nap layout is not required but recommended; pattern will need matching

Seams: plain, neatened with overlocker or zigzag stitch

Thread: polyester all-purpose thread

Needle: machine size 11/12; sharps for hand sewing

Pressing: steam iron on a cotton setting; a pressing cloth should not be required

Use for: children's wear, dresses, shirts, home furnishings

JERSEY

A fine cotton yarn that has been knitted to give stretch, making the fabric very comfortable to wear. Jersey will also drape well.

Cutting out: a nap layout is recommended

Seams: 4-thread overlock stitch; or plain seam stitched with a small zigzag stitch and then seam allowances stitched together with a zigzag

Thread: polyester all-purpose thread

Needle: machine size 12/14; a ballpoint needle may be required for overlocker and a milliner's for hand sewing

Pressing: steam iron on a wool setting as jersey may shrink on a cotton setting

Use for: underwear, drapey dresses, leisurewear, bedding

MADRAS

A check fabric made from a fine cotton yarn, usually from India. Often found in bright colours featuring an uneven check. An inexpensive cotton fabric.

Cutting out: use a nap layout and match the checks

Seams: plain, neatened with overlocker or zigzag stitch

Thread: polyester all-purpose thread

Needle: machine size 12/14; sharps for hand sewing

Pressing: steam iron on a cotton setting; a pressing cloth is not required

Use for: shirts, skirts, home furnishings

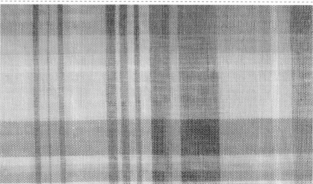

MUSLIN

A fine, plain, open-weave cotton. Can be found in colours but usually sold a natural/unbleached or white. Makes great pressing cloths and interlinings. It is a good idea to wash prior to use.

Cutting out: a nap layout is not required

Seams: 4-thread overlock stitch; or plain seam, neatened with overlocker or zigzag stitch; a French seam could also be used

Thread: polyester all-purpose thread

Needle: machine size 11; milliner's for hand sewing

Pressing: steam iron on a cotton setting; a cloth is not required

Use for: curtaining and other household uses

SEERSUCKER

A woven cotton that has a bubbly appearance woven into it, due to stripes of puckers. Do not over-press, or the surface effect will be damaged.

Cutting out: use a nap layout, due to puckered surface effect

Seams: plain, neatened with overlocker or zigzag stitch

Thread: polyester all-purpose thread

Needle: machine size 11/12; milliner's for hand sewing

Pressing: steam iron on a cotton setting (be careful not to press out the wrinkles)

Use for: summer clothing, skirts, shirts, children's wear

SHIRTING

A closely woven, fine cotton, with coloured warp and weft yarns making stripes or checks.

Cutting out: use a nap layout if fabric has uneven stripes

Seams: plain, neatened with overlocker or zigzag stitch; a run and fell seam can also be used

Thread: polyester all-purpose thread

Needle: machine size 12; milliner's for hand sewing

Pressing: steam iron on a cotton setting; a pressing cloth is not required

Use for: ladies' and men's shirts

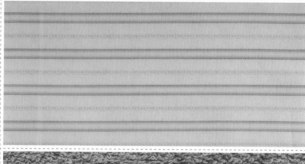

TOWELLING

A cotton fabric with loops on the surface; top-quality towelling has loops on both sides. It is highly absorbent. Wash before use to preshrink and make it fluffy.

Cutting out: use a nap layout

Seams: 4-thread overlock stitch; or plain seam, neatened with overlocker or zigzag stitch

Thread: polyester all-purpose thread

Needle: machine size 14; sharps for hand sewing

Pressing: steam iron on a cotton setting; a pressing cloth is not required

Use for: bathrobes, beachwear

VELVET

A pile-weave fabric, made by using an additional yarn that is then cut to produce the pile. Difficult to handle and can be easily damaged if seams have to be unpicked.

Cutting out: use a nap layout with the pile brushing up from hem to neck, to give depth of colour

Seams: plain, stitched using a walking foot (stitch all seams from hem to neck) and neatened with overlocker or zigzag stitch

Thread: polyester all-purpose thread

Needle: machine size 14; milliner's for hand sewing

Pressing: only if you have to; use a velvet board, a bit of steam, toe of iron, and silk organza cloth

Use for: jackets, coats

TOOLS

Silk fabrics

Often referred to as the queen of all fabrics, silk is made from the fibres of the silkworm's cocoon. This strong and luxurious fabric dates back thousands of years to its first development in China, and the secret of silk production was well protected by the Chinese until 300AD. Silk fabrics can be very fine or thick and chunky. They need careful handling as some silk fabrics can be easily damaged.

PROPERTIES OF SILK

- keeps you warm in winter and cool in summer
- absorbs moisture and dries quickly
- dyes well, producing deep, rich colours
- static electricity can build up and fabric may cling
- will fade in prolonged strong sunlight
- prone to shrinkage
- best dry-cleaned
- weaker when wet than dry
- may water-mark

CHIFFON
A very strong and very fine, transparent silk with a plain weave. Will gather and ruffle well. Difficult to handle.

Cutting out: place tissue paper under the fabric and pin the fabric to the tissue, cutting through all layers if necessary; use extra-fine pins

Seams: French

Thread: polyester all-purpose thread

Needle: machine size 9/11; fine milliner's for hand sewing

Pressing: dry iron on a wool setting

Use for: special-occasion wear, over-blouses

CREPE DE CHINE
Medium weight, with an uneven surface due to the twisted silk yarn used. Drapes well and often used on bias-cut garments.

Cutting out: if to be bias-cut, use a single layer layout; otherwise use a nap layout

Seams: a seam for a difficult fabric or French

Thread: polyester all-purpose thread

Needle: machine size 11; milliner's or betweens for hand sewing

Pressing: dry iron on a wool setting

Use for: blouses, dresses, special-occasion wear

DUCHESSE SATIN
A heavy, expensive satin fabric used almost exclusively for special-occasion wear.

Cutting out: use a nap layout

Seams: plain, with pinked edges

Thread: polyester all-purpose thread

Needle: machine size 12/14; milliner's for hand sewing

Pressing: steam iron on a wool setting with a pressing cloth; use a seam roll under the seams to prevent shadowing

Use for: special-occasion wear

DUPION
Similar to hand-woven dupion (see page 48) but woven using a much smoother yarn to reduce the amount of nubbly bits in the weft.

Cutting out: use a nap layout to prevent shadowing

Seams: plain, neatened with overlocker or zigzag stitch

Thread: polyester all-purpose thread

Needle: machine size 12; milliner's for hand sewing

Pressing: steam iron on a wool setting, with a pressing cloth as fabric may water-mark

Use for: dresses, skirts, jackets, special-occasion wear, soft furnishings

Cutting out pp76–83   Machine stitches and seams pp92–103   》》》

DUPION, HAND-WOVEN

The most popular of all the silks. A distinctive weft yarn with many nubbly bits. Available in hundreds of colours. Easy to handle, but it does fray badly.

Cutting out: use a nap layout as the fabric shadows

Seams: plain, neatened with overlocker or zigzag stitch

Thread: polyester all-purpose thread

Needle: machine size 12; milliner's for hand sewing

Pressing: steam iron on a wool setting, with a pressing cloth to avoid water-marking

Use for: dresses, special-occasion wear, jackets, soft furnishings

GEORGETTE

A soft, filmy silk fabric that has a slight transparency. Does not crease easily.

Cutting out: place tissue paper under the fabric and pin fabric to tissue, cutting through all layers if necessary; use extra-fine pins

Seams: French

Thread: polyester all-purpose thread

Needle: machine size 11; milliner's for hand sewing

Pressing: dry iron on a wool setting (fabric can be damaged by steam)

Use for: special-occasion wear, loose-fitting overshirts

HABUTAI

Originally from Japan, a smooth, fine silk that can have a plain or a twill weave. Fabric is often used for silk painting.

Cutting out: a nap layout is not required

Seams: French

Thread: polyester all-purpose thread

Needle: machine size 9/11; very fine milliner's or betweens for hand sewing

Pressing: steam iron on a wool setting

Use for: lining, shirts, blouses

MATKA

A silk suiting fabric with an uneven-looking yarn. Matka can be mistaken for linen.

Cutting out: use a nap layout as silk may shadow

Seams: plain, neatened with overlocker or zigzag stitch or Hong Kong finish

Thread: polyester all-purpose thread

Needle: machine size 12/14; milliner's for hand sewing

Pressing: steam iron on a wool setting with a pressing cloth; a seam roll is recommended to prevent the seams from showing through

Use for: dresses, jackets, trousers

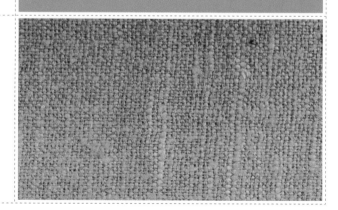

ORGANZA

A sheer fabric with a crisp appearance that will crease easily.

Cutting out: a nap layout is not required

Seams: French or a seam for a difficult fabric

Thread: polyester all-purpose thread

Needle: machine size 11; milliner's or betweens for hand sewing

Pressing: steam iron on a wool setting; a pressing cloth should not be required

Use for: sheer blouses, shrugs, interlining, interfacing

SATIN

A silk with a satin weave that can be very light to quite heavy in weight.

Cutting out: use a nap layout in a single layer as fabric is slippy

Seams: French; on thicker satins, a seam for a difficult fabric

Thread: polyester all-purpose thread (not silk thread as it becomes weak with wear)

Needle: machine size 11/12; milliner's or betweens for hand sewing

Pressing: steam iron on a wool setting, with a pressing cloth as fabric may water-mark

Use for: blouses, dresses, special-occasion wear

SILK AND WOOL MIX

A fabric made by mixing wool and silk fibres or wool and silk yarns. The fabric made may be fine in quality or thick, like a coating.

Cutting out: use a nap layout

Seams: plain, neatened with overlocker or zigzag stitch

Thread: polyester all-purpose thread

Needle: machine size 11/14, depending on fabric; sharps for hand sewing

Pressing: steam iron on a wool setting; seams will require some steam to make them lie flat

Use for: suits, skirts, trousers, coats

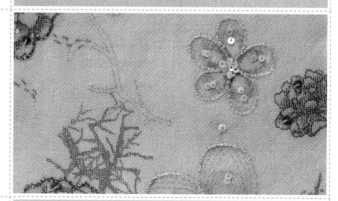

TAFFETA

A smooth, plain-weave fabric with a crisp appearance. It makes a rustling sound when worn. Can require special handling and does not wear well.

Cutting out: use a nap layout, with extra-fine pins in seams as they will mark the fabric

Seams: plain; fabric may pucker, so sew from the hem upwards, keeping the fabric taut under the machine; neaten with overlocker or pinking shears

Thread: polyester all-purpose thread

Needle: machine size 11; milliner's or betweens for hand sewing

Pressing: cool iron, with a seam roll under the seams

Use for: special-occasion wear

Cutting out pp76–83   Machine stitches and seams pp92–103   〉〉〉〉

Linen fabrics

Linen is a natural fibre that is derived from the stem of the flax plant. It is available in a variety of qualities and weights, from very fine linen to heavy suiting weights. Coarser than cotton, it is sometimes woven with cotton as well as being mixed with silk.

PROPERTIES OF LINEN

- cool and comfortable to wear
- absorbs moisture well
- shrinks when washed
- does not ease well

- has a tendency to crease
- prone to fraying
- resists moths but is damaged by mildew

COTTON AND LINEN MIX

Two fibres may have been mixed together in the yarn or may have mixed warp and weft yarns. It has lots of texture in the weave. Silk and linen mix is treated in the same way.

Cutting out: a nap layout should not be required

Seams: plain, neatened with overlocker or zigzag stitch

Thread: polyester all-purpose thread

Needle: machine size 14; sharps for hand sewing

Pressing: a steam iron on a steam setting, with a silk organza pressing cloth

Use for: summer-weight jackets, tailored dresses

DRESS-WEIGHT LINEN

A medium-weight linen with a plain weave. The yarn is often uneven, which causes slubs in the weave.

Cutting out: a nap layout is not required

Seams: plain, neatened with overlocker or zigzag stitch or a Hong Kong finish

Thread: polyester all-purpose thread with a top-stitching thread for top-stitching

Needle: machine size 14; sharps for hand sewing

Pressing: steam iron on a cotton setting (steam is required to remove creases)

Use for: dresses, trousers, skirts

PRINTED LINENS

Many linens today feature prints or even embroidery. The fabric may be light to medium weight, with a smooth yarn that has few slubs.

Cutting out: use a nap layout

Seams: plain, neatened with overlocker or zigzag stitch

Thread: polyester all-purpose thread

Needle: machine size 14; sharps for hand sewing

Pressing: steam iron on a cotton setting (steam is required to remove creases)

Use for: dresses, skirts

SUITING LINEN

A heavier yarn is used to produce a linen suitable for suits for men and women. Can be a firm, tight weave or a looser weave.

Cutting out: a nap layout is not required

Seams: plain, neatened with overlocker or a zigzag stitch and sharps hand-sewing needle

Thread: polyester all-purpose thread with a top-stitch thread for top-stitching

Needle: machine size 14; sharps for hand sewing

Pressing: steam iron on a cotton setting (steam is required to remove creases)

Use for: men's and women's suits, trousers, coats

«« Needles and pins pp22–23   Threads pp24–25   Pressing aids pp28–29

Leather and suede

Leather and suede are natural fabrics derived from either a pig or a cow and are sold as skins. Depending on the curing process that has been used, the skin will be either a suede or a leather. The fabrics require special handling.

LEATHER AND SUEDE
As the pattern pieces cannot be pinned on to leather and suede, you will need to draw around them using tailor's chalk. After cutting out, the chalk will rub off and will not damage the skin.

Cutting out: a complete pattern is required, left and right-hand halves; use a nap layout for suede, as it will brush one way

Seams: lapped or plain, using a walking foot or an ultra-glide foot; neatening is not required

Thread: polyester all-purpose thread

Needle: machine size 14 (a special leather needle may actually damage the skin); hand sewing is not recommended

Pressing: steam iron, with a silk organza pressing cloth

Use for: skirts, trousers, jackets, soft furnishings

Man-made fabrics

The term "man-made" applies to any fabric that is not 100 per cent natural. Many of these fabrics have been developed over the last hundred years, which means they are new compared to natural fibres. Some man-made fabrics are made from natural elements mixed with chemicals while others are made entirely from non-natural substances. The properties of man-made fabrics vary from fabric to fabric.

ACETATE
Introduced in 1924, acetate is made from cellulose and chemicals. The fabric has a slight shine and is widely used for linings. Acetate can also be woven into fabrics such as acetate taffeta, acetate satin, and acetate jersey.

Properties of acetate:
· dyes well
· can be heat-set into pleats
· washes well

Cutting out: use a nap layout due to sheen on fabric

Seams: plain, neatened with overlocker or zigzag stitch, or 4-thread overlock stitch

Thread: polyester all-purpose thread

Needle: machine size 11; sharps for hand sewing

Pressing: steam iron on a cool setting (fabric can melt)

Use for: special-occasion wear, linings

ACRYLIC
Introduced in 1950, acrylic fibres are made from ethylene and acrylonitrile. The fabric resembles wool and makes a good substitute for machine-washable wool. Often seen as a knitted fabric, the fibres can be mixed with wool.

Properties of acrylic:
· little absorbency
· tends to retain odours
· not very strong

Cutting out: a nap layout may be required

Seams: 4-thread overlock stitch on knitted fabrics; plain seam on woven fabrics

Thread: polyester all-purpose thread

Needle: machine size 12/14, but a ballpoint needle may be required on knitted fabrics; sharps for hand sewing

Pressing: steam iron on a wool setting (fabric can be damaged by heat)

Use for: knitted yarns for sweaters; wovens for skirts, blouses

NYLON
Developed by DuPont in 1938, the fabric takes its name from a collaboration between New York and London. Nylon is made from polymer chips that are melted and extruded into fibres. The fabric can be knitted or woven.

Properties of nylon:
· very hard-wearing
· does not absorb moisture

· washes easily, although white nylon can discolour easily
· very strong

Cutting out: a nap layout is not required unless the fabric is printed

Seams: plain, neatened with overlocker or zigzag stitch

Thread: polyester all-purpose thread

Needle: machine size 14, but a ballpoint needle may be required for knitted nylons; sharps for hand sewing

Pressing: steam iron on a silk setting (fabric can melt)

Use for: sportswear, underwear

Cutting out pp76-83   Machine stitches and seams pp92-103 »»»

POLYESTER

One of the most popular of the man-made fibres, polyester was introduced in 1951 as a washable man's suit! Polyester fibres are made from petroleum by-products and can take on any form, from a very fine sheer fabric to a thick, heavy suiting.

Properties of polyester:
· non-absorbent
· does not crease
· can build up static
· may "pill"

Cutting out: a nap layout is only required if the fabric is printed

Seams: French, plain, or 4-thread overlock, depending on the weight of the fabric

Thread: polyester all-purpose thread

Needle: machine size 11/14; sharps for hand sewing

Pressing: steam iron on a wool setting

Use for: workwear, school uniforms

RAYON

Also known as viscose and often referred to as artificial silk, this fibre was developed in 1889. It is made from wood pulp or cotton linters mixed with chemicals. Rayon can be knitted or woven and made into a wide range of fabrics. It is often blended with other fibres.

Properties of rayon:
· is absorbent
· is not static
· dyes well
· frays badly

Cutting out: a nap layout is only required if the fabric is printed

Seams: plain, neatened with overlocker or zigzag stitch

Thread: polyester all-purpose thread

Needle: machine size 12/14; sharps for hand sewing

Pressing: steam iron on a silk setting

Use for: dresses, blouses, jackets

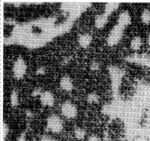

SPANDEX

Introduced in 1958, this is a lightweight, soft fibre than can be stretched 500% without breaking. A small amount of spandex is often mixed with other fibres to produce wovens with a slight stretch.

Properties of spandex:
· resistant to body oils, detergents, sun, sea, and sand

· can be difficult to sew
· can be damaged by heat
· not suitable for hand sewing

Cutting out: use a nap layout

Seams: 4-thread overlock stitch or a seam stitched with a small zigzag

Thread: polyester all-purpose thread

Needle: machine ballpoint size 14 or a machine stretch needle

Pressing: steam iron on a wool setting (spandex can be damaged by a hot iron)

Use for: swimwear, foundation wear, sportswear

SYNTHETIC FURS

Created using a looped yarn that is then cut on a knitted or a woven base, synthetic fur can be made from nylon or acrylic fibres. The furs vary tremendously in quality and some are very difficult to tell from the real thing.

Properties of synthetic furs:
· easy to sew
· require careful sewing

· can be heat-damaged by pressing
· not as warm as real fur

Cutting out: use a nap layout, with the fur pile brushed from the neck to the hem; cut just the backing carefully and not through the fur pile

Seams: plain, with a longer stitch and a walking foot; no neatening is required

Thread: polyester all-purpose thread

Needle: machine size 14; sharps for hand sewing

Pressing: if required, use a cool iron (synthetic fur can melt under a hot iron)

Use for: outerwear

SYNTHETIC LEATHER AND SUEDE

Made from polymers, these are non-woven fabrics. Some synthetic leathers and suedes can closely resemble the real thing.

Properties of synthetic leather and suede:
· do not fray
· do not ease well

· can be difficult to sew by hand, so this is not recommended

Cutting out: use a nap layout

Seams: plain, stitched using a walking foot and neatened with pinking shears; can also use top-stitched seams and lapped seams

Thread: polyester all-purpose thread

Needle: machine size 11/14

Pressing: steam iron on a wool setting, with a pressing cloth

Use for: jackets, skirts, trousers, soft furnishings

⟪⟪ Needles and pins pp22–23   Threads pp24–25   Pressing aids pp28–29

Fabric construction

Most fabric is made by either knitting or weaving. A knitted fabric is constructed by interlocking looped yarns. For a woven fabric, horizontal and vertical yarns go under and over each other. The warp yarn, which is the strongest, runs vertically and the weft crosses it at right angles. There are also non-woven fabrics created by a felting process where tiny fibres are mixed and squeezed together, then rolled out.

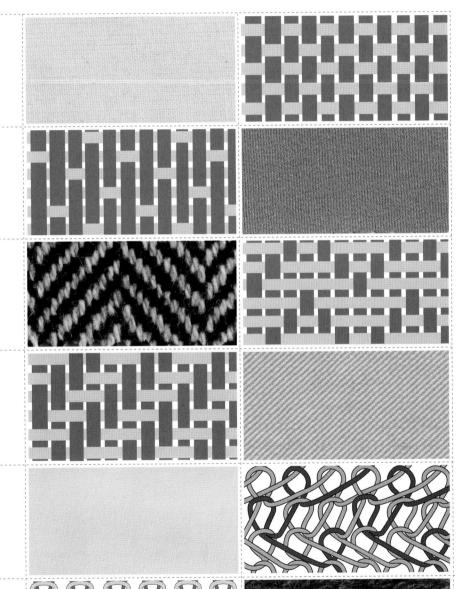

PLAIN WEAVE
As the name suggests, this is the simplest of all the weaves. The weft yarn passes under one warp yarn, then over another one.

SATIN WEAVE
This has a long strand known as a float on the warp yarn. The weft goes under four warp yarns, then over one. This weave gives a sheen on the fabric.

HERRINGBONE WEAVE
The distinctive herringbone zigzag weave is made by the weft yarn going under and over warp yarns in a staggered pattern.

TWILL WEAVE
The diagonal twill weave is made by the weft yarn going under two warp yarns, then over another two, with the pattern moved one yarn across each time.

WARP KNIT
This is made on a knitting machine, where one yarn is set to each needle (latch). The knit is formed in a vertical and diagonal direction.

WEFT KNIT
Made in the same way as knitting by hand on needles, this uses one yarn that runs horizontally.

Cutting out pp76–83   Machine stitches and seams pp92–103 »»»

Interfacings

An interfacing is a piece of fabric that is attached to the main fabric to give it support or structure. An interfacing fabric may be woven, knitted, or non-woven. It may also be fusible or non-fusible. A fusible interfacing (also called iron-on) can be bonded to the fabric by applying heat, whereas a non-fusible interfacing needs to be sewn to the fabric with a tacking stitch. Always cut interfacings on the same grain as the fabric, regardless of its construction.

FUSIBLE INTERFACINGS

Be sure to buy fusibles designed for the home sewer, because the adhesive on the back of fusible interfacings for commercial use cannot be released with a normal steam iron. Do all pattern marking after the interfacing has been applied to the fabric.

WOVEN
A woven fusible is always a good choice for a woven fabric as the two weaves will work together. Always cut on the same grain as the fabric. This type of interfacing is suitable for crafts and for more structured garments.

LIGHTWEIGHT WOVEN
A very light, woven fusible that is almost sheer, this can be difficult to cut out as it tends to stick to the scissors. It is suitable for all light to medium-weight fabrics.

KNITTED
A knitted fusible is ideally suited to a knit fabric as the two will be able to stretch together. Some knitted fusibles only stretch one way, while others will stretch in all directions. A knitted fusible is also a good choice on fabrics that have a percentage of stretch.

NON-WOVEN
Non-woven fusibles are available in a wide variety of weights – choose one that feels lighter than your fabric. You can always add a second layer if one interfacing proves to be too light. This interfacing is suitable for supporting collars and cuffs, and facings on garments.

HOW TO APPLY A FUSIBLE INTERFACING

1 Place fabric on pressing surface, wrong side up, making sure it is straight and not wrinkled.

2 Place the chosen interfacing sticky side down on the fabric (the sticky side feels gritty).

3 Cover with a dry pressing cloth and spray the cloth with a fine mist of water.

4 Place a steam iron, on a steam setting, on top of the pressing cloth.

5 Leave the iron in place for at least 10 seconds before moving it to the next area of fabric.

6 Check to see if the interfacing is fused to the fabric by rolling the fabric – if the interfacing is still loose in places, repeat the pressing process.

7 When the fabric has cooled down, the fusing process will be complete. Then pin the pattern back on to the fabric and transfer the pattern markings as required.

《《《 Pressing aids pp28–29

NON-FUSIBLE INTERFACINGS

These sew-in interfacings require tacking to the wrong side of facings or the main garment fabric around the seam allowances. They are useful for sheer or fine fabrics where the adhesive from a fusible interfacing might show through.

ALPACA
A tailorings canvas made from wool and alpaca, this interfacing is excellent to use in difficult fabrics such as velvet, because the alpaca can be steamed into shape.

COLLAR CANVAS
A firm, white cotton canvas, this will stiffen shirt collars and also boned bodices. It is available as firm and soft collar canvas although there is little difference between the two. Collar canvas is also useful in crafts, such as handbags.

MUSLIN
A cotton muslin interfacing is a good choice on summer dresses as well as for special-occasion wear. Muslin can also be used to line fine cotton dresses.

ORGANZA
A pure silk organza makes an excellent interfacing for sheer fabric to give support and structure. It can also be used for structure in much larger areas such as bridal skirts.

NON-WOVEN SEW-IN INTERFACING
A non-woven material is ideal for crafts and small areas of garments, such as cuffs and collars. Use it in garments when a woven or fusible alternative is not available.

HOW TO APPLY A NON-FUSIBLE INTERFACING

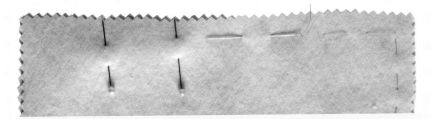

1 Place the interfacing on to the wrong side of the fabric, aligning the cut edges.

2 Pin in place.

3 Using a basic tacking stitch, tack the interfacing to the fabric or facing at 1cm (⅜in) within the seam allowance.

Stitches for hand sewing pp88–91   Applying interfacing to a facing p145   Linings and interfacings pp274–279   »»»

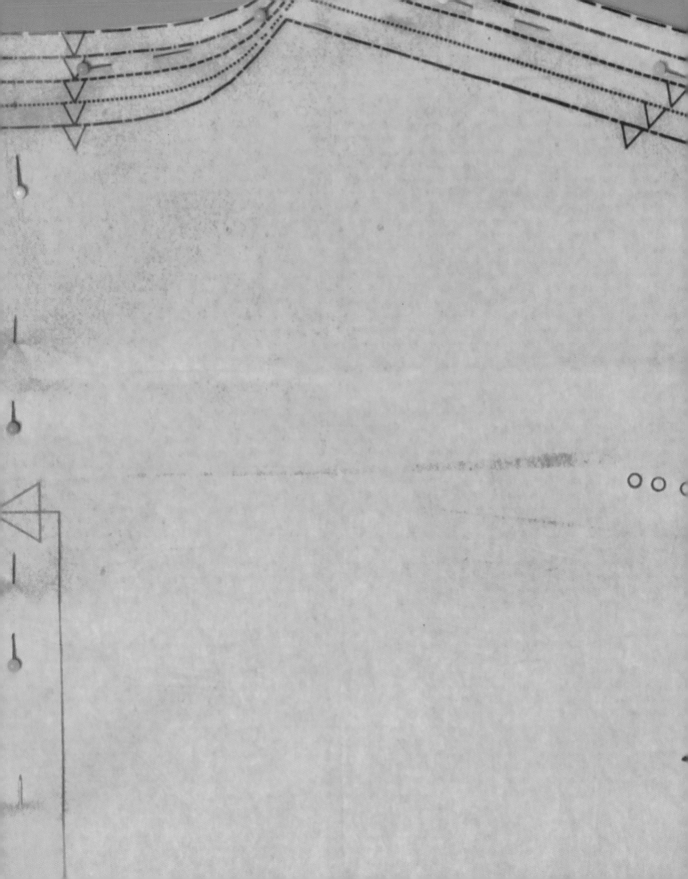

PATTERNS

- -

Patterns are available not only for clothes but for a whole range of crafts and soft furnishing projects. When using a paper pattern to create a garment, you'll need to take your body measurements so that you can compare them to those of the pattern. The pattern may then have to be altered prior to cutting out your fabric. It is always a good idea to test out a pattern in calico before using the real fabric – this is known as making a toile. The toile will help you analyse the fit and whether or not the style chosen suits your figure type. The final step is to pin the pattern on the fabric, cut out the pieces, and transfer all the marks from the pattern to the fabric.

READING PATTERNS

Paper patterns are available for clothing, crafts, and home furnishings. A pattern has three main components: the envelope, the pattern, and the instructions. The envelope gives an illustration of the item that can be made from the contents, together with fabric suggestions and requirements. The pattern sheets inside the envelope are normally printed on tissue and contain a wealth of information, while the instructions tell you how to construct the item.

Reading a pattern envelope

The envelope front illustrates the finished garment or item that can be made from the contents of the envelope. This may be a line drawing or a photograph. The different versions are known as views. On the reverse of the envelope there is usually an illustration of the back view and the standard body measurement chart that has been used for this pattern, plus a chart that will help you purchase the correct amount of fabric for each view. Suitable fabrics are also suggested alongside "notions", or haberdashery, which are all the bits and pieces you need to complete the project.

Number of pattern pieces

Code number for ordering

Description of garment or item, giving details of style and different views included in pattern

List of pattern sizes in metric and imperial measurements for bust, waist, and hips in each size

Suggested fabrics suitable for garment or item as well as unsuitable fabrics

Notions required for each view

5678
15 PIECES

MISSES' UNLINED JACKET, SKIRT, SHORTS, AND PANTS. Unlined, semi-fitted, V-neck jacket has short sleeves, front buttons, optional waistline darts, and optional breast pocket. Straight skirt, above mid-knee, and trousers or shorts with straight legs, have waistband, front pleats, side seam pockets, and back zip.

FABRICS: Jacket, skirt, shorts, and trousers: wool crepe, soft cottons, sheeting, linen, silk, silk types, and lightweight woollens. Skirt, shorts, and trousers also challis, jacquards, and crepe. Unsuitable for fabrics printed with obvious diagonals. Allow extra fabric in order to match plaids, stripes, or one-way design fabrics.

Use nap yardages/layouts for shaded, pile, or one-way design fabrics. *with nap. ** without nap
NOTIONS: Thread. Jacket: three 1.2 cm (7/8 in) buttons; 6mm (1/4 in) shoulder pads. Skirt, trousers: pkg of 3.2 cm (1 1/4 in) waistband interfacing; 18 cm (7 in) zip; and one hook and eye closure.

METRIC

Body measurements	(6	8	10)	(12	14	16)	(18	20	22)	
Bust	78	80	83	87	92	97	102	107	112	cm
Waist	58	61	63.5	66	71	76	81	86	94	cm
Hip	81	84	86	91	96.5	102	107	112	117	cm

Fabric needed		(6	8	10)	(12	14	16)	(18	20	22)	
Jacket	115 cm*/**	1.70	1.70	1.70	1.80	1.80	2.10	2.20	2.20	2.20	m
	150 cm*/**	1.30	1.30	1.30	1.40	1.70	1.70	1.70	1.80	1.80	m
Interfacing		1 m of 55–90 cm lightweight fusible or non-fusible									
Skirt A	115 cm*/**	1.6	1.6	1.6	1.6	1.9	1.9	1.9	1.9	2	m
	150 cm*/**	1.2	1.2	1.3	1.3	1.3	1.3	1.4	1.4	1.5	m
Shorts B	115 cm*/**	1.6	1.6	1.6	1.6	1.9	1.9	1.9	2	2	m
	150 cm*/**	1.2	1.2	1.3	1.3	1.3	1.3	1.4	1.4	1.5	m
Pants B	115 cm*/**	2.4	2.4	2.4	2.4	2.4	2.4	2.7	2.7	2.7	m
	150 cm*	2	2	2	2	2.1	2.1	2.2	2.3	2.3	m
	150 cm**	1.6	1.6	1.8	2	2	2.1	2.2	2.3	2.3	m

Garment measurements	(6	8	10)	(12	14	16)	(18	20	22)	
Jacket bust	92	94.5	97	101	106	111	116	121	126	cm
Jacket waist	81	83	86	89.5	94.5	100	105	110	116	cm
Jacket back length	73	73.5	74	75	75.5	76	77	77.5	78	cm
Skirt A lower edge	99	101	104	106	112	117	122	127	132	cm
Skirt A length	61	61	61	63	63	63	65	65	65	cm
Shorts B leg width	71	73.5	76	81	86.5	94	99	104	109	cm
Shorts B side length	49.5	50	51	51.5	52	52.5	53.5	54	54.5	cm
Pants B leg width	53.5	53.5	56	56	58.5	58.5	61	61	63.5	cm
Pants B side length	103	103	103	103	103	103	103	103	103	cm

IMPERIAL

Body measurements	(6	8	10)	(12	14	16)	(18	20	22)	
Bust	30 1/2	31 1/2	32 1/2	34	36	38	40	42	44	in
Waist	23	24	25	26 1/2	28	30	32	34	37	in
Hip	32 1/2	33 1/2	34 1/2	36	38	40	42	44	46	in

Fabric needed		(6	8	10)	(12	14	16)	(18	20	22)	
Jacket	45 in*/**	1 7/8	1 7/8	1 7/8	1 7/8	2	2 3/8	2 3/8	2 3/8	2 3/8	yd
	60 in*/**	1 3/8	1 3/8	1 3/8	1 1/2	1 7/8	1 7/8	1 7/8	1 7/8	2	yd
Interfacing		1 1/8 yd of 22–36 in lightweight fusible or non-fusible									
Skirt A	45 in*/**	1 3/4	1 3/4	1 3/4	1 7/8	2	2	2	2	2 1/8	yd
	60 in*/**	1 1/4	1 1/4	1 3/8	1 3/8	1 3/8	1 3/8	1 1/2	1 1/2	1 5/8	yd
Shorts B	45 in*/**	1 3/4	1 3/4	1 3/4	1 3/4	2	2	2	2	2 1/8	yd
	60 in*/**	1 1/4	1 1/4	1 3/8	1 3/8	1 3/8	1 3/8	1 1/2	1 1/2	1 5/8	yd
Pants B	45 in*/**	2 5/8	2 5/8	2 5/8	2 5/8	2 5/8	2 5/8	2 7/8	2 7/8	2 7/8	yd
	60 in*	2 1/8	2 1/8	2 1/8	2 1/8	2 1/4	2 1/4	2 3/8	2 1/2	2 1/2	yd
	60 in **	1 3/4	1 3/4	1 7/8	2 1/8	2 1/8	2 1/4	2 3/8	2 1/2	2 1/2	yd

Garment measurements	(6	8	10)	(12	14	16)	(18	20	22)	
Jacket bust	36 1/4	37 1/4	38 1/4	39 3/4	41 3/4	43 3/4	45 1/4	47 3/4	49 3/4	in
Jacket waist	31 3/4	32 3/4	33 3/4	35 1/4	37 1/4	39 1/4	41 1/4	43 1/4	45 1/4	in
Jacket back length	28 3/4	29	29 1/4	29 1/2	29 3/4	30	30 1/4	30 1/2	30 3/4	in
Skirt A lower edge	39	40	41	42	44	46	48	50	52	in
Skirt A length	24	24	24	24 3/4	24 3/4	24 3/4	25 1/2	25 1/2	25 1/2	in
Shorts B leg width	28	29	30	32	34	37	39	41	43	in
Shorts B side length	19 1/2	19 3/4	20	20 1/4	20 1/4	20 3/4	21	21 1/4	21 1/2	in
Pants B leg width	21	21	22	22	23	23	24	24	25	in
Pants B side length	40 1/2	40 1/2	40 1/2	40 1/2	40 1/2	40 1/2	40 1/2	40 1/2	40 1/2	in

Outline drawing of garment or item, including back views, showing darts and zip positions

Garment measurements box gives actual size of finished garment

Chart to follow for required fabric quantity, indicating size across top, and chosen view and correct width down the side

Figure shapes

Most people fall into one of these four basic figure shapes. Pattern books and envelopes may feature these symbols and they can be used to help you choose suitable patterns for your figure.

 THE WEDGE
Upper body (bust and shoulders) is larger than lower body (hips).

 THE TRIANGLE
Lower body (hips) is larger than upper body (bust and shoulders).

 THE RECTANGLE
Upper and lower body are of similar proportions.

 THE HOURGLASS
Upper and lower body similar in proportion with a small, neat waist.

Pattern markings

Each pattern piece will have a series of lines, dots, and other symbols printed on it. These symbols are to help you alter the pattern and join the pattern pieces together. The symbols are universal across all major paper patterns.

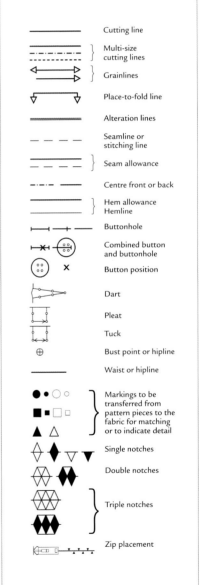

Single-size patterns

Some patterns contain a garment or craft project of one size only. If you are using a single-size pattern, cut around the tissue on the thick black cutting line before making any alterations.

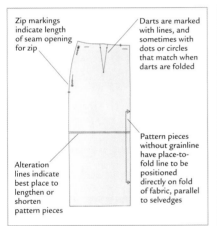

Zip markings indicate length of seam opening for zip

Darts are marked with lines, and sometimes with dots or circles that match when darts are folded

Alteration lines indicate best place to lengthen or shorten pattern pieces

Pattern pieces without grainline have place-to-fold line to be positioned directly on fold of fabric, parallel to selvedges

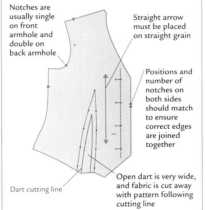

Notches are usually single on front armhole and double on back armhole

Straight arrow must be placed on straight grain

Positions and number of notches on both sides should match to ensure correct edges are joined together

Dart cutting line

Open dart is very wide, and fabric is cut away with pattern following cutting line

Multi-size patterns

Many patterns today have more than one size printed on the tissue. Each size is clearly labelled and the cutting lines are marked with a different type of line for each size.

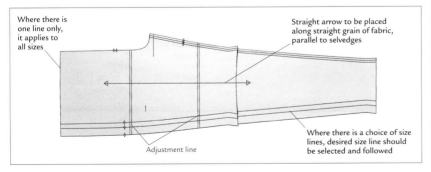

Where there is one line only, it applies to all sizes

Straight arrow to be placed along straight grain of fabric, parallel to selvedges

Adjustment line

Where there is a choice of size lines, desired size line should be selected and followed

Body measuring p60–61 Altering patterns pp62–73 Pattern marking pp82–83 »»

BODY MEASURING

Accurate body measurements are needed to determine the correct pattern size to use and if any alterations are required. Pattern sizes are usually chosen by the hip or bust measurement; for tops follow the bust measurement, but for skirts or trousers use the hip measurement. If you are choosing a dress pattern, go by whichever measurement is the largest.

TAKING BODY MEASUREMENTS

You'll need a tape measure and ruler as well as a helper for some of the measuring, and a hard chair or stool.

Wear close-fitting clothes such as a leotard and leggings.

Do not wear any shoes.

HOW TO MEASURE YOUR HEIGHT

Most paper patterns are designed for a woman 165 to 168cm (5ft 5in to 5ft 6in). If you are shorter or taller than this you may need to adjust the pattern prior to cutting out your fabric.

1 Remove your shoes.

2 Stand straight, with your back against the wall.

3 Place a ruler flat on your head, touching the wall, and mark the wall at this point.

4 Step away and measure the distance from the floor to the marked point.

Chest

Measure above the bust, high under the arms, keeping the tape measure flat and straight across the back.

Full bust

Make sure you are wearing a good-fitting bra and measure over the fullest part of the bust. If your cup size is in excess of a B, you will probably need to do a bust alteration, although some patterns are now cut to accommodate larger cup sizes.

Waist

This is the measurement around the smallest part of your waist. Wrap the tape around first to find your natural waist, then measure.

Hips

This measurement must be taken around the fullest part of the hips, between the waist and legs.

High hip

Take this just below the waist and just above the hip bones to give a measurement across the tummy.

Shoulder

Hold the end of the tape measure at the base of your neck (where a necklace would lie) and measure to the dent at the end of your shoulder. To find this dent raise your arm slightly.

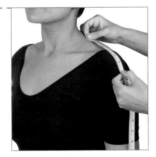

Neck

Measure around the neck – snugly but not too tight – to determine collar size.

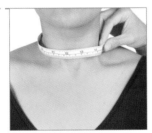

Arm

Bend your elbow and place your hand on your hip, then measure from the end of the shoulder over the elbow to the wrist bone.

Back waist

Take this measurement down the centre of the back, from the lumpy bit at the top of the spine, in line with the shoulders, to the waist.

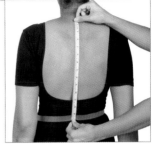

Outside leg

Measure the side of the leg from the waist, over the hip, and straight down the leg to the ankle bone.

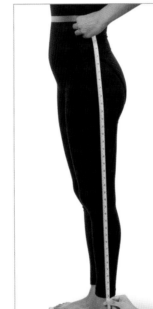

Inside leg

Stand with your legs apart and measure the inside of one leg from the crotch to the ankle bone.

Crotch depth

Sit upright on a hard chair or stool and measure from the waist vertically down to the chair.

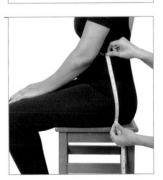

Altering patterns pp62-73   Making a toile pp74-75   Marking a hemline p229   »»

ALTERING PATTERNS

It is unlikely that your body measurements will be exactly the same as those of your chosen pattern, so you will need to alter the pattern to accommodate your figure. Here is how to lengthen and shorten pattern pieces, and how to make specific alterations at the bust, waist and hips, shoulders and back, and to sleeves and trousers.

Equipment

In addition to scissors and pins or tape, you will need a pencil, an eraser, a ruler that is clearly marked, and possibly a set square. For many alterations you will also need pattern paper. After pinning or taping the piece of pattern tissue to the paper, you can redraw the pattern lines. Trim away the excess tissue or paper before pinning the pattern pieces to the fabric for cutting out.

Easy multi-size pattern alterations

Using a multi-size pattern has many advantages, as you can cut it to suit your unique individual shape – for example, to accommodate a hip measurement that may be two sizes different to a waist measurement, or your not being precisely one size or another.

INDIVIDUAL PATTERN ADJUSTMENT

To adjust for a wider hip measurement, when cutting from one size to another, make the lines a gentle curve to follow the contours of the body.

BETWEEN SIZES

If your body measurements fall between two pattern sizes, cut carefully between the two cutting lines for the different sizes.

Lengthening and shortening patterns

If you are shorter or taller, or your arms or legs are shorter or longer, than the pattern pieces, you will need to adjust the paper pattern prior to cutting out. There are lines printed on the pattern pieces that will guide you as to the best places to adjust. However, you will need to compare your body shape against the pattern. Alter the front and back by the same amount at the same points, and always check finished lengths.

FOR A FITTED SLEEVE

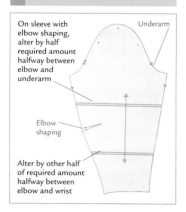

On sleeve with elbow shaping, alter by half required amount halfway between elbow and underarm

Underarm

Elbow shaping

Alter by other half of required amount halfway between elbow and wrist

FOR A STRAIGHT SLEEVE

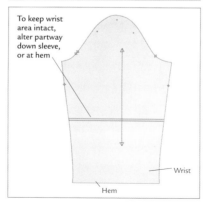

To keep wrist area intact, alter partway down sleeve, or at hem

Wrist

Hem

FOR A BODICE

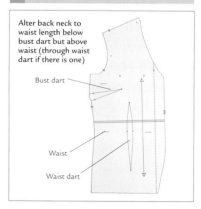

Alter back neck to waist length below bust dart but above waist (through waist dart if there is one)

Bust dart

Waist

Waist dart

⟪⟪   Measuring tools and marking aids pp18–19   Body measuring pp60–61

FOR A FITTED DRESS

Mark between bust and waist to alter back neck to waist length

Bust dart

Waist

Hipline

Alter below hipline if not altering at hem

Alter below hem if not altering at hipline

FOR A PRINCESS DRESS

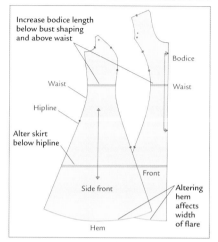

Increase bodice length below bust shaping and above waist

Bodice

Waist

Waist

Hipline

Alter skirt below hipline

Front

Side front

Altering hem affects width of flare

Hem

FOR SHORTS

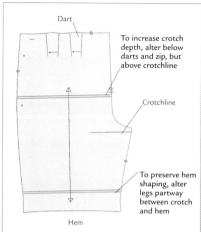

Dart

To increase crotch depth, alter below darts and zip, but above crotchline

Crotchline

To preserve hem shaping, alter legs partway between crotch and hem

Hem

FOR A SKIRT

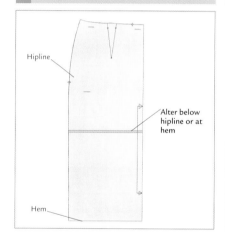

Hipline

Alter below hipline or at hem

Hem

FOR SHAPED-LEG TROUSERS

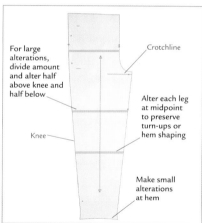

For large alterations, divide amount and alter half above knee and half below

Crotchline

Alter each leg at midpoint to preserve turn-ups or hem shaping

Knee

Make small alterations at hem

FOR STRAIGHT TROUSERS

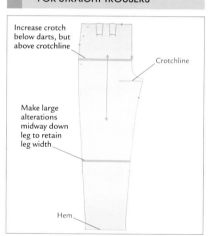

Increase crotch below darts, but above crotchline

Crotchline

Make large alterations midway down leg to retain leg width

Hem

HOW TO LENGTHEN A PATTERN PIECE

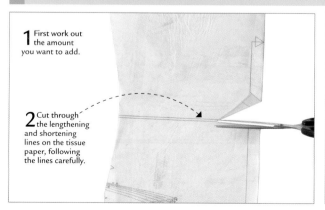

1 First work out the amount you want to add.

2 Cut through the lengthening and shortening lines on the tissue paper, following the lines carefully.

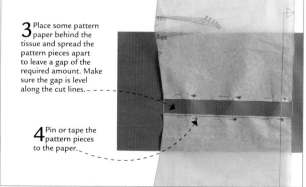

3 Place some pattern paper behind the tissue and spread the pattern pieces apart to leave a gap of the required amount. Make sure the gap is level along the cut lines.

4 Pin or tape the pattern pieces to the paper.

Making a toile pp74–75   Marking a hemline p229 »»»

HOW TO SHORTEN A PATTERN PIECE

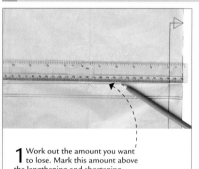

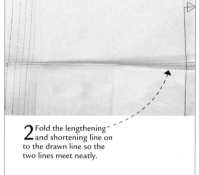

1 Work out the amount you want to lose. Mark this amount above the lengthening and shortening lines, then draw a line through the marks using the ruler as a guide.

2 Fold the lengthening and shortening line on to the drawn line so the two lines meet neatly.

3 Press with your fingers to crease the fold sharply, then secure the fold in the pattern piece with tape.

HOW TO LENGTHEN ACROSS DARTS

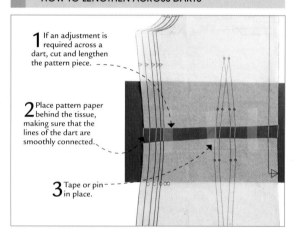

1 If an adjustment is required across a dart, cut and lengthen the pattern piece.

2 Place pattern paper behind the tissue, making sure that the lines of the dart are smoothly connected.

3 Tape or pin in place.

HOW TO SHORTEN ACROSS DARTS

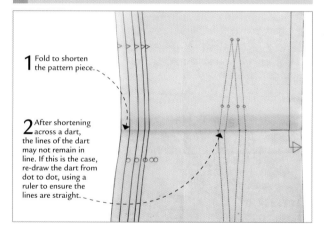

1 Fold to shorten the pattern piece.

2 After shortening across a dart, the lines of the dart may not remain in line. If this is the case, re-draw the dart from dot to dot, using a ruler to ensure the lines are straight.

HOW TO LENGTHEN A HEM EDGE

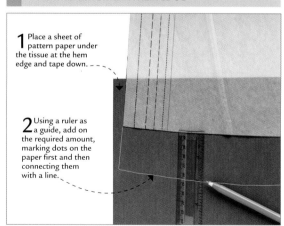

1 Place a sheet of pattern paper under the tissue at the hem edge and tape down.

2 Using a ruler as a guide, add on the required amount, marking dots on the paper first and then connecting them with a line.

HOW TO SHORTEN A HEM EDGE

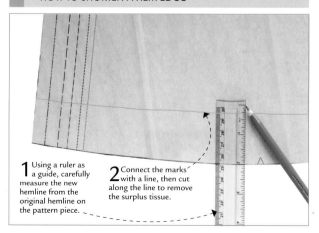

1 Using a ruler as a guide, carefully measure the new hemline from the original hemline on the pattern piece.

2 Connect the marks with a line, then cut along the line to remove the surplus tissue.

《《《 Measuring tools and marking aids pp18–19 Body measuring pp60–61

Bust

Some paper patterns today feature various cup sizes, but the majority of patterns are cut to accommodate a B cup. If you are larger than this, you will probably need to adjust your pattern before cutting out. As a general rule, when spreading the pattern pieces apart, try adjusting by 6mm (¼in) per cup size over a B cup. Other pattern alterations can be made for bust position, raising it higher or lowering it. If the bust dart is altered, the waist dart may also need to be adjusted.

RAISING A BUST DART

1 If you have a high bust you may need to raise the point of the darts. The bust point is nearly always marked on the pattern pieces. Mark the new bust point on the tissue.

2 Redraw the lines of the dart to this point.

Lengthened waist dart

RAISING A BUST DART SUBSTANTIALLY

1 If the dart has to be raised quite a lot, it is easier to cut a rectangle out of the part of the pattern that contains the dart and then move it higher.

2 Mark the new bust point on the tissue first.

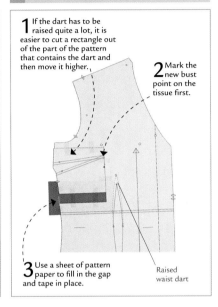

3 Use a sheet of pattern paper to fill in the gap and tape in place.

Raised waist dart

INCREASING A BUST DART

1 Cut the pattern as indicated, straight through the bust point.

3 Tape securely in place.

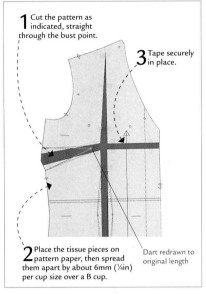

2 Place the tissue pieces on pattern paper, then spread them apart by about 6mm (¼in) per cup size over a B cup.

Dart redrawn to original length

LOWERING A BUST DART

1 Mark the new lower bust point on your pattern piece.

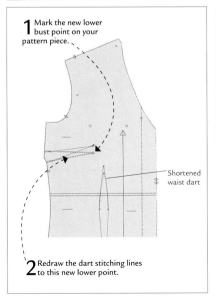

2 Redraw the dart stitching lines to this new lower point.

Shortened waist dart

LOWERING A BUST DART SUBSTANTIALLY

1 First mark the new bust point on the tissue.

2 Cut out a rectangle from the pattern piece that contains the dart and move it to the lower position.

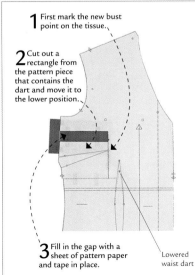

3 Fill in the gap with a sheet of pattern paper and tape in place.

Lowered waist dart

INCREASING A FRENCH DART

1 Cut the pattern piece along the dart line from the side seam, straight through the bust point to the centre front line.

2 Spread the tissue apart and tape to pattern paper.

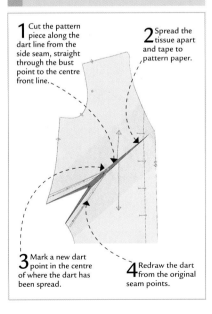

3 Mark a new dart point in the centre of where the dart has been spread.

4 Redraw the dart from the original seam points.

TOOLS

RAISING A CURVED BUST SEAM

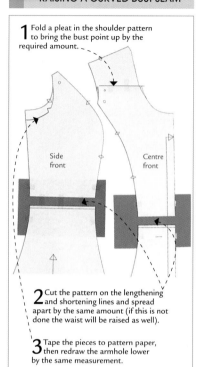

1 Fold a pleat in the shoulder pattern to bring the bust point up by the required amount.

Side front

Centre front

2 Cut the pattern on the lengthening and shortening lines and spread apart by the same amount (if this is not done the waist will be raised as well).

3 Tape the pieces to pattern paper, then redraw the armhole lower by the same measurement.

LOWERING A CURVED BUST SEAM

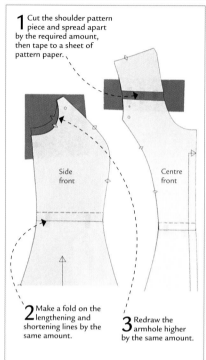

1 Cut the shoulder pattern piece and spread apart by the required amount, then tape to a sheet of pattern paper.

Side front

Centre front

2 Make a fold on the lengthening and shortening lines by the same amount.

3 Redraw the armhole higher by the same amount.

ADJUSTING A CURVED SEAM

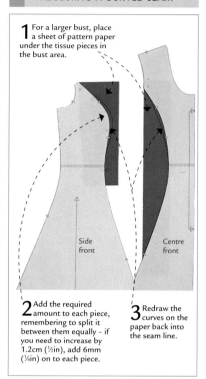

1 For a larger bust, place a sheet of pattern paper under the tissue pieces in the bust area.

Side front

Centre front

2 Add the required amount to each piece, remembering to split it between them equally – if you need to increase by 1.2cm (½in), add 6mm (¼in) on to each piece.

3 Redraw the curves on the paper back into the seam line.

Waist and hips

Most people's waists and hips are out of proportion when compared to the measurements of a paper pattern. To alter the pattern to suit your body shape, adjust the pieces for the waist first and then do the hip pieces.

INCREASING THE WAIST AT A SEAM

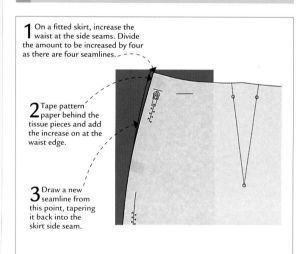

1 On a fitted skirt, increase the waist at the side seams. Divide the amount to be increased by four as there are four seamlines.

2 Tape pattern paper behind the tissue pieces and add the increase on at the waist edge.

3 Draw a new seamline from this point, tapering it back into the skirt side seam.

INCREASING THE WAIST ON A GORED SKIRT

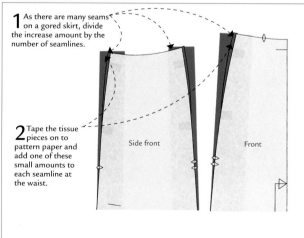

1 As there are many seams on a gored skirt, divide the increase amount by the number of seamlines.

2 Tape the tissue pieces on to pattern paper and add one of these small amounts to each seamline at the waist.

Side front

Front

≪≪≪ Measuring tools and marking aids pp18–19 Body measuring pp60–61

INCREASING THE WAIST ON A FULL-CIRCLE SKIRT

1 First carefully check the waist circumference on the pattern against your body measurements.

2 Make the waist larger by drawing a new, lower waist stitching line on the pattern pieces.

3 Be sure to adjust the finished length of the skirt, if necessary.

INCREASING THE WAIST ON A FITTED DRESS

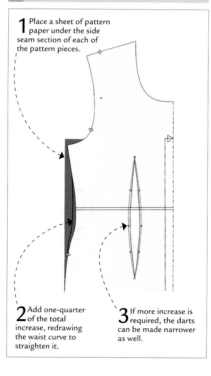

1 Place a sheet of pattern paper under the side seam section of each of the pattern pieces.

2 Add one-quarter of the total increase, redrawing the waist curve to straighten it.

3 If more increase is required, the darts can be made narrower as well.

INCREASING THE WAIST ON A PRINCESS-LINE DRESS

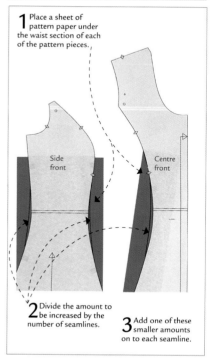

Side front

Centre front

1 Place a sheet of pattern paper under the waist section of each of the pattern pieces.

2 Divide the amount to be increased by the number of seamlines.

3 Add one of these smaller amounts on to each seamline.

DECREASING THE WAIST AT A SEAM

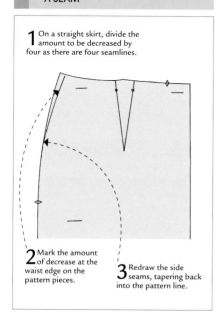

1 On a straight skirt, divide the amount to be decreased by four as there are four seamlines.

2 Mark the amount of decrease at the waist edge on the pattern pieces.

3 Redraw the side seams, tapering back into the pattern line.

DECREASING THE WAIST ON A GORED SKIRT

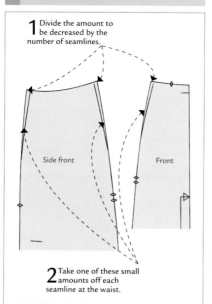

Side front

Front

1 Divide the amount to be decreased by the number of seamlines.

2 Take one of these small amounts off each seamline at the waist.

DECREASING THE WAIST ON A FULL-CIRCLE SKIRT

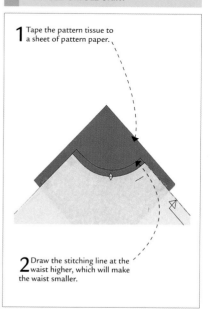

1 Tape the pattern tissue to a sheet of pattern paper.

2 Draw the stitching line at the waist higher, which will make the waist smaller.

TOOLS

DECREASING THE WAIST ON A FITTED DRESS

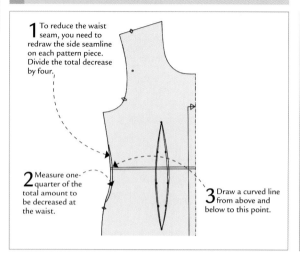

1 To reduce the waist seam, you need to redraw the side seamline on each pattern piece. Divide the total decrease by four.

2 Measure one-quarter of the total amount to be decreased at the waist.

3 Draw a curved line from above and below to this point.

DECREASING THE WAIST ON A PRINCESS-LINE DRESS

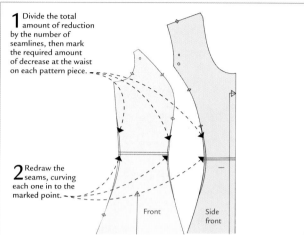

1 Divide the total amount of reduction by the number of seamlines, then mark the required amount of decrease at the waist on each pattern piece.

2 Redraw the seams, curving each one in to the marked point.

Front   Side front

WIDENING A FITTED SKIRT AT THE HIPLINE

1 To increase the hip dimension on a fitted skirt, divide the amount of the increase by four. Place the tissue pieces on pattern paper and increase each side seam at the hip point by the required amount.

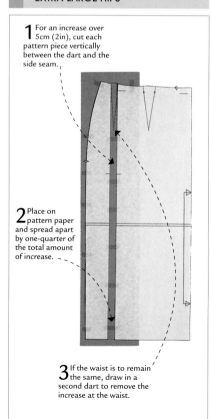

2 Redraw the seamline from the hip increase, gradually tapering into the waistline.

3 It is more flattering to take the adjustment all the way down the skirt, so redraw the seamline straight down from the hip to the hem.

ADJUSTING A FITTED SKIRT FOR EXTRA-LARGE HIPS

1 For an increase over 5cm (2in), cut each pattern piece vertically between the dart and the side seam.

2 Place on pattern paper and spread apart by one-quarter of the total amount of increase.

3 If the waist is to remain the same, draw in a second dart to remove the increase at the waist.

ADJUSTING A FITTED SKIRT FOR PROMINENT HIPS

1 Place the tissue on pattern paper and add the required amount from the waist to the hip point as for a fitted skirt (see left), tapering the line back into the seam.

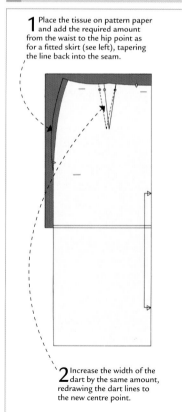

2 Increase the width of the dart by the same amount, redrawing the dart lines to the new centre point.

ADJUSTING A FITTED SKIRT FOR A LARGE BOTTOM

1 Cut through the skirt back pattern piece, vertically through the dart to the hem.

2 Cut across the hipline, but not through the side seam.

3 Spread apart the tissue on pattern paper as much as needed and tape in place.

4 Redraw the dart.

DECREASING THE HIPLINE ON A FITTED SKIRT

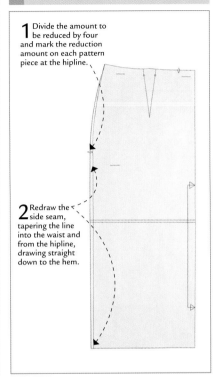

1 Divide the amount to be reduced by four and mark the reduction amount on each pattern piece at the hipline.

2 Redraw the side seam, tapering the line into the waist and from the hipline, drawing straight down to the hem.

ADJUSTING THE HIPLINE ON A GORED SKIRT OR PRINCESS DRESS

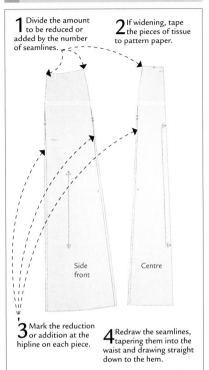

1 Divide the amount to be reduced or added by the number of seamlines.

2 If widening, tape the pieces of tissue to pattern paper.

Side front

Centre

3 Mark the reduction or addition at the hipline on each piece.

4 Redraw the seamlines, tapering them into the waist and drawing straight down to the hem.

MAKING A LARGE INCREASE AT THE HIPLINE ON A FITTED DRESS

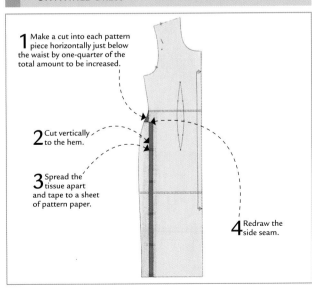

1 Make a cut into each pattern piece horizontally just below the waist by one-quarter of the total amount to be increased.

2 Cut vertically to the hem.

3 Spread the tissue apart and tape to a sheet of pattern paper.

4 Redraw the side seam.

ADJUSTING AT THE HIPLINE TO ALLOW FOR A HOLLOW BACK

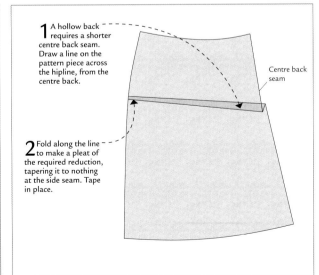

1 A hollow back requires a shorter centre back seam. Draw a line on the pattern piece across the hipline, from the centre back.

Centre back seam

2 Fold along the line to make a pleat of the required reduction, tapering it to nothing at the side seam. Tape in place.

TOOLS

Shoulders, back, and sleeves

Alterations can be made to accommodate sloping shoulders, square shoulders, and backs that may be wider or narrower than the pattern allowances. It's important to ensure that these alterations have a minimum effect on the armhole. Sleeves need to allow for movement, so should not be too tight, and pattern pieces can be enlarged as necessary. Alterations can also be made for thin arms.

ADJUSTING TO FIT SQUARE SHOULDERS

1 Starting at the armhole, slash the pattern piece about 3cm (1¼in) below and parallel with the shoulder line, not cutting through the neck seamline.

2 Spread the tissue apart to make the shoulder line straighter. Tape to pattern paper.

3 Redraw the line across the gap created.

4 Raise the armhole by the amount added at the shoulder.

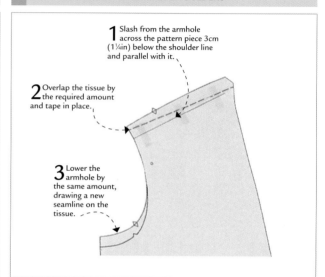

ADJUSTING TO FIT SLOPING SHOULDERS

1 Slash from the armhole across the pattern piece 3cm (1¼in) below the shoulder line and parallel with it.

2 Overlap the tissue by the required amount and tape in place.

3 Lower the armhole by the same amount, drawing a new seamline on the tissue.

PREPARING THE PATTERN FOR BROAD OR NARROW SHOULDER ALTERATIONS

1 Draw a vertical line 20cm (8in) long from the middle of the shoulder line.

2 Next, draw a second line horizontally from the end of this line to the armhole.

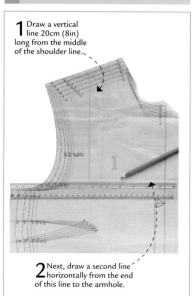

ADJUSTING TO FIT BROAD SHOULDERS

1 Cut along the lines that have been drawn and spread the pieces of tissue apart on pattern paper, to accommodate the increase in shoulder length.

2 Tape in place and redraw the shoulder line.

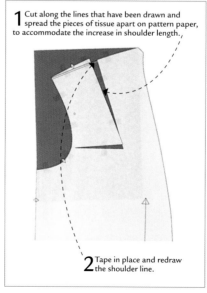

ADJUSTING TO FIT NARROW SHOULDERS

1 Cut along the drawn lines.

2 Slide the cut-out piece of tissue in to overlap the cut edges and reduce the shoulder length.

3 Tape on to pattern paper and redraw the shoulder line.

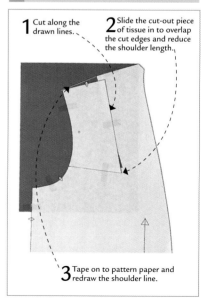

ENLARGING A FITTED SLEEVE

1 Cut the sleeve pattern piece vertically down the centre.

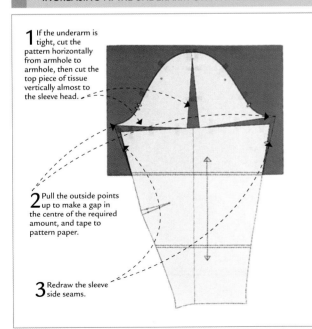

2 Spread apart as much as required to make the sleeve wider. Tape to pattern paper.

ENLARGING THE HEAD ON A FITTED SLEEVE

1 Cut the pattern piece vertically down the centre, not cutting through the wrist seamline.

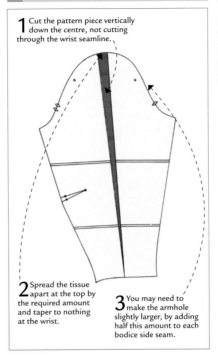

2 Spread the tissue apart at the top by the required amount and taper to nothing at the wrist.

3 You may need to make the armhole slightly larger, by adding half this amount to each bodice side seam.

ENLARGING A FITTED SLEEVE AT THE ELBOW

1 Cut horizontally at an angle from just above the elbow dart to the centre, then cut vertically almost to the top.

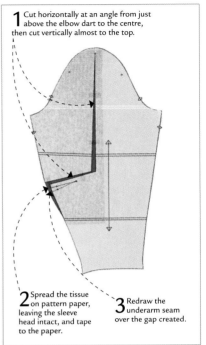

2 Spread the tissue on pattern paper, leaving the sleeve head intact, and tape to the paper.

3 Redraw the underarm seam over the gap created.

INCREASING AT THE UNDERARM ON A FITTED SLEEVE

1 If the underarm is tight, cut the pattern horizontally from armhole to armhole, then cut the top piece of tissue vertically almost to the sleeve head.

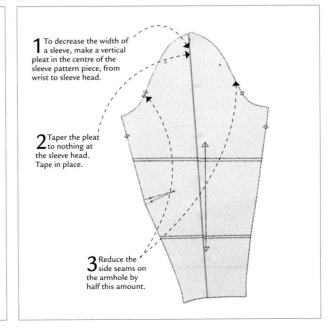

2 Pull the outside points up to make a gap in the centre of the required amount, and tape to pattern paper.

3 Redraw the sleeve side seams.

DECREASING A FITTED SLEEVE FOR THIN ARMS

1 To decrease the width of a sleeve, make a vertical pleat in the centre of the sleeve pattern piece, from wrist to sleeve head.

2 Taper the pleat to nothing at the sleeve head. Tape in place.

3 Reduce the side seams on the armhole by half this amount.

Making a toile pp74–75   Sleeves pp190–195

Trousers

Trouser alterations, to accommodate a large stomach, wide hips, or a prominent or flat bottom, can be more complicated than those on other pattern pieces, and need to be done in the correct order. Crotch depth alterations are done first, followed by width alterations, then crotch length alterations, and finally trouser leg length. The crotch depth line is only marked on the back pattern pieces.

TOOLS

INCREASING DEPTH AT CROTCH SEAM

1 Adjust both back and front pattern pieces by the same amount. Cut along the upper lengthening and shortening lines.

2 Spread the pattern tissue apart by the required amount at the centre back and centre front seams, tapering to nothing at the side seam. Tape the tissue to pattern paper.

3 Redraw the crotch edge.

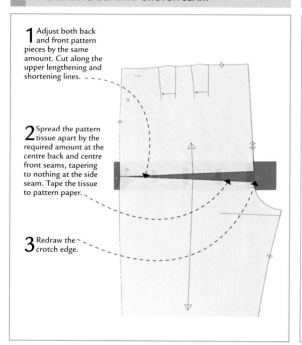

DECREASING DEPTH AT CROTCH SEAM

1 Adjust both back and front pattern pieces by the same amount. Cut each of the pattern pieces along the lengthening and shortening lines.

2 Overlap by the amount to be reduced, working from the centre and tapering to nothing at the side seam.

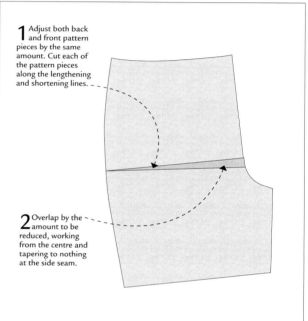

INCREASING THE WAISTLINE

1 Divide the amount to be increased by eight (there are eight seamlines that you can add on to). Tape the tissue to pattern paper.

2 Add an equal amount to each seamline at the waist, tapering the new drawn line back into the seam.

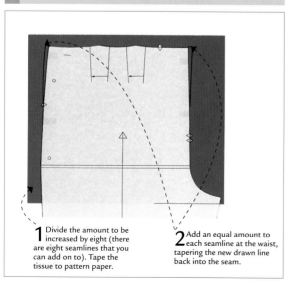

DECREASING THE WAISTLINE

1 Take the amount to be decreased and divide it by eight.

2 Reduce each of the waist seamlines by this amount.

3 Draw a new line from the decrease point back into the seamline on the pattern.

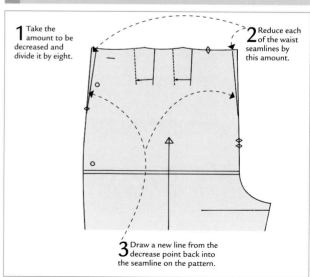

INCREASING AT THE HIPLINE

1 Take the amount to be increased and divide it by four.

2 Place a sheet of pattern paper under the hip area on the side seam of each pattern piece.

3 Add the required amount to each of the seamlines at the hip, tapering the new seamline into the waist and thigh.

4 For straight trousers, draw the new seamline straight down from the hip to the hem.

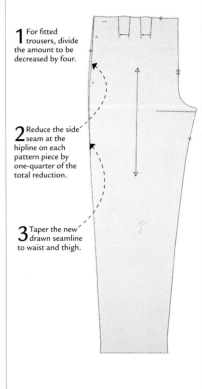

ADJUSTING FOR A LARGE BOTTOM

1 Cut through the trouser back pattern pieces at the hipline.

2 Place the tissue on pattern paper and spread apart by the required amount, then tape the tissue to the paper.

3 Redraw the crotch edge. This adjustment may be in addition to a crotch depth adjustment.

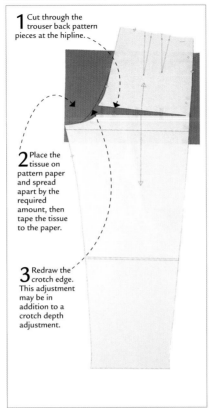

DECREASING AT THE HIPLINE

1 For fitted trousers, divide the amount to be decreased by four.

2 Reduce the side seam at the hipline on each pattern piece by one-quarter of the total reduction.

3 Taper the new drawn seamline to waist and thigh.

INCREASING LENGTH AT CROTCH POINT

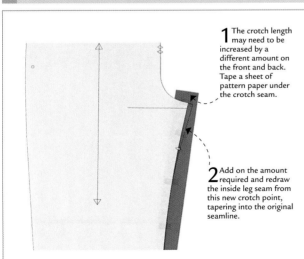

1 The crotch length may need to be increased by a different amount on the front and back. Tape a sheet of pattern paper under the crotch seam.

2 Add on the amount required and redraw the inside leg seam from this new crotch point, tapering into the original seamline.

DECREASING LENGTH AT CROTCH POINT

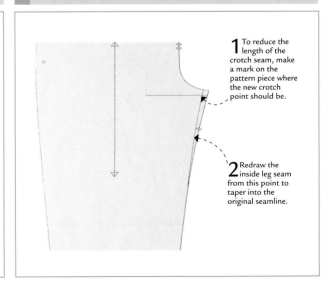

1 To reduce the length of the crotch seam, make a mark on the pattern piece where the new crotch point should be.

2 Redraw the inside leg seam from this point to taper into the original seamline.

Making a toile pp74–75 Waistlines pp170–179 »»»

MAKING A TOILE

When using a new pattern for the first time, or if you have made pattern alterations, it is always a good idea to try out the pattern in calico, to make a test garment called a toile. This will tell you if the garment is going to fit you, or whether more alterations are required. It is also a good opportunity to confirm that the style suits your figure type. You will need a helper, or failing that a dressmaker's dummy.

Toile too big

When you try the toile on, if it is too big there will be surplus fabric. Pleat and pin out the surplus fabric, making the pleating equal on both the left and right-hand sides of the garment. Take off the toile and measure the surplus amount. Alter the pattern pieces to match, by pinning out the surplus tissue.

BACK ADJUSTMENT
If the back is too big, pleat and pin out the surplus fabric parallel to the centre back seam, doing this equally on both sides. The alteration can then be made down the centre back seam on the appropriate pattern pieces.

THE WAIST ON THE BODICE AND SKIRT
If the waist is too big, this can easily be adjusted by taking more fabric into the bust dart, thus making the waist smaller. If you adjust the bust dart on the bodice, you will need to alter the skirt dart too, so they join up.

SHOULDER ADJUSTMENT
If the shoulder is too wide it will need a sloping shoulder adjustment (see page 70).

THE HIP ON THE SKIRT
If the hip is too loose, pleat and pin out the surplus fabric, doing this equally on both side seams. Measure the surplus amount and take in the hipline on the pattern pieces accordingly (see Decreasing the hipline on a fitted skirt, page 69).

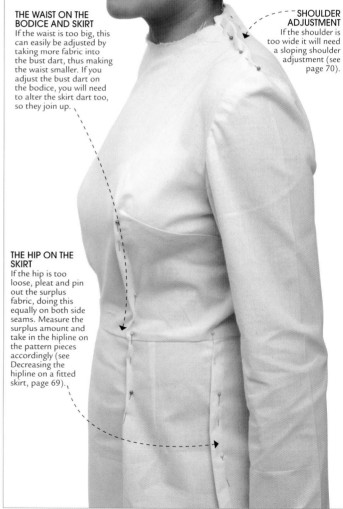

⫷⫷⫷ Measuring tools and marking aids pp18–19   Useful extras p21   Cotton fabrics p43   Body measuring pp60–61   Altering patterns pp62–73

Toile too small

If the toile is too small, the fabric will "pull" where it is too tight. The garment shown below is too tight over the bust and also over the high hip area. The pattern will need adjusting to allow more fabric in these areas. It is also snug at the top of the sleeve, which will need adjusting.

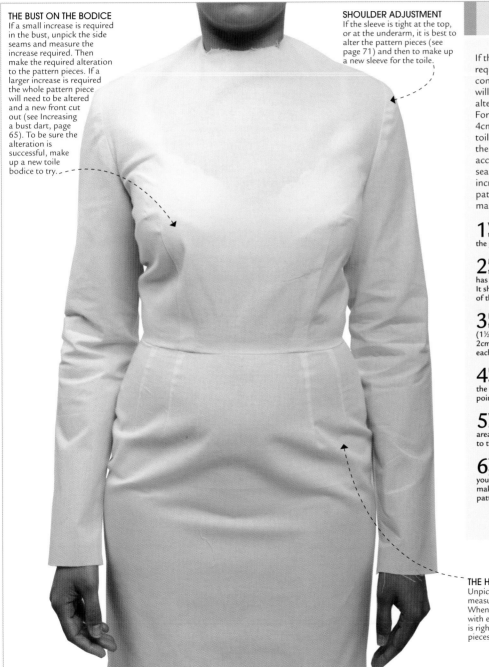

THE BUST ON THE BODICE
If a small increase is required in the bust, unpick the side seams and measure the increase required. Then make the required alteration to the pattern pieces. If a larger increase is required the whole pattern piece will need to be altered and a new front cut out (see Increasing a bust dart, page 65). To be sure the alteration is successful, make up a new toile bodice to try.

SHOULDER ADJUSTMENT
If the sleeve is tight at the top, or at the underarm, it is best to alter the pattern pieces (see page 71) and then to make up a new sleeve for the toile.

THE HIP ON THE SKIRT
Unpick the side seams and measure the increase required. When you have adjusted the toile with extra calico to be sure the fit is right, you can alter the pattern pieces accordingly (see page 68).

HOW TO ADJUST A TOILE THAT IS TOO SMALL

If the toile is too tight, it will require more fabric to cover the contours of the body and you will need to make further alterations to the pattern pieces. For small increases (up to 4cm/1½in), you can adjust the toile as described below and then alter the pattern pieces accordingly, redrawing the seamlines. For more substantial increases, after altering the pattern pieces you will need to make up a new toile to try on.

1 Where the toile is too tight, unpick the side seam on either side, until the garment will hang without pulling.

2 Measure the gap between the stitching lines where the seam has been opened at the fullest point. It should be the same on both sides of the body.

3 Divide this measurement in half – for example, if the gap is 4cm (1½in) at the fullest point, then 2cm (¾in) needs to be added to each seamline.

4 Using a marker pen, mark directly on the toile the top and bottom of the alteration. Also mark the fullest point of the alteration.

5 When the toile has been removed, add calico to the seam in the given area at the fullest point, tapering back to the original seam at either end.

6 Try the toile on again to be sure your alterations have made it fit you properly, then measure them and make adjustments to the relevant pattern pieces.

CUTTING OUT

Cutting out correctly can make or break your project. But first you need to examine the fabric in the shop, looking for any flaws, such as a crooked pattern, and checking to see if the fabric has been cut properly from the roll – that is at a right angle to the selvedge. If not you will need to straighten the edge. If the fabric is creased, press it; if washable, wash it to avoid shrinkage later. After this preparation, you will be ready to lay the pattern pieces on the fabric, pin in place, and cut out.

Fabric grain and nap

It is important that the pattern pieces are cut on the correct grain, as this will make the fabric hang correctly and produce a longer-lasting item. The grain of the fabric is the direction in which the yarns or threads that make up the fabric lie. The majority of pattern pieces need to be placed with the straight of grain symbol running parallel to the warp yarn. Some fabrics have a nap due to the pile, which means the fabric shadows when it is smoothed in one direction. A fabric with a one-way design or uneven stripes is also described as being with nap. Fabrics with nap are generally cut out with the nap running down, whereas those without nap can be cut out at any angle.

GRAIN ON WOVEN FABRICS

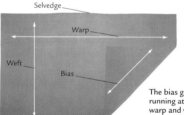

The selvedge is the woven, non-frayable edge that runs parallel to the warp grain.

Weft yarns run crossways, over and under the warp yarns.

Selvedge

Warp

Weft

Bias

Selvedge

Yarns that run the length of the fabric are called warp yarns. They are stronger than weft yarns and less likely to stretch.

The bias grain is diagonal – running at 45 degrees to the warp and weft. A garment cut on the bias will follow the contours of the body.

GRAIN ON KNITTED FABRICS

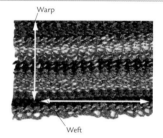

Warp

Weft

A knitted fabric also has a grain. Some knit fabrics stretch only one way while others stretch in both directions. Patterns for knit fabrics often need to be cut following the direction of the greatest stretch.

NAP DUE TO PILE

Fabrics such as velvet, corduroy, and velour will show a difference in colour, depending on whether the nap is running up or down.

NAP IF ONE-WAY DESIGN

A one-way pattern – in this case flowers – that runs lengthways in the fabric will be upside-down on one side when the fabric is folded back on itself.

NAP IF STRIPED

If the stripes do not match on both sides when the fabric is folded back, they are uneven and the fabric will need a nap layout.

Fabric preparation

To check if the fabric has been cut properly from the roll, smooth it out flat, with the selvedges lying together. If the cut ends are uneven and do not match, use one of the following methods to make the edge straight. Then press the fabric.

PULLING A THREAD TO OBTAIN A STRAIGHT EDGE

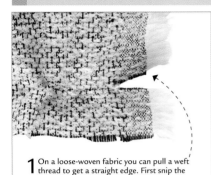

1 On a loose-woven fabric you can pull a weft thread to get a straight edge. First snip the selvedge, then find a single thread and tug it gently to pull it out.

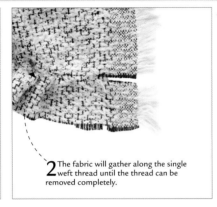

2 The fabric will gather along the single weft thread until the thread can be removed completely.

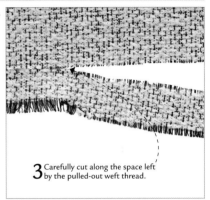

3 Carefully cut along the space left by the pulled-out weft thread.

CUTTING ON A STRIPE LINE

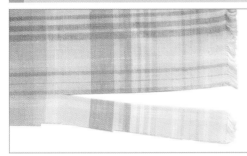

On checks and stripes, cut along the edge of one of the boldest stripes to achieve a straight edge.

CUTTING ON A STITCH LINE ON KNIT FABRICS

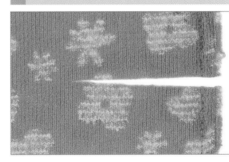

On jersey and other knit fabrics, if you look carefully you can cut along a row of stitches.

Pattern preparation

Before cutting out, sort out all the pattern pieces that are required for the item you are making. Check them to see if any have special cutting instructions. Make pattern alterations, if necessary. If there are no alterations, just trim patterns to your size.

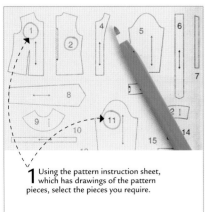

1 Using the pattern instruction sheet, which has drawings of the pattern pieces, select the pieces you require.

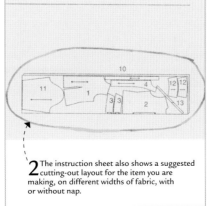

2 The instruction sheet also shows a suggested cutting-out layout for the item you are making, on different widths of fabric, with or without nap.

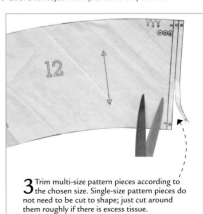

3 Trim multi-size pattern pieces according to the chosen size. Single-size pattern pieces do not need to be cut to shape; just cut around them roughly if there is excess tissue.

Pattern layout pp78–79   Stripes and checks pp80–81   Cutting out accurately p82 »»

Pattern layout

Fabric is usually folded selvedge to selvedge. With the fabric folded, the pattern is pinned on top, and both the right and left-side pieces are cut out at the same time. If pattern pieces have to be cut from single layer fabric, remember to cut matching pairs. For a fabric with a design it is a good idea to have this on the outside so that you can arrange the pattern pieces to show off the design. If you have left and right-side pattern pieces, they are cut on single fabric with the fabric right side up and the pattern right side up.

PINNING THE PATTERN TO THE FABRIC

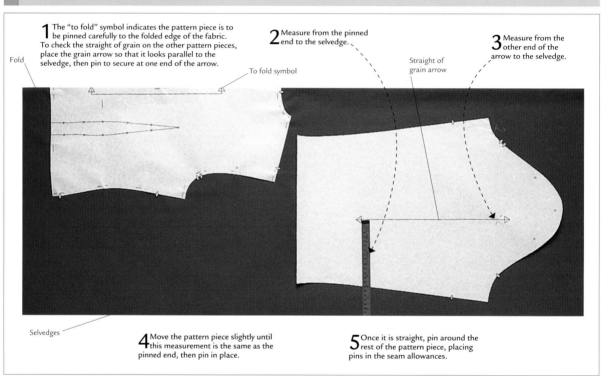

1 The "to fold" symbol indicates the pattern piece is to be pinned carefully to the folded edge of the fabric. To check the straight of grain on the other pattern pieces, place the grain arrow so that it looks parallel to the selvedge, then pin to secure at one end of the arrow.

Fold

To fold symbol

2 Measure from the pinned end to the selvedge.

Straight of grain arrow

3 Measure from the other end of the arrow to the selvedge.

Selvedges

4 Move the pattern piece slightly until this measurement is the same as the pinned end, then pin in place.

5 Once it is straight, pin around the rest of the pattern piece, placing pins in the seam allowances.

GENERAL GUIDE TO LAYOUT

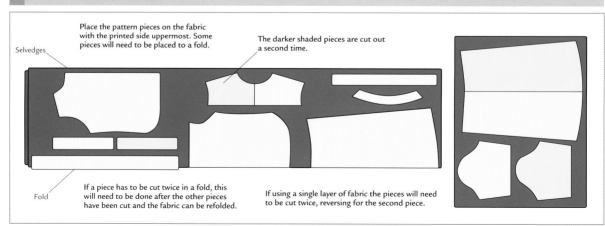

Place the pattern pieces on the fabric with the printed side uppermost. Some pieces will need to be placed to a fold.

Selvedges

The darker shaded pieces are cut out a second time.

Fold

If a piece has to be cut twice in a fold, this will need to be done after the other pieces have been cut and the fabric can be refolded.

If using a single layer of fabric the pieces will need to be cut twice, reversing for the second piece.

《《《 Cutting tools pp16–17   Measuring tools p18   Fabrics pp40–52

LAYOUT FOR FABRICS WITH A NAP OR A ONE-WAY DESIGN

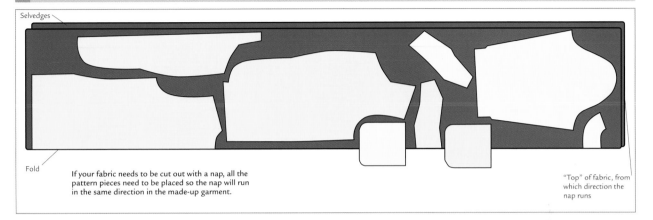

Selvedges

Fold

If your fabric needs to be cut out with a nap, all the pattern pieces need to be placed so the nap will run in the same direction in the made-up garment.

"Top" of fabric, from which direction the nap runs

LAYOUT ON A CROSSWAYS FOLD

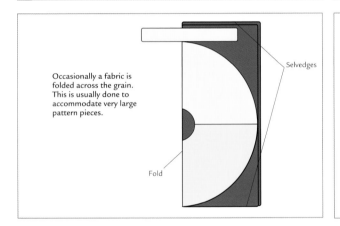

Occasionally a fabric is folded across the grain. This is usually done to accommodate very large pattern pieces.

Selvedges

Fold

LAYOUT ON A CROSSWAYS FOLD WITH A NAP

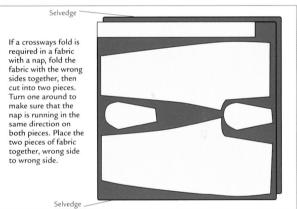

Selvedge

If a crossways fold is required in a fabric with a nap, fold the fabric with the wrong sides together, then cut into two pieces. Turn one around to make sure that the nap is running in the same direction on both pieces. Place the two pieces of fabric together, wrong side to wrong side.

Selvedge

LAYOUT ON A PARTIAL FOLD

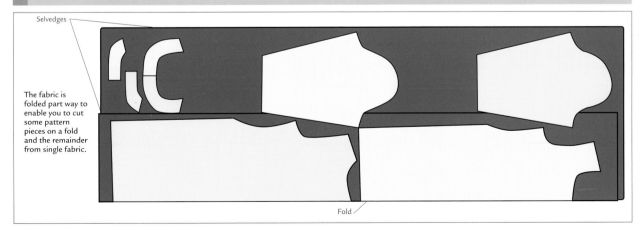

Selvedges

The fabric is folded part way to enable you to cut some pattern pieces on a fold and the remainder from single fabric.

Fold

Stripes and checks

For fabrics with a stripe or check pattern, a little more care is needed when laying out the pattern pieces. If the checks and stripes are running across or down the length of the fabric when cutting out, they will run the same direction in the finished garment. So it is important to place the pattern pieces to ensure that the checks and stripes match and that they run together at the seams. If possible, try to place the pattern pieces so each has a stripe down the centre. With a check, be aware of the hemline placement on the pattern.

EVEN OR UNEVEN STRIPES

EVEN STRIPES

When a corner of the fabric is folded back diagonally, the stripes will meet up at the fold.

UNEVEN STRIPES

When a corner of the fabric is folded back diagonally, the stripes will not match at the fold.

EVEN OR UNEVEN CHECKS

EVEN CHECKS

When a corner is folded back diagonally, the checks will be symmetrical on both of the fabric areas.

UNEVEN CHECKS

When a corner of the fabric is folded back diagonally, the checks will be uneven lengthways, widthways, or both.

MATCHING STRIPES OR CHECKS ON A SKIRT

1 Place one of the skirt pattern pieces on the fabric and pin in place.

2 Mark on the tissue the position of the boldest lines of the checks or stripes.

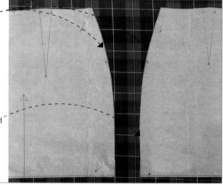

3 Place the adjoining skirt pattern piece alongside, with notches matching and side seams even. Transfer the marks across.

4 Move the second pattern piece away, matching up the bold lines, and pin it in place.

MATCHING STRIPES OR CHECKS AT THE SHOULDER

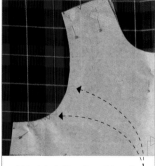

1 Mark the boldest lines of the stripes or checks around the armhole on the front bodice pattern.

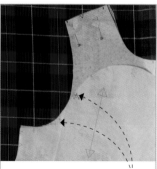

2 Place the sleeve pattern on to the armhole, matching the notches, and copy the marks on to the sleeve pattern.

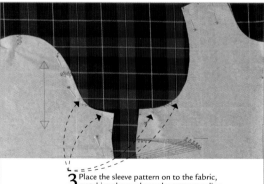

3 Place the sleeve pattern on to the fabric, matching the marks to the corresponding bold lines, and pin in place.

LAYOUT FOR EVEN CHECKS ON FOLDED FABRIC

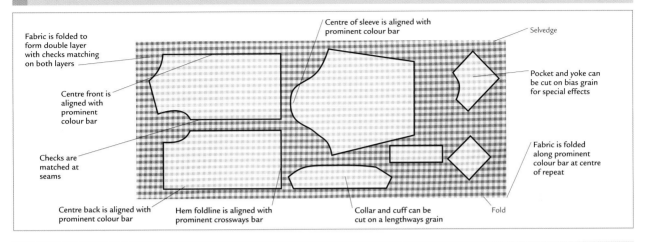

Fabric is folded to form double layer with checks matching on both layers

Centre of sleeve is aligned with prominent colour bar

Selvedge

Pocket and yoke can be cut on bias grain for special effects

Centre front is aligned with prominent colour bar

Fabric is folded along prominent colour bar at centre of repeat

Checks are matched at seams

Centre back is aligned with prominent colour bar

Hem foldline is aligned with prominent crossways bar

Collar and cuff can be cut on a lengthways grain

Fold

LAYOUT FOR EVEN STRIPES ON FOLDED FABRIC

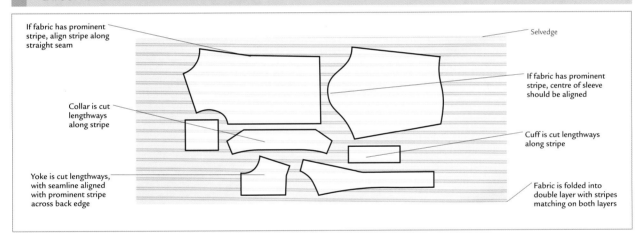

If fabric has prominent stripe, align stripe along straight seam

Selvedge

Collar is cut lengthways along stripe

If fabric has prominent stripe, centre of sleeve should be aligned

Cuff is cut lengthways along stripe

Yoke is cut lengthways, with seamline aligned with prominent stripe across back edge

Fabric is folded into double layer with stripes matching on both layers

LAYOUT FOR UNEVEN CHECKS OR STRIPES ON UNFOLDED FABRIC

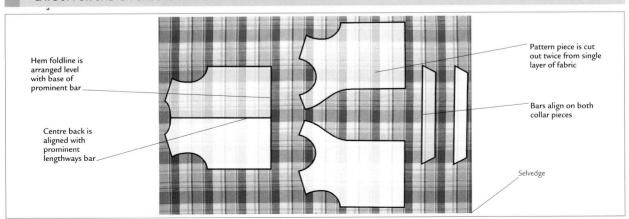

Hem foldline is arranged level with base of prominent bar

Pattern piece is cut out twice from single layer of fabric

Centre back is aligned with prominent lengthways bar

Bars align on both collar pieces

Selvedge

TOOLS

Cutting out accurately

Careful, smooth cutting around the pattern pieces will ensure that they join together accurately. Always cut out on a smooth, flat surface such as a table – the floor is not ideal – and be sure your scissors are sharp. Use the full blade of the scissors on long, straight edges, sliding the blades along the fabric; use smaller cuts around curves. Do not nibble or snip at the fabric.

HOW TO CUT

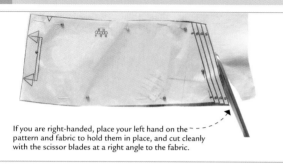

If you are right-handed, place your left hand on the pattern and fabric to hold them in place, and cut cleanly with the scissor blades at a right angle to the fabric.

MARKING NOTCHES

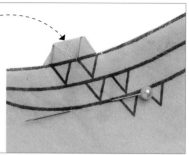

These symbols need to be marked on to the fabric as they are matching points. One of the easiest ways to do this is to cut the mirror image of the notches out into the fabric. Rather than cutting out each notch separately, cut straight across from point to point.

MARKING DOTS

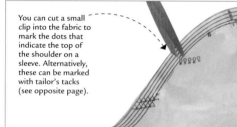

You can cut a small clip into the fabric to mark the dots that indicate the top of the shoulder on a sleeve. Alternatively, these can be marked with tailor's tacks (see opposite page).

CLIPPING LINES

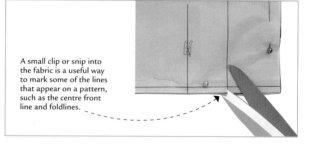

A small clip or snip into the fabric is a useful way to mark some of the lines that appear on a pattern, such as the centre front line and foldlines.

Pattern marking

Once the pattern pieces have been cut out, you will need to mark the symbols shown on the tissue through to the fabric. There are various methods to do this. Tailor's tacks are good for circles and dots, or mark these with a water or air-soluble pen (when using a pen, it's a good idea to test it on a piece of scrap fabric first). For lines, you can use trace tacking or a tracing wheel with dressmaker's carbon paper.

TRACE TACKING

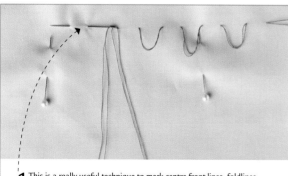

1 This is a really useful technique to mark centre front lines, foldlines, and placement lines. With double thread in your needle, stitch a row of loopy stitches, sewing along the line marked on the pattern.

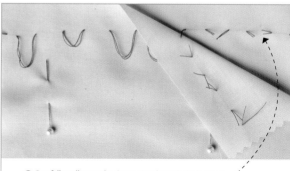

2 Carefully pull away the tissue. Cut through the loops, then gently separate the layers of fabric to show the threads. Snip apart to leave thread tails in both of the fabric layers.

««« Cutting tools pp16–17 Marking aids p19

TAILOR'S TACKS

1 As there are often dots of different sizes, it is a good idea to choose a different colour thread for each dot size. It is then easy to match the colours as well as the dots. Have double thread in your needle, unknotted. Insert the needle through the dot from right to left, leaving a tail of thread. Be sure to go through the tissue and both layers of fabric.

2 Now stitch through the dot again, this time from top to bottom to make a loop. Cut through the loop, then snip off excess thread to leave a tail.

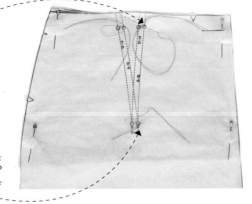

3 Carefully pull the pattern tissue away. On the top side you will have four threads marking each dot. When you turn the fabric over, the dot positions will be marked with an X.

4 Gently turn back the two layers of fabric to separate them, then cut through the threads so that thread tails are left in both pieces of fabric.

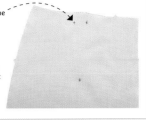

TRACING PAPER AND WHEEL

1 This method is not suitable for all fabrics as the marks may not be able to be removed easily. Slide dressmaker's carbon paper against the wrong side of the fabric.

2 Run a tracing wheel along the pattern lines (a ruler will help you make straight lines).

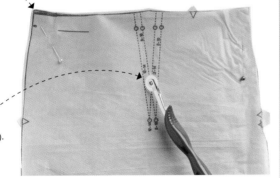

3 Remove the carbon paper and carefully pull off the pattern tissue. You will have dotted lines marked on your fabric.

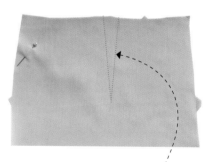

MARKER PENS

1 This method can only be used with a single layer of fabric. Press the point of the pen into the centre of the dot marked on the pattern piece.

2 Carefully remove the pattern. The pen marks will have gone through the tissue on to the fabric. Be sure not to press the fabric before the pen marks are removed or they may become permanent.

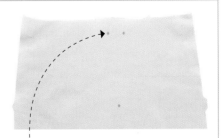

TECHNIQUES

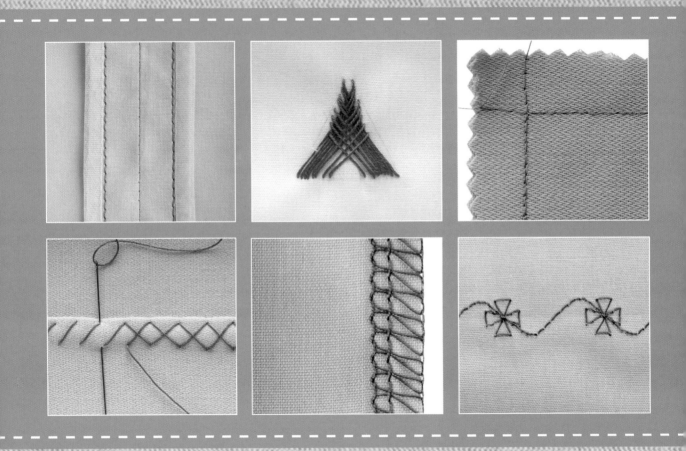

STITCH ESSENTIALS

Seams and stitches are the essential construction elements of your work. Some stitches are created by hand, while others are made on the sewing machine or overlocker.

STITCHES FOR HAND SEWING

Although modern sewing machines have eliminated the need for a lot of hand sewing, it is still necessary to use hand stitching to prepare the fabric prior to permanent stitching – these temporary pattern marking and tacking stitches will eventually be removed. Permanent hand stitching is used to finish a garment and to attach fasteners, as well as to help out with a quick repair.

HOW TO THREAD A NEEDLE

When sewing by hand, cut your piece of thread to be no longer than the distance from your fingertips to your elbow. If the thread is much longer than this, it will knot as you sew.

1 Hold your needle in your right hand and the end of the thread in your left. Keeping the thread still, place the eye of the needle over the thread.

2 If the needle will not slip over the thread, dampen your fingers and run the moisture across the eye of the needle.

3 Pull the thread through the eye of the needle.

4 At the other end of the thread, tie a knot as shown below or secure the thread as shown right.

Threading the needle

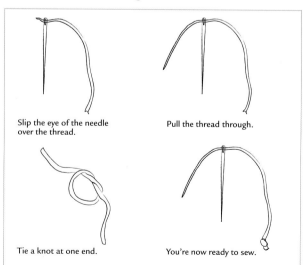

Slip the eye of the needle over the thread.

Pull the thread through.

Tie a knot at one end.

You're now ready to sew.

Securing the thread

The ends of the thread must be secured firmly, especially if the hand stitching is to be permanent. A knot (see left) is frequently used and is the preferred choice for temporary stitches. For permanent stitching a double stitch is a better option.

DOUBLE STITCH

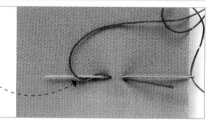

1 Take a stitch.

2 Go back through the stitch with the thread wrapped under the needle.

3 Pull through to make a knot.

BACK STITCH

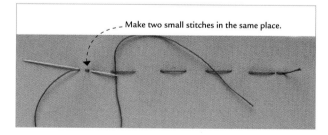

Make two small stitches in the same place.

LOCKING STITCH

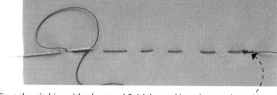

Start the stitching with a knot and finish by working a knot at the end.

TECHNIQUES

Tacking stitches

Each of the many types of tacking stitches has its own individual use. Trace tacks are used to transfer pattern markings to fabric. Basic tacks and bar tacks hold two or more pieces of fabric together. Long and short tacks are an alternative version of the basic tacking stitch, often used when the tacking will stay in the work for some time. Thread chain tacks work in a similar way to bar tacks but are much finer as they are made by looping a single thread through itself. Diagonal tacks hold folds or overlaid fabrics together, while slip tacks are used to hold a fold in fabric to another piece of fabric.

BASIC TACKS

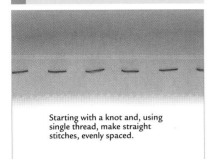

Starting with a knot and, using single thread, make straight stitches, evenly spaced.

DIAGONAL TACKS

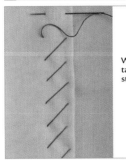

Work vertically, taking horizontal stitches.

SLIP TACKS

Take a stitch into the fold and then a stitch into the base fabric.

LONG AND SHORT TACKS

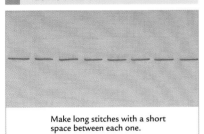

Make long stitches with a short space between each one.

BAR TACKS

1 Using double thread, make two or three loops between the two layers of fabric.

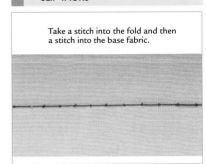

2 Work a buttonhole stitch (see page 91) across the loops.

THREAD CHAIN TACKS

1 Start with a stitch in the fabric and make a loop.

2 Make another loop from the thread and push through the first loop, then pull to tighten the first loop.

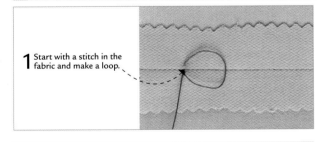

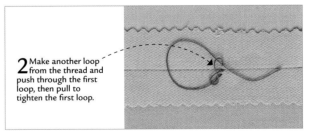

3 Repeat the process. Eventually you will have made a thread chain.

4 To finish, take a single thread through the last loop and pull to tighten. Use the thread end to stitch the loop as required.

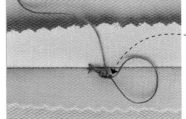

Hand stitches

There are a number of hand stitches that can be used during construction of a garment or other item. Some are for decorative purposes while others are more functional.

BACK STITCH

A strong stitch that could be used to construct a piece of work. Work from right to left. Bring the needle up, leaving a space, and then take the thread back to the end of the last stitch.

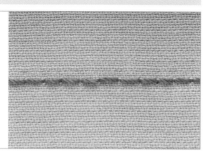

RUNNING STITCH

Very similar to tacking (see page 89), but used more for decorative purposes. Work from right to left. Run the needle in and out of the fabric to create even stitches and spaces.

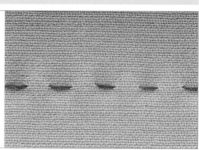

PRICK STITCH

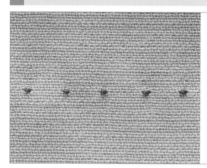

Often used to highlight the edge of a completed garment, such as a collar. Work from right to left. Make small stitches about 2mm (⅟₁₆in) long, with spaces between of at least three times that length.

WHIP STITCH

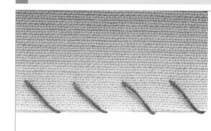

A diagonal stitch sewn with a single thread along a raw edge to prevent fraying. Work from right to left. Take a stitch through the edge of the fabric. The depth of the stitch depends on the thickness of the fabric – for a thin fabric take a shallow stitch.

HERRINGBONE STITCH

A very useful stitch as it is secure yet has some movement in it. It is used to secure hems and interlinings. Work from left to right. Take a small horizontal stitch into one layer and then the other, so the thread crosses itself.

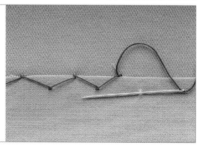

FLAT FELL STITCH

A strong, secure stitch to hold two layers permanently together. This stitch is often used to secure bias bindings and linings. Work from right to left. Make a short, straight stitch at the edge of the fabric.

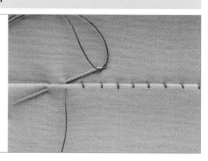

SLIP HEM STITCH

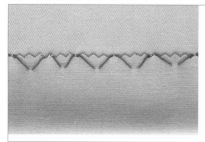

Also called a catch stitch, this is used primarily for securing hems. It looks similar to herringbone (above). Work from right to left. Take a short horizontal stitch into one layer and then the other.

BLIND HEM STITCH

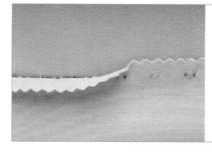

As the name suggests this is for hemming a garment. As the stitch is under the edge of the fabric it should be discreet. Work from right to left and use a slip hem stitch (left).

BUTTONHOLE STITCH

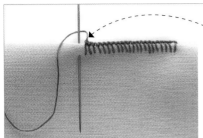

1 Used to make hand-worked buttonholes and also to secure fastenings. It is always stitched on an edge with no spaces between the stitches. Work from right to left. Push the needle from the top edge into the fabric.

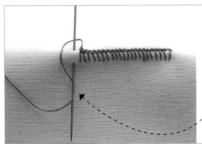

2 Wrap the thread behind the needle as the needle goes in and again as the needle leaves the fabric. Pull through and a knot will appear at the edge. This is an essential stitch for all sewers and is not difficult to master.

BLANKET STITCH

Similar to buttonhole stitch (above) but without the knot. Blanket stitch is useful to neaten edges and for decorative purposes. Always leave a space between the stitches. Push the needle into the fabric and, as it appears at the edge, wrap the thread under the needle.

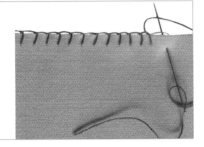

CROSS STITCH

A temporary securing stitch used to hold pleats in place after construction. It can also be used to secure linings. Work a row of even diagonal stitches in one direction and then a row back over them to make crosses.

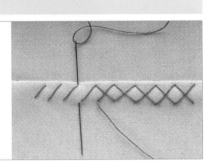

Hand-stitched arrowheads

LEVEL OF DIFFICULTY ★★★★

An arrowhead is a triangular shape made by working straight stitches in a set order. This is a permanent stitch placed at an area of strain or stress, such as the top of a split.

1 Mark a triangle with sides about 8mm (⁵⁄₁₆in) long on the fabric. Start with a knot. Bring the needle up through 1 and down through 2.

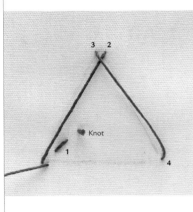

2 Then bring the needle up through 3 and down through 4. Repeat the stitch.

3 Continue the stitches, up through 5 and down through 6, up through 7 and down through 8.

4 Make about 10 alternating stitches to complete the arrowhead.

Machine-made buttonholes p264 ⟩⟩⟩

TECHNIQUES

MACHINE STITCHES AND SEAMS

Fabric is joined together using seams – whether it be for an item of clothing, craft work, or soft furnishings. The most common seam is a plain seam, which is suitable for a wide variety of fabrics and items. However, there are many other seams to be used as appropriate, depending on the fabric and item being constructed. Some seams are decorative and can add detail to structured garments.

Securing the thread

Machine stitches need to be secured at the end of a seam to prevent them from coming undone. This can be done by hand, tying the ends of the thread, or using the machine with a reverse stitch or a locking stitch, which stitches three or four stitches in the same place.

TIE THE ENDS

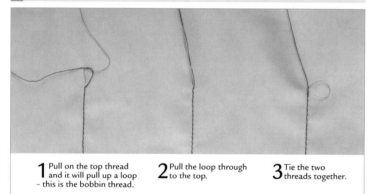

1 Pull on the top thread and it will pull up a loop – this is the bobbin thread.

2 Pull the loop through to the top.

3 Tie the two threads together.

REVERSE STITCH

1 When starting, stitch a couple of stitches forward, then hold in the reverse button and reverse over them. Continue forward again.

2 At the end of the seam, reverse again to secure the stitches.

LOCKING STITCH

1 When starting, press the locking stitch and stitch, then continue forward.

2 At the end of the seam, press the locking stitch again.

Stitches made with a machine

The sewing machine will stitch plain seams and decorative seams as well as buttonholes of various styles. The length and width of all buttonholes can be altered to suit the garment or craft item.

STRAIGHT STITCH

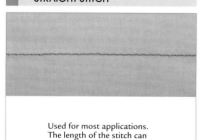

Used for most applications. The length of the stitch can be altered from 0.5 to 5.0 on most sewing machines.

ZIGZAG STITCH

To neaten seam edges and for securing and decorative purposes. Both the width and the length of this stitch can be altered.

3-STEP ZIGZAG STITCH

Made up of small, straight stitches. This stitch is decorative as well as functional, and is often found in lingerie. The stitch length and width can be altered.

≪≪≪   Sewing machine pp30–31   Sewing-machine accessories pp32–33   Overlocker pp34–35   Seam neatening pp94–95

BLIND HEM STITCH

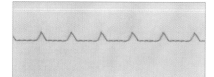

Made in conjunction with the blind hem foot. A combination of straight stitches and a zigzag stitch (see opposite page). Used to secure hems.

OVEREDGE STITCH

Made in conjunction with the overedge foot. The stitch is used for neatening the edge of fabric. The width and length of the stitch can be altered.

STRETCH STITCH

Also known as a lightening stitch. This stitch is recommended for stretch knits but is better used to help control difficult fabrics.

BASIC BUTTONHOLE STITCH

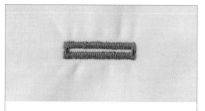

Square on both ends. Used on all styles of garment.

ROUND-END BUTTONHOLE STITCH

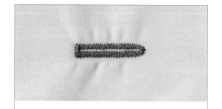

One square end and one round end. Used on jackets.

KEYHOLE BUTTONHOLE STITCH

One square end and one end shaped like a loop. Used on jackets.

DECORATIVE STITCHES

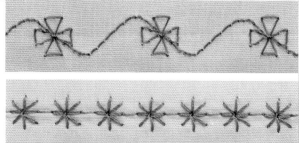

Sewing machines are capable of producing decorative linear stitches. These can be used to enhance the surface of work or a seam as they add interest to edges. Or, when worked as many rows together, they can be used to create a piece of embroidered fabric.

3-THREAD OVERLOCK STITCH

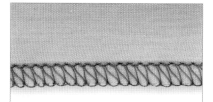

Stitched using three threads on the overlocker. Used to neaten the edge of fabric to prevent fraying.

4-THREAD OVERLOCK STITCH

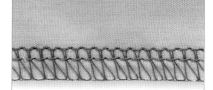

Made using four threads on the overlocker. Used to neaten edges and to construct stretch knits.

MACHINE ARROWHEADS

This is a built-in stitch on many sewing machines. Used to secure weak points.

Machined hems p234 Buttonholes pp262–267 »»

How to make a plain seam

LEVEL OF DIFFICULTY **✱**

A plain seam is 1.5cm (⅝in) wide. It is important that the seam is stitched accurately at this measurement, otherwise the item being made will come out the wrong size and shape. There are guides on the plate of the sewing machine that can be used to help align the fabric.

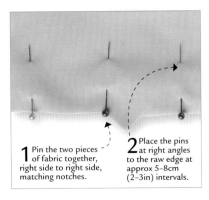

1 Pin the two pieces of fabric together, right side to right side, matching notches.

2 Place the pins at right angles to the raw edge at approx 5–8cm (2–3in) intervals.

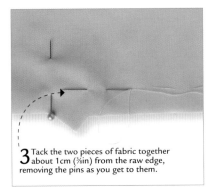

3 Tack the two pieces of fabric together about 1cm (⅜in) from the raw edge, removing the pins as you get to them.

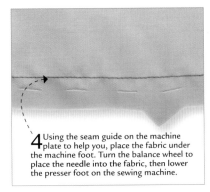

4 Using the seam guide on the machine plate to help you, place the fabric under the machine foot. Turn the balance wheel to place the needle into the fabric, then lower the presser foot on the sewing machine.

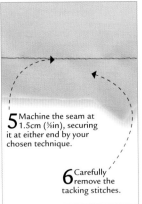

5 Machine the seam at 1.5cm (⅝in), securing it at either end by your chosen technique.

6 Carefully remove the tacking stitches.

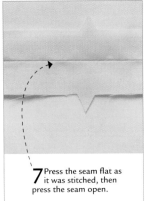

7 Press the seam flat as it was stitched, then press the seam open.

Making a seam with the overlocker

LEVEL OF DIFFICULTY **✱✱**

Use this when constructing stretch knits.

1 Put the fabric together, right side to right side.

2 Stitch the seam with a 4-thread overlock stitch.

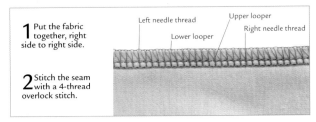

Left needle thread · Upper looper · Lower looper · Right needle thread

Seam neatening

LEVEL OF DIFFICULTY **✱**

It is important that the raw edges of the seam are neatened or finished – this will make the seam hard-wearing and prevent fraying. The method of neatening will depend on the style of item that is being made and the fabric you are using.

PINKED

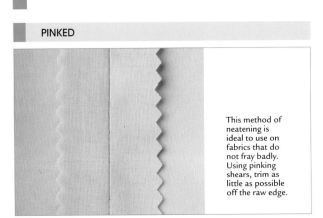

This method of neatening is ideal to use on fabrics that do not fray badly. Using pinking shears, trim as little as possible off the raw edge.

ZIGZAGGED

All sewing machines will make a zigzag stitch. It is an ideal stitch to use to stop the edges fraying and is suitable for all types of fabric. Stitch in from the raw edge, then trim back to the zigzag stitch. On most fabrics, use a stitch width of 2.0 and a stitch length of 1.5.

⟪⟪⟪ Cutting tools p16   Overlocker pp34–35   Tacking stitches p89   Stitches made with a machine pp92–93

TECHNIQUES

OVEREDGE STITCHED

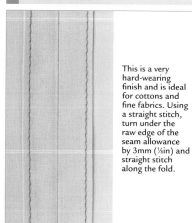

This is found on most sewing machines. Select the overedge stitch on your machine. Using the overedge machine foot and the pre-set stitch length and width, machine along the raw edge of the seam.

CLEAN FINISH

This is a very hard-wearing finish and is ideal for cottons and fine fabrics. Using a straight stitch, turn under the raw edge of the seam allowance by 3mm (⅛in) and straight stitch along the fold.

3-THREAD OVERLOCKED

If you have an overlocker, you can neaten seams with a 3-thread overlock stitch. It is one of the most professional ways to finish seams and is suitable for all types of fabrics and items.

Hong Kong finish

LEVEL OF DIFFICULTY **

This is a great finish to use on wools and linens, to neaten the seams on unlined jackets. It is made by wrapping the raw edge with bias-cut strips.

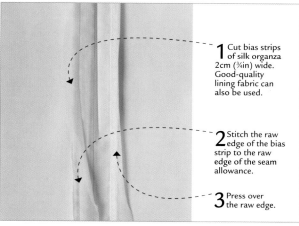

1 Cut bias strips of silk organza 2cm (¾in) wide. Good-quality lining fabric can also be used.

2 Stitch the raw edge of the bias strip to the raw edge of the seam allowance.

3 Press over the raw edge.

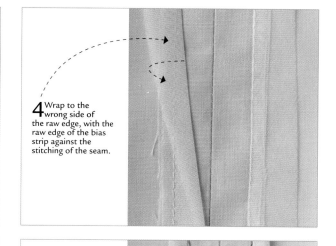

4 Wrap to the wrong side of the raw edge, with the raw edge of the bias strip against the stitching of the seam.

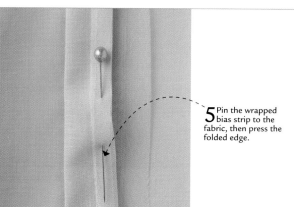

5 Pin the wrapped bias strip to the fabric, then press the folded edge.

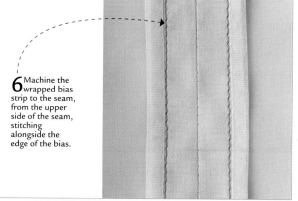

6 Machine the wrapped bias strip to the seam, from the upper side of the seam, stitching alongside the edge of the bias.

How to cut bias strips p147 »»»

French seam

LEVEL OF DIFFICULTY **

A French seam is a seam that is stitched twice, first on the right side of the work and then on the wrong side, enclosing the first seam. The French seam has traditionally been used on delicate garments such as lingerie and on sheer and silk fabrics.

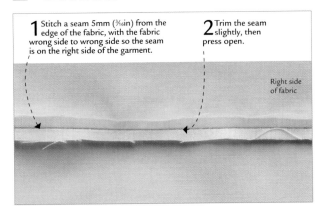

1 Stitch a seam 5mm (³⁄₁₆in) from the edge of the fabric, with the fabric wrong side to wrong side so the seam is on the right side of the garment.

2 Trim the seam slightly, then press open.

Right side of fabric

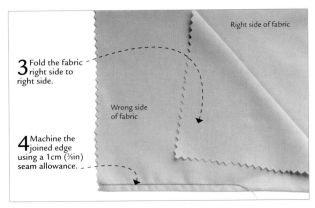

3 Fold the fabric right side to right side.

4 Machine the joined edge using a 1cm (³⁄₈in) seam allowance.

Right side of fabric

Wrong side of fabric

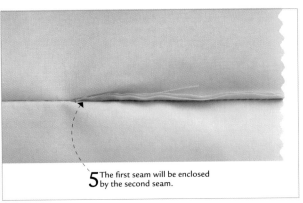

5 The first seam will be enclosed by the second seam.

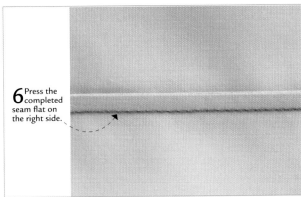

6 Press the completed seam flat on the right side.

Run and fell seam

LEVEL OF DIFFICULTY **

Some garments require a strong seam that will withstand frequent washing and wear and tear. A run and fell seam, also known as a flat fell seam, is very strong. It is made on the right side of a garment and is used on the inside leg seam of jeans, and on men's tailored shirts.

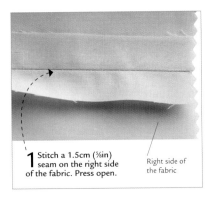

1 Stitch a 1.5cm (⁵⁄₈in) seam on the right side of the fabric. Press open.

Right side of the fabric

2 Trim the side of the seam allowance that is towards the back of the garment down to one-third of its width.

3 Wrap the other side of the seam allowance around the trimmed side and pin in position.

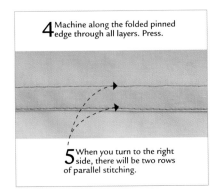

4 Machine along the folded pinned edge through all layers. Press.

5 When you turn to the right side, there will be two rows of parallel stitching.

Self-bound seam
LEVEL OF DIFFICULTY **

Another strong seam, this is constructed in a similar way to the run and fell seam (see opposite page), but on the wrong side of the work. It is used in children's wear.

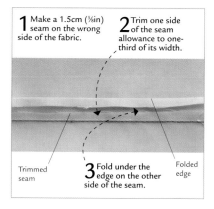

1 Make a 1.5cm (⅝in) seam on the wrong side of the fabric.

2 Trim one side of the seam allowance to one-third of its width.

Trimmed seam

3 Fold under the edge on the other side of the seam.

Folded edge

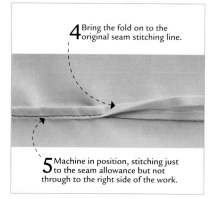

4 Bring the fold on to the original seam stitching line.

5 Machine in position, stitching just to the seam allowance but not through to the right side of the work.

6 The finished seam can only be seen on the wrong side. On the right side there is just a seamline.

Mock French seam
LEVEL OF DIFFICULTY **

When this seam is completed, it looks very similar to the French seam. A mock French seam is best used on cotton or firmer fine fabrics. It is constructed on the wrong side of the work.

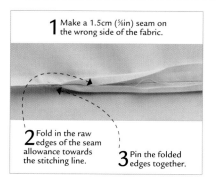

1 Make a 1.5cm (⅝in) seam on the wrong side of the fabric.

2 Fold in the raw edges of the seam allowance towards the stitching line.

3 Pin the folded edges together.

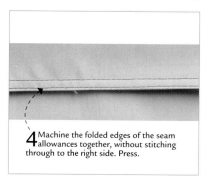

4 Machine the folded edges of the seam allowances together, without stitching through to the right side. Press.

Slotted seam
LEVEL OF DIFFICULTY **

A slotted seam is a decorative seam, shown on the right side. The edges of the seam open to reveal an under layer, which could be a contrasting fabric.

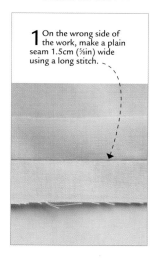

1 On the wrong side of the work, make a plain seam 1.5cm (⅝in) wide using a long stitch.

2 Cut through every fifth stitch using a seam ripper. Press the seam open.

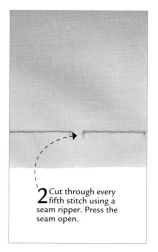

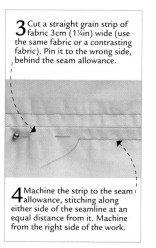

3 Cut a straight grain strip of fabric 3cm (1¼in) wide (use the same fabric or a contrasting fabric). Pin it to the wrong side, behind the seam allowance.

4 Machine the strip to the seam allowance, stitching along either side of the seamline at an equal distance from it. Machine from the right side of the work.

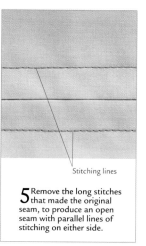

Stitching lines

5 Remove the long stitches that made the original seam, to produce an open seam with parallel lines of stitching on either side.

Stitches made with a machine pp92–93 «««

TECHNIQUES

Top-stitched seam

LEVEL OF DIFFICULTY **

A top-stitched seam is very useful as it is both decorative and practical. This seam is often used on crafts and soft furnishings as well as garments.

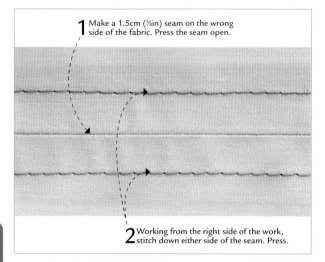

1 Make a 1.5cm (⅝in) seam on the wrong side of the fabric. Press the seam open.

2 Working from the right side of the work, stitch down either side of the seam. Press.

Lapped seam

LEVEL OF DIFFICULTY **

Also called an overlaid seam, a lapped seam is constructed on the right side of the garment. It is a very flat seam when it is finished.

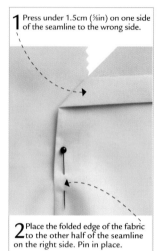

1 Press under 1.5cm (⅝in) on one side of the seamline to the wrong side.

2 Place the folded edge of the fabric to the other half of the seamline on the right side. Pin in place.

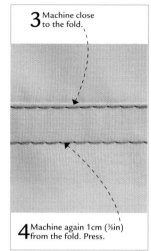

3 Machine close to the fold.

4 Machine again 1cm (⅜in) from the fold. Press.

Corded seam

LEVEL OF DIFFICULTY **

A seam with piping in it can add interest to an otherwise plain garment. This is also a useful technique if you are joining two fabrics that are different. The piping is made first, prior to its being inserted in the seam.

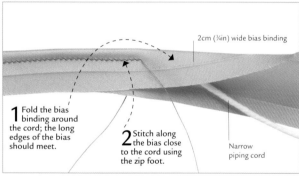

2cm (¾in) wide bias binding

1 Fold the bias binding around the cord; the long edges of the bias should meet.

2 Stitch along the bias close to the cord using the zip foot.

Narrow piping cord

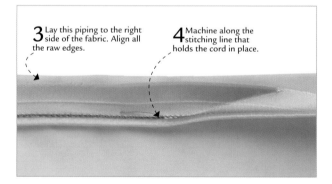

3 Lay this piping to the right side of the fabric. Align all the raw edges.

4 Machine along the stitching line that holds the cord in place.

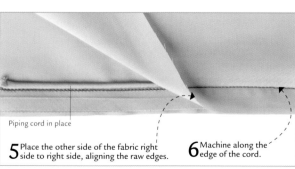

Piping cord in place

5 Place the other side of the fabric right side to right side, aligning the raw edges.

6 Machine along the edge of the cord.

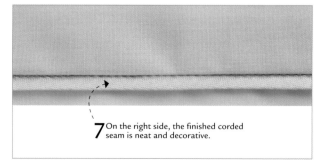

7 On the right side, the finished corded seam is neat and decorative.

Seams on difficult fabrics

LEVEL OF DIFFICULTY **

Some fabrics require specialist care for seam construction because they are very bulky, as you find with a fur fabric, or so soft and delicate that they appear too soft to sew. On a sheer fabric, the seam used is an alternative to a French seam; it is very narrow when finished and presses very flat. Making a seam on suede is done by means of a lapped seam. As some suede-effect fabric has a fake fur on the other side, the seam is reversible.

A SEAM ON SHEER FABRIC

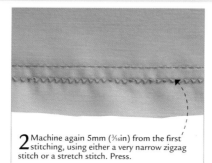

1 On the wrong side of the work, make a 1.5cm (⅝in) seam.

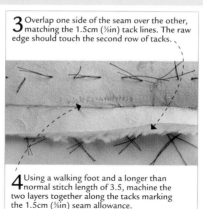

2 Machine again 5mm (³⁄₁₆in) from the first stitching, using either a very narrow zigzag stitch or a stretch stitch. Press.

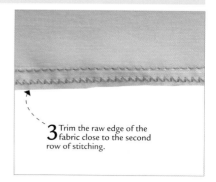

3 Trim the raw edge of the fabric close to the second row of stitching.

A SEAM ON SUEDE OR SUEDE-EFFECT FABRIC

1 On all seams, trace tack the stitching line 1.5cm (⅝in) from the edge.

2 Trace tack again 1.5cm (⅝in) away from the first row of stitching.

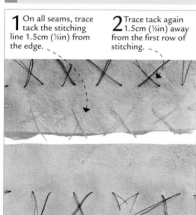

3 Overlap one side of the seam over the other, matching the 1.5cm (⅝in) tack lines. The raw edge should touch the second row of tacks.

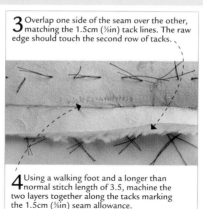

4 Using a walking foot and a longer than normal stitch length of 3.5, machine the two layers together along the tacks marking the 1.5cm (⅝in) seam allowance.

5 Stitch again 1cm (⅜in) from the first stitching line.

6 Trim the raw edge by about 3mm (⅛in).

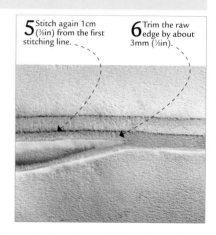

A SEAM ON FUR FABRIC

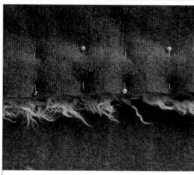

1 Pin the fabric together right side to right side, placing the pins in alternate directions to stop the fur moving.

2 Using a walking foot and a longer than normal stitch length, machine the seam.

3 Finger press the seam open.

4 Trim the surplus fur fabric off the seam allowances.

Stitches made with a machine pp92–93 How to make a plain seam p94

TECHNIQUES

Stitching corners and curves

LEVEL OF DIFFICULTY ✱✱

Not all sewing is straight lines. The work will have curves and corners that require negotiation, to produce sharp clean angles and curves on the right side. The technique for stitching a corner shown below applies to corners of all angles. On a thick fabric, the technique is slightly different, with a stitch taken across the corner, and on a fabric that frays badly the corner is reinforced with a second row of stitches.

STITCHING A CORNER

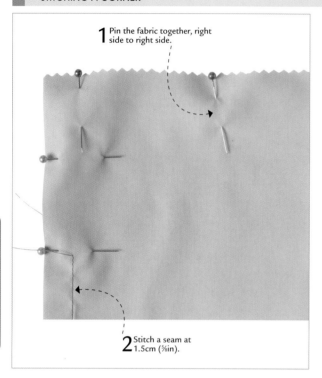

1 Pin the fabric together, right side to right side.

2 Stitch a seam at 1.5cm (⅝in).

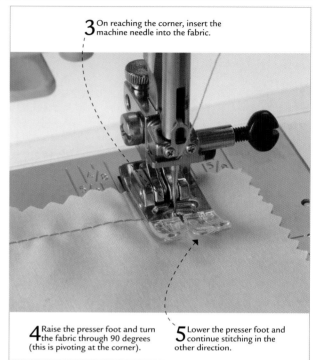

3 On reaching the corner, insert the machine needle into the fabric.

4 Raise the presser foot and turn the fabric through 90 degrees (this is pivoting at the corner).

5 Lower the presser foot and continue stitching in the other direction.

6 The stitching lines are at right angles to each other, which means the finished corner have a sharp point when turned through to the right side.

STITCHING A CORNER ON HEAVY FABRIC

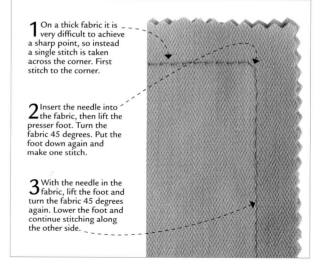

1 On a thick fabric it is very difficult to achieve a sharp point, so instead a single stitch is taken across the corner. First stitch to the corner.

2 Insert the needle into the fabric, then lift the presser foot. Turn the fabric 45 degrees. Put the foot down again and make one stitch.

3 With the needle in the fabric, lift the foot and turn the fabric 45 degrees again. Lower the foot and continue stitching along the other side.

⟪⟪⟪ Sewing-machine accessories pp32–33   Stitches made with a machine pp92–93   How to make a plain seam p94

STITCHING A REINFORCED CORNER

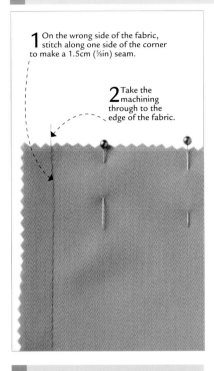

1 On the wrong side of the fabric, stitch along one side of the corner to make a 1.5cm (⅝in) seam.

2 Take the machining through to the edge of the fabric.

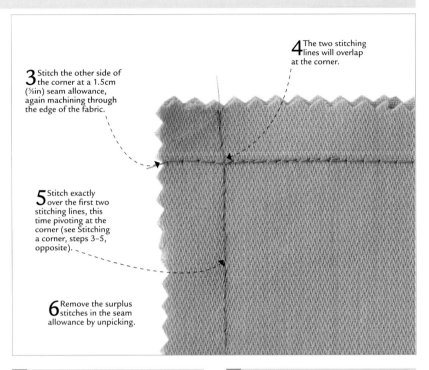

3 Stitch the other side of the corner at a 1.5cm (⅝in) seam allowance, again machining through the edge of the fabric.

4 The two stitching lines will overlap at the corner.

5 Stitch exactly over the first two stitching lines, this time pivoting at the corner (see Stitching a corner, steps 3–5, opposite).

6 Remove the surplus stitches in the seam allowance by unpicking.

STITCHING AN INNER CORNER

1 Machine accurately at 1.5cm (⅝in) from the edge, pivoting at the corner (see Stitching a corner, steps 3–5, opposite page).

2 Clip through the seam allowance into the corner.

STITCHING AN INNER CURVE

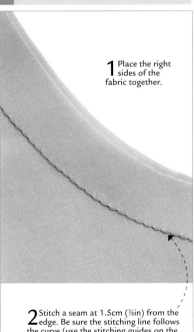

1 Place the right sides of the fabric together.

2 Stitch a seam at 1.5cm (⅝in) from the edge. Be sure the stitching line follows the curve (use the stitching guides on the plate of the machine to help).

STITCHING AN OUTER CURVE

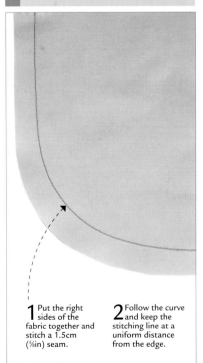

1 Put the right sides of the fabric together and stitch a 1.5cm (⅝in) seam.

2 Follow the curve and keep the stitching line at a uniform distance from the edge.

Reducing seam bulk pp102–103 ⟫⟫⟫

REDUCING SEAM BULK

It is important that the seams used for construction do not cause bulk on the right side. To make sure this does not happen, the seam allowances need to be reduced in size by a technique known as layering a seam. They may also require V shapes to be removed, which is known as notching, or the seam allowance may be clipped.

Layering a seam

On the majority of fabrics, if the seam is on the edge of the work, the fabric in the seam needs reducing. The seam allowance closest to the outside of the garment or item stays full width, while the seam allowance closest to the body or inside is reduced.

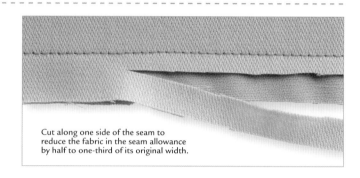

Cut along one side of the seam to reduce the fabric in the seam allowance by half to one-third of its original width.

Reducing seam bulk on an inner curve

LEVEL OF DIFFICULTY *

For an inner curve to lie flat, the seam will need to be layered and notched, then understitched to hold it in place (see opposite page).

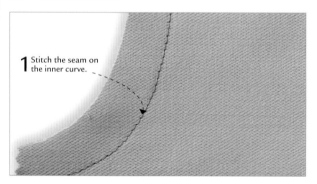

1 Stitch the seam on the inner curve.

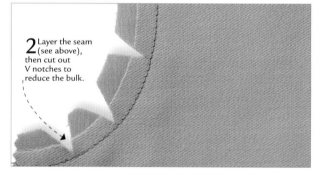

2 Layer the seam (see above), then cut out V notches to reduce the bulk.

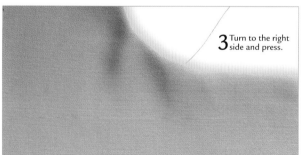

3 Turn to the right side and press.

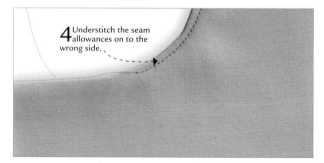

4 Understitch the seam allowances on to the wrong side.

TECHNIQUES

Reducing seam bulk on an outer curve

LEVEL OF DIFFICULTY ✱

An outer curve also needs layering and notching or clipping to allow the fabric to turn to the right side, after which it is understitched.

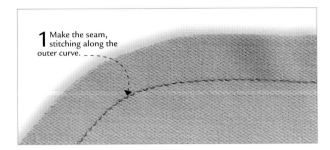

1 Make the seam, stitching along the outer curve.

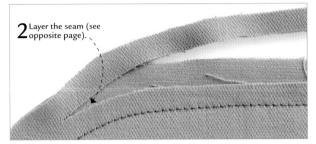

2 Layer the seam (see opposite page).

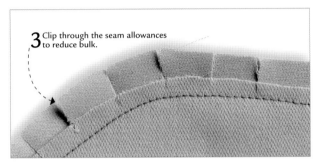

3 Clip through the seam allowances to reduce bulk.

4 Turn through to the right side and press.

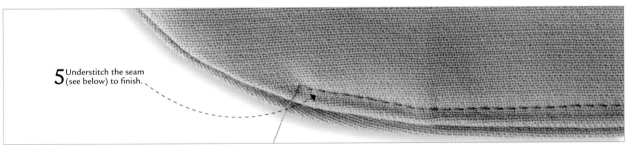

5 Understitch the seam (see below) to finish.

Stitch finishes

LEVEL OF DIFFICULTY ✱✱

Top-stitching and understitching are two methods to finish edges. Top-stitching is meant to be seen on the right side of the work, whereas understitching is not visible from the right side.

TOP-STITCHING

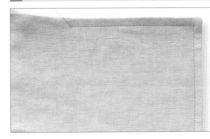

A top-stitch is a decorative, sharp finish to an edge. Use a longer stitch length, of 3.0 or 3.5, and machine on the right side of the work, using the edge of the machine foot as a guide.

UNDERSTITCHING

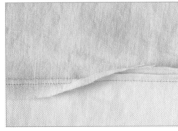

Understitching is used to secure a seam that is on the edge of a piece of fabric. It helps to stop the seam from rolling to the right side. First make the seam, then layer, turn, and press on to the right side. Open the seam again and push the seam allowance over the layered seam allowance. Machine the seam allowance down.

Combination neck and armhole facing p151   Inserting a set-in sleeve p191   »»

DARTS, TUCKS, PLEATS, AND GATHERS

Shape is put into a piece of flat fabric by means of a dart, a tuck, a pleat, or a gather. It may be to shape the fabric around the body or shape for crafts or soft furnishings.

DARTS

A dart is used to give shape to a piece of fabric so that it can fit around the contours of the body. Some darts are stitched using straight stitching lines and other darts are stitched using a slightly curved line. Always stitch a dart from the point to the wide end because you are able to sink the machine needle into the point accurately and securely.

Directory of darts

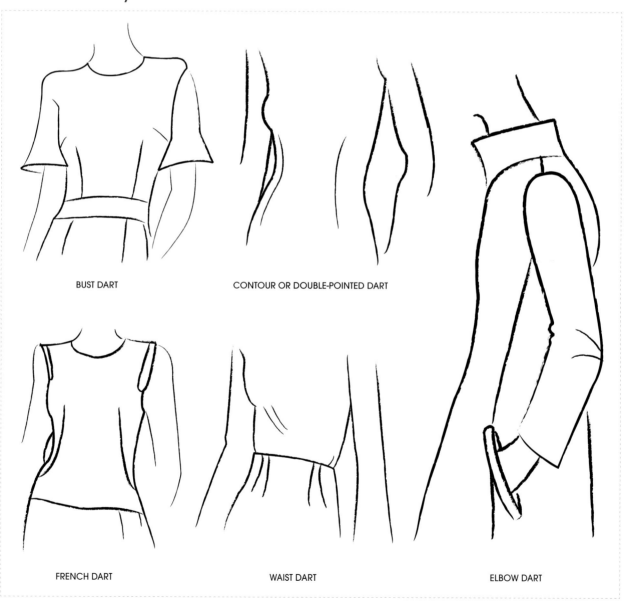

BUST DART

CONTOUR OR DOUBLE-POINTED DART

FRENCH DART

WAIST DART

ELBOW DART

«««   Body measuring pp60–61   Altering patterns pp64–65

Plain dart

LEVEL OF DIFFICULTY *

This is the most common type of dart and is used to give shaping to the bust in the bodice. It is also found at the waist in skirts and trousers to give shape from the waist to the hip.

Shaping darts to fit

LEVEL OF DIFFICULTY **

Our bodies often curve, and the straight line of the dart may not sit closely enough to our own personal shape. The dart can be stitched slightly concave or convex so it follows our contours. Do not move the curve out by more than 3mm (⅛in).

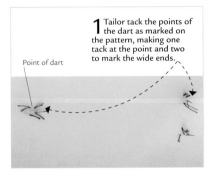

1 Tailor tack the points of the dart as marked on the pattern, making one tack at the point and two to mark the wide ends.

Point of dart

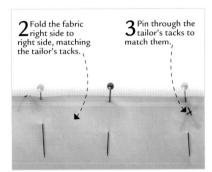

2 Fold the fabric right side to right side, matching the tailor's tacks.

3 Pin through the tailor's tacks to match them.

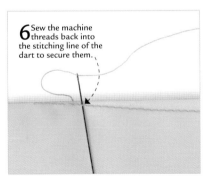

4 Tack along the dart line, joining the tailor's tacks. Remove the pins.

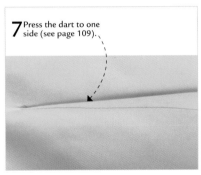

5 Machine stitch alongside the tacking line. Remove the tacks.

CONVEX DART

Use this for fuller shapes. Stitch the dart slightly inside the normal stitching line, to make a smooth convex curve.

6 Sew the machine threads back into the stitching line of the dart to secure them.

7 Press the dart to one side (see page 109).

CONCAVE DART

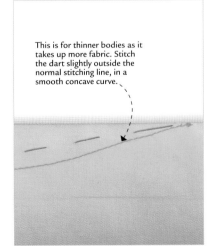

This is for thinner bodies as it takes up more fabric. Stitch the dart slightly outside the normal stitching line, in a smooth concave curve.

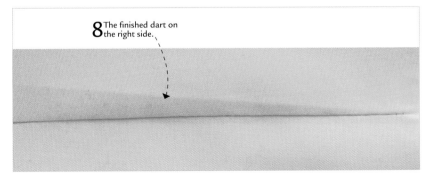

8 The finished dart on the right side.

Making a toile pp74–75   Pattern marking pp82–83 ≪≪

Contour or double-pointed dart

This type of dart is like two darts joined together at the fat end. It is used to give shape at the waist of a garment. It will contour the fabric from the bust into the waist and then out again for the hip.

LEVEL OF DIFFICULTY **

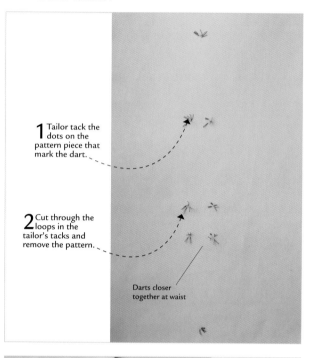

1 Tailor tack the dots on the pattern piece that mark the dart.

2 Cut through the loops in the tailor's tacks and remove the pattern.

Darts closer together at waist

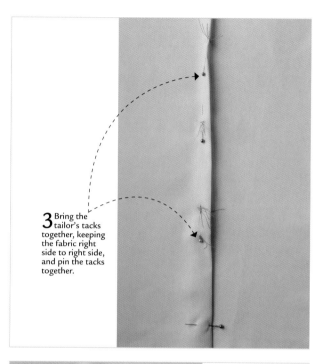

3 Bring the tailor's tacks together, keeping the fabric right side to right side, and pin the tacks together.

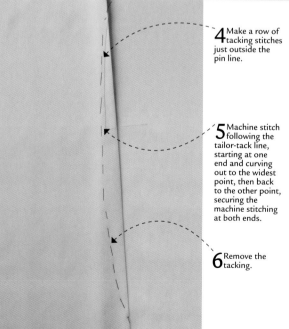

4 Make a row of tacking stitches just outside the pin line.

5 Machine stitch following the tailor-tack line, starting at one end and curving out to the widest point, then back to the other point, securing the machine stitching at both ends.

6 Remove the tacking.

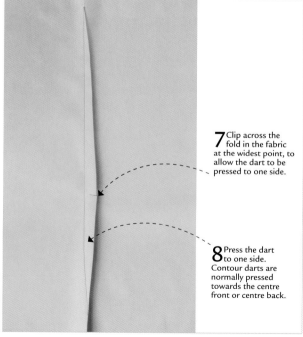

7 Clip across the fold in the fabric at the widest point, to allow the dart to be pressed to one side.

8 Press the dart to one side. Contour darts are normally pressed towards the centre front or centre back.

≪≪ Pressing aids pp28–29   Altering patterns   pp64–65   Pattern marking pp82–83

French dart

LEVEL OF DIFFICULTY ***

A French dart is used on the front of a garment only. It is a curved dart that extends from the side seam at the waist to the bust point. As this is a long dart that is shaped, it will need to be slashed prior to construction, in order for it to fit together and then lie flat when pressed.

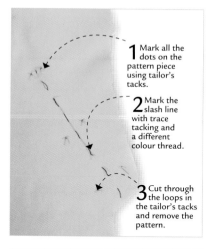

1 Mark all the dots on the pattern piece using tailor's tacks.

2 Mark the slash line with trace tacking and a different colour thread.

3 Cut through the loops in the tailor's tacks and remove the pattern.

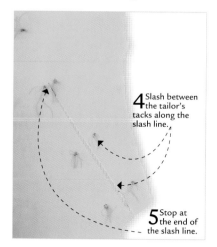

4 Slash between the tailor's tacks along the slash line.

5 Stop at the end of the slash line.

6 Bring the tailor's tacks together, right side to right side, and pin.

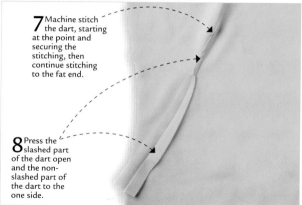

7 Machine stitch the dart, starting at the point and securing the stitching, then continue stitching to the fat end.

8 Press the slashed part of the dart open and the non-slashed part of the dart to the one side.

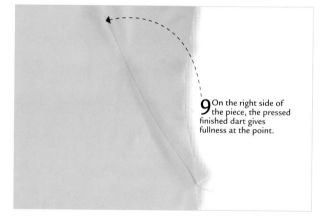

9 On the right side of the piece, the pressed finished dart gives fullness at the point.

Pressing a dart

If a dart is pressed incorrectly, this can spoil the look of a garment. For successful pressing you will need a tailor's ham and a steam iron on a steam setting. A pressing cloth may be required for delicate fabrics such as silk, satin, and chiffon, and for lining fabrics.

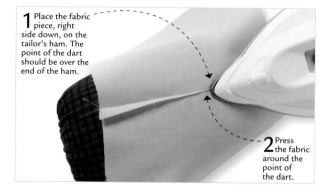

1 Place the fabric piece, right side down, on the tailor's ham. The point of the dart should be over the end of the ham.

2 Press the fabric around the point of the dart.

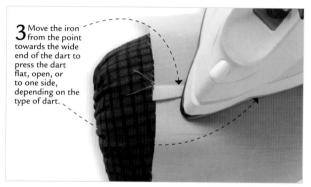

3 Move the iron from the point towards the wide end of the dart to press the dart flat, open, or to one side, depending on the type of dart.

TUCKS

A tuck is a decorative addition to any piece of fabric, and can be big and bold or very delicate. Tucks are made by stitching evenly spaced folds into the fabric on the right side, normally on the straight grain of the fabric. As the tucks take up additional fabric, it is advisable to make them prior to cutting out.

Directory of tucks

BLIND TUCKS

CROSS TUCKS

PLAIN TUCKS

SHELL TUCKS

SPACED TUCKS

PLAIN DARTED TUCKS

Plain tucks

LEVEL OF DIFFICULTY **

A plain tuck is made by marking and creasing the fabric at regular intervals. A row of machine stitches are then worked adjacent to the fold.

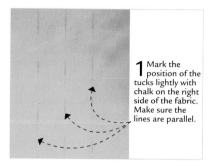

1 Mark the position of the tucks lightly with chalk on the right side of the fabric. Make sure the lines are parallel.

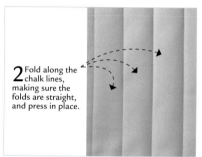

2 Fold along the chalk lines, making sure the folds are straight, and press in place.

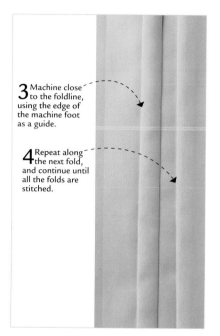

3 Machine close to the foldline, using the edge of the machine foot as a guide.

4 Repeat along the next fold, and continue until all the folds are stitched.

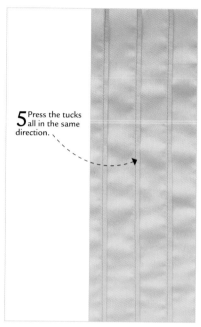

5 Press the tucks all in the same direction.

Other simple tucks

LEVEL OF DIFFICULTY **

These tucks are also made by marking and creasing the fabric. The positioning of the machine stitching determines the type of tuck.

SPACED TUCKS

These are similar to a plain tuck but with wider regular spacing. Press the tucks in place along the foldlines and pin. Machine 1cm (⅜in) from the foldline. Press all the tucks in one direction.

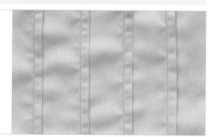

PIN TUCKS

These narrow, regularly spaced tucks are stitched very close to the foldline, which may require moving the machine needle closer to the fold. Use the pintuck foot on the sewing machine.

TWIN NEEDLE TUCKS

For these regularly spaced tucks, stitch along the foldlines using the twin needle on the sewing machine. The twin needle produces a shallow tuck that looks very effective when multiple rows are stitched.

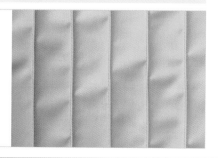

BLIND TUCKS

Blind tucks are stitched so that they touch, and no machining lines show. Fold back all but one tuck and stitch it in place. Continue stitching the tucks in this way so that the folded edge of each covers the machine line of the previous tuck.

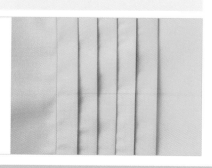

Stitches made with a machine pp92–93 ≪≪≪

Shell tucks

LEVEL OF DIFFICULTY **

A shell tuck is very decorative as it has a scalloped edge. Shell tucks can be easily stitched using the sewing machine. On heavy fabric and delicate fabrics it may be preferable to make the tucks by hand.

MACHINE SHELL TUCKS

1 Mark the foldlines on the fabric, then fold and press.

2 Tack the folds in place.

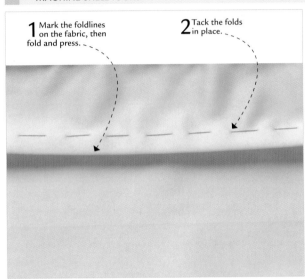

3 Use the embroidery foot on the sewing machine and set the sewing machine to a shell hem stitch.

4 Stitch along the fold, keeping the fold close to the inside opening of the machine foot.

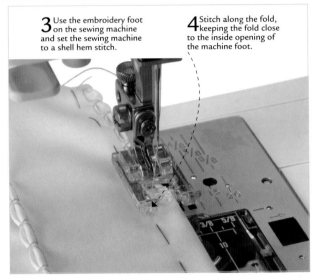

5 The finished tucks should be stitched at regular intervals.

SHELL TUCKS BY HAND

1 Tack the foldlines for the tucks in place.

2 Using a double thread in the needle, make two or three running stitches.

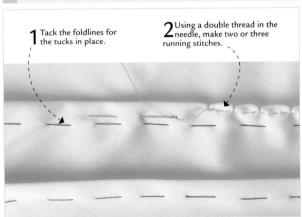

3 Every 1.25cm (½in), make an over-stitch through the fold to produce a scallop.

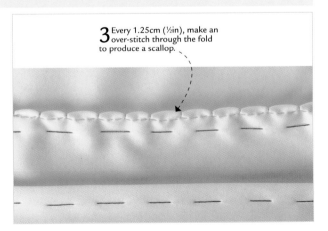

TECHNIQUES

Corded or piped tucks

LEVEL OF DIFFICULTY **

These are very substantial tucks that stand proud of the fabric. This type of tuck is best used in soft furnishings.

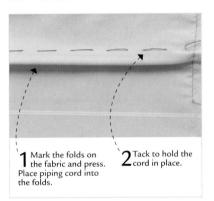

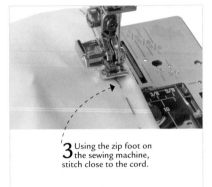

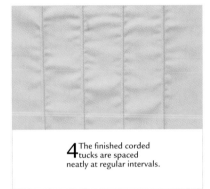

1 Mark the folds on the fabric and press. Place piping cord into the folds.

2 Tack to hold the cord in place.

3 Using the zip foot on the sewing machine, stitch close to the cord.

4 The finished corded tucks are spaced neatly at regular intervals.

Darted tucks

LEVEL OF DIFFICULTY **

A tuck that stops to release the fullness is known as a darted tuck. It can be used to give fullness at the bust or hip. The shaped darted tuck is stitched at an angle to release less fabric, while the plain darted tuck is stitched straight on the grainline.

SHAPED DARTED TUCKS

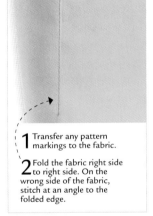

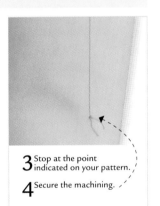

1 Transfer any pattern markings to the fabric.

2 Fold the fabric right side to right side. On the wrong side of the fabric, stitch at an angle to the folded edge.

3 Stop at the point indicated on your pattern.

4 Secure the machining.

PLAIN DARTED TUCKS

1 Make in the same way as a shaped darted tuck (see left), but stitch parallel to the folded edge.

2 Stop as indicated on the pattern.

3 The tuck as seen from the right side.

Cross tucks

LEVEL OF DIFFICULTY **

These are tucks that cross over each other by being stitched in opposite directions.

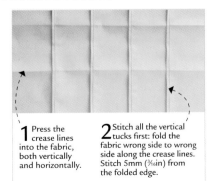

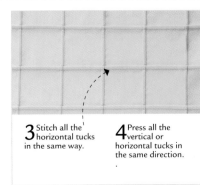

1 Press the crease lines into the fabric, both vertically and horizontally.

2 Stitch all the vertical tucks first: fold the fabric wrong side to wrong side along the crease lines. Stitch 5mm (³⁄₁₆in) from the folded edge.

3 Stitch all the horizontal tucks in the same way.

4 Press all the vertical or horizontal tucks in the same direction.

PLEATS

A pleat is a fold or series of folds in fabric. Pleats are most commonly found in skirts where the pleats are made to fit around the waist and hip and then left to fall in crisply pressed folds, giving fullness at the hemline. It is important that pleats are made accurately, otherwise they will not fit the body and will look uneven. Foldlines and placement lines, or foldlines and crease lines, are marked on the fabric from the pattern. It is by using a combination of these lines and the spaces between them that the pleats are made.

Directory of pleats

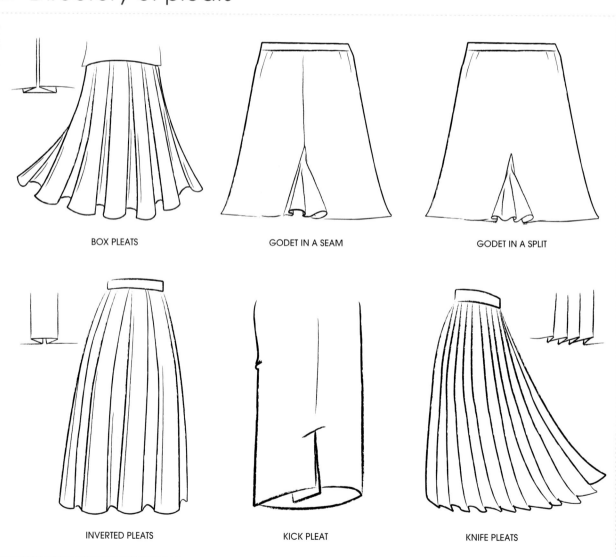

BOX PLEATS

GODET IN A SEAM

GODET IN A SPLIT

INVERTED PLEATS

KICK PLEAT

KNIFE PLEATS

Pleats on the right side

LEVEL OF DIFFICULTY **

Knife pleats are normally formed on the right side of fabric. They can all face the same direction or may face opposite directions from opposite sides of the garment. Knife pleats have foldlines and placement lines.

1 Mark the placement lines and foldlines with trace tacks. Use one colour thread, such as red, for placement lines.

2 Use a contrasting colour thread, such as blue, to mark foldlines.

3 Cut through the thread loops and remove the pattern pieces carefully.

Placement line   Foldline

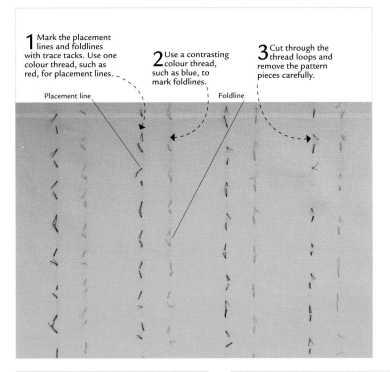

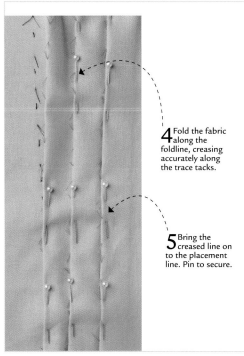

4 Fold the fabric along the foldline, creasing accurately along the trace tacks.

5 Bring the creased line on to the placement line. Pin to secure.

6 Tack along the foldlines about 2mm (⅟₁₆in) from the folded edge, through all the layers.

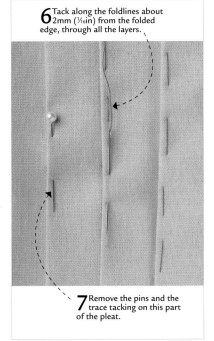

7 Remove the pins and the trace tacking on this part of the pleat.

8 With the right side of the fabric uppermost, cover with a silk organza pressing cloth.

9 Using a steam iron on a steam setting, press the pleats in place. Keep the iron still as opposed to moving it around, and eject a shot of steam each time you lift it to a new position. Repeat this action across all of the pleats.

10 Turn the fabric to the wrong side and insert thin strips of manila card or brown paper under the pleat fabric.

11 Press again with the steam iron and a silk organza cloth. The card or paper will prevent the fabric from leaving an imprint on the right side.

Pleats on the wrong side

LEVEL OF DIFFICULTY **

Some pleats, including box (shown below) and inverted pleats, are formed on the wrong side of the fabric. As the pleats are made on the wrong side, you can mark the crease lines and foldlines with a tracing wheel and dressmaker's carbon paper. Use a ruler to guide the tracing wheel, because these pleats need to be straight lines.

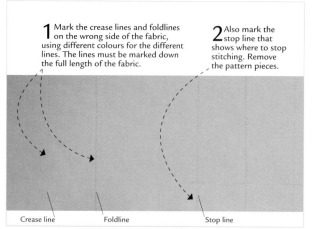

1 Mark the crease lines and foldlines on the wrong side of the fabric, using different colours for the different lines. The lines must be marked down the full length of the fabric.

2 Also mark the stop line that shows where to stop stitching. Remove the pattern pieces.

Crease line Foldline Stop line

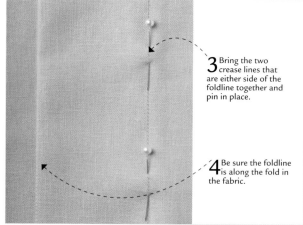

3 Bring the two crease lines that are either side of the foldline together and pin in place.

4 Be sure the foldline is along the fold in the fabric.

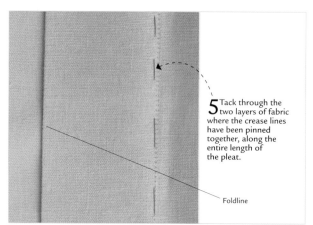

5 Tack through the two layers of fabric where the crease lines have been pinned together, along the entire length of the pleat.

Foldline

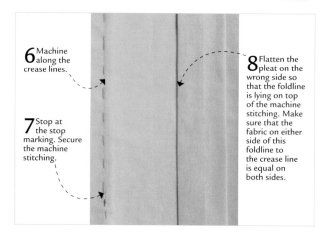

6 Machine along the crease lines.

7 Stop at the stop marking. Secure the machine stitching.

8 Flatten the pleat on the wrong side so that the foldline is lying on top of the machine stitching. Make sure that the fabric on either side of this foldline to the crease line is equal on both sides.

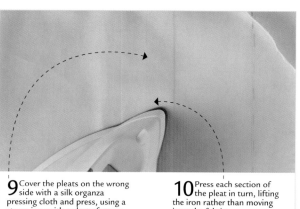

9 Cover the pleats on the wrong side with a silk organza pressing cloth and press, using a steam iron with a shot of steam.

10 Press each section of the pleat in turn, lifting the iron rather than moving it on the fabric.

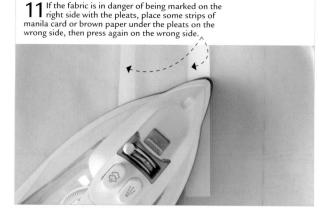

11 If the fabric is in danger of being marked on the right side with the pleats, place some strips of manila card or brown paper under the pleats on the wrong side, then press again on the wrong side.

Pleats with a separate underlay

LEVEL OF DIFFICULTY ★★★

Sometimes a box pleat is constructed with a separate piece of fabric or underlay. This technique is usually done on large, single box pleats or on a pleat made using thicker fabric, because it reduces the bulk. The seam to make this pleat is much wider than normal, as it is the width of the pleat.

1 Mark the stitching line with trace tacks. Cut through the thread loops and carefully pull away the pattern piece.

2 Place the two pieces of fabric together, right side to right side. Match the notches and trace tacking.

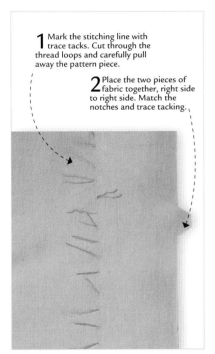

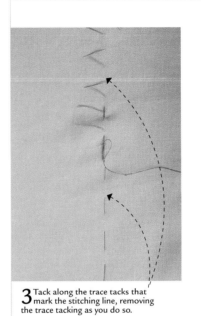

3 Tack along the trace tacks that mark the stitching line, removing the trace tacking as you do so.

4 Machine the seam to the stop point.

5 Press the seam open along its full length.

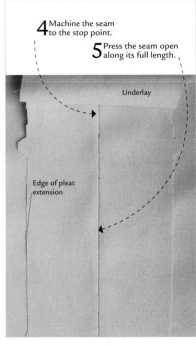

Underlay

Edge of pleat extension

6 Take the underlay and place carefully on to the pressed seam, matching the notches. The wrong side of the underlay should be uppermost.

7 Pin the underlay in place, being careful to pin it just to the edge of the seam and not through to the main fabric.

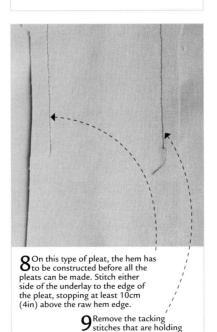

8 On this type of pleat, the hem has to be constructed before all the pleats can be made. Stitch either side of the underlay to the edge of the pleat, stopping at least 10cm (4in) above the raw hem edge.

9 Remove the tacking stitches that are holding the pleat together.

10 Turn up the hem including the pleat. Separately turn up the underlay to match.

11 Pin the underlay and the pleat back together from where the machine stitching stopped, down through the hem. Make sure that on the right side the hem is even through this area.

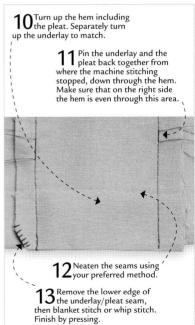

12 Neaten the seams using your preferred method.

13 Remove the lower edge of the underlay/pleat seam, then blanket stitch or whip stitch. Finish by pressing.

Top-stitching and edge-stitching pleats

LEVEL OF DIFFICULTY ✱✱

If a pleat is top-stitched or edge-stitched, it will hang correctly and always look crisp. It will also help the pleats on the skirt to stay in shape when you are sitting. Try to stitch both the top-stitching and the edge-stitching the entire length of the skirt, from the hem to the waist.

TOP-STITCHING KNIFE PLEATS

1 Once the knife pleats have been pressed and all tacks and markings removed, place some pins across the pleat to stop it from moving.

2 Machine stitch from the right side approx 2mm (¹⁄₁₆in) from the fold.

3 Start the stitching at the lower end of the pleat and stitch to the waist.

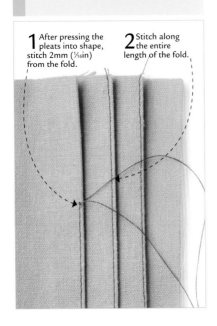

TOP-STITCHING BOX PLEATS THAT HAVE A SQUARE END

1 This requires stitching down on either side of the foldline. Stitch down one side about 5mm (³⁄₁₆in) from the foldline.

2 Pivot and stitch horizontally across the end of the stitching of the pleat.

3 Pivot again and stitch up the other side of the foldline about 5mm (³⁄₁₆in) from the foldline.

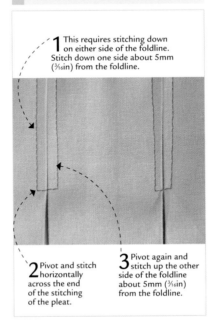

TOP-STITCHING BOX PLEATS THAT HAVE A POINTED END

1 Stitch down one side 5mm (³⁄₁₆in) from the foldline, then pivot and stitch diagonally to the centre.

2 Pivot again and stitch diagonally the other side and back to the waist 5mm (³⁄₁₆in) from the foldline.

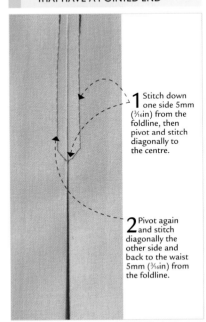

EDGE-STITCHING KNIFE PLEATS

1 After pressing the pleats into shape, stitch 2mm (¹⁄₁₆in) from the fold.

2 Stitch along the entire length of the fold.

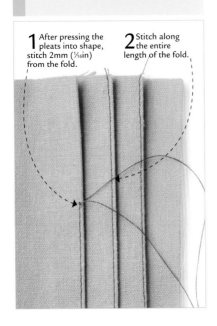

EDGE-STITCHING AND TOP-STITCHING PLEATS

1 Edge-stitch first the edge of the pleat about 2mm (¹⁄₁₆in) from the folded edge.

2 Stop the edge-stitching just above the point where the pleat is to be top-stitched.

3 Place the machine needle into the pleat, through all layers, four or five stitches below where the edge-stitching stops.

4 Top-stitch through all the layers, continuing at 2mm (¹⁄₁₆in) from the fold, to the waist.

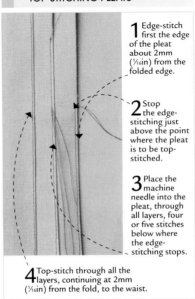

TOP-STITCHING KICK PLEATS OR INVERTED PLEATS

1 This pleat is pressed to the right. Just below the stitching line that makes the pleat, stitch a line diagonally, to secure the pleat fabric at the back.

2 Make sure the stitching line finishes exactly on the foldline.

3 Pull the ends of the machine stitching through to the reverse.

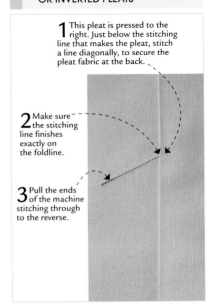

Staying pleats

LEVEL OF DIFFICULTY ★★★

Staying a pleat is a technique used to reduce the bulk of the pleat, especially in the hip area. There are various ways of doing this and the method chosen will depend on the type of pleat, the fabric used, and your personal preference.

SELF-STAYING BOX PLEATS OR INVERTED PLEATS

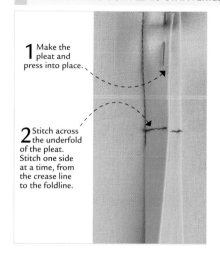

1 Make the pleat and press into place.

2 Stitch across the underfold of the pleat. Stitch one side at a time, from the crease line to the foldline.

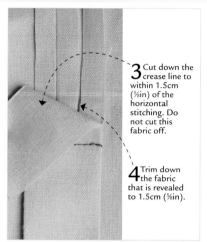

3 Cut down the crease line to within 1.5cm (⅝in) of the horizontal stitching. Do not cut this fabric off.

4 Trim down the fabric that is revealed to 1.5cm (⅝in).

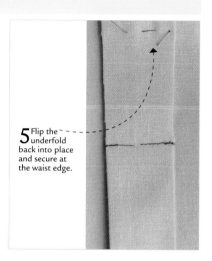

5 Flip the underfold back into place and secure at the waist edge.

STAYING KNIFE PLEATS ON THICKER FABRIC

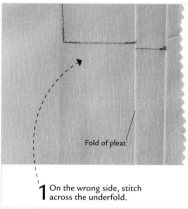

Fold of pleat

1 On the wrong side, stitch across the underfold.

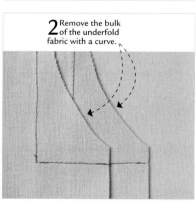

2 Remove the bulk of the underfold fabric with a curve.

3 Cut a piece of lining large enough to cover the pleated section.

4 Clean finish the lower edge.

5 Tack to secure along the waist edge (to make this fabric fit at the waist, tuck the lining at the waist).

6 Using a flat fell stitch, hand stitch the edge of the lining to the stitching on the underfold.

Hand-stitched hems – clean finish p230 »»

Hemming pleats

LEVEL OF DIFFICULTY ★★★

Most pleated garments or soft furnishings are hemmed after the pleats have been constructed; however, in some cases pleats can be hemmed first. This technique is only used for garments with all-around pleats or that have to follow a check or stripe.

HEMMING KNIFE PLEATS OR INVERTED PLEATS

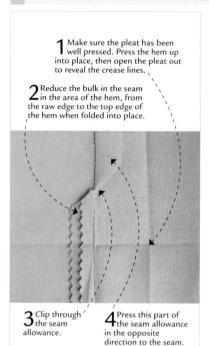

1 Make sure the pleat has been well pressed. Press the hem up into place, then open the pleat out to reveal the crease lines.

2 Reduce the bulk in the seam in the area of the hem, from the raw edge to the top edge of the hem when folded into place.

3 Clip through the seam allowance.

4 Press this part of the seam allowance in the opposite direction to the seam.

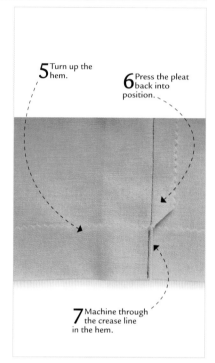

5 Turn up the hem.

6 Press the pleat back into position.

7 Machine through the crease line in the hem.

HEMMING BOX PLEATS BEFORE THE GARMENT IS FINISHED

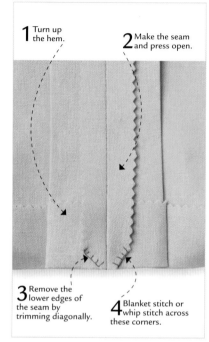

1 Turn up the hem.

2 Make the seam and press open.

3 Remove the lower edges of the seam by trimming diagonally.

4 Blanket stitch or whip stitch across these corners.

HEMMING BOX PLEATS AFTER THE GARMENT IS FINISHED

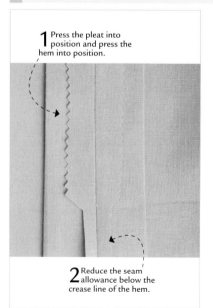

1 Press the pleat into position and press the hem into position.

2 Reduce the seam allowance below the crease line of the hem.

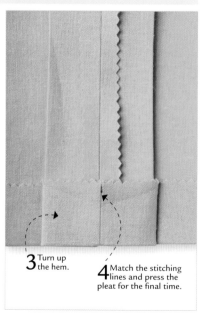

3 Turn up the hem.

4 Match the stitching lines and press the pleat for the final time.

SECURING PLEATS AT THE HEM

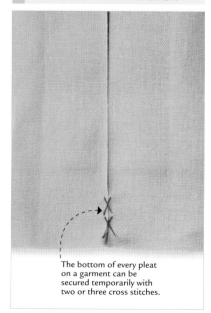

The bottom of every pleat on a garment can be secured temporarily with two or three cross stitches.

⟪⟪ Altering patterns pp66–67   Pattern marking pp82–83   Hand stitches pp90–91   Reducing seam bulk pp102–103

Adjusting pleats to fit

LEVEL OF DIFFICULTY ***

If a pleated skirt is either too big or too tight at the waist or hip, a small adjustment on each pleat can make a huge difference. Simply take the amount to be added or removed and divide it by the number of pleats. If the adjustment is not the same on all the pleats, they will look unbalanced.

LETTING OUT PLEATS FORMED ON THE RIGHT SIDE

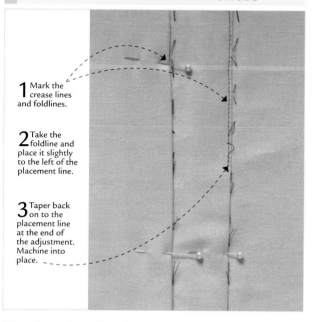

1 Mark the crease lines and foldlines.

2 Take the foldline and place it slightly to the left of the placement line.

3 Taper back on to the placement line at the end of the adjustment. Machine into place.

TAKING IN PLEATS FORMED ON THE RIGHT SIDE

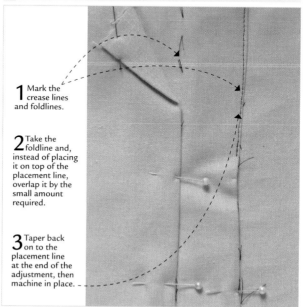

1 Mark the crease lines and foldlines.

2 Take the foldline and, instead of placing it on top of the placement line, overlap it by the small amount required.

3 Taper back on to the placement line at the end of the adjustment, then machine in place.

LETTING OUT PLEATS FORMED ON THE WRONG SIDE

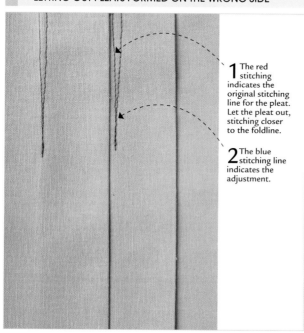

1 The red stitching indicates the original stitching line for the pleat. Let the pleat out, stitching closer to the foldline.

2 The blue stitching line indicates the adjustment.

TAKING IN PLEATS FORMED ON THE WRONG SIDE

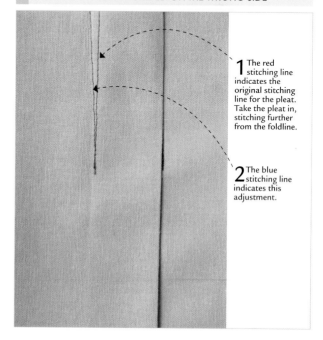

1 The red stitching line indicates the original stitching line for the pleat. Take the pleat in, stitching further from the foldline.

2 The blue stitching line indicates this adjustment.

Godet in a seam

LEVEL OF DIFFICULTY ***

A godet is a type of pleat that is inserted into a garment to give fullness at the hem edge. It is a segment of a circle, usually triangular in shape but also sometimes a half circle – the size of the godet depends on the fullness required. The godet may go from hem to knee or even hem to thigh, according to the style of the skirt. The easiest way to insert a godet is in a seam.

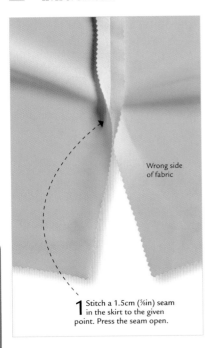

Wrong side of fabric

1 Stitch a 1.5cm (⅝in) seam in the skirt to the given point. Press the seam open.

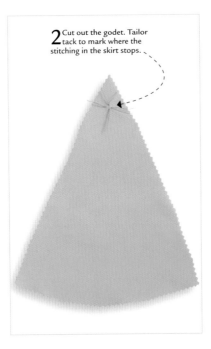

2 Cut out the godet. Tailor tack to mark where the stitching in the skirt stops.

3 Place the godet to the split in the skirt seam, right side to right side.

4 Join one side of the godet to the skirt, machining along the edge, from the hem to the tailor's tack.

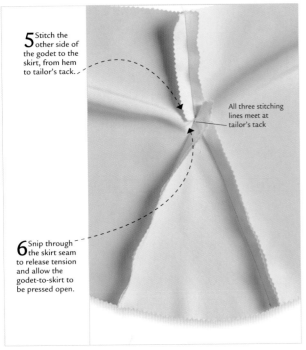

5 Stitch the other side of the godet to the skirt, from hem to tailor's tack.

All three stitching lines meet at tailor's tack

6 Snip through the skirt seam to release tension and allow the godet-to-skirt to be pressed open.

7 Finish the godet by pressing carefully on the right side.

Godet in a split

LEVEL OF DIFFICULTY ★★★★

Sometimes there are not enough seams in a garment for the number of godets that you would like to insert. If that is the case, a split must be made in the fabric at the hemline to accommodate each godet. A piece of silk organza is sewn on to the point of the split to strengthen it.

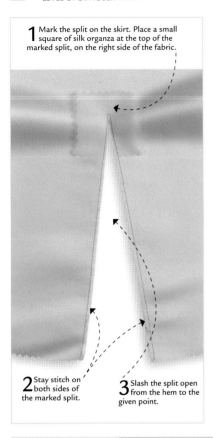

1 Mark the split on the skirt. Place a small square of silk organza at the top of the marked split, on the right side of the fabric.

2 Stay stitch on both sides of the marked split.

3 Slash the split open from the hem to the given point.

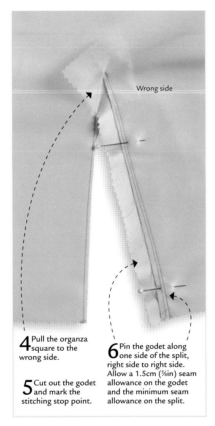

Wrong side

4 Pull the organza square to the wrong side.

5 Cut out the godet and mark the stitching stop point.

6 Pin the godet along one side of the split, right side to right side. Allow a 1.5cm (⅝in) seam allowance on the godet and the minimum seam allowance on the split.

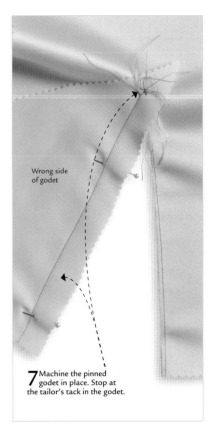

Wrong side of godet

7 Machine the pinned godet in place. Stop at the tailor's tack in the godet.

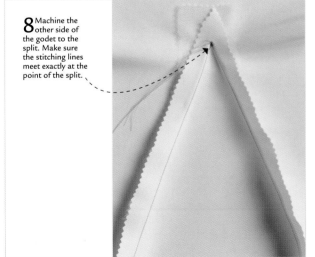

8 Machine the other side of the godet to the split. Make sure the stitching lines meet exactly at the point of the split.

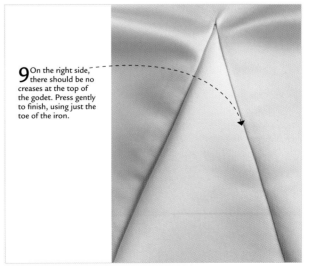

9 On the right side, there should be no creases at the top of the godet. Press gently to finish, using just the toe of the iron.

Stitches made with a machine pp92–93 How to make a plain seam p94 《《《

Pleats on curtains

LEVEL OF DIFFICULTY **

Pleats are used in soft furnishings, particularly at the top of curtains, to reduce the fabric so that the curtain will fit on to its track and fit the window. The easiest way to pleat the upper edge of a curtain is to apply a curtain tape. Tapes are available in various depths and will pull the curtain into pencil pleats or goblet pleats. The most common tape used for pencil pleating is 8cm (3¼in) deep. A curtain is normally cut two and a half to three times the width of the window. The curtain tape will reduce the fabric by this much as it pleats up.

PREPARING THE CURTAIN TO TAKE THE TAPE

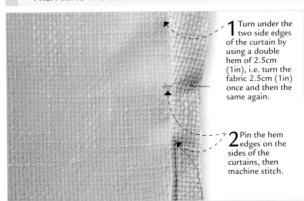

1 Turn under the two side edges of the curtain by using a double hem of 2.5cm (1in), i.e. turn the fabric 2.5cm (1in) once and then the same again.

2 Pin the hem edges on the sides of the curtains, then machine stitch.

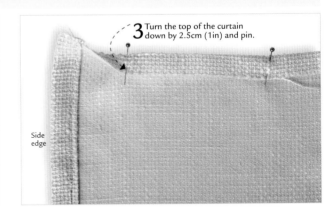

3 Turn the top of the curtain down by 2.5cm (1in) and pin.

Side edge

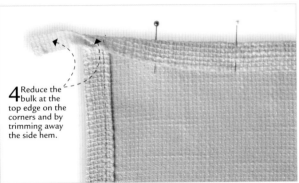

4 Reduce the bulk at the top edge on the corners and by trimming away the side hem.

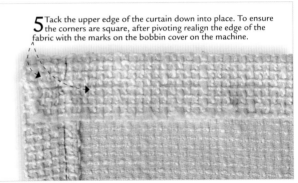

5 Tack the upper edge of the curtain down into place. To ensure the corners are square, after pivoting realign the edge of the fabric with the marks on the bobbin cover on the machine.

MAKING A POCKET FOR THE STRINGS

1 Before the tape is applied, a small pocket needs to be made to take the strings that are used to pull up the tape. Cut a rectangle of spare fabric 15 x 8cm (6 x 3¼in).

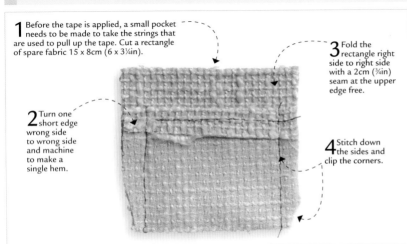

2 Turn one short edge wrong side to wrong side and machine to make a single hem.

3 Fold the rectangle right side to right side with a 2cm (¾in) seam at the upper edge free.

4 Stitch down the sides and clip the corners.

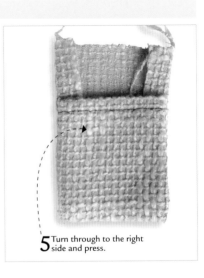

5 Turn through to the right side and press.

PENCIL PLEATS

1 Take the curtain tape and release the strings at the one end, making sure they are all visible on the same side.

2 Place the top of the tape 5mm (³⁄₁₆in) down from the folded edge of the curtain. Pin in place, stretching the tape as you do so. Turn under the short end, avoiding the strings and pin.

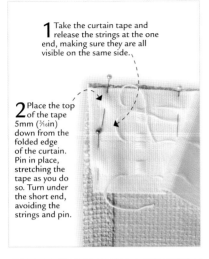

3 Machine the upper edge of the tape to the curtain fabric. Make sure the strings stay free.

4 Before stitching the lower edge of the tape, place the pocket you made under the end of the tape.

5 Pin the tape and the pocket in place. Machine stitch the tape and pocket.

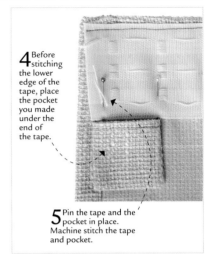

6 Pull up the strings in the tape from the end with the pocket to make the pleats.

7 Tie the strings together and place in the pocket.

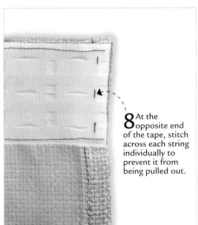

8 At the opposite end of the tape, stitch across each string individually to prevent it from being pulled out.

9 Turn the curtain over to check that the pencil pleats are evenly spaced and will fit the window. Adjust if necessary.

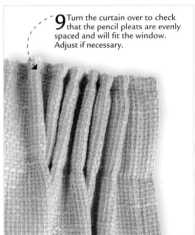

GOBLET PLEATS

1 Goblet pleats are three pleats together at regular intervals. When the tape is pulled up, the pleats are close together at the base and fan out at the top. Prepare the curtain to take the tape and make the pocket (see opposite page).

2 Attach the tape in the same way as for pencil pleats (above).

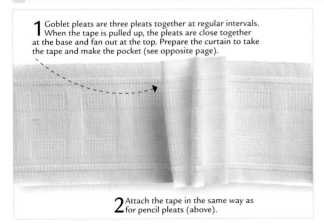

3 After pulling up the tape, secure it by hand on the right side at the base of the tape.

4 Hand stitch the upper edge of the pleats at the back.

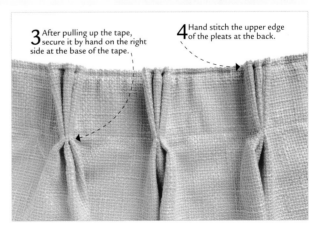

Unlined patch pocket p213 Machined curtain hems p234 »»»

GATHERS

Gathers are an easy way to draw up a piece of larger fabric so that it will fit on to a smaller piece of fabric. They often appear at waistlines or yoke lines. The gather stitch is inserted after the major seams have been constructed, and it is best worked on the sewing machine using the longest stitch length that is available. On the majority of fabrics two rows of gather stitches are required, but for very heavy fabrics it is advisable to make three rows. Try to stitch the rows so that the stitches line up under one another.

Directory of gathers

GATHERS

SMOCKING

WAFFLE SHIRRING

CORDED SHIRRING

How to make and fit gathers
LEVEL OF DIFFICULTY ✱

Once all the main seams have been sewn, stitch the two rows of gathers so that the stitches are inside the seam allowance. This should avoid the need to remove them because removing gathers after they have been pulled up can damage the fabric.

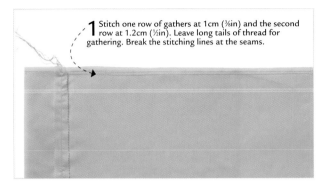

1 Stitch one row of gathers at 1cm (⅜in) and the second row at 1.2cm (½in). Leave long tails of thread for gathering. Break the stitching lines at the seams.

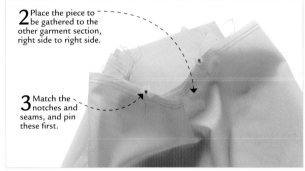

2 Place the piece to be gathered to the other garment section, right side to right side.

3 Match the notches and seams, and pin these first.

4 Gently pull on the two ends of the thread on the wrong side – the fabric will gather along the thread.

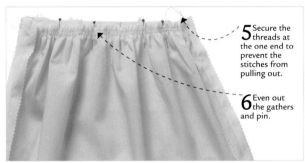

5 Secure the threads at the one end to prevent the stitches from pulling out.

6 Even out the gathers and pin.

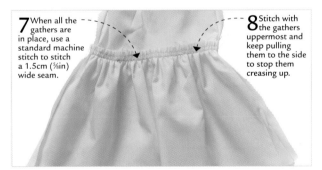

7 When all the gathers are in place, use a standard machine stitch to stitch a 1.5cm (⅝in) wide seam.

8 Stitch with the gathers uppermost and keep pulling them to the side to stop them creasing up.

9 Turn the bodice of the garment inside. Using a mini iron, press the seam very carefully to avoid creasing the gathers.

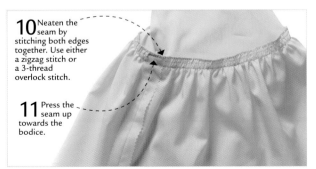

10 Neaten the seam by stitching both edges together. Use either a zigzag stitch or a 3-thread overlock stitch.

11 Press the seam up towards the bodice.

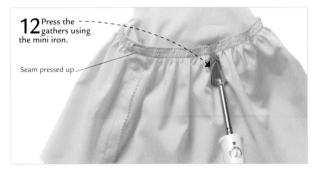

12 Press the gathers using the mini iron.

Seam pressed up

Stitches made with a machine pp92–93   How to make a plain seam p94 ⟪⟪⟪

TECHNIQUES

Corded gathers

LEVEL OF DIFFICULTY **

Corded gathers are gathers that are pulled up over a narrow cord or thick thread. This technique is used for thicker fabrics, such as for soft furnishings, where machine gathers may not be strong enough.

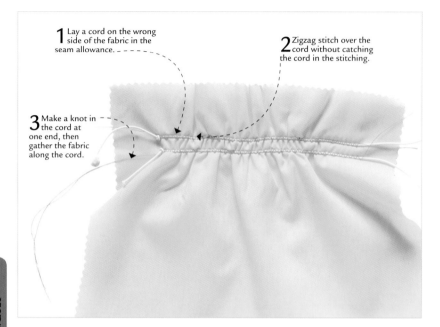

1 Lay a cord on the wrong side of the fabric in the seam allowance.

2 Zigzag stitch over the cord without catching the cord in the stitching.

3 Make a knot in the cord at one end, then gather the fabric along the cord.

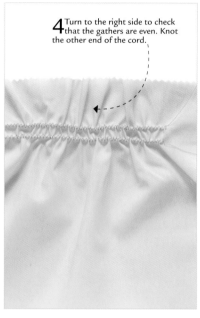

4 Turn to the right side to check that the gathers are even. Knot the other end of the cord.

Gathers on the overlocker

LEVEL OF DIFFICULTY ***

An attachment can be purchased for the overlocker that will enable you to gather fine fabrics, such as net, chiffon, and georgettes, on to other fabrics. This is a really useful technique if large quantities of a fine fabric are to be gathered, such as bridal petticoats and frills in soft furnishings.

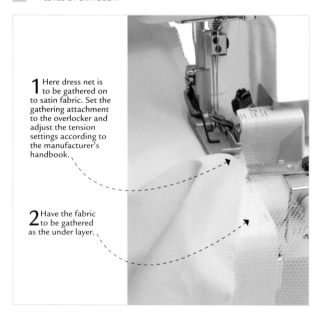

1 Here dress net is to be gathered on to satin fabric. Set the gathering attachment to the overlocker and adjust the tension settings according to the manufacturer's handbook.

2 Have the fabric to be gathered as the under layer.

3 Feed the two fabrics through the overlocker. The under layer will gather automatically to the top layer.

Staying a gathered seam
LEVEL OF DIFFICULTY **

A gathered seam is often stayed by stitching on cotton stay tape, to ensure the gathers remain in place and also to help strengthen the seam.

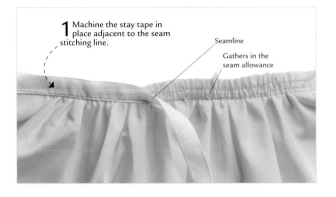

1 Machine the stay tape in place adjacent to the seam stitching line.

Seamline

Gathers in the seam allowance

2 Using a zigzag stitch, machine the top of the stay tape to the raw edge of the seam.

Joining two gathered edges together
LEVEL OF DIFFICULTY ***

On some garments it may be necessary to join together two gathered edges. This usually happens when gathering a skirt on to a gathered bodice. The one side, usually the skirt, is gathered first on to a stay tape and the second side is gathered to fit, then stitched in place.

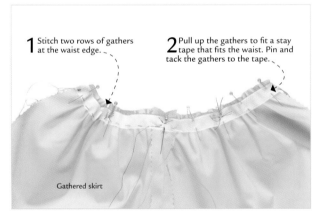

1 Stitch two rows of gathers at the waist edge.

2 Pull up the gathers to fit a stay tape that fits the waist. Pin and tack the gathers to the tape.

Gathered skirt

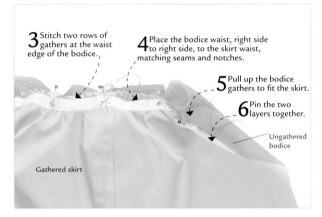

3 Stitch two rows of gathers at the waist edge of the bodice.

4 Place the bodice waist, right side to right side, to the skirt waist, matching seams and notches.

5 Pull up the bodice gathers to fit the skirt.

6 Pin the two layers together.

Ungathered bodice

Gathered skirt

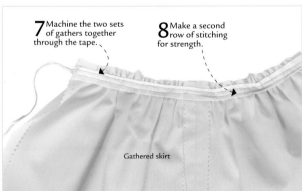

7 Machine the two sets of gathers together through the tape.

8 Make a second row of stitching for strength.

Gathered skirt

9 The waist of the bodice is now gathered to fit the skirt waist.

Bodice

Interlinings p276 〉〉〉

Shirring

LEVEL OF DIFFICULTY **

Shirring is the name given to multiple rows of gathers. It is an excellent way to give fullness in a garment. If made using shirring elastic in the bobbin, shirring gathers can stretch. On heavier fabrics, such as for soft furnishings, static shirring is more suitable.

MACHINE SHIRRING

1 Hand wind shirring elastic on to the bobbin.

2 Insert the bobbin into the sewing machine and pull the elastic through the tension on the bobbin case.

3 Set the machine to a stitch length of 5.0.

4 Stitch a row of machining across the fabric.

5 Stitch a second row of machining. Make sure the rows of stitching are parallel.

6 Continue stitching as many rows of shirring as required.

7 Knot the ends of the elastic together.

WAFFLE SHIRRING

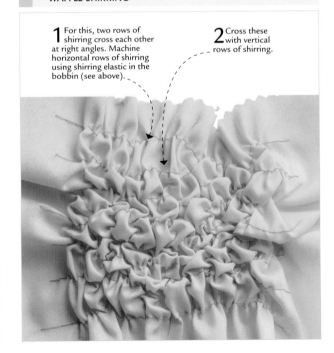

1 For this, two rows of shirring cross each other at right angles. Machine horizontal rows of shirring using shirring elastic in the bobbin (see above).

2 Cross these with vertical rows of shirring.

TECHNIQUES

CORDED SHIRRING

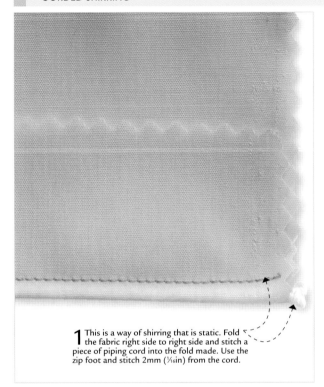

1 This is a way of shirring that is static. Fold the fabric right side to right side and stitch a piece of piping cord into the fold made. Use the zip foot and stitch 2mm (⅙in) from the cord.

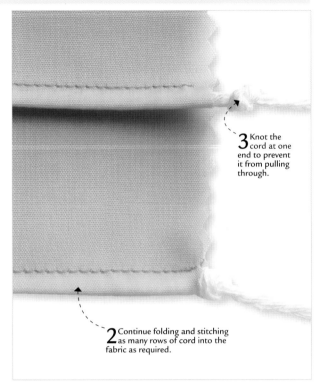

3 Knot the cord at one end to prevent it from pulling through.

2 Continue folding and stitching as many rows of cord into the fabric as required.

4 Push the fabric along the cord to create the shirred gathers.

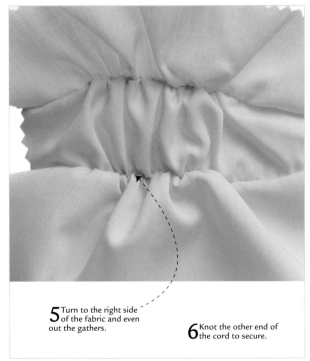

5 Turn to the right side of the fabric and even out the gathers.

6 Knot the other end of the cord to secure.

Smocking

LEVEL OF DIFFICULTY **

Smocking is one of the oldest ways of gathering fabric. It is very decorative and can add interest to a garment. Smocking involves pulling up multiple rows of gathers that have been stitched in by hand, in line with each other, to produce fine tubes in the fabric. These tubes are then stitched over. Smocking dots that can be heat-transferred to the fabric are used as a guide for the hand gathers. Dots can be purchased with different spaces between them.

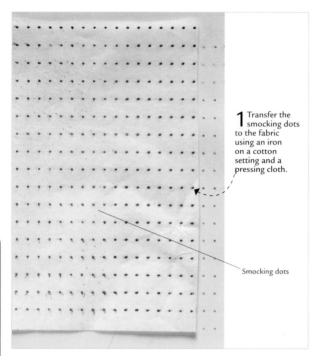

1 Transfer the smocking dots to the fabric using an iron on a cotton setting and a pressing cloth.

Smocking dots

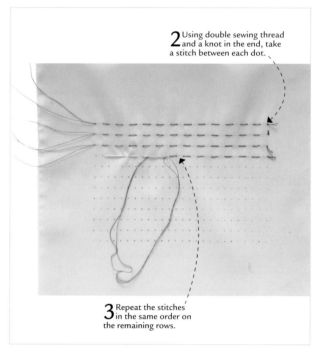

2 Using double sewing thread and a knot in the end, take a stitch between each dot.

3 Repeat the stitches in the same order on the remaining rows.

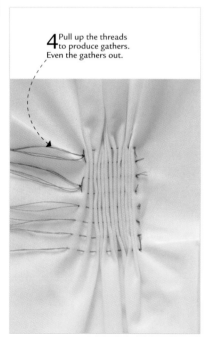

4 Pull up the threads to produce gathers. Even the gathers out.

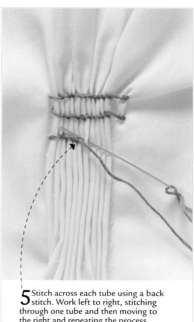

5 Stitch across each tube using a back stitch. Work left to right, stitching through one tube and then moving to the right and repeating the process.

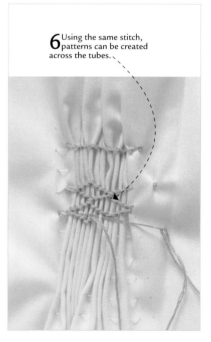

6 Using the same stitch, patterns can be created across the tubes.

Smocking for cushions

LEVEL OF DIFFICULTY **

Smocking can be used in a much larger format to produce a decorative effect on cushions. Patterns and templates can be purchased for this effect.

1 Mark the dots on the wrong side of the fabric with chalk. Use two different colours to distinguish the different kinds of dots.

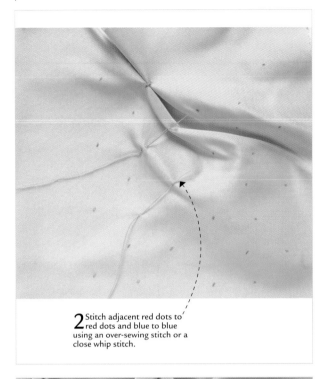

2 Stitch adjacent red dots to red dots and blue to blue using an over-sewing stitch or a close whip stitch.

3 Continue working across the fabric, joining the blue dots to blue dots and red dots to red dots.

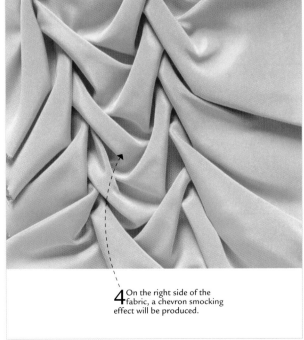

4 On the right side of the fabric, a chevron smocking effect will be produced.

RUFFLES

Ruffles can be single layer or double layer and are used to give a decorative gathered effect to a garment. The amount of fullness in a ruffle depends on the fabric used – to achieve a similar result, a fine, thin fabric will need twice the fullness of a thicker fabric.

Directory of ruffles

PLAIN RUFFLE

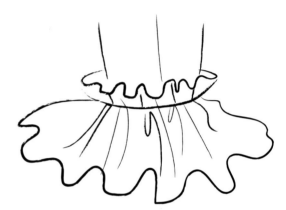

RUFFLE WITH A HEADING

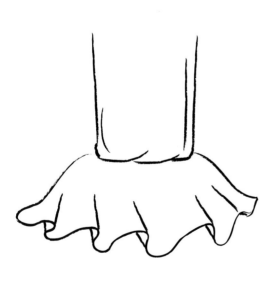

CIRCULAR RUFFLE

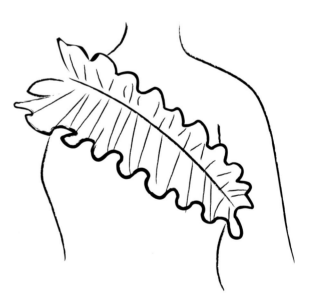

DOUBLE RUFFLE

TECHNIQUES

Plain ruffle

LEVEL OF DIFFICULTY **

A plain ruffle is normally made from a single layer of fabric cut on the straight of the grain. The length of the fabric needs to be at least two and a half times the length of the seam into which it is to be inserted or of the edge to which it is to be attached. The width of the ruffle depends on where it is to be used.

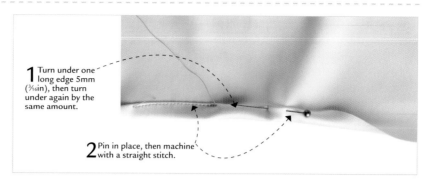

1 Turn under one long edge 5mm (³⁄₁₆in), then turn under again by the same amount.

2 Pin in place, then machine with a straight stitch.

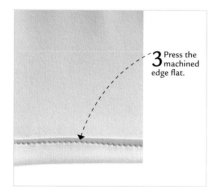

3 Press the machined edge flat.

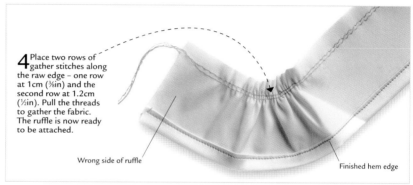

4 Place two rows of gather stitches along the raw edge – one row at 1cm (³⁄₈in) and the second row at 1.2cm (¹⁄₂in). Pull the threads to gather the fabric. The ruffle is now ready to be attached.

Wrong side of ruffle

Finished hem edge

Ruffle with a heading

LEVEL OF DIFFICULTY **

This type of ruffle can give a decorative effect on clothing and soft furnishings.

1 Neaten one long edge as for a plain ruffle (see steps 1–3 above).

2 Turn down the other long edge – the amount of the turn down is the depth of the required heading plus a seam allowance of 1.5cm (⅝in).

3 Tack the heading in place.

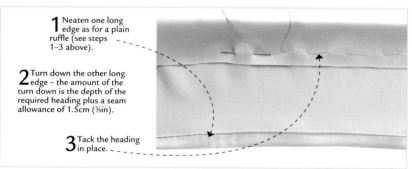

Threads to pull up gathers

4 Insert the two rows of gather stitches.

Tacking stitches

5 Pull up the stitches to make the gathers.

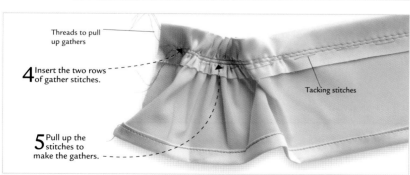

6 After gathering, there will be gathers with a ruffle on one side of the stitch line and a short gathered heading on the other. Pull out the tacking stitches.

Double ruffle version 1

LEVEL OF DIFFICULTY ✳✳

This is a great ruffle on fine fabrics as it can be highly decorative. Attach to the garment by stitching through the centre of the gather lines.

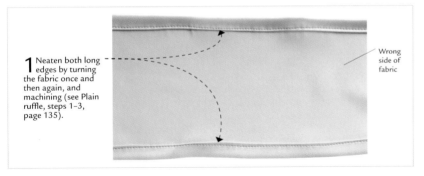

1 Neaten both long edges by turning the fabric once and then again, and machining (see Plain ruffle, steps 1–3, page 135).

Wrong side of fabric

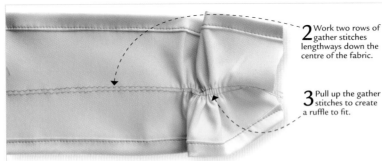

2 Work two rows of gather stitches lengthways down the centre of the fabric.

3 Pull up the gather stitches to create a ruffle to fit.

4 Turn the ruffle over to the right side to check that the gathers are equally spaced. Adjust if necessary, then attach to the garment.

Double ruffle version 2

LEVEL OF DIFFICULTY ✳✳

This ruffle has one side longer than the other and is fashioned from two plain ruffles.

1 Cut two pieces of fabric for the ruffle, one wider than the other. Neaten one long edge of each piece (see Plain ruffle, steps 1–3, page 135).

2 Pin the pieces of fabric together along the raw edges, right sides up, making sure the shorter piece is on the top.

3 Insert two rows of gather stitches through the two layers.

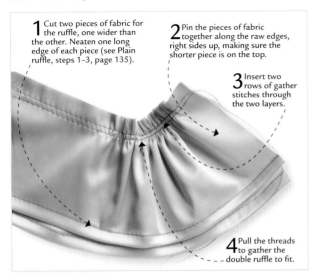

4 Pull the threads to gather the double ruffle to fit.

Double ruffle version 3

LEVEL OF DIFFICULTY ✳✳

This is a useful ruffle on a fabric that is prone to fraying.

1 Cut the fabric for the ruffle twice the required depth.

2 Fold the fabric lengthways, wrong side to wrong side.

3 Pin the raw edges together.

4 Insert gathers along the raw edge.

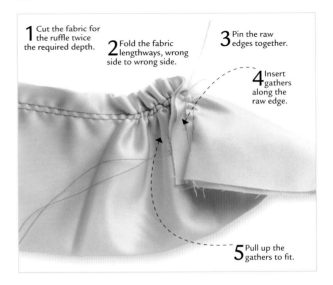

5 Pull up the gathers to fit.

TECHNIQUES

Stitching into a seam

LEVEL OF DIFFICULTY **✷✷**

Once the ruffle has been constructed it can either be inserted into a seam or attached to the edge of the fabric (see page 138). The two techniques below apply to both single and double ruffles.

1 Insert two rows of gathers at the edge of the ruffle.

2 Pull up the gathers to fit along one side of the fabric seam and pin.

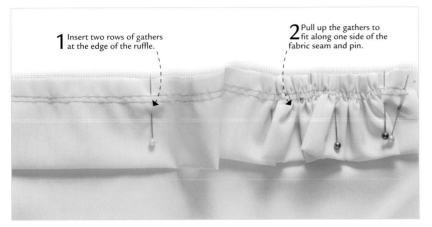

3 Even out the gathers and pin again.

4 Tack to secure.

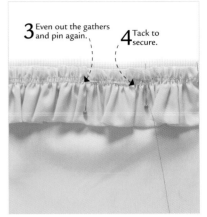

5 Place the other piece of fabric over the ruffle, right side to right side.

6 Pin all the layers together.

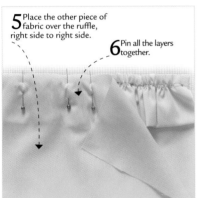

7 Machine through all the layers using a 1.5cm (⅝in) seam allowance.

8 Layer the seam.

9 Turn the fabric and ruffle through to the right side.

Stitching around a corner

LEVEL OF DIFFICULTY **✷✷✷**

It can be difficult to stitch a ruffle to a corner and achieve a sharp point. It is easier to fit the gathers into a tight curve, which can be done as the ruffle is being applied to the corner.

1 Pull up the gathers to fit along one side of the fabric seam and pin in place.

2 Fit the gathers into a tight curve at the corner.

3 Machine the ruffle in place.

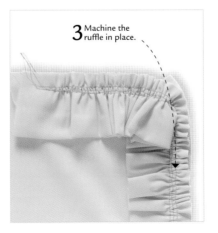

4 Attach the other piece of fabric and machine in place. Layer the seam.

5 Turn the fabric and ruffle through to the right side. The corner will have a tight curve.

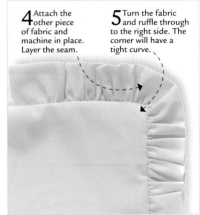

Layering a seam p102   How to make and fit gathers p127 ◀◀◀

Stitching a ruffle to an edge

LEVEL OF DIFFICULTY ★★★

If a ruffle is not in a seam then it will be attached to an edge. The edge of the seam will require neatening, which is often best done by using a binding method as it is more discreet. A self-bound edge, where the seam is wrapped on to itself, is suitable for fine, delicate fabrics. For thicker fabrics, use a bias binding to finish the edge.

SELF-BOUND FINISH

1 Place the gathered ruffle to the edge of the fabric, right side to right side. Pin in place.

2 Machine the ruffle to the fabric using a 1.5cm (⅝in) seam allowance.

3 Trim the gathered side of the seam allowance down to half.

4 Wrap the longer, fabric side of the seam over the gathered seam, tucking under the raw edge. Pin in place.

5 Machine the wrapped seam to secure. Make sure it is attached to the seam only.

BIAS-BOUND FINISH

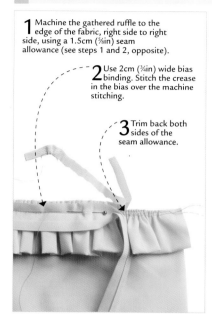

1 Machine the gathered ruffle to the edge of the fabric, right side to right side, using a 1.5cm (⅝in) seam allowance (see steps 1 and 2, opposite).

2 Use 2cm (¾in) wide bias binding. Stitch the crease in the bias over the machine stitching.

3 Trim back both sides of the seam allowance.

4 Wrap the bias over to the wrong side of the seam. Pin in place.

Wrong side of fabric

5 Machine stitch the other side of the bias close to the fold.

Right side of fabric

Attaching a double frill to an edge

This is a very neat way to attach a double ruffle to an edge as the seam is hidden. The ruffle is stitched first to the wrong side of the work and then folded on to the right side.

LEVEL OF DIFFICULTY ★★★

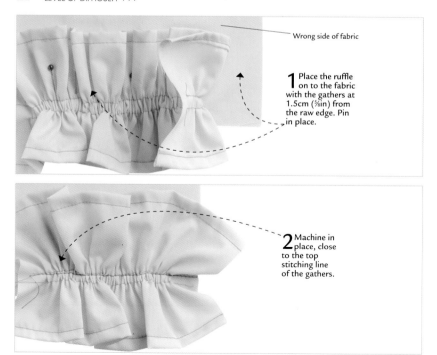

Wrong side of fabric

1 Place the ruffle on to the fabric with the gathers at 1.5cm (⅝in) from the raw edge. Pin in place.

2 Machine in place, close to the top stitching line of the gathers.

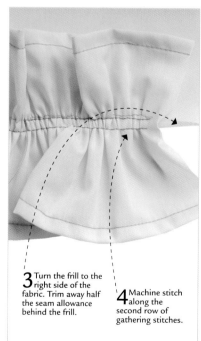

3 Turn the frill to the right side of the fabric. Trim away half the seam allowance behind the frill.

4 Machine stitch along the second row of gathering stitches.

Circular ruffle

LEVEL OF DIFFICULTY ***

A ruffle can be cut using a circular shape. The advantage is that there are no gathers because the centre part of the circle is cut out to make a seam. The fullness occurs as the inner edge of the circle is stretched and attached. For a circular ruffle you will need a pattern.

MAKING THE PATTERN FOR A CIRCULAR RUFFLE

You need pattern paper to cut your circle and a compass created from a pencil with a piece of string tied on to it.

1 Draw an inner circle, the circumference of which will be the length of the seam into which the ruffle is to be attached. You can join several ruffles together to achieve this measurement.

2 Draw in the seam allowance.

3 From the seamline measure out the depth of the ruffle, then draw to make another circle.

4 Cut out the larger circle, then cut out the inner circle. Cut through the pattern, from the outer edge to the inner edge.

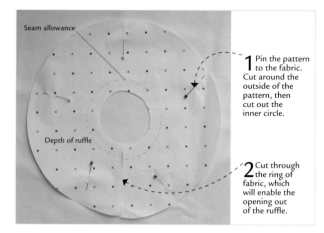

Seam allowance

Depth of ruffle

1 Pin the pattern to the fabric. Cut around the outside of the pattern, then cut out the inner circle.

2 Cut through the ring of fabric, which will enable the opening out of the ruffle.

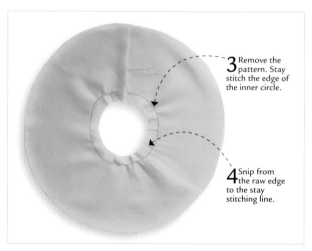

3 Remove the pattern. Stay stitch the edge of the inner circle.

4 Snip from the raw edge to the stay stitching line.

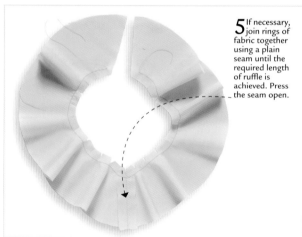

5 If necessary, join rings of fabric together using a plain seam until the required length of ruffle is achieved. Press the seam open.

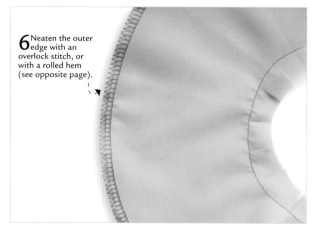

6 Neaten the outer edge with an overlock stitch, or with a rolled hem (see opposite page).

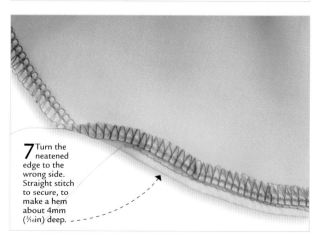

7 Turn the neatened edge to the wrong side. Straight stitch to secure, to make a hem about 4mm (³⁄₁₆in) deep.

8 Place the ruffle to the edge where it is to be attached, right side to right side. Pin in place.

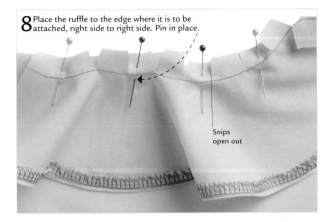

Snips
open out

Double circular ruffle
LEVEL OF DIFFICULTY ★★★

On very lightweight fabrics such as chiffon or silk, it is advisable to make a double-layer ruffle as it will hang better. With this method there is no edge to neaten.

1 Cut two circular ruffles (see opposite) and join them together, right side to right side. Pin to secure.

2 Machine the outer edges together with a 1.5cm (⅝in) seam allowance. Continue the stitching along the short ends.

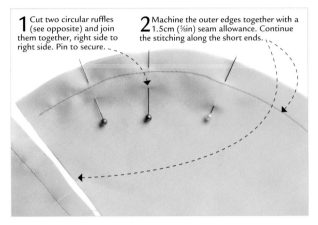

9 Machine in place just below the stay stitching.

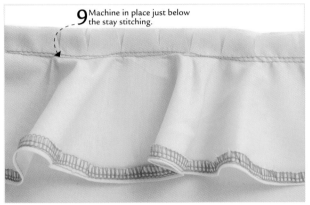

4 Cut out V shapes to reduce the bulk.

3 Trim down one half of the seam allowance.

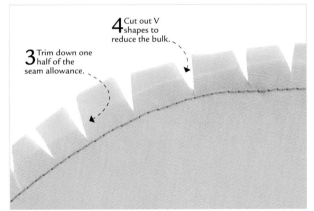

NEATENING THE RUFFLE EDGE WITH A ROLLED HEM

An alternative way to neaten the outer edge is to use the sewing machine with the rolled hem foot and a straight stitch.

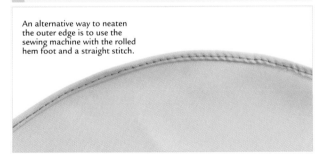

Another alternative is a rolled hem on the sewing machine using the rolled hem foot and a zigzag stitch.

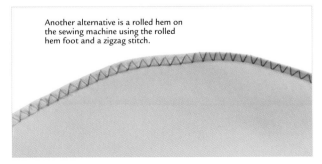

5 Turn through to the right side, pushing out the corners. Press.

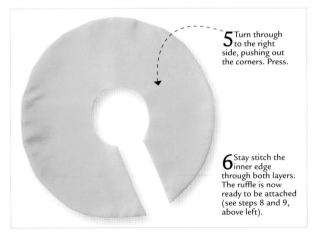

6 Stay stitch the inner edge through both layers. The ruffle is now ready to be attached (see steps 8 and 9, above left).

FACINGS AND NECKLINES

Edges on garments are often neatened by means of a facing. This is a shaped piece of fabric, which may be stiffened with interfacing, attached to a neckline – or to an armhole or at a waist edge – for a strong finish.

FACINGS AND NECKLINES

The simplest way to finish the neck or armhole of a garment is to apply a facing. The neckline can be any shape to have a facing applied, from a curve to a square to a V, and many more. Some facings and necklines can add interest to the centre back or centre front of a garment.

Directory of necklines

ROUND NECK

SCOOP NECK

SQUARE NECK

SWEETHEART NECK

U-NECK

V-NECK

Applying interfacing to a facing

LEVEL OF DIFFICULTY ∗

All facings require interfacing. The interfacing is to give structure to the facing and to hold it in shape. A fusible interfacing is the best choice and it should be cut on the same grain as the facing. Choose an interfacing that is lighter in weight than the main fabric.

INTERFACING FOR HEAVY FABRIC

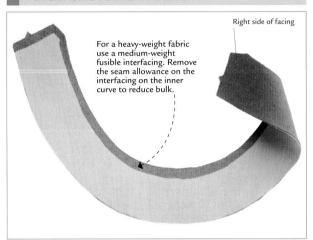

Right side of facing

For a heavy-weight fabric use a medium-weight fusible interfacing. Remove the seam allowance on the interfacing on the inner curve to reduce bulk.

INTERFACING FOR LIGHT FABRIC

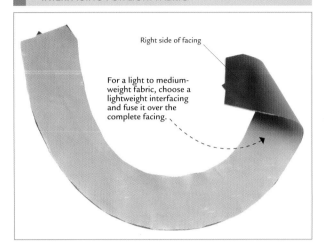

Right side of facing

For a light to medium-weight fabric, choose a lightweight interfacing and fuse it over the complete facing.

Construction of a facing

LEVEL OF DIFFICULTY ∗

The facing may be in two or three pieces in order to fit around a neck or armhole edge. The facing sections need to be joined together prior to being attached. The photographs here show an interfaced neck facing in three pieces.

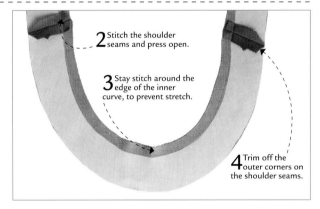

2 Stitch the shoulder seams and press open.

3 Stay stitch around the edge of the inner curve, to prevent stretch.

4 Trim off the outer corners on the shoulder seams.

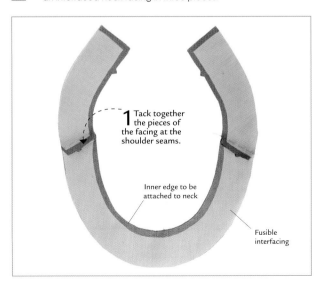

1 Tack together the pieces of the facing at the shoulder seams.

Inner edge to be attached to neck

Fusible interfacing

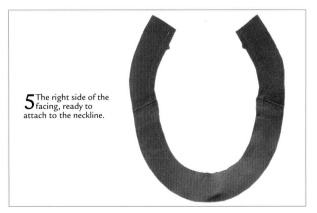

5 The right side of the facing, ready to attach to the neckline.

Neatening the edge of a facing

The outer edge of a facing will require neatening to prevent it from fraying, and there are several ways to do this. Binding the lower edge of a facing with a bias strip makes the garment a little more luxurious and can add a designer touch inside the garment. Alternatively, the edge can be stitched or pinked (see opposite page).

LEVEL OF DIFFICULTY **

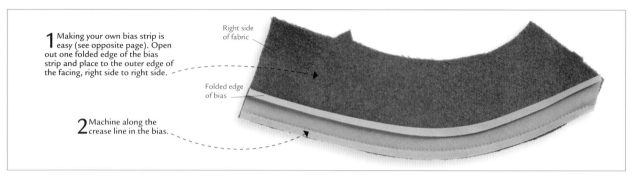

1 Making your own bias strip is easy (see opposite page). Open out one folded edge of the bias strip and place to the outer edge of the facing, right side to right side.

Right side of fabric

Folded edge of bias

2 Machine along the crease line in the bias.

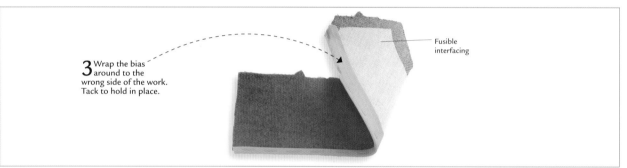

3 Wrap the bias around to the wrong side of the work. Tack to hold in place.

Fusible interfacing

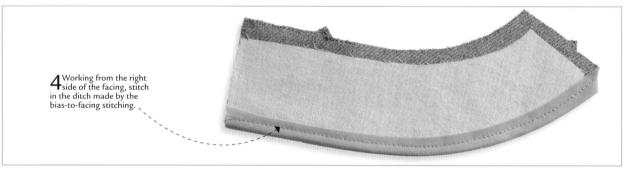

4 Working from the right side of the facing, stitch in the ditch made by the bias-to-facing stitching.

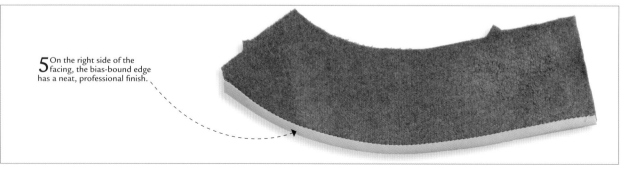

5 On the right side of the facing, the bias-bound edge has a neat, professional finish.

« Marking aids p19 Useful extras pp20–21 Overlocker pp34–35

HOW TO CUT BIAS STRIPS

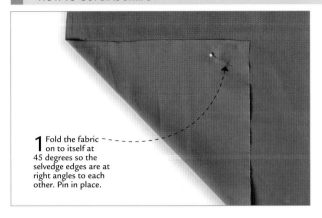

1 Fold the fabric on to itself at 45 degrees so the selvedge edges are at right angles to each other. Pin in place.

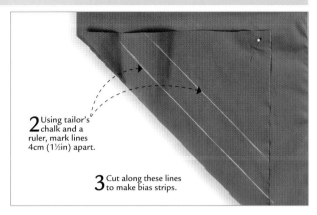

2 Using tailor's chalk and a ruler, mark lines 4cm (1½in) apart.

3 Cut along these lines to make bias strips.

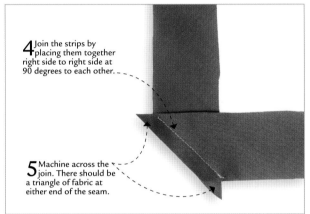

4 Join the strips by placing them together right side to right side at 90 degrees to each other.

5 Machine across the join. There should be a triangle of fabric at either end of the seam.

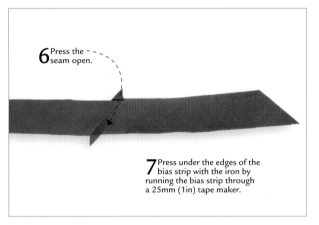

6 Press the seam open.

7 Press under the edges of the bias strip with the iron by running the bias strip through a 25mm (1in) tape maker.

Other neatening methods

LEVEL OF DIFFICULTY ✱

The following techniques are alternative popular ways to neaten the edge of a facing. The one you choose depends upon the garment being made and the fabric used.

OVERLOCKED

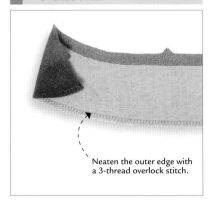

Neaten the outer edge with a 3-thread overlock stitch.

PINKED

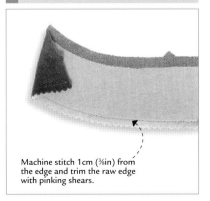

Machine stitch 1cm (⅜in) from the edge and trim the raw edge with pinking shears.

ZIGZAGGED

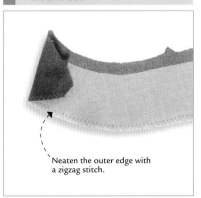

Neaten the outer edge with a zigzag stitch.

TECHNIQUES

Attaching a neck facing

LEVEL OF DIFFICULTY **

This technique applies to all shapes of neckline, from round to square to sweetheart.

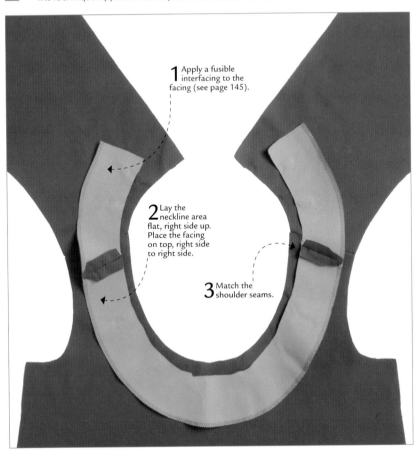

1 Apply a fusible interfacing to the facing (see page 145).

2 Lay the neckline area flat, right side up. Place the facing on top, right side to right side.

3 Match the shoulder seams.

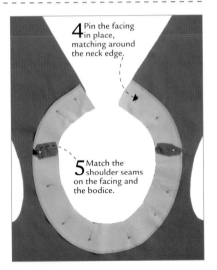

4 Pin the facing in place, matching around the neck edge.

5 Match the shoulder seams on the facing and the bodice.

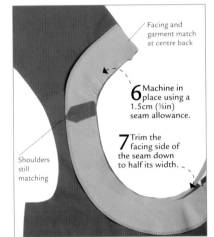

Facing and garment match at centre back

Shoulders still matching

6 Machine in place using a 1.5cm (⅝in) seam allowance.

7 Trim the facing side of the seam down to half its width.

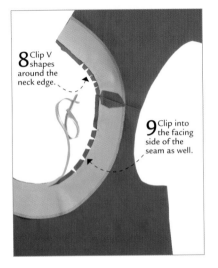

8 Clip V shapes around the neck edge.

9 Clip into the facing side of the seam as well.

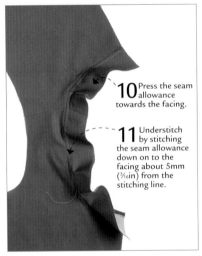

10 Press the seam allowance towards the facing.

11 Understitch by stitching the seam allowance down on to the facing about 5mm (³⁄₁₆in) from the stitching line.

12 Press the finished neck edge and turn the facing towards the wrong side.

Facing a slashed neckline

LEVEL OF DIFFICULTY ★★★

A slashed neckline occurs at either the centre front or the centre back neck edge. It enables a close-fitting neckline to open sufficiently to go over the head.

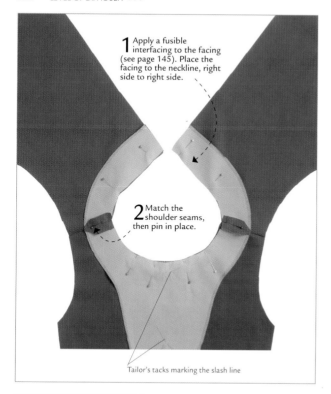

1 Apply a fusible interfacing to the facing (see page 145). Place the facing to the neckline, right side to right side.

2 Match the shoulder seams, then pin in place.

Tailor's tacks marking the slash line

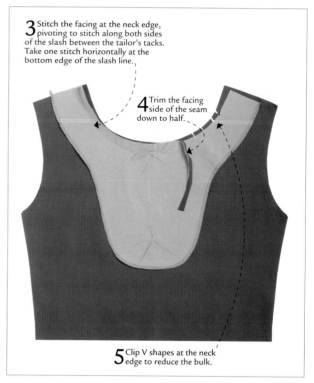

3 Stitch the facing at the neck edge, pivoting to stitch along both sides of the slash between the tailor's tacks. Take one stitch horizontally at the bottom edge of the slash line.

4 Trim the facing side of the seam down to half.

5 Clip V shapes at the neck edge to reduce the bulk.

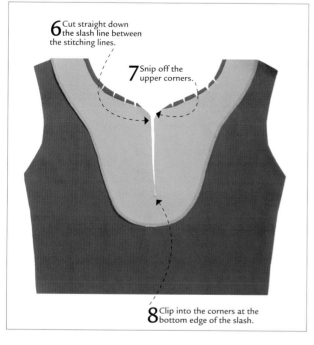

6 Cut straight down the slash line between the stitching lines.

7 Snip off the upper corners.

8 Clip into the corners at the bottom edge of the slash.

9 Turn the facing to the inside of the neckline and press.

Armhole facing

LEVEL OF DIFFICULTY **

On sleeveless garments, a facing is an excellent way of neatening an armhole because it is not bulky. Also, as the facing is made in the same fabric as the garment, it does not show.

1 Construct the interfaced armhole facing (see page 145) and neaten the edge by your preferred method.

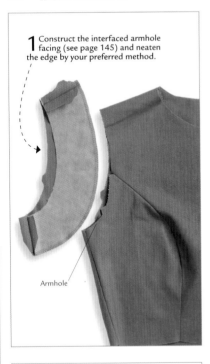

Armhole

2 Place the facing to the armhole, right side to right side. Match at the shoulder seams and at the underarm seam.

3 Match the notches, one at the front and two at the back. Pin the facing in place.

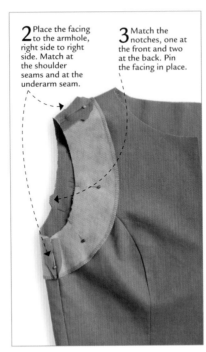

4 Machine around the armhole to attach the facing, taking a 1.5cm (⅝in) seam allowance.

5 Trim the facing side of the seam allowance down to half.

6 Clip out some V shapes in the seam allowance to reduce bulk.

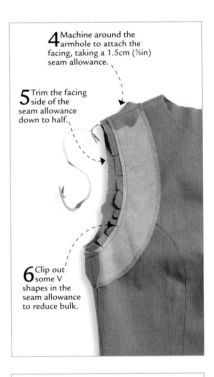

7 Turn the facing into position on the wrong side. Understitch by pressing the seam allowance on to the facing and machining down.

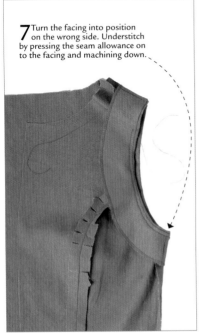

Understitching

8 On the underarm and shoulder seams, secure the facing to the seam allowance with cross stitches.

9 Press the stitched edge. On the right side the armhole will have a neat finish.

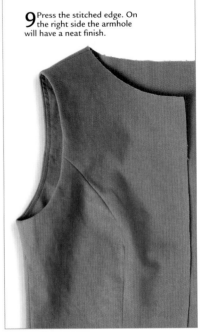

Combination neck and armhole facing

LEVEL OF DIFFICULTY ★★★

This type of facing neatens the neck and the armhole edge at the same time. It needs to be stitched in place before the centre back seam or the side seams are constructed.

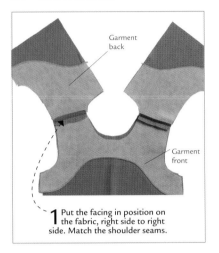

Garment back

Garment front

1 Put the facing in position on the fabric, right side to right side. Match the shoulder seams.

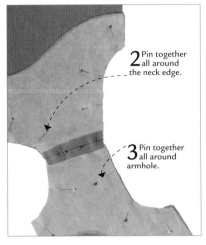

2 Pin together all around the neck edge.

3 Pin together all around armhole.

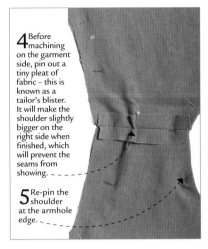

4 Before machining on the garment side, pin out a tiny pleat of fabric – this is known as a tailor's blister. It will make the shoulder slightly bigger on the right side when finished, which will prevent the seams from showing.

5 Re-pin the shoulder at the armhole edge.

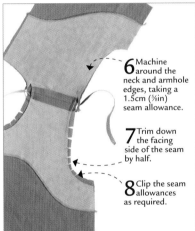

6 Machine around the neck and armhole edges, taking a 1.5cm (⅝in) seam allowance.

7 Trim down the facing side of the seam by half.

8 Clip the seam allowances as required.

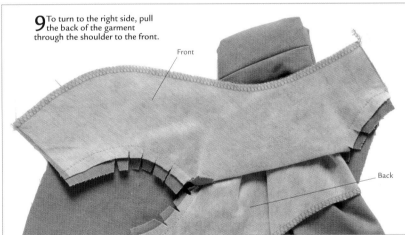

9 To turn to the right side, pull the back of the garment through the shoulder to the front.

Front

Back

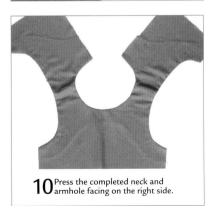

10 Press the completed neck and armhole facing on the right side.

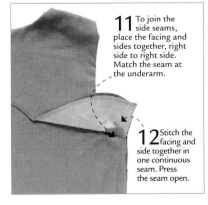

11 To join the side seams, place the facing and sides together, right side to right side. Match the seam at the underarm.

12 Stitch the facing and side together in one continuous seam. Press the seam open.

13 The faced neckline and armholes from the right side.

Grown-on facing

LEVEL OF DIFFICULTY **

A facing is not always a separate unit. Many garments, especially blouses, feature what is known as a grown-on facing, which is where the facing is an extension of the front of the garment, cut out at the same time.

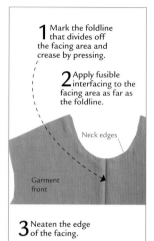

1 Mark the foldline that divides off the facing area and crease by pressing.

2 Apply fusible interfacing to the facing area as far as the foldline.

Neck edges

Garment front

3 Neaten the edge of the facing.

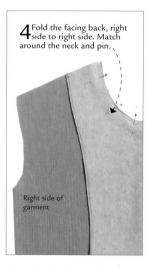

4 Fold the facing back, right side to right side. Match around the neck and pin.

Right side of garment

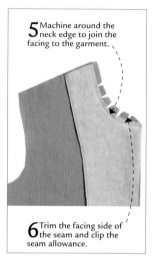

5 Machine around the neck edge to join the facing to the garment.

6 Trim the facing side of the seam and clip the seam allowance.

7 Turn through to the right side and press.

Bound neck edge

LEVEL OF DIFFICULTY **

Binding is an excellent way to finish a raw neck edge. It has the added advantage of being a method that can be used if you are short of fabric or you would like a contrast or decorative finish. You can use bought bias binding or a bias strip cut from the same or a contrasting fabric (see page 147). A double bias strip is used on fine fabrics.

BIAS-BOUND NECK EDGE VERSION 1

1 Open out one edge of the bias strip and place the crease line on the 1.5cm (⅝in) stitching line. Pin in place.

2 Machine in place along the crease line.

3 Trim away the surplus fabric from the seam allowance.

4 Clip the neck seam if required.

5 Wrap the bias strip over the neck to the wrong side of the garment.

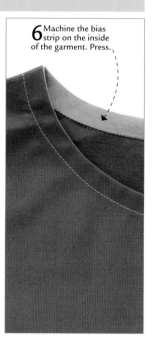

6 Machine the bias strip on the inside of the garment. Press.

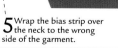 How to apply a fusible interfacing p54 Hand stitches pp90–91

BIAS-BOUND NECK EDGE VERSION 2

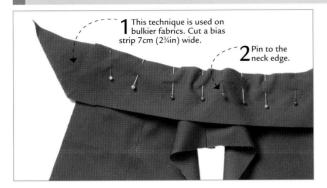

1 This technique is used on bulkier fabrics. Cut a bias strip 7cm (2¾in) wide.

2 Pin to the neck edge.

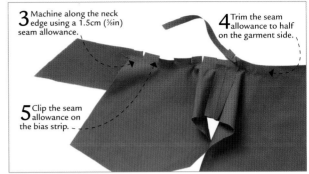

3 Machine along the neck edge using a 1.5cm (⅝in) seam allowance.

4 Trim the seam allowance to half on the garment side.

5 Clip the seam allowance on the bias strip.

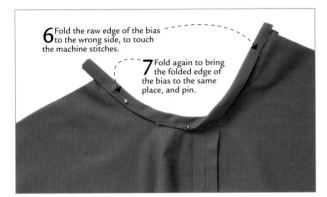

6 Fold the raw edge of the bias to the wrong side, to touch the machine stitches.

7 Fold again to bring the folded edge of the bias to the same place, and pin.

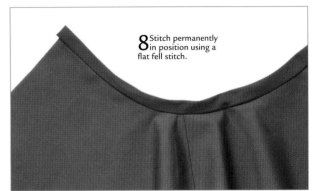

8 Stitch permanently in position using a flat fell stitch.

DOUBLE BIAS-BOUND NECK EDGE

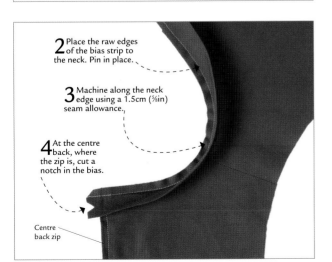

1 Cut a bias strip 6cm (2⅜in) wide. Press in half.

2 Place the raw edges of the bias strip to the neck. Pin in place.

3 Machine along the neck edge using a 1.5cm (⅝in) seam allowance.

4 At the centre back, where the zip is, cut a notch in the bias.

Centre back zip

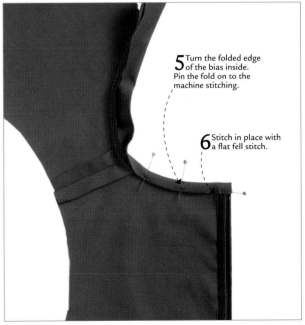

5 Turn the folded edge of the bias inside. Pin the fold on to the machine stitching.

6 Stitch in place with a flat fell stitch.

Piped neck edge

LEVEL OF DIFFICULTY **

This technique features a piping around the neck as well as a facing. A piped neckline looks very good on special-occasion wear.

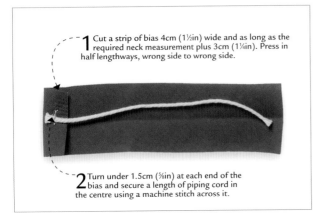

1 Cut a strip of bias 4cm (1½in) wide and as long as the required neck measurement plus 3cm (1¼in). Press in half lengthways, wrong side to wrong side.

2 Turn under 1.5cm (⅝in) at each end of the bias and secure a length of piping cord in the centre using a machine stitch across it.

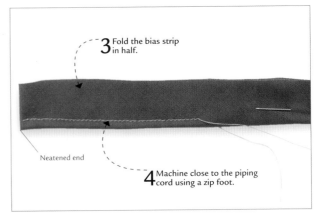

3 Fold the bias strip in half.

Neatened end

4 Machine close to the piping cord using a zip foot.

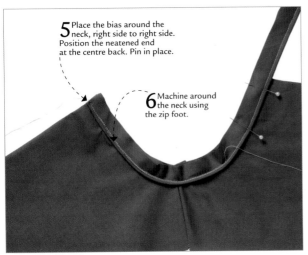

5 Place the bias around the neck, right side to right side. Position the neatened end at the centre back. Pin in place.

6 Machine around the neck using the zip foot.

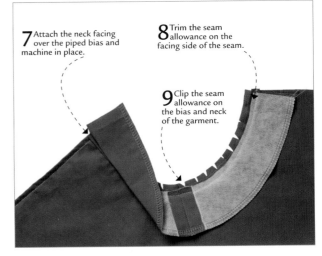

7 Attach the neck facing over the piped bias and machine in place.

8 Trim the seam allowance on the facing side of the seam.

9 Clip the seam allowance on the bias and neck of the garment.

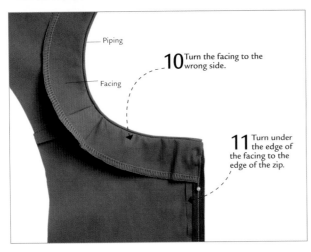

Piping

Facing

10 Turn the facing to the wrong side.

11 Turn under the edge of the facing to the edge of the zip.

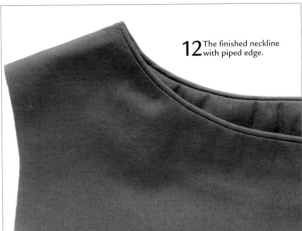

12 The finished neckline with piped edge.

«« Sewing-machine accessories pp32–33   How to apply a fusible interfacing p54   Pattern marking pp82–83

Plackets

LEVEL OF DIFFICULTY ★★★

A placket is an opening that stops partway down a bodice. It is made by applying two separate bands of fabric to the bodice. Care must be taken to ensure that the pattern pieces are accurately marked. A placket opening is popular on sportswear.

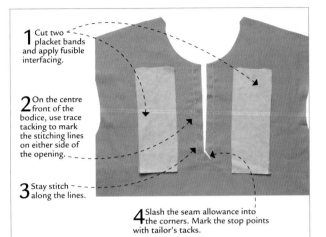

1 Cut two placket bands and apply fusible interfacing.

2 On the centre front of the bodice, use trace tacking to mark the stitching lines on either side of the opening.

3 Stay stitch along the lines.

4 Slash the seam allowance into the corners. Mark the stop points with tailor's tacks.

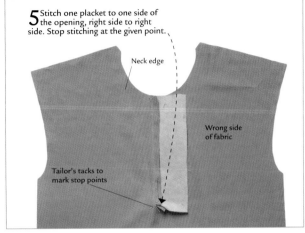

5 Stitch one placket to one side of the opening, right side to right side. Stop stitching at the given point.

Neck edge

Wrong side of fabric

Tailor's tacks to mark stop points

6 Repeat with the other placket, stitching it on to the other side of the opening.

7 Trim the placket side of the seam down on both plackets.

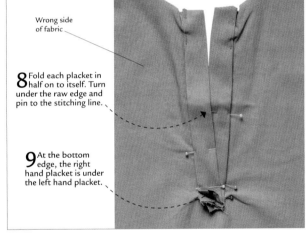

Wrong side of fabric

8 Fold each placket in half on to itself. Turn under the raw edge and pin to the stitching line.

9 At the bottom edge, the right hand placket is under the left hand placket.

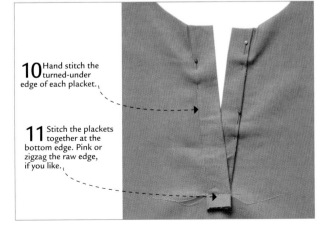

10 Hand stitch the turned-under edge of each placket.

11 Stitch the plackets together at the bottom edge. Pink or zigzag the raw edge, if you like.

12 Turn to the right side and press.

Necklines in stretch knits

LEVEL OF DIFFICULTY ★★★

When working with a stretch knit fabric, the neckline can be finished with a single banding or a more decorative double banding. The banding is usually attached with a 4-thread overlock stitch, which enables the neck to stretch over the head. If you do not have an overlocker you can use a 3-step zigzag stitch on the sewing machine.

SINGLE BANDING WITH OVERLOCKER

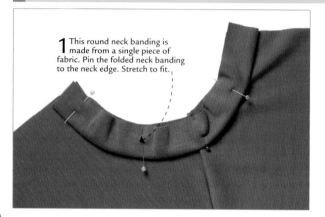

1 This round neck banding is made from a single piece of fabric. Pin the folded neck banding to the neck edge. Stretch to fit.

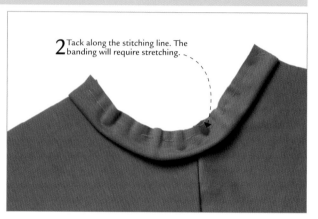

2 Tack along the stitching line. The banding will require stretching.

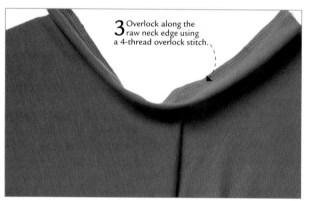

3 Overlock along the raw neck edge using a 4-thread overlock stitch.

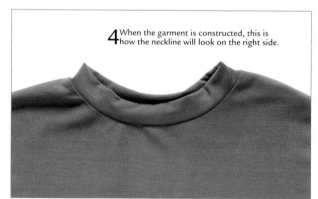

4 When the garment is constructed, this is how the neckline will look on the right side.

DOUBLE BANDING WITH OVERLOCKER

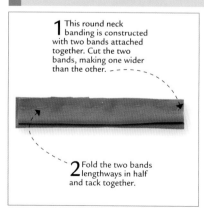

1 This round neck banding is constructed with two bands attached together. Cut the two bands, making one wider than the other.

2 Fold the two bands lengthways in half and tack together.

3 Attach to the neckline as for a single band (see above), with the wider banding against the neck.

ATTACHING BANDING WITH A SEWING MACHINE

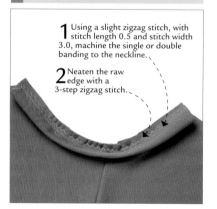

1 Using a slight zigzag stitch, with stitch length 0.5 and stitch width 3.0, machine the single or double banding to the neckline.

2 Neaten the raw edge with a 3-step zigzag stitch.

TECHNIQUES

BANDING FOR A V NECK

1 Tailor tack the centre of the V on the neckline.

2 Stay stitch on the sewing machine through this point.

3 Snip through the seam allowance to the stay stitching.

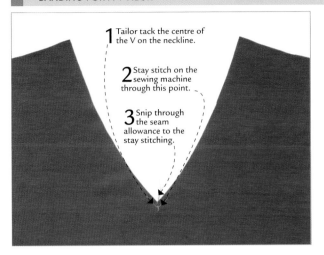

4 Cut the band as a straight strip, not as a V shape.

5 Pin the band to the V neckline, straightening out the garment front as you do so. Tack in place.

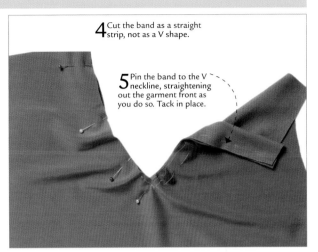

6 Straighten out the band and stitch to the neckline using a 4-thread overlock stitch. (If you do not have access to an overlocker, use a zigzag stitch as described on the opposite page.)

7 Snip the seam allowance in the centre.

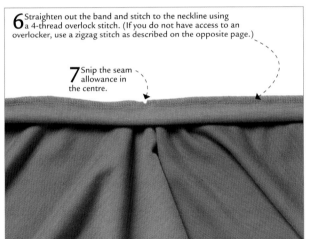

8 Turn to the wrong side and place a pin in line with the centre front of the garment.

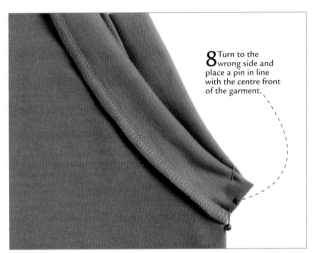

9 Stitch through the band in line with the centre front. Press flat.

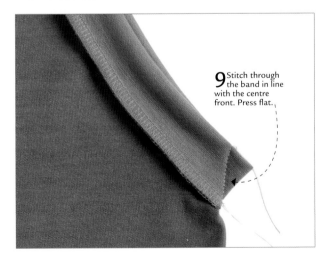

10 When turned to the right side, there will be a sharp V.

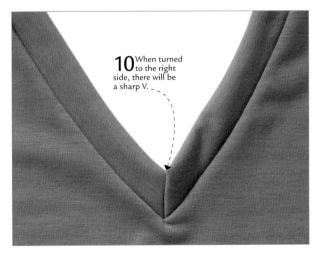

COLLARS

Collars frame the face and neck, and are always a focal point on any garment. There are three main types: flat, stand, and rolled. To construct a symmetrical collar, careful and accurate marking and stitching are essential.

COLLARS

All collars consist of a minimum of two pieces, the upper collar (which will be on the outside) and the under collar. Interfacing, which is required to give the collar shape and structure, is often applied to the upper collar to give a smoother appearance to the fabric.

Directory of collars

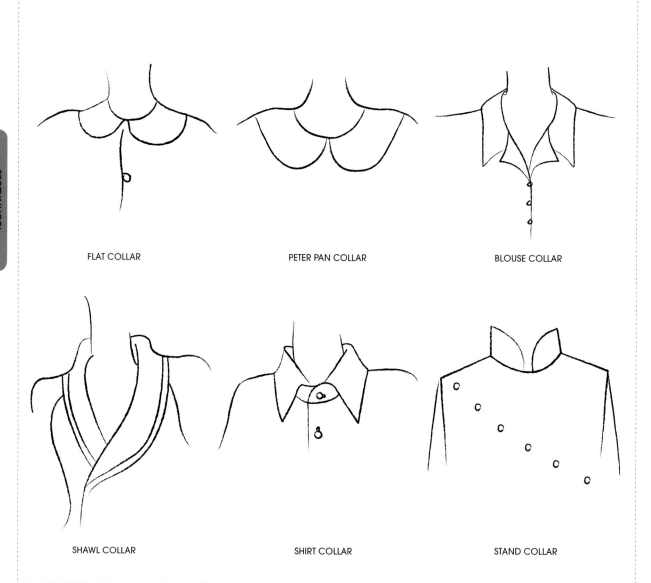

FLAT COLLAR

PETER PAN COLLAR

BLOUSE COLLAR

SHAWL COLLAR

SHIRT COLLAR

STAND COLLAR

⟪⟪ How to apply a fusible interfacing p54   Pattern marking pp82–83   Stitches made with a machine pp92–93

TECHNIQUES

Flat collar

A flat collar is the easiest of all the collars to construct, and the techniques used are the same for most other shapes of flat collar and facings.

LEVEL OF DIFFICULTY **

1 Cut out the fabric for the collar accurately. Make sure the two halves match.

2 Cut out a fusible interfacing, being sure to cut on the same grain as the collar. Apply the interfacing to the upper collar.

3 Insert tailor's tacks at the centre front point of the collar where indicated by a dot on the pattern piece.

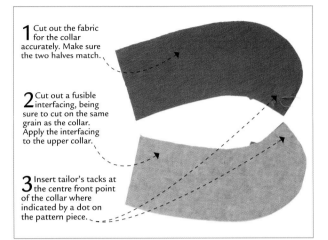

4 Pin the upper collar and under collar together, right side to right side. Match any notches and make sure the cut edges match.

5 Machine stitch 1.5cm (⅝in) along the raw outer curved edge to the lower edge of the collar. Make sure the machining at the centre front goes through the tailor's tack. If you have problems stitching a curve, mark the fabric first with chalk.

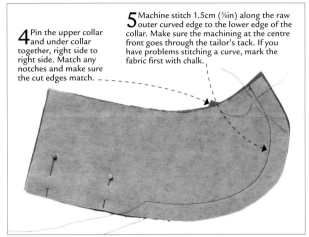

6 Trim the under collar seam allowance to half of its width, which will reduce the bulk.

7 Trim around the curve with pinking shears, reducing both layers. This will allow the fabric to turn.

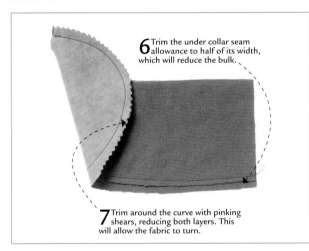

8 Clip the curve on the collar using small cuts at 90 degrees to the stitching line, clipping through the pinked seam.

9 Press the seam allowance of the upper collar on to the collar.

10 While the collar is still warm from the steam iron, turn to the right side.

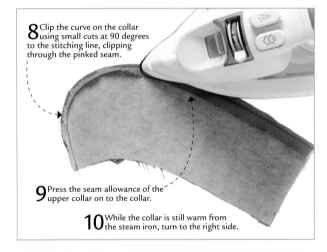

11 Working from the inside of the collar, push all the seam allowance towards the under collar and machine it to the under collar. This is called understitching and will hold the collar in shape.

12 Understitch as far through the curve as you can.

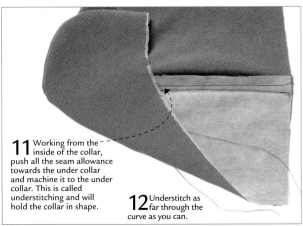

13 Press the curved edge flat on the right side, making sure the seam is pushed out completely.

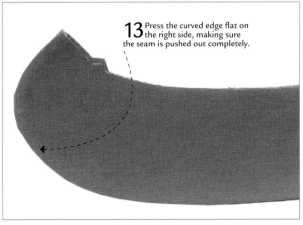

Attaching a flat collar

LEVEL OF DIFFICULTY ★★★

A flat collar can be attached to the neckline by means of a facing. Depending upon the style of the garment, the facing may go all around the neck, which is usually found on garments with centre back openings, or just be at the front. The collar with no back facing has to be attached to the garment in stages.

FLAT ROUND COLLAR WITH NO BACK FACING

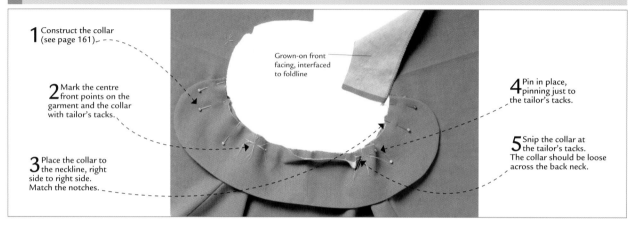

1 Construct the collar (see page 161).

2 Mark the centre front points on the garment and the collar with tailor's tacks.

3 Place the collar to the neckline, right side to right side. Match the notches.

Grown-on front facing, interfaced to foldline

4 Pin in place, pinning just to the tailor's tacks.

5 Snip the collar at the tailor's tacks. The collar should be loose across the back neck.

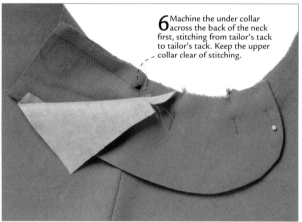

6 Machine the under collar across the back of the neck first, stitching from tailor's tack to tailor's tack. Keep the upper collar clear of stitching.

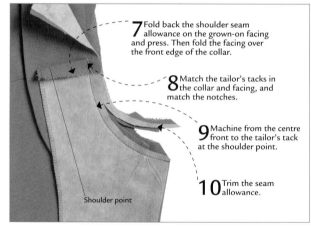

7 Fold back the shoulder seam allowance on the grown-on facing and press. Then fold the facing over the front edge of the collar.

8 Match the tailor's tacks in the collar and facing, and match the notches.

9 Machine from the centre front to the tailor's tack at the shoulder point.

10 Trim the seam allowance.

Shoulder point

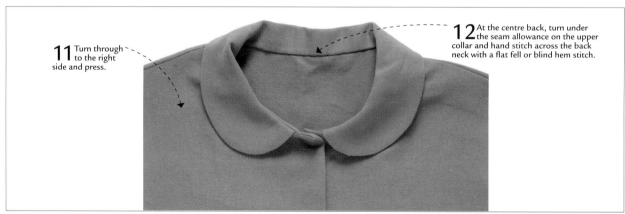

11 Turn through to the right side and press.

12 At the centre back, turn under the seam allowance on the upper collar and hand stitch across the back neck with a flat fell or blind hem stitch.

‹‹‹ Pattern marking pp82–83 Hand stitches pp90–91 Stitches made with a machine pp92–93

FLAT ROUND COLLAR WITH A FULL FACING

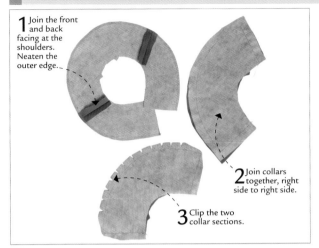

1 Join the front and back facing at the shoulders. Neaten the outer edge.

2 Join collars together, right side to right side.

3 Clip the two collar sections.

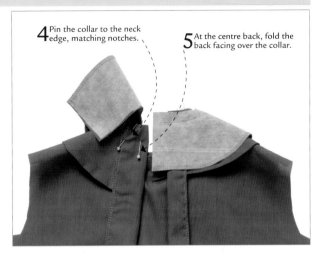

4 Pin the collar to the neck edge, matching notches.

5 At the centre back, fold the back facing over the collar.

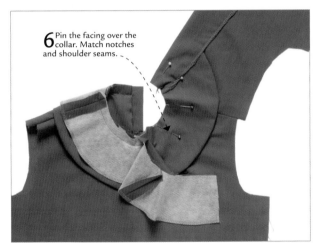

6 Pin the facing over the collar. Match notches and shoulder seams.

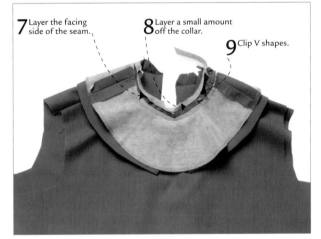

7 Layer the facing side of the seam.

8 Layer a small amount off the collar.

9 Clip V shapes.

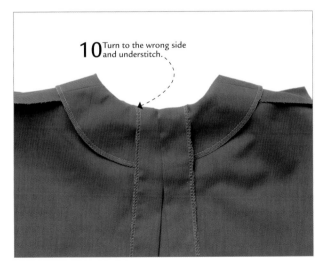

10 Turn to the wrong side and understitch.

11 Turn to the right side and press.

Seam neatening pp94–95   Reducing seam bulk pp102–103   Stitch finishes p103   Grown-on facing p152   ≪≪

Stand collar

LEVEL OF DIFFICULTY ✱✱✱

Also called a mandarin collar, this collar stands upright around the neck. It is normally cut from a straight piece of fabric, with shaping at the centre front edges. For a very close-fitting stand collar, the collar is cut with a slight curve.

1 Apply a fusible interfacing to the upper collar (see page 161). Insert any tailor's tacks as indicated on the pattern.

2 Pin the upper collar, interfacing side out, to the neckline of the garment, matching any notches and tailor's tacks at the centre front edge.

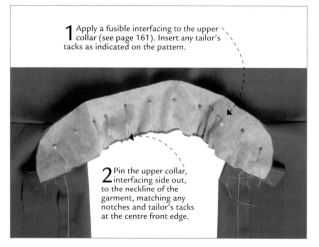

3 Machine the upper collar to the neckline using a 1.5cm (⅝in) seam allowance. Make sure the stitching stops at the tailor's tack at the front edge.

4 Reduce the seam allowance on the upper collar by half.

5 Clip though the seam allowances – this will allow the fabric to relax into shape when pressed later.

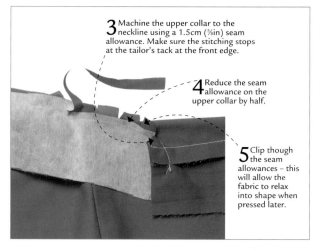

6 Working from the wrong side of the garment, turn in the centre front edge as indicated by the pattern. This will leave the front edge of the collar proud of the garment.

Wrong side of collar

7 Pin the under collar to the upper collar, right side to right side, along the top edge.

8 Machine the two pieces together using a 1.5cm (⅝in) seam allowance.

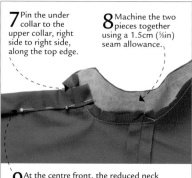

9 At the centre front, the reduced neck seam allowance needs to be pointing up into the collar, so that the machining attaching the two collar sections together goes over it. Be sure the machining is in line with the centre front of the garment.

10 Reduce the seam allowance to half its width on the under collar side of the seam (the non-interfaced side).

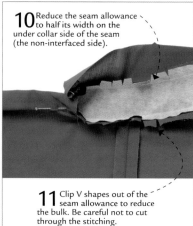

11 Clip V shapes out of the seam allowance to reduce the bulk. Be careful not to cut through the stitching.

12 Press the seam as it has been stitched, and while warm turn to the right side.

Wrong side

13 Turn under the lower edge seam allowance on the under collar and tack in place around the neck edge.

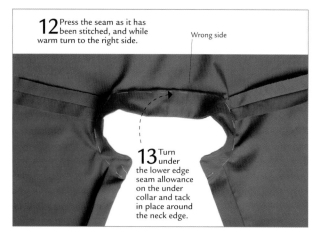

14 Make sure the two leading front edges of the collar are symmetrical.

15 Use a flat fell stitch to secure the under collar at the neck edge.

⟪⟪⟪ How to apply a fusible interfacing p54   Pattern marking pp82–83

Shawl collar

LEVEL OF DIFFICULTY ★★★

A shawl collar, which is a deep V-neck shape that combines both collar and rever in one, gives a flattering neckline that is often found on blouses and jackets. Although the collar looks complicated, it is straightforward to make. The under collar is usually part of the front of the garment.

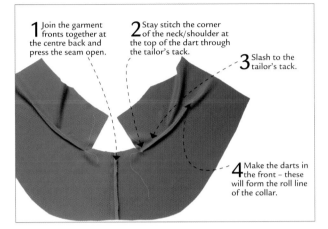

1 Join the garment fronts together at the centre back and press the seam open.

2 Stay stitch the corner of the neck/shoulder at the top of the dart through the tailor's tack.

3 Slash to the tailor's tack.

4 Make the darts in the front – these will form the roll line of the collar.

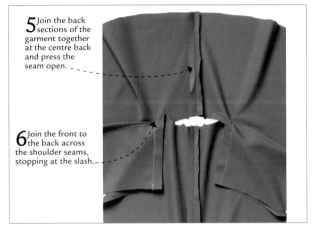

5 Join the back sections of the garment together at the centre back and press the seam open.

6 Join the front to the back across the shoulder seams, stopping at the slash.

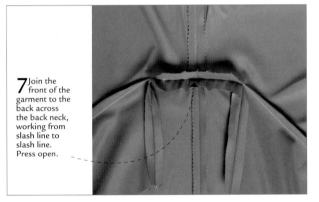

7 Join the front of the garment to the back across the back neck, working from slash line to slash line. Press open.

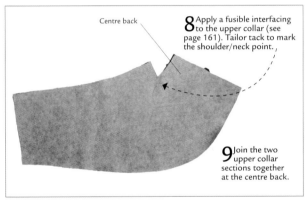

Centre back

8 Apply a fusible interfacing to the upper collar (see page 161). Tailor tack to mark the shoulder/neck point.

9 Join the two upper collar sections together at the centre back.

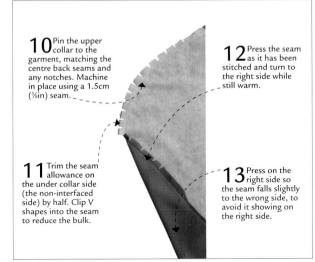

10 Pin the upper collar to the garment, matching the centre back seams and any notches. Machine in place using a 1.5cm (⅝in) seam.

11 Trim the seam allowance on the under collar side (the non-interfaced side) by half. Clip V shapes into the seam to reduce the bulk.

12 Press the seam as it has been stitched and turn to the right side while still warm.

13 Press on the right side so the seam falls slightly to the wrong side, to avoid it showing on the right side.

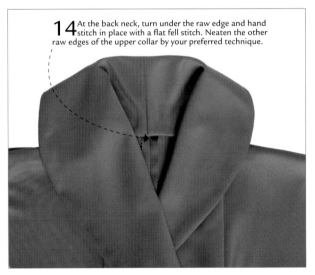

14 At the back neck, turn under the raw edge and hand stitch in place with a flat fell stitch. Neaten the other raw edges of the upper collar by your preferred technique.

Blouse collar with revers

LEVEL OF DIFFICULTY **

A blouse collar can have rounded or pointed centre front edges, depending on the style of blouse chosen. A blouse collar forms a V neckline with revers. When constructing the collar, before fusing the interfacing to the upper collar, trim the corners of the interfacing to reduce bulk.

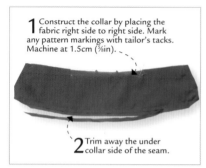

1 Construct the collar by placing the fabric right side to right side. Mark any pattern markings with tailor's tacks. Machine at 1.5cm (⅝in).

2 Trim away the under collar side of the seam.

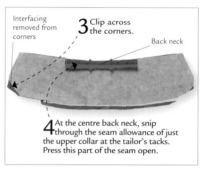

3 Clip across the corners.

Interfacing removed from corners

Back neck

4 At the centre back neck, snip through the seam allowance of just the upper collar at the tailor's tacks. Press this part of the seam open.

Sharp corners

5 Turn the collar through to the right side and press. The seam allowance on the back neck is pressed under between the clips.

6 Place the collar to the neck, matching the tailor's tacks. Pin to secure.

7 Tack in place through the double collar edges at the front and through the single layer collar at the back neck.

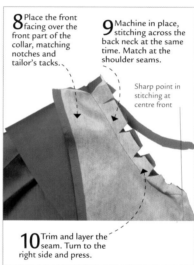

8 Place the front facing over the front part of the collar, matching notches and tailor's tacks.

9 Machine in place, stitching across the back neck at the same time. Match at the shoulder seams.

Sharp point in stitching at centre front

10 Trim and layer the seam. Turn to the right side and press.

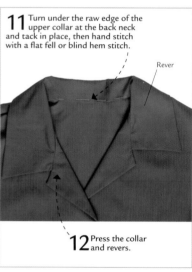

11 Turn under the raw edge of the upper collar at the back neck and tack in place, then hand stitch with a flat fell or blind hem stitch.

Rever

12 Press the collar and revers.

Two-piece shirt collar

LEVEL OF DIFFICULTY ***

A traditional-style shirt has a collar that consists of two pieces: a collar and a stand, both of which require interfacing. The stand fits close around the neck and the collar is attached to the stand. This type of collar is found on men's and ladies' shirts. On a man's shirt, the stand accommodates the tie.

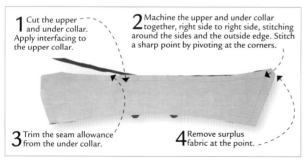

1 Cut the upper and under collar. Apply interfacing to the upper collar.

2 Machine the upper and under collar together, right side to right side, stitching around the sides and the outside edge. Stitch a sharp point by pivoting at the corners.

3 Trim the seam allowance from the under collar.

4 Remove surplus fabric at the point.

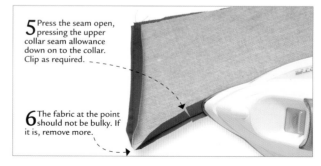

5 Press the seam open, pressing the upper collar seam allowance down on to the collar. Clip as required.

6 The fabric at the point should not be bulky. If it is, remove more.

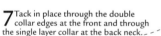

TECHNIQUES

7 Turn the collar to the right side and press.

8 Top-stitch the sides and outside edge using the edge of the machine foot as a guide.

9 Construct the stand, applying interfacing to one side.

Collar fits between the tailor's tacks

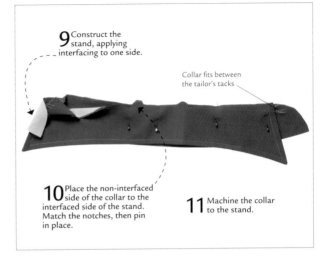

10 Place the non-interfaced side of the collar to the interfaced side of the stand. Match the notches, then pin in place.

11 Machine the collar to the stand.

12 Place the stand to the shirt neck, matching the notches, and pin in place.

13 Tack the stand to the neckline. The seam allowance on the stand extends at the centre front.

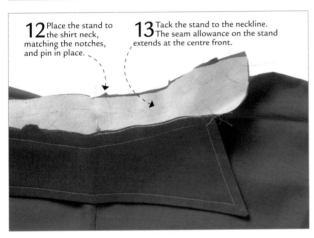

14 Pin the non-interfaced side of the collar stand to the neck edge, so that there is a collar stand on either side of the shirt

15 Tack the collar stand to the neckline.

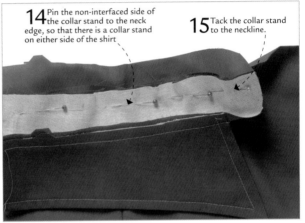

16 Reposition the stand so that the front edges come together right side to right side.

17 Machine along the neck edge and around the centre front curve to the collar.

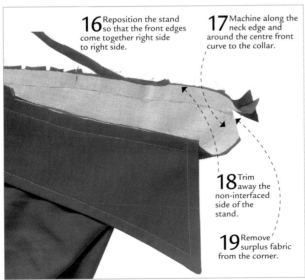

18 Trim away the non-interfaced side of the stand.

19 Remove surplus fabric from the corner.

20 Turn and press.

21 Bring the raw edge of the stand to the collar and turn under. Pin in place.

22 Secure this edge with a flat fell stitch.

23 Top-stitch the stand, if required. The stand fits snugly under the collar at the centre front.

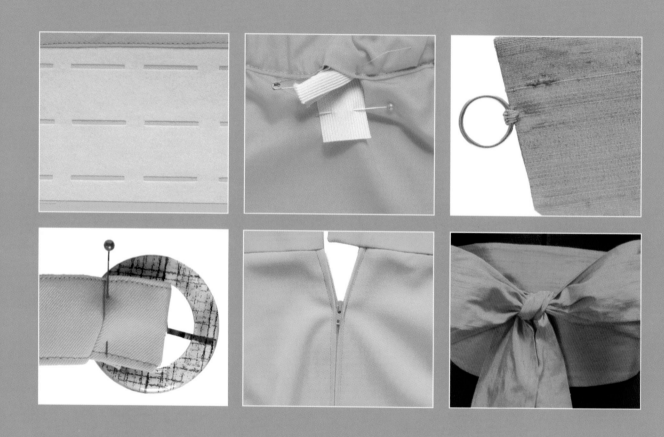

WAISTLINES, BELTS, AND TIE-BACKS

Bodice and skirt sections are often joined together at the waist. However, on some garments a "waist" needs to be created to take a piece of elastic. A waist may be enhanced by making a matching belt. Curtain tie-backs are also covered in this section.

WAISTLINES

Waistlines can be formed where a bodice and skirt join together or at the waist edge of a skirt or pair of trousers. Some waistlines are attached separately to the garment to create a feature and others are more discreet. They may be shaped to follow the contours of the body.

Directory of waistlines

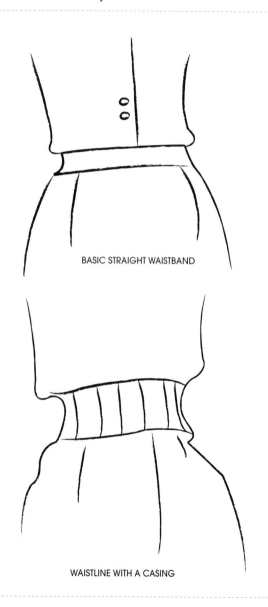

BASIC STRAIGHT WAISTBAND

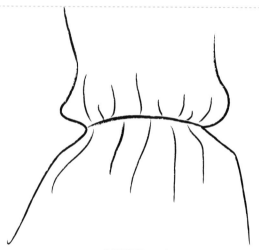

GATHERED WAISTLINE

WAISTLINE WITH A CASING

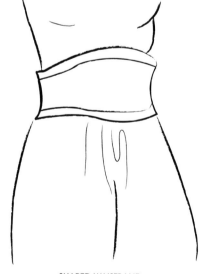

SHAPED WAISTBAND

≪≪   How to make a plain seam p94   Plain dart p107

TECHNIQUES

Joining a fitted skirt to a bodice
LEVEL OF DIFFICULTY **

Many dresses feature a straight fitted skirt attached to a fitted dress bodice. When joining them together, it is important that the darts or seamlines on the bodice line up with those on the skirt.

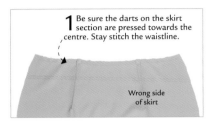

1 Be sure the darts on the skirt section are pressed towards the centre. Stay stitch the waistline.

Wrong side of skirt

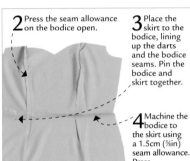

2 Press the seam allowance on the bodice open.

3 Place the skirt to the bodice, lining up the darts and the bodice seams. Pin the bodice and skirt together.

4 Machine the bodice to the skirt using a 1.5cm (⅝in) seam allowance. Press.

5 Neaten the skirt/bodice seam using either a 3-thread overlock stitch or a zigzag stitch.

6 Press the seam up towards the bodice.

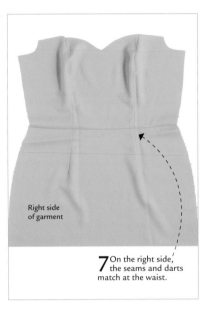

Right side of garment

7 On the right side, the seams and darts match at the waist.

Joining a gathered skirt to a bodice
LEVEL OF DIFFICULTY **

When attaching a gathered skirt to a fitted bodice, the gathers must be distributed evenly around the waist. If there are seams on the gathered skirt these must be matched to the bodice seams and darts.

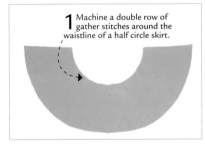

1 Machine a double row of gather stitches around the waistline of a half circle skirt.

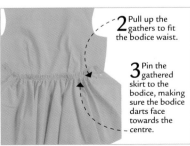

2 Pull up the gathers to fit the bodice waist.

3 Pin the gathered skirt to the bodice, making sure the bodice darts face towards the centre.

4 Machine the gathered skirt to the bodice using a 1.5cm (⅝in) seam allowance. Neaten the seam using either a 3-thread overlock stitch or a zigzag stitch.

5 Press the seam up towards the bodice. On the right side the skirt seam is gathered into a smooth bodice seam.

How to make and fit gathers p127 ≪≪

Making a casing at the waist edge

LEVEL OF DIFFICULTY **

An elasticated waist edge is featured on both skirts and trousers and also at the waist edge on casual jackets. The casing can be made by using a deep waist seam or by attaching a facing. The facing will form a complete circle that will be attached to the waist edge.

USING A DEEP WAIST SEAM AS A CASING

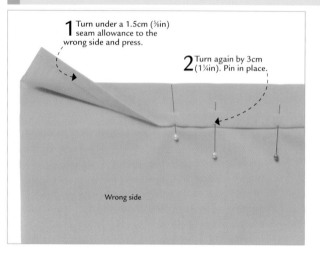

1 Turn under a 1.5cm (⅝in) seam allowance to the wrong side and press.

2 Turn again by 3cm (1¼in). Pin in place.

Wrong side

3 Stitch 2mm (¹⁄₁₆in) from the top folded edge.

Wrong side

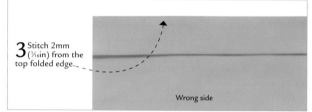

4 Machine the lower edge of the fold 2mm (¹⁄₁₆in) from the edge. Leave a gap of about 3cm (1¼in) to insert the elastic through.

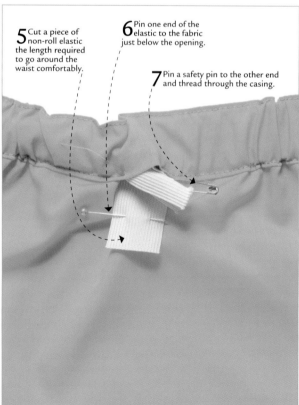

5 Cut a piece of non-roll elastic the length required to go around the waist comfortably.

6 Pin one end of the elastic to the fabric just below the opening.

7 Pin a safety pin to the other end and thread through the casing.

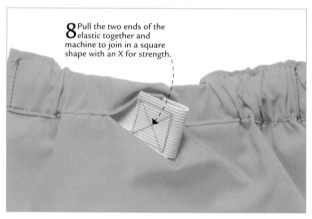

8 Pull the two ends of the elastic together and machine to join in a square shape with an X for strength.

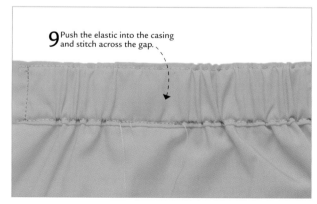

9 Push the elastic into the casing and stitch across the gap.

≪≪≪ Tacking stitches p89   How to make a plain seam p94   Layering a seam p102

USING A FACING AS A CASING

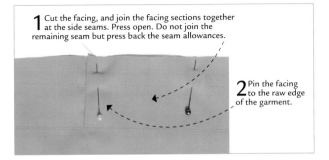

1 Cut the facing, and join the facing sections together at the side seams. Press open. Do not join the remaining seam but press back the seam allowances.

2 Pin the facing to the raw edge of the garment.

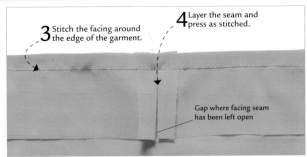

3 Stitch the facing around the edge of the garment.

4 Layer the seam and press as stitched.

Gap where facing seam has been left open

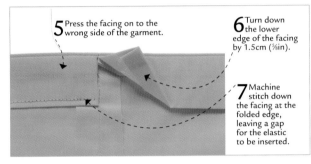

5 Press the facing on to the wrong side of the garment.

6 Turn down the lower edge of the facing by 1.5cm (⅝in).

7 Machine stitch down the facing at the folded edge, leaving a gap for the elastic to be inserted.

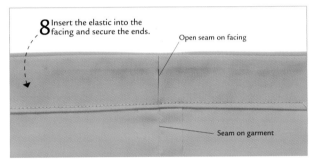

8 Insert the elastic into the facing and secure the ends.

Open seam on facing

Seam on garment

Applied casings
LEVEL OF DIFFICULTY ★★

Some elasticated waist edges will require the application of extra fabric to make a casing into which the elastic can be inserted. The casing may be applied to the inside or the outside of the garment. A quick way is to make the casing with bias binding. The casing can also be made from the same fabric as the garment or from a facing.

INTERNAL CASING

1 This type of casing is often used on a shirt-waisted dress or on a blouson-style jacket. Cut a strip of fabric on the straight of grain wide enough to accommodate your elastic and turnings.

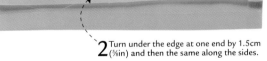

2 Turn under the edge at one end by 1.5cm (⅝in) and then the same along the sides.

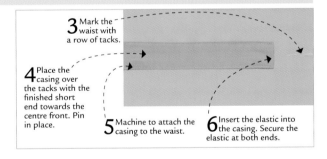

3 Mark the waist with a row of tacks.

4 Place the casing over the tacks with the finished short end towards the centre front. Pin in place.

5 Machine to attach the casing to the waist.

6 Insert the elastic into the casing. Secure the elastic at both ends.

INTERNAL CASING USING BIAS BINDING

1 Be sure to use bias binding that will be wide enough to insert an elastic through after it has been stitched down. Apply the bias to the waistline and stitch at 2mm (¹⁄₁₆in) from either edge.

2 Insert the elastic and knot the ends.

2cm (¾in) wide bias binding

EXTERNAL CASING

1 Cut a strip of straight grain fabric 3.5cm (1⅜in) wide x the waist measurement on the garment. Turn under all raw edges by 5mm (³⁄₁₆in) and press.

2 Place this casing over the garment waistline, with the short ends to the centre front.

3 Machine in place along the long edges. Insert elastic to fit the waist.

Construction of a facing p145   How to cut bias strips p147 ‹‹‹

Mock casings

LEVEL OF DIFFICULTY ★★★

There are several ways to construct mock casings. The simplest is to stitch on elastic at the waist. An alternative, if a bodice and skirt have a waist seam joining them together, is to insert elastic between the seam allowances. On many garments, there is elastic at the back only, in a partial casing, and a waistband interfacing at the front.

TECHNIQUES

STITCHING ON ELASTIC TO MAKE A WAISTLINE

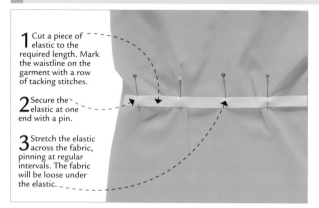

1 Cut a piece of elastic to the required length. Mark the waistline on the garment with a row of tacking stitches.

2 Secure the elastic at one end with a pin.

3 Stretch the elastic across the fabric, pinning at regular intervals. The fabric will be loose under the elastic.

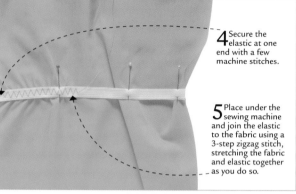

4 Secure the elastic at one end with a few machine stitches.

5 Place under the sewing machine and join the elastic to the fabric using a 3-step zigzag stitch, stretching the fabric and elastic together as you do so.

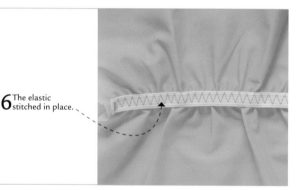

6 The elastic stitched in place.

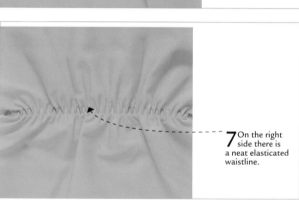

7 On the right side there is a neat elasticated waistline.

CASING IN A WAIST SEAM ALLOWANCE

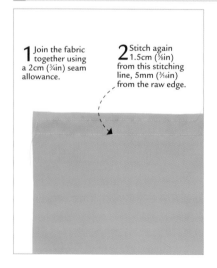

1 Join the fabric together using a 2cm (¾in) seam allowance.

2 Stitch again 1.5cm (⅝in) from this stitching line, 5mm (³⁄₁₆in) from the raw edge.

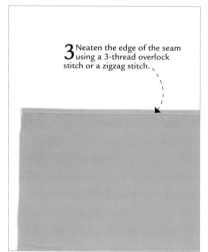

3 Neaten the edge of the seam using a 3-thread overlock stitch or a zigzag stitch.

4 Insert elastic into the casing that you have made, with the help of a safety pin.

ALTERNATIVE CASING USING A SEAM ALLOWANCE

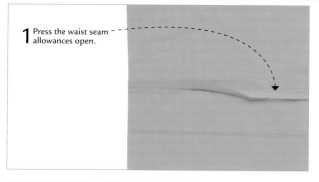

1 Press the waist seam allowances open.

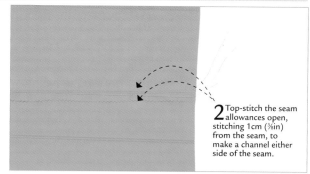

2 Top-stitch the seam allowances open, stitching 1cm (⅜in) from the seam, to make a channel either side of the seam.

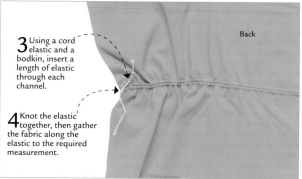

3 Using a cord elastic and a bodkin, insert a length of elastic through each channel.

4 Knot the elastic together, then gather the fabric along the elastic to the required measurement.

Back

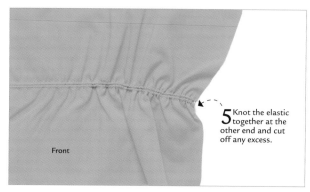

Front

5 Knot the elastic together at the other end and cut off any excess.

PARTIAL CASING

1 The front waist is made by using a grown-on waistband. This means the waistband has been cut in one piece together with the skirt front. Apply a fusible interfacing to the waistband allowance.

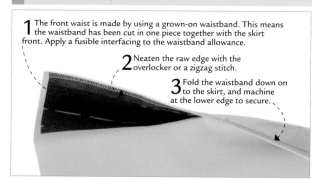

2 Neaten the raw edge with the overlocker or a zigzag stitch.

3 Fold the waistband down on to the skirt, and machine at the lower edge to secure.

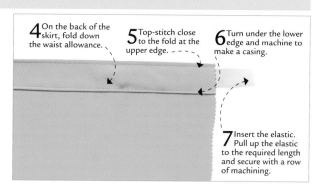

4 On the back of the skirt, fold down the waist allowance.

5 Top-stitch close to the fold at the upper edge.

6 Turn under the lower edge and machine to make a casing.

7 Insert the elastic. Pull up the elastic to the required length and secure with a row of machining.

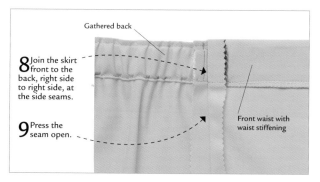

Gathered back

8 Join the skirt front to the back, right side to right side, at the side seams.

9 Press the seam open.

Front waist with waist stiffening

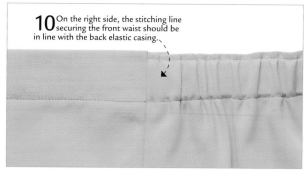

10 On the right side, the stitching line securing the front waist should be in line with the back elastic casing.

A waist with a facing

LEVEL OF DIFFICULTY **

Many waistlines on skirts and trousers are finished with a facing, which will follow the contours of the waist but will have had the dart shaping removed to make it smooth. A faced waistline always sits comfortably to the body. The facing is attached after all the main sections of the skirt or trousers have been constructed.

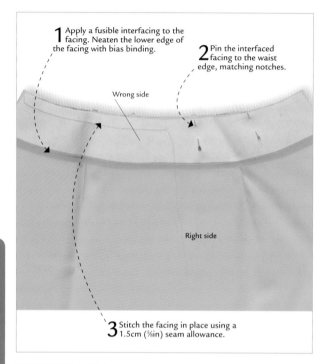

1 Apply a fusible interfacing to the facing. Neaten the lower edge of the facing with bias binding.

2 Pin the interfaced facing to the waist edge, matching notches.

Wrong side

Right side

3 Stitch the facing in place using a 1.5cm (⅝in) seam allowance.

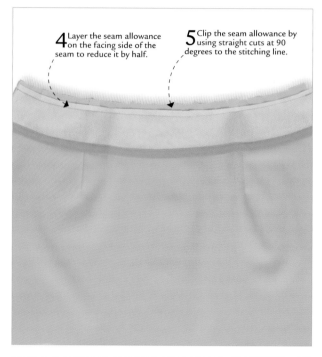

4 Layer the seam allowance on the facing side of the seam to reduce it by half.

5 Clip the seam allowance by using straight cuts at 90 degrees to the stitching line.

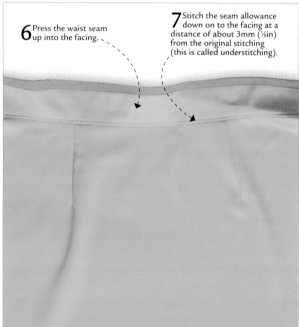

6 Press the waist seam up into the facing.

7 Stitch the seam allowance down on to the facing at a distance of about 3mm (⅛in) from the original stitching (this is called understitching).

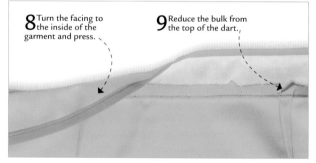

8 Turn the facing to the inside of the garment and press.

9 Reduce the bulk from the top of the dart.

10 The right side of the waistline.

Petersham-faced waist

LEVEL OF DIFFICULTY ∗∗∗

Petersham is an alternative finish to a facing if you do not have enough fabric to cut a facing. Available in black and white, it is a stiff, ridged tape that is 2.5cm (1in) wide and curved – the tighter curve is the top edge. Like a facing, petersham is attached to the waist after the skirt or trousers have been constructed.

1 Stay stitch around the waist 1.2cm (½in) from the raw edge.

2 Trim back the raw edge to 6mm (¼in).

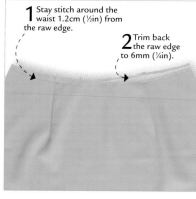

3 Pin the top edge of the petersham (the tighter curve) to the waist so that it overlaps the stay stitching by 2mm (¹⁄₁₆in).

4 Tack in place.

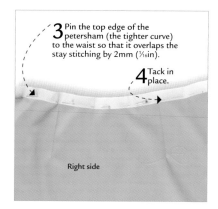

Right side

5 Machine the petersham in place, stitching about 2mm (¹⁄₁₆in) from the edge of the petersham. Do not worry if the other edge looks wavy.

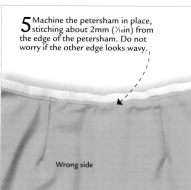

Wrong side

6 Turn over and roll the petersham to the inside of the waist.

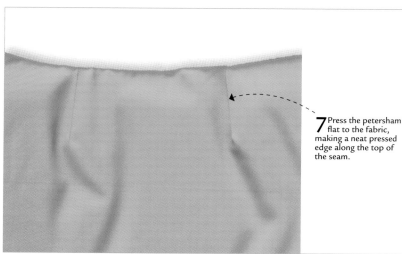

7 Press the petersham flat to the fabric, making a neat pressed edge along the top of the seam.

Finishing the edge of a waistband

LEVEL OF DIFFICULTY ∗

One long edge of the waistband will be stitched to the garment waist. The other edge will need to be finished, to prevent fraying and reduce bulk inside. .

TURNING UNDER

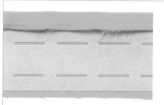

This method is suitable for fine fabrics only. Turn under 1.5cm (⅝in) along the edge of the waistband and press in place. After the waistband has been attached to the garment, hand stitch the pressed-under edge in place.

OVERLOCK STITCHING

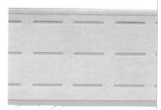

This method is suitable for heavier fabrics as it is left flat inside the garment after construction. Neaten one long edge of the waistband with a 3-thread overlock stitch.

BIAS BINDING

This method is ideal for fabrics that fray badly and can add a feature inside the garment. It is left flat inside the garment after construction. Apply a 2cm (¾in) bias binding to one long edge of the waistband.

Attaching a straight waistband

LEVEL OF DIFFICULTY **

A waistband is designed to fit snugly but not tight to the waist. Whether it is shaped or straight or slightly curved, it will be constructed and attached in a similar way. Every waistband will require a fusible interfacing to give it structure and support. Special waistband interfacings are available, usually featuring slot lines that will guide you where to fold the fabric. Make sure the slots on the outer edge correspond to a 1.5cm (⅝in) seam allowance. If a specialist waistband fusible interfacing is not available you can use a medium-weight fusible interfacing.

1 Cut the waistband and apply the interfacing. Neaten one long edge.

2 Pin the waistband to the skirt waist edge, right side to right side. Match the notches.

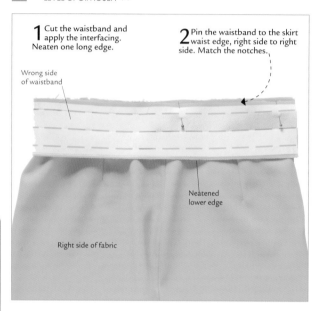

Wrong side of waistband

Neatened lower edge

Right side of fabric

3 Stitch the waistband to the waist edge using a 1.5cm (⅝in) seam allowance. The waistband will extend beyond the zip by 1.5cm (⅝in) on the left and 5cm (2in) on the right.

4 Press the waistband away from the skirt.

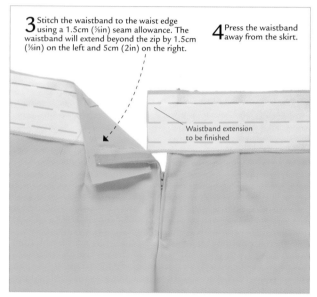

Waistband extension to be finished

5 Fold the waistband along the crease in the interfacing, right side to right side. The neatened edge of the waistband should extend 1.5cm (⅝in) below the stitching line.

6 Pin the end of the waistband in line with the centre back.

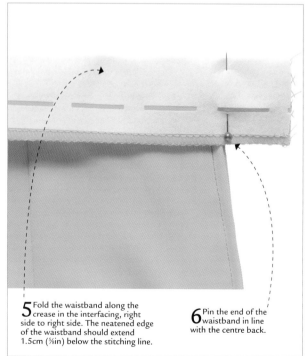

7 On the right-hand back at the waist, fold the waistband in half, right side to right side.

8 Extend the waist/skirt stitching line through the waistband and through the end.

9 Turn the ends of the waistband to the right side. The extension on the waistband should be on the right-hand back.

10 Add your chosen fasteners.

11 To complete the waistband, stitch through the band to the skirt seam. This is known as stitching in the ditch.

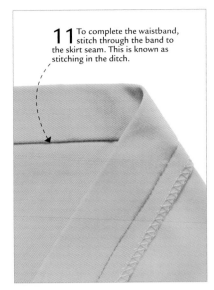

12 The finished straight waistband.

Ribbon-faced waistband

LEVEL OF DIFFICULTY ★★★

On a bulky fabric, you can replace the inner side of the waistband with a ribbon. This will not affect the structure and stability of the waistband, but will produce a less bulky finish. Use a grosgrain ribbon that is 2.5cm (1in) wide. Grosgrain ribbon looks like petersham (see page 177) but is ribbed and much softer.

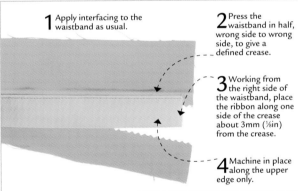

1 Apply interfacing to the waistband as usual.

2 Press the waistband in half, wrong side to wrong side, to give a defined crease.

3 Working from the right side of the waistband, place the ribbon along one side of the crease about 3mm (⅛in) from the crease.

4 Machine in place along the upper edge only.

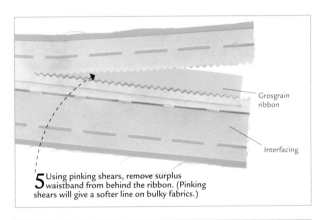

Grosgrain ribbon

Interfacing

5 Using pinking shears, remove surplus waistband from behind the ribbon. (Pinking shears will give a softer line on bulky fabrics.)

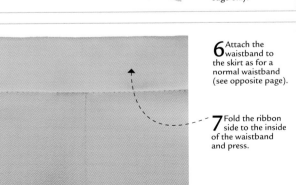

6 Attach the waistband to the skirt as for a normal waistband (see opposite page).

7 Fold the ribbon side to the inside of the waistband and press.

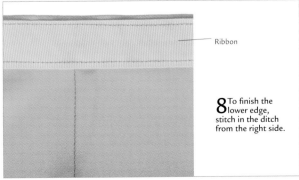

Ribbon

8 To finish the lower edge, stitch in the ditch from the right side.

Fasteners pp250–273 »»»

BELTS

A belt in a fabric that matches the garment can add the perfect finishing touch. Whether it be a soft tie belt or a stiff structured belt, it will be best if it has an interfacing of some kind – the firmer and more structured the belt, the firmer the interfacing should be. A belt will also need belt carriers to support it and prevent it from drooping.

Directory of belts and tie-backs

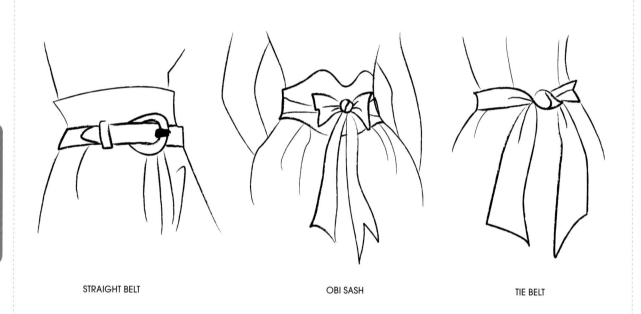

STRAIGHT BELT

OBI SASH

TIE BELT

RUCHED CURTAIN TIE-BACK

STRUCTURED CURTAIN TIE-BACK

TECHNIQUES

Belt carriers
LEVEL OF DIFFICULTY ***

Belt carriers can be made from fabric strips and machined to the garment, or they can be made more simply from thread loops fashioned by hand stitching. Fabric carriers are designed to support a heavier belt.

HAND-STITCHED BELT LOOPS

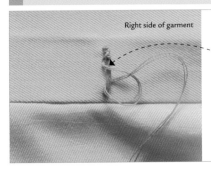

Right side of garment

1 Work the belt loop prior to the waistband being finished on the inside. Using double bold machine thread, work several strands of thread long enough to slot a belt through.

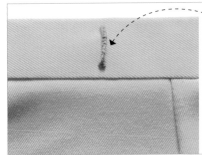

2 Use a buttonhole stitch and work the stitches across the loops.

3 When the loops are covered with buttonhole stitches, take the thread to the reverse and finish securely.

MACHINE-STITCHED BELT CARRIERS

1 Cut the fabric strips 3cm (1¼in) wide and long enough to allow for the depth of the belt plus turnings of 1.5cm (⅝in) at each end.

2 Press the long edges of the fabric carriers to the centre, wrong side to wrong side.

3 Press the carriers in half lengthways.

4 Machine along the centre of each carrier, securing the folded edges.

5 Press again to be sure the stitch line runs down the centre of the carrier.

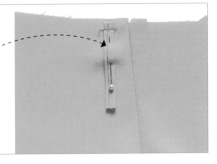

6 Starting at each side seam and then at regular intervals between, place the carriers to the waist of the garment, on the right side. Stitch to secure at the waist inside the seam allowance.

7 Apply the waistband to the garment, stitching across the carriers as you do so.

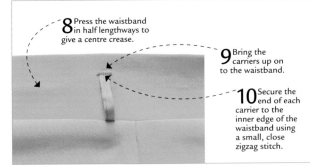

8 Press the waistband in half lengthways to give a centre crease.

9 Bring the carriers up on to the waistband.

10 Secure the end of each carrier to the inner edge of the waistband using a small, close zigzag stitch.

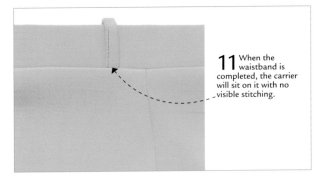

11 When the waistband is completed, the carrier will sit on it with no visible stitching.

Reinforced straight belt

LEVEL OF DIFFICULTY ★★★

This is a straightforward way to make a belt to match a garment. It can be of any width as it is reinforced with a very firm fusible interfacing, such as a craft interfacing. If one layer of interfacing is not firm enough, try adding another layer. The interfacing should be cut along its length to avoid joins. To ensure that it is cut straight, use a rotary cutter on a self-healing mat.

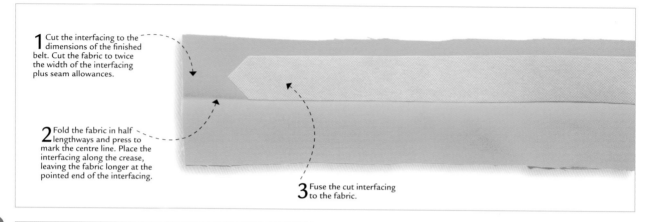

1 Cut the interfacing to the dimensions of the finished belt. Cut the fabric to twice the width of the interfacing plus seam allowances.

2 Fold the fabric in half lengthways and press to mark the centre line. Place the interfacing along the crease, leaving the fabric longer at the pointed end of the interfacing.

3 Fuse the cut interfacing to the fabric.

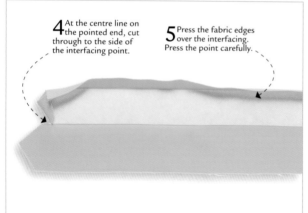

4 At the centre line on the pointed end, cut through to the side of the interfacing point.

5 Press the fabric edges over the interfacing. Press the point carefully.

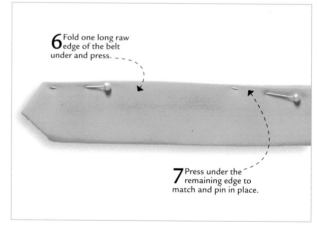

6 Fold one long raw edge of the belt under and press.

7 Press under the remaining edge to match and pin in place.

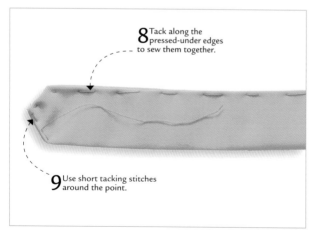

8 Tack along the pressed-under edges to sew them together.

9 Use short tacking stitches around the point.

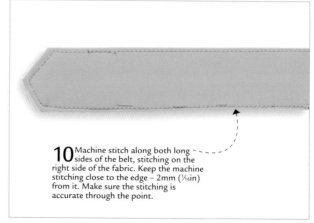

10 Machine stitch along both long sides of the belt, stitching on the right side of the fabric. Keep the machine stitching close to the edge – 2mm (⅟₁₆in) from it. Make sure the stitching is accurate through the point.

⫷⫷⫷ Useful extras p21   How to apply a fusible interfacing p54   Tacking stitches p89   Stitches made with a machine pp92–93

TECHNIQUES

11 Measure the positioning of the eyelets towards the pointed end of the belt.

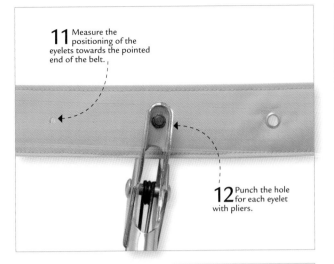

12 Punch the hole for each eyelet with pliers.

13 Insert a 4mm (³⁄₁₆in) eyelet into the hole, working from the right side of the belt.

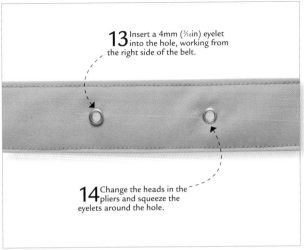

14 Change the heads in the pliers and squeeze the eyelets around the hole.

15 Insert one eyelet at the other end of the belt about 5cm (2in) from the end, placing it centrally on the right side of the belt.

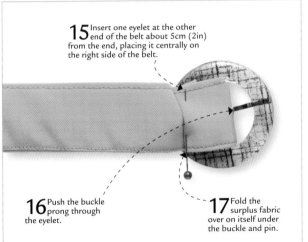

16 Push the buckle prong through the eyelet.

17 Fold the surplus fabric over on itself under the buckle and pin.

18 Secure with a machine or hand stitch, then turn the belt over.

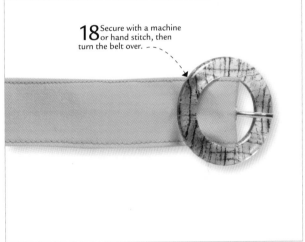

19 When the belt is placed around the waist, check that the fit is correct. Add extra eyelets if required.

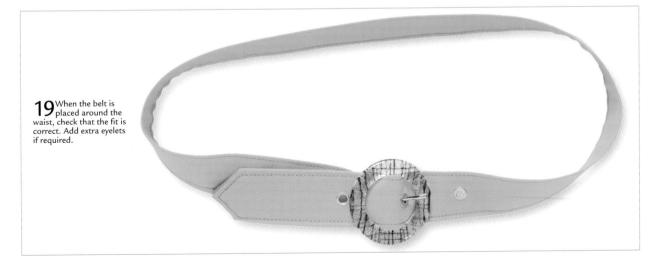

Tie belt

LEVEL OF DIFFICULTY **

A tie belt is the easiest of all the belts to make. It can be any width and made of most fabrics, from cottons for summer dresses to satin and silks for bridal wear. Most tie belts will require a light to medium-weight interfacing for support. A fusible interfacing is the best choice as it will stay in place when tied repeatedly. If a very long tie belt is required, the belt can be joined at the centre back.

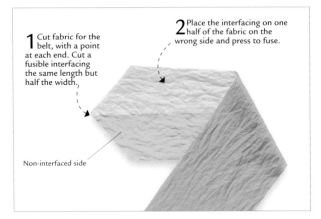

1 Cut fabric for the belt, with a point at each end. Cut a fusible interfacing the same length but half the width.

Non-interfaced side

2 Place the interfacing on one half of the fabric on the wrong side and press to fuse.

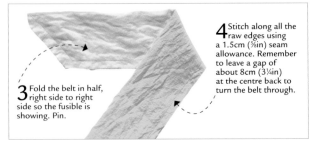

3 Fold the belt in half, right side to right side so the fusible is showing. Pin.

4 Stitch along all the raw edges using a 1.5cm (⅝in) seam allowance. Remember to leave a gap of about 8cm (3¼in) at the centre back to turn the belt through.

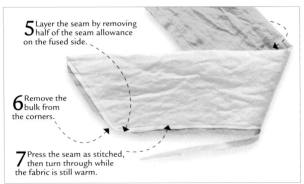

5 Layer the seam by removing half of the seam allowance on the fused side.

6 Remove the bulk from the corners.

7 Press the seam as stitched, then turn through while the fabric is still warm.

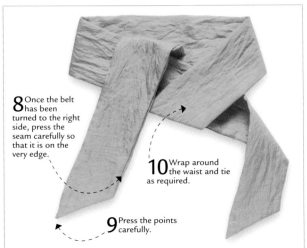

8 Once the belt has been turned to the right side, press the seam carefully so that it is on the very edge.

9 Press the points carefully.

10 Wrap around the waist and tie as required.

Obi sash

LEVEL OF DIFFICULTY ***

An obi sash is a variation of the traditional sash that is worn with a kimono. This type of sash has a stiffened centre piece with softer ties that cross at the back and then wrap to the front and tie. If you are using a firm fabric, such as silk dupion or heavy cotton, interfacing will not be required for the ties.

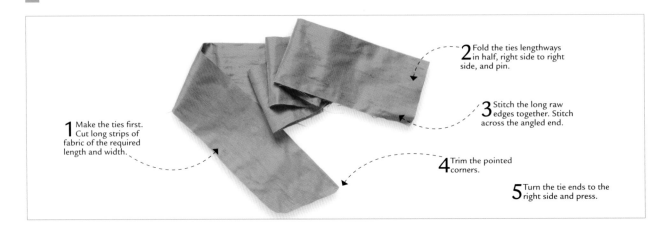

1 Make the ties first. Cut long strips of fabric of the required length and width.

2 Fold the ties lengthways in half, right side to right side, and pin.

3 Stitch the long raw edges together. Stitch across the angled end.

4 Trim the pointed corners.

5 Turn the tie ends to the right side and press.

⫷⫷⫷   How to apply a fusible interfacing p54 Hand stitches pp90–91

6 Next make the centre section. Cut out two shaped pieces of fabric and a matching piece of very firm fusible interfacing.

Right side

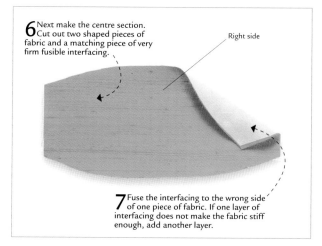

7 Fuse the interfacing to the wrong side of one piece of fabric. If one layer of interfacing does not make the fabric stiff enough, add another layer.

8 Centre the tie ends to the short ends of the stiffened centre piece on the right side. Machine stitch to secure, using a 1cm (⅜in) seam allowance.

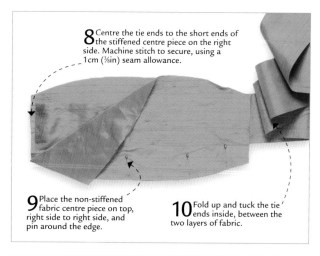

9 Place the non-stiffened fabric centre piece on top, right side to right side, and pin around the edge.

10 Fold up and tuck the tie ends inside, between the two layers of fabric.

11 Machine stitch around the centre section, leaving a gap at the lower edge for turning through.

13 Clip the curved edges of the centre section in the seam allowance.

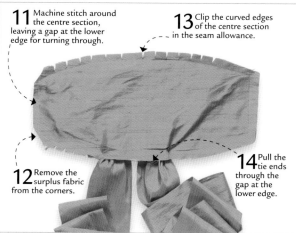

12 Remove the surplus fabric from the corners.

14 Pull the tie ends through the gap at the lower edge.

15 Turn the centre section through to the right side and press.

16 Hand stitch the gap at the lower edge with a flat fell or blind hem stitch.

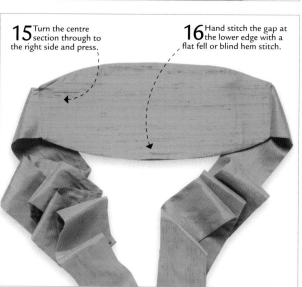

17 The finished obi sash.

Curtain tie-backs

LEVEL OF DIFFICULTY **✳✳**

Tie-backs are used to hold the drape of a curtain in position. Some are structured, with an interfacing, and follow a predetermined shape, while others are softer and more decorative. The construction of a tie-back is similar to that of a tie belt.

STRUCTURED TIE-BACK

1 Cut out two pieces of fabric for the tie-back. Use a heavy fusible interfacing and cut it to the same size as the fabric, minus the seam allowances of 1.5cm (⅝in) on all sides.

2 Fuse the interfacing to the wrong side of one piece of fabric.

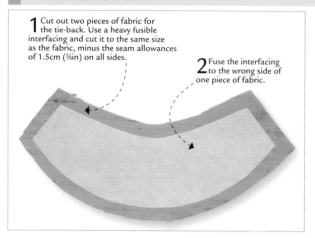

3 Pin the non-interfaced piece of fabric to the interfaced piece, right side to right side.

4 Stitch around the two pieces, taking a 1.5cm (⅝in) seam allowance. The machining should follow the edge of the interfacing, but not go through it.

5 Leave a gap of about 8cm (3¼in) at the lower edge to turn through.

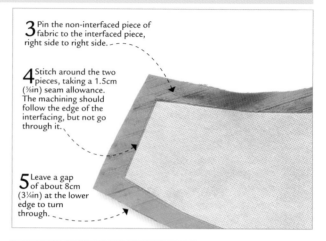

6 Remove the corners from the fabric layers.

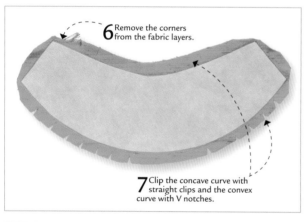

7 Clip the concave curve with straight clips and the convex curve with V notches.

8 Turn the tie-back through to the right side.

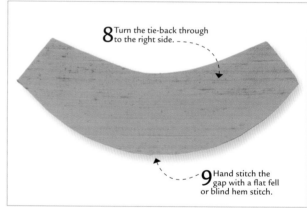

9 Hand stitch the gap with a flat fell or blind hem stitch.

10 On the two short ends of the tie-back, sew on a curtain ring. Use a buttonhole stitch to secure it.

TECHNIQUES

DECORATIVE RUCHED TIE-BACK

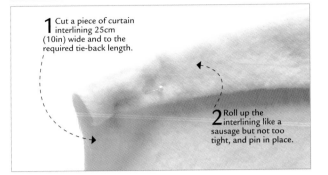

1 Cut a piece of curtain interlining 25cm (10in) wide and to the required tie-back length.

2 Roll up the interlining like a sausage but not too tight, and pin in place.

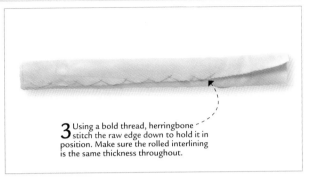

3 Using a bold thread, herringbone stitch the raw edge down to hold it in position. Make sure the rolled interlining is the same thickness throughout.

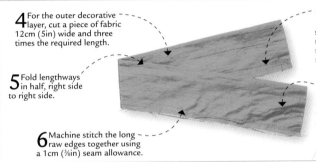

4 For the outer decorative layer, cut a piece of fabric 12cm (5in) wide and three times the required length.

5 Fold lengthways in half, right side to right side.

6 Machine stitch the long raw edges together using a 1cm (⅜in) seam allowance.

7 Stitch again, between the stitching line and the raw edge. The double stitching is for strength.

8 Turn the decorative top layer fabric through to the right side and press.

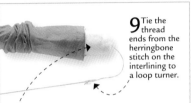

9 Tie the thread ends from the herringbone stitch on the interlining to a loop turner.

10 Using the loop turner, pull the interlining sausage through the decorative layer. This is difficult as it will stick. Work the decorative fabric gently down the interlining.

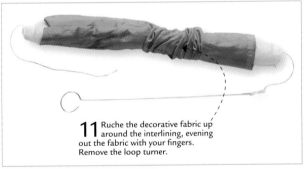

11 Ruche the decorative fabric up around the interlining, evening out the fabric with your fingers. Remove the loop turner.

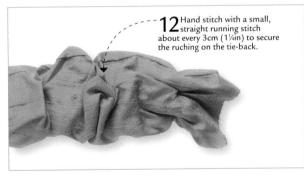

12 Hand stitch with a small, straight running stitch about every 3cm (1¼in) to secure the ruching on the tie-back.

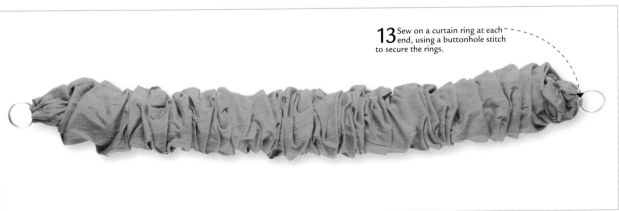

13 Sew on a curtain ring at each end, using a buttonhole stitch to secure the rings.

SLEEVES AND SLEEVE FINISHES

Sleeves come in all shapes and lengths, and form an important part of the design of a garment. They should always hang properly from the end of the wearer's shoulder, without wrinkles. The lower end of the sleeve is normally finished by means of a cuff or a facing.

SLEEVES

A few sleeves, such as the dolman, are cut as part of the garment, but most sleeves, including set-in and raglan, are made separately and then inserted into the armhole. Whichever type of sleeve is being inserted, always place it to the armhole and not the armhole to the sleeve – in other words, always work with the sleeve facing you.

Directory of sleeves

SET-IN SLEEVE (SHORT)   SET-IN SLEEVE (LONG)   SHORT TRUMPET SLEEVE   BISHOP SLEEVE

CAP SLEEVE   DOLMAN SLEEVE   KIMONO SLEEVE

LEG-OF-MUTTON SLEEVE   PUFF SLEEVE   RAGLAN SLEEVE

Inserting a set-in sleeve

LEVEL OF DIFFICULTY ★★★

A set-in sleeve should feature a smooth sleeve head that fits on the end of your shoulder accurately. This is achieved by the use of ease stitches, which are long stitches used to tighten the fabric but not gather it.

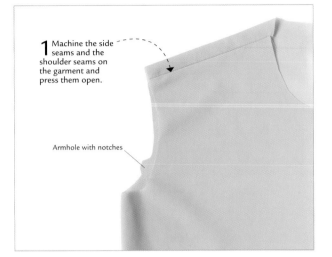

1 Machine the side seams and the shoulder seams on the garment and press them open.

Armhole with notches

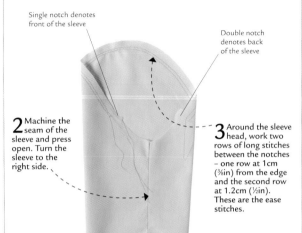

Single notch denotes front of the sleeve

Double notch denotes back of the sleeve

2 Machine the seam of the sleeve and press open. Turn the sleeve to the right side.

3 Around the sleeve head, work two rows of long stitches between the notches – one row at 1cm (⅜in) from the edge and the second row at 1.2cm (½in). These are the ease stitches.

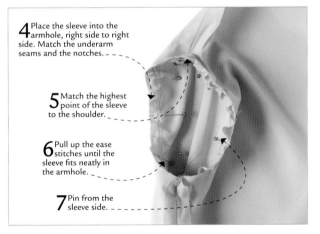

4 Place the sleeve into the armhole, right side to right side. Match the underarm seams and the notches.

5 Match the highest point of the sleeve to the shoulder.

6 Pull up the ease stitches until the sleeve fits neatly in the armhole.

7 Pin from the sleeve side.

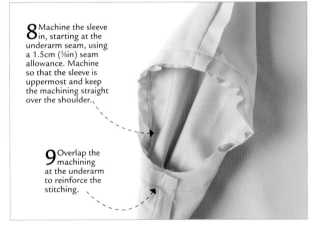

8 Machine the sleeve in, starting at the underarm seam, using a 1.5cm (⅝in) seam allowance. Machine so that the sleeve is uppermost and keep the machining straight over the shoulder.

9 Overlap the machining at the underarm to reinforce the stitching.

10 Stitch around the sleeve again inside the seam allowance.

11 Trim the raw edges of the sleeve.

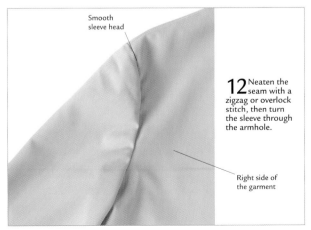

Smooth sleeve head

12 Neaten the seam with a zigzag or overlock stitch, then turn the sleeve through the armhole.

Right side of the garment

Seam neatening pp94–95 Reducing seam bulk pp102–103 ⟪⟪⟪

Puff sleeve

LEVEL OF DIFFICULTY ✶✶

A sleeve that has a gathered sleeve head is referred to as a puff sleeve or gathered sleeve. It is one of the easiest sleeves to insert because the gathers take up any spare fabric.

1 Machine stitch the sleeve, right side to right side, using a 1.5cm (⅝in) seam allowance. Press the seam open.

2 Between the sleeve notches, insert two rows of gather stitches, one row at 1cm (⅜in) from the raw edge and the second row at 1.2cm (½in).

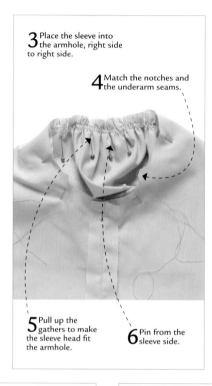

3 Place the sleeve into the armhole, right side to right side.

4 Match the notches and the underarm seams.

5 Pull up the gathers to make the sleeve head fit the armhole.

6 Pin from the sleeve side.

7 Working with the sleeve uppermost, machine the sleeve to the armhole. Use a 1.5cm (⅝in) seam allowance. Overlap the machining at the underarm.

8 Stitch around the sleeve seam again between the seam stitching and the raw edge.

9 Trim away the surplus fabric by 5mm (³⁄₁₆in).

10 Neaten the seam.

11 Turn right side out – all the gathers will be at the top of the sleeve.

⟨⟨⟨ Stitches made with a machine pp92–93   Seam neatening pp94–95

Flat sleeve construction
LEVEL OF DIFFICULTY **

On shirts and children's clothes, sleeves are inserted flat prior to the side seams being constructed. This technique can be difficult on some fabrics, such as those firmly woven, because no ease stitches are used.

1 The shoulder seam on the garment should be stitched and pressed open. Place the sleeve to the armhole of the garment, right side to right side.

2 Match the notches and pin.

3 Stitch the sleeve to the armhole at a 1.5cm (⅝in) seam allowance.

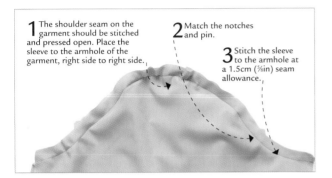

4 Stitch again between the stitching line and the raw edge.

5 Neaten the seam.

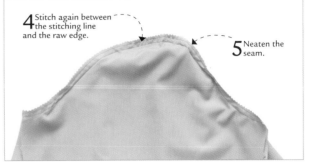

6 Press the sleeve seam towards the sleeve.

7 Fold the garment and sleeve right side to right side. Match the underarm seams.

8 Stitch together with a 1.5cm (⅝in) seam allowance.

9 Press the seam open, then turn the sleeve through the armhole, right side out.

Raglan sleeve
LEVEL OF DIFFICULTY **

A raglan sleeve can be constructed as a one-piece sleeve or a two-piece sleeve. The armhole seam on a raglan sleeve runs diagonally from the armhole to the neck.

1 Join the front and back sleeves together, right side to right side.

2 Press the seam open.

Sleeve front

Sleeve back

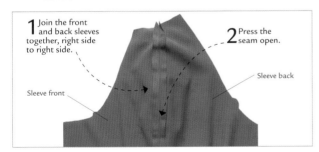

3 Pin the sleeve to the front and back of the garment, matching the notches.

4 Stitch together using a 1.5cm (⅝in) seam allowance.

5 Press the seams open.

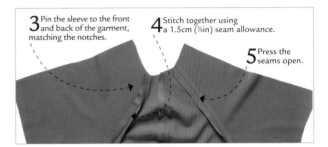

6 Bring the front and the back of the garment together, right side to right side.

7 Machine the side seam of the garment and continue stitching down the sleeve.

8 Press the seam open, then turn the sleeve through the armhole to the right side.

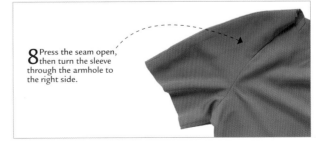

Reducing seam bulk pp102–103   How to make and fit gathers p127   «««

Kimono sleeve

LEVEL OF DIFFICULTY **

A kimono sleeve is a very large, deep sleeve that is inserted on to a garment prior to its construction. Some kimono sleeves are cut with a curve and others are cut straight, but they are made the same way.

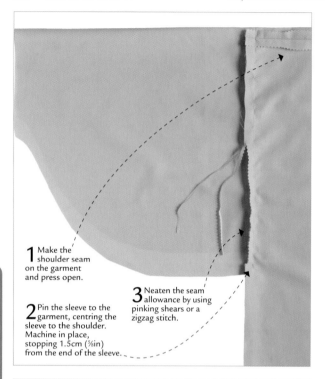

1 Make the shoulder seam on the garment and press open.

2 Pin the sleeve to the garment, centring the sleeve to the shoulder. Machine in place, stopping 1.5cm (⅝in) from the end of the sleeve.

3 Neaten the seam allowance by using pinking shears or a zigzag stitch.

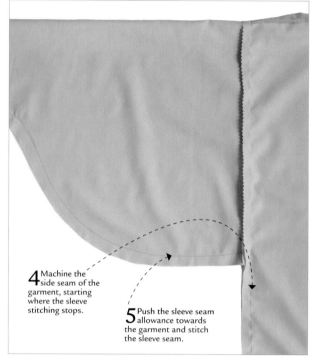

4 Machine the side seam of the garment, starting where the sleeve stitching stops.

5 Push the sleeve seam allowance towards the garment and stitch the sleeve seam.

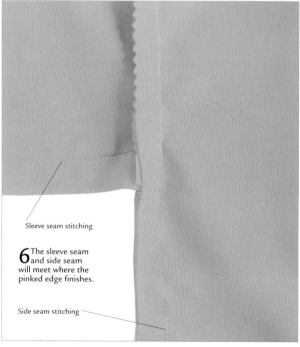

Sleeve seam stitching

6 The sleeve seam and side seam will meet where the pinked edge finishes.

Side seam stitching

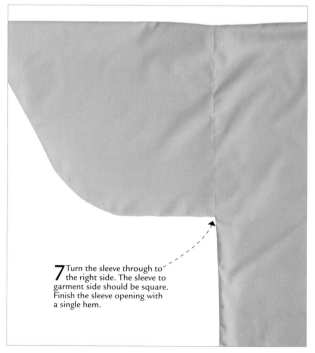

7 Turn the sleeve through to the right side. The sleeve to garment side should be square. Finish the sleeve opening with a single hem.

⫷⫷⫷ Pattern marking pp82–83   Stitches made with a machine pp92–93   How to make a plain seam p94

TECHNIQUES

Dolman sleeve

LEVEL OF DIFFICULTY *

A dolman sleeve is cut as an extension to a garment. As the armhole is very loose, it is ideal for a coat or jacket. The dolman sleeve often has a raglan shoulder pad to define the shoulder end.

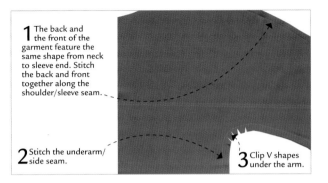

1 The back and the front of the garment feature the same shape from neck to sleeve end. Stitch the back and front together along the shoulder/sleeve seam.

2 Stitch the underarm/ side seam.

3 Clip V shapes under the arm.

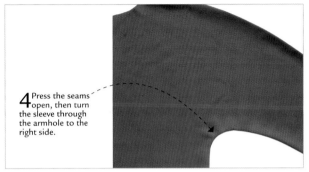

4 Press the seams open, then turn the sleeve through the armhole to the right side.

Dolman sleeve with a gusset

LEVEL OF DIFFICULTY ***

A dolman sleeve can be cut through, to give a tight sleeve. However a tight dolman sleeve will require an underarm gusset to allow movement. The gusset requires accurate stitching and marking if it is to be inserted correctly.

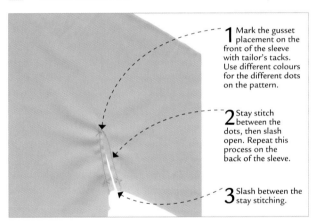

1 Mark the gusset placement on the front of the sleeve with tailor's tacks. Use different colours for the different dots on the pattern.

2 Stay stitch between the dots, then slash open. Repeat this process on the back of the sleeve.

3 Slash between the stay stitching.

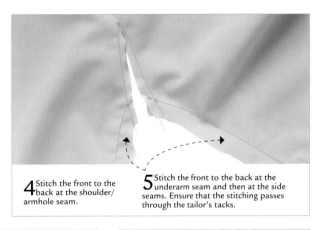

4 Stitch the front to the back at the shoulder/ armhole seam.

5 Stitch the front to the back at the underarm seam and then at the side seams. Ensure that the stitching passes through the tailor's tacks.

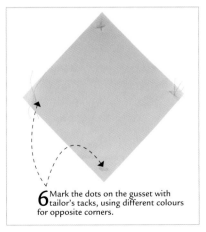

6 Mark the dots on the gusset with tailor's tacks, using different colours for opposite corners.

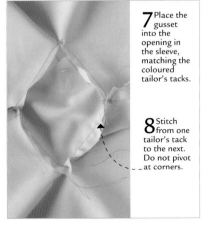

7 Place the gusset into the opening in the sleeve, matching the coloured tailor's tacks.

8 Stitch from one tailor's tack to the next. Do not pivot at corners.

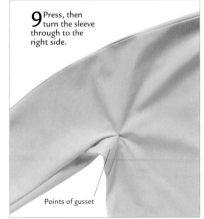

9 Press, then turn the sleeve through to the right side.

Points of gusset

Seam neatening pp94–95   Reducing seam bulk pp102–103 «««

SLEEVE EDGE FINISHES

The lower edge of a sleeve has to be finished according to the style of the garment being made. Some sleeves are finished tight into the arm or wrist, while others may have a more decorative or functional finish.

Directory of sleeve edge finishes

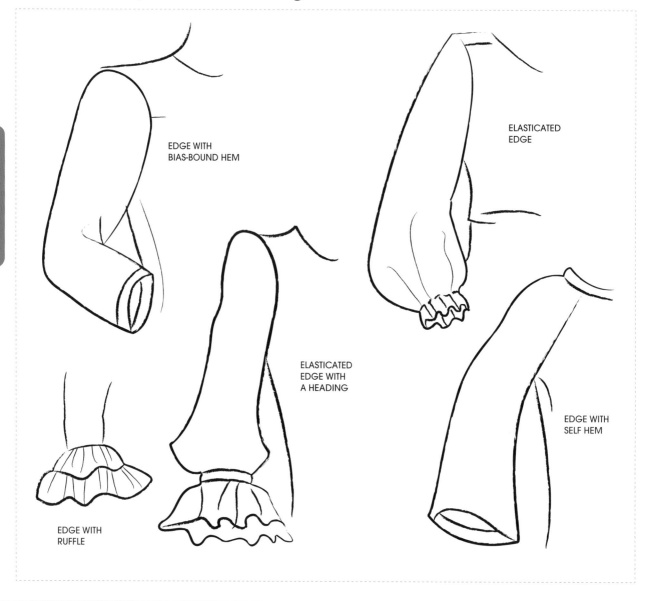

EDGE WITH
BIAS-BOUND HEM

ELASTICATED
EDGE

ELASTICATED
EDGE WITH
A HEADING

EDGE WITH
SELF HEM

EDGE WITH
RUFFLE

Sleeve hems

LEVEL OF DIFFICULTY **

The simplest way to finish a sleeve is to make a small hem, which can be part of the sleeve or additional fabric that is attached to turn up. A self hem is where the edge of the sleeve is turned up on to itself. If there is insufficient fabric to turn up, a bias binding can be used to create the hem. You can use purchased bias binding or make your own bias strips.

SELF HEM

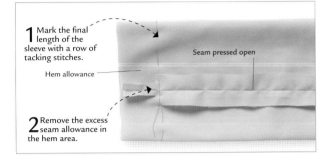

1 Mark the final length of the sleeve with a row of tacking stitches.

Hem allowance

Seam pressed open

2 Remove the excess seam allowance in the hem area.

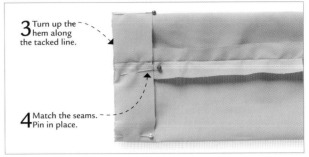

3 Turn up the hem along the tacked line.

4 Match the seams. Pin in place.

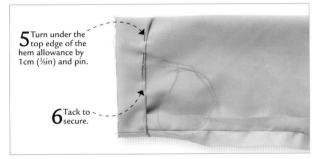

5 Turn under the top edge of the hem allowance by 1cm (⅜in) and pin.

6 Tack to secure.

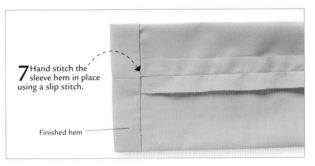

7 Hand stitch the sleeve hem in place using a slip stitch.

Finished hem

BIAS-BOUND HEM

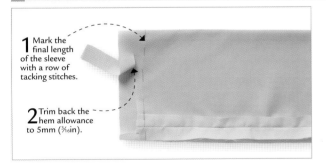

1 Mark the final length of the sleeve with a row of tacking stitches.

2 Trim back the hem allowance to 5mm (³⁄₁₆in).

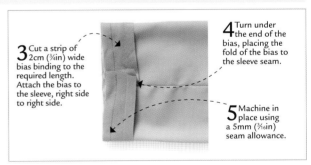

3 Cut a strip of 2cm (¾in) wide bias binding to the required length. Attach the bias to the sleeve, right side to right side.

4 Turn under the end of the bias, placing the fold of the bias to the sleeve seam.

5 Machine in place using a 5mm (³⁄₁₆in) seam allowance.

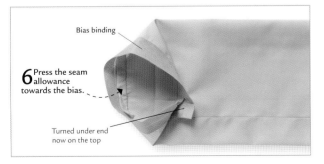

Bias binding

6 Press the seam allowance towards the bias.

Turned under end now on the top

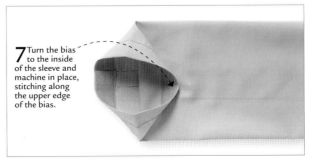

7 Turn the bias to the inside of the sleeve and machine in place, stitching along the upper edge of the bias.

Reducing seam bulk pp102–103   How to cut bias strips p147 ⫷

A casing on a sleeve edge

LEVEL OF DIFFICULTY **

A casing is often used on the edge of a sleeve to insert elastic into, which will allow you to gather the sleeve in a specific place. The casing may be grown-on, which means it is part of the sleeve, or it may be applied separately. The photographs below show an applied casing of bias binding.

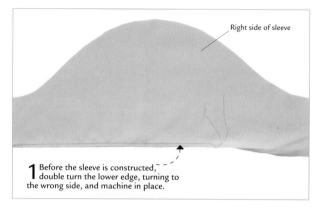

Right side of sleeve

1 Before the sleeve is constructed, double turn the lower edge, turning to the wrong side, and machine in place.

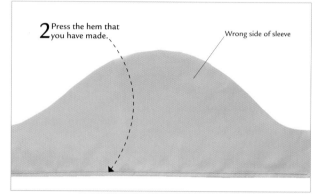

2 Press the hem that you have made.

Wrong side of sleeve

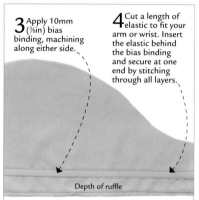

3 Apply 10mm (⅜in) bias binding, machining along either side.

4 Cut a length of elastic to fit your arm or wrist. Insert the elastic behind the bias binding and secure at one end by stitching through all layers.

Depth of ruffle

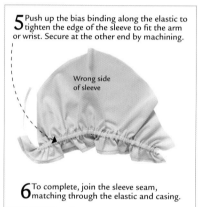

5 Push up the bias binding along the elastic to tighten the edge of the sleeve to fit the arm or wrist. Secure at the other end by machining.

Wrong side of sleeve

6 To complete, join the sleeve seam, matching through the elastic and casing.

7 Press the seam open, then turn the sleeve through the armhole to the right side. You can adjust the ruffles if they are not evenly placed.

Elasticated edge with a heading

LEVEL OF DIFFICULTY **

This is an alternative method for making a ruffle or heading at the end of a sleeve, using a casing that is part of the sleeve.

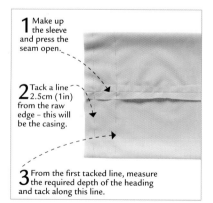

1 Make up the sleeve and press the seam open.

2 Tack a line 2.5cm (1in) from the raw edge – this will be the casing.

3 From the first tacked line, measure the required depth of the heading and tack along this line.

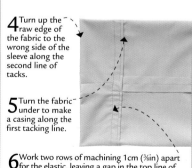

4 Turn up the raw edge of the fabric to the wrong side of the sleeve along the second line of tacks.

5 Turn the fabric under to make a casing along the first tacking line.

6 Work two rows of machining 1cm (⅜in) apart for the elastic, leaving a gap in the top line of stitching where the elastic will be inserted.

7 Cut a piece of elastic to fit the arm or wrist. Insert it into the gap between the two stitching lines. Secure the ends of the elastic together.

8 Turn the sleeve through to the right side and even out the elasticated gathers.

Elasticated sleeve edge

LEVEL OF DIFFICULTY **

The ends of sleeves on workwear and children's clothes are often elasticated to produce a neat and functional finish. Elastic that is 12mm (½in) or 25mm (1in) wide will be most suitable.

1 Make up the sleeve and press the seam open.

2 Work a row of tacking stitches on the foldline of the hem.

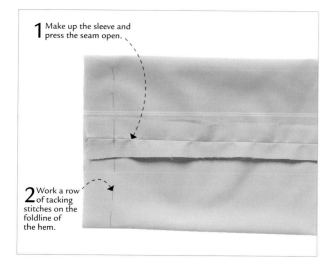

3 Turn up 5mm (³⁄₁₆in) at the raw edge and press.

4 Turn again on to the tacking line.

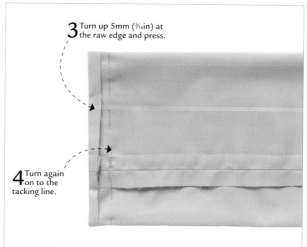

5 Machine to hold the turn-up in place, 2mm (¹⁄₁₆in) from the folded edge. Leave a gap next to the seam allowance through which you will insert the elastic.

Gap to insert the elastic

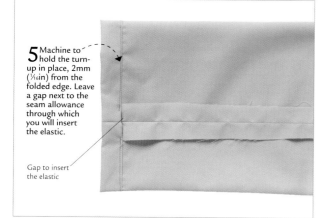

6 Machine the bottom of the sleeve 2mm (¹⁄₁₆in) from the edge, to give a neat finish. This will also help prevent the elastic from twisting.

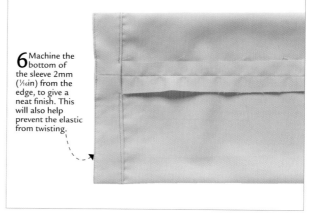

7 Cut a piece of elastic to fit the arm or wrist and insert it into the sleeve end between the two rows of machining.

8 Secure the ends of the elastic together, stitching an X for strength.

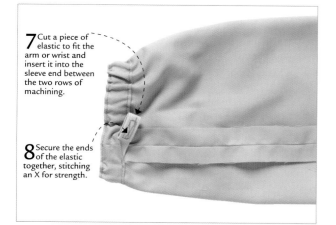

9 Turn the sleeve through the armhole and check that the elasticated edge is even.

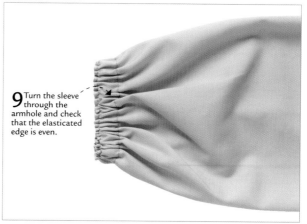

Sleeve edge with ruffle

LEVEL OF DIFFICULTY **

A ruffle at the end of a sleeve is a very feminine finish. It is used on a set-in sleeve that may or may not have a gathered sleeve head.

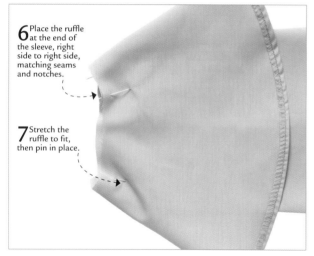

1 First, cut out the ruffle according to your pattern.

2 Neaten the outer edge of the ruffle with a 3-thread overlock stitch or a zigzag stitch.

3 Turn the neatened edge to the wrong side of the ruffle and machine in place.

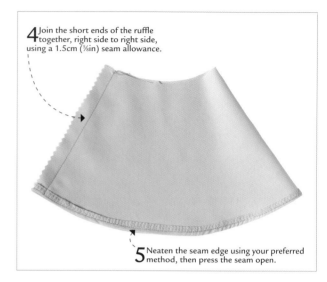

4 Join the short ends of the ruffle together, right side to right side, using a 1.5cm (⅝in) seam allowance.

5 Neaten the seam edge using your preferred method, then press the seam open.

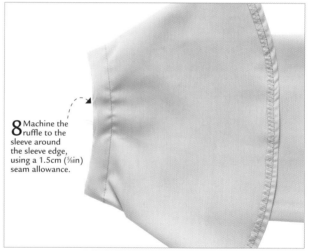

6 Place the ruffle at the end of the sleeve, right side to right side, matching seams and notches.

7 Stretch the ruffle to fit, then pin in place.

8 Machine the ruffle to the sleeve around the sleeve edge, using a 1.5cm (⅝in) seam allowance.

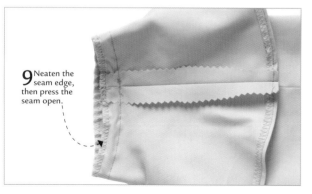

9 Neaten the seam edge, then press the seam open.

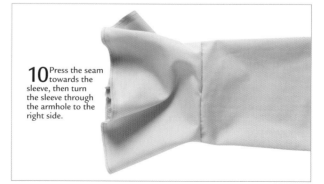

10 Press the seam towards the sleeve, then turn the sleeve through the armhole to the right side.

Faced sleeve edge

LEVEL OF DIFFICULTY **

Adding a facing to the end of a sleeve produces a very clean and bulk-free finish. This technique is particularly suitable for dress sleeves and sleeves on unlined jackets.

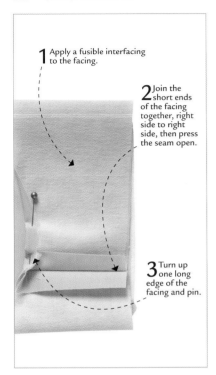

1 Apply a fusible interfacing to the facing.

2 Join the short ends of the facing together, right side to right side, then press the seam open.

3 Turn up one long edge of the facing and pin.

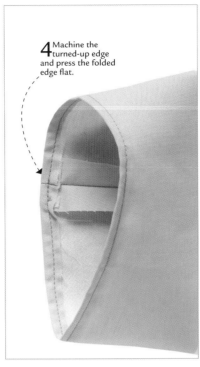

4 Machine the turned-up edge and press the folded edge flat.

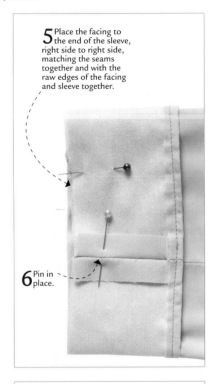

5 Place the facing to the end of the sleeve, right side to right side, matching the seams together and with the raw edges of the facing and sleeve together.

6 Pin in place.

7 Trim the facing seam allowance down to half its width.

8 Press the whole seam allowance towards the facing. Use a seam roll to help the pressing.

9 Understitch the seam allowance to the facing.

10 Turn the facing through to the inside of the sleeve.

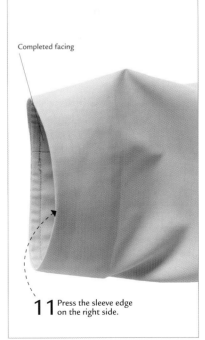

Completed facing

11 Press the sleeve edge on the right side.

Seam neatening pp94–95 Reducing seam bulk pp102–103 Stitch finishes p103

CUFFS AND OPENINGS

A cuff and an opening are ways of producing a sleeve finish that will fit neatly around the wrist. The opening enables the hand to fit through the end of the sleeve, and it allows the sleeve to be rolled up. There are various types of cuffs – single or double, and with pointed or curved edges. All cuffs are interfaced, with the interfacing attached to the upper cuff. The upper cuff is sewn to the sleeve.

Directory of cuffs and openings

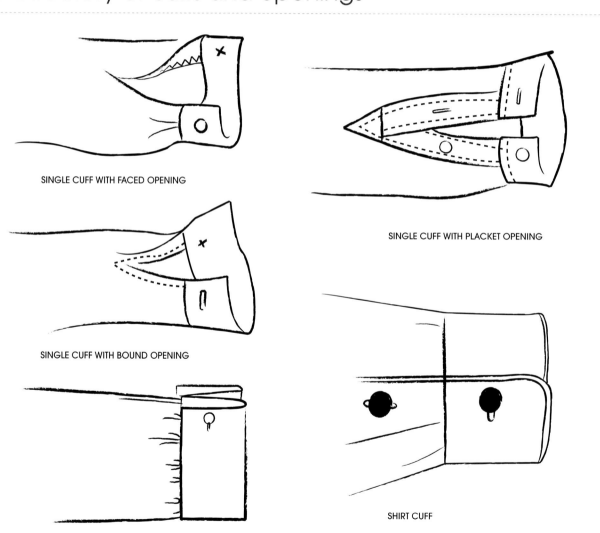

SINGLE CUFF WITH FACED OPENING

SINGLE CUFF WITH PLACKET OPENING

SINGLE CUFF WITH BOUND OPENING

DOUBLE CUFF

SHIRT CUFF

One-piece cuff

LEVEL OF DIFFICULTY **

A one-piece cuff is cut out from the fabric in one piece, and in most cases only half of it is interfaced. The exception is the one-piece double cuff (see page 209).

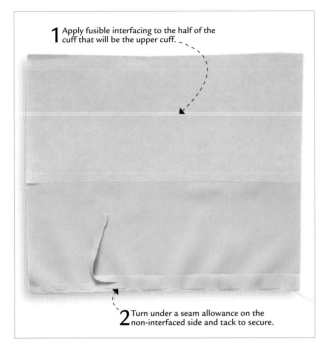

1 Apply fusible interfacing to the half of the cuff that will be the upper cuff.

2 Turn under a seam allowance on the non-interfaced side and tack to secure.

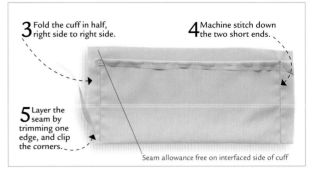

3 Fold the cuff in half, right side to right side.

4 Machine stitch down the two short ends.

5 Layer the seam by trimming one edge, and clip the corners.

Seam allowance free on interfaced side of cuff

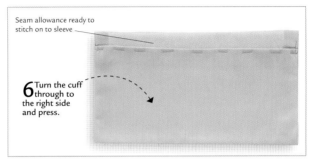

Seam allowance ready to stitch on to sleeve

6 Turn the cuff through to the right side and press.

Two-piece cuff

LEVEL OF DIFFICULTY **

Some cuffs are cut in two pieces: an upper cuff and an under cuff. The upper cuff piece is interfaced.

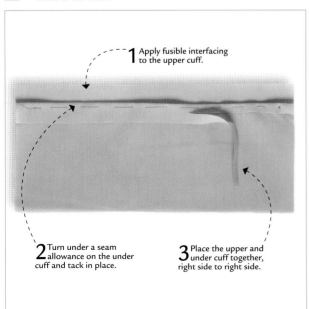

1 Apply fusible interfacing to the upper cuff.

2 Turn under a seam allowance on the under cuff and tack in place.

3 Place the upper and under cuff together, right side to right side.

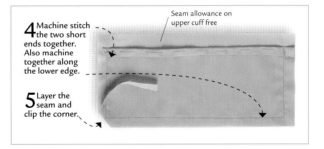

Seam allowance on upper cuff free

4 Machine stitch the two short ends together. Also machine together along the lower edge.

5 Layer the seam and clip the corner.

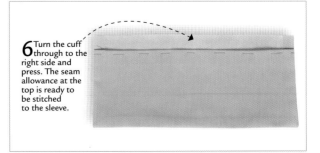

6 Turn the cuff through to the right side and press. The seam allowance at the top is ready to be stitched to the sleeve.

Faced opening

LEVEL OF DIFFICULTY **

Adding a facing to the area of the sleeve where the opening is to be is a neat method of finishing. This type of opening is appropriate to use with a one-piece cuff.

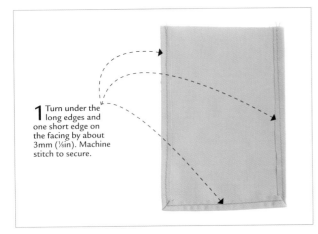

1 Turn under the long edges and one short edge on the facing by about 3mm (⅛in). Machine stitch to secure.

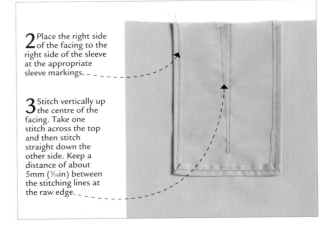

2 Place the right side of the facing to the right side of the sleeve at the appropriate sleeve markings.

3 Stitch vertically up the centre of the facing. Take one stitch across the top and then stitch straight down the other side. Keep a distance of about 5mm (³⁄₁₆in) between the stitching lines at the raw edge.

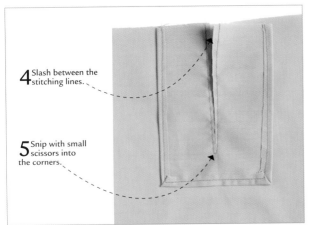

4 Slash between the stitching lines.

5 Snip with small scissors into the corners.

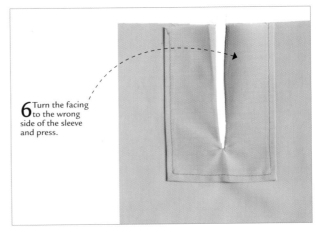

6 Turn the facing to the wrong side of the sleeve and press.

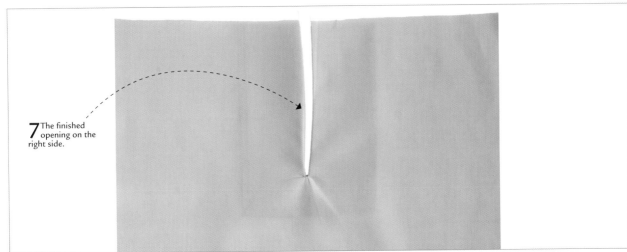

7 The finished opening on the right side.

Bound opening

LEVEL OF DIFFICULTY **

On a fabric that frays badly or a sleeve that may get a great deal of wear, a strong bound opening is a good idea. It involves binding a slash in the sleeve with a matching bias strip.

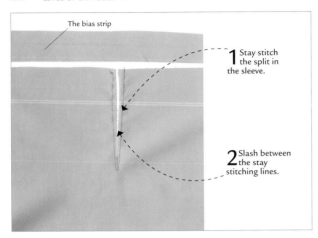

The bias strip

1 Stay stitch the split in the sleeve.

2 Slash between the stay stitching lines.

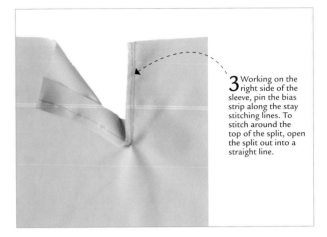

3 Working on the right side of the sleeve, pin the bias strip along the stay stitching lines. To stitch around the top of the split, open the split out into a straight line.

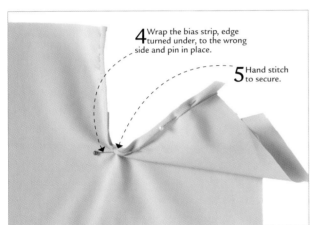

4 Wrap the bias strip, edge turned under, to the wrong side and pin in place.

5 Hand stitch to secure.

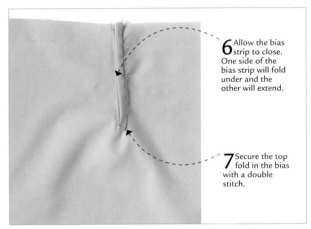

6 Allow the bias strip to close. One side of the bias strip will fold under and the other will extend.

7 Secure the top fold in the bias with a double stitch.

8 Tailor tack to aid the placement of the cuff.

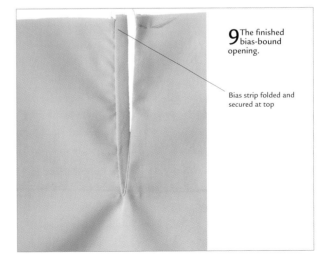

9 The finished bias-bound opening.

Bias strip folded and secured at top

Machined hems p232 〉〉〉〉

TECHNIQUES

Shirt sleeve placket

This is the opening that is found on the sleeves of men's shirts and tailored ladies' shirts. It looks complicated but is straightforward if you take it one step at a time.

LEVEL OF DIFFICULTY ★★★

1 Cut out the placket and mark the pattern dots with tailor's tacks. Only these four tailor's tacks are required.

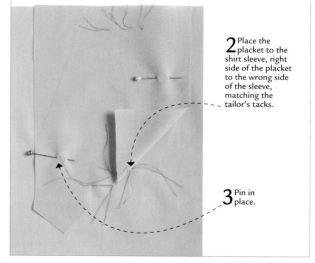

2 Place the placket to the shirt sleeve, right side of the placket to the wrong side of the sleeve, matching the tailor's tacks.

3 Pin in place.

4 Machine a rectangular box, joining the tailor's tacks together. Make sure the rows of stitching are parallel. Remove the tacks.

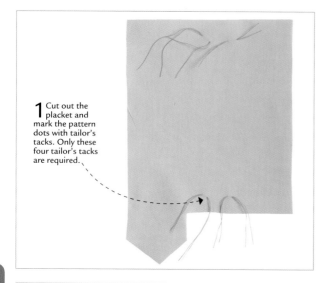

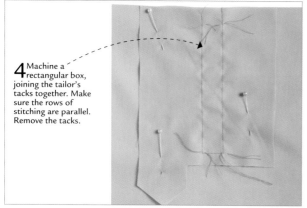

5 Slash though the placket and sleeve straight down the centre, between the rows of stitching.

6 Slash into the corners of the rectangle.

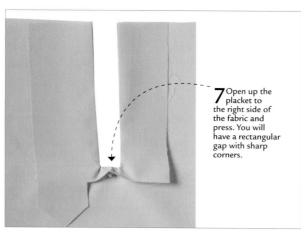

7 Open up the placket to the right side of the fabric and press. You will have a rectangular gap with sharp corners.

8 Fold back the long edge of the shorter side of the placket.

9 Place the folded edge on top of the machine stitching and pin in place.

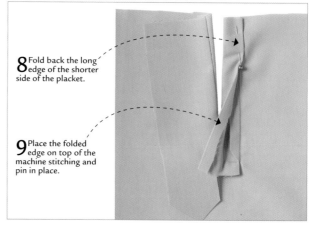

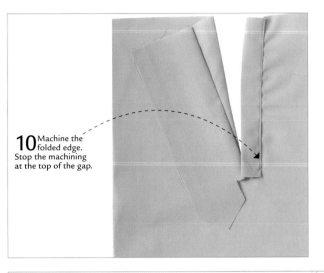

10 Machine the folded edge. Stop the machining at the top of the gap.

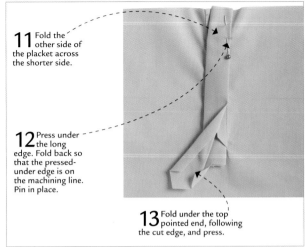

11 Fold the other side of the placket across the shorter side.

12 Press under the long edge. Fold back so that the pressed-under edge is on the machining line. Pin in place.

13 Fold under the top pointed end, following the cut edge, and press.

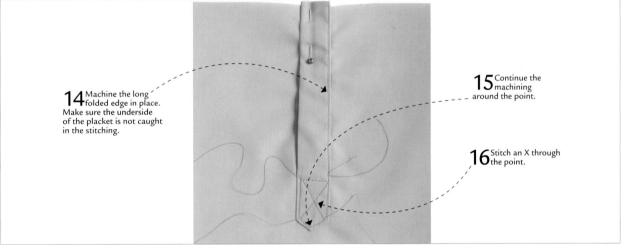

14 Machine the long folded edge in place. Make sure the underside of the placket is not caught in the stitching.

15 Continue the machining around the point.

16 Stitch an X through the point.

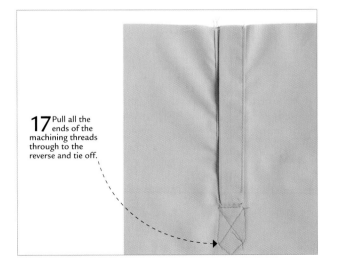

17 Pull all the ends of the machining threads through to the reverse and tie off.

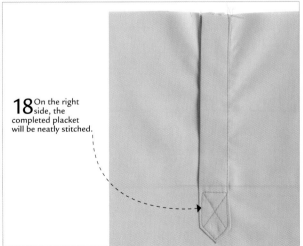

18 On the right side, the completed placket will be neatly stitched.

Attaching a cuff

LEVEL OF DIFFICULTY ✱✱✱

There are various types of cuff that can be attached to sleeve openings. The one-piece lapped cuff works well with a bound or faced opening. A two-piece shirt cuff is usually on a sleeve with a placket opening, but works equally well on a bound opening. The double cuff, or French cuff, is for men's dress shirts and tailored shirts for both ladies and men, and may be cut in one or two sections. It is usually found with a placket or bound opening.

LAPPED CUFF

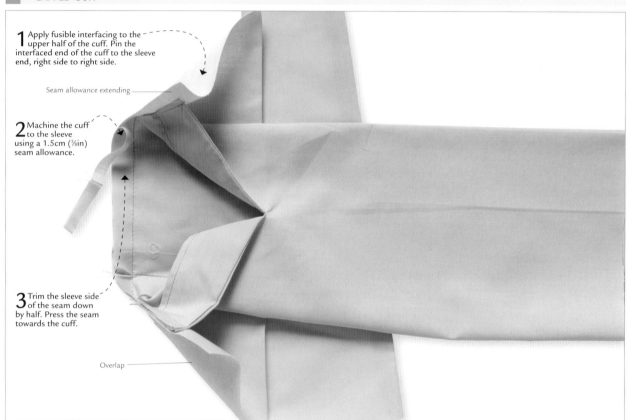

1 Apply fusible interfacing to the upper half of the cuff. Pin the interfaced end of the cuff to the sleeve end, right side to right side.

Seam allowance extending

2 Machine the cuff to the sleeve using a 1.5cm (⅝in) seam allowance.

3 Trim the sleeve side of the seam down by half. Press the seam towards the cuff.

Overlap

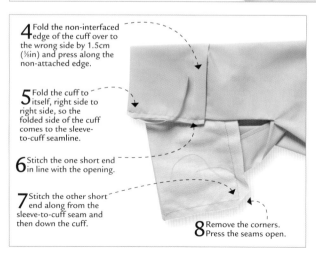

4 Fold the non-interfaced edge of the cuff over to the wrong side by 1.5cm (⅝in) and press along the non-attached edge.

5 Fold the cuff to itself, right side to right side, so the folded side of the cuff comes to the sleeve-to-cuff seamline.

6 Stitch the one short end in line with the opening.

7 Stitch the other short end along from the sleeve-to-cuff seam and then down the cuff.

8 Remove the corners. Press the seams open.

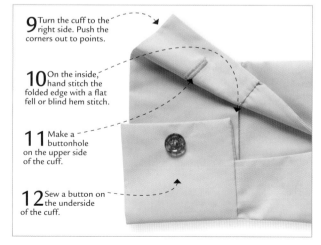

9 Turn the cuff to the right side. Push the corners out to points.

10 On the inside, hand stitch the folded edge with a flat fell or blind hem stitch.

11 Make a buttonhole on the upper side of the cuff.

12 Sew a button on the underside of the cuff.

⟨⟨⟨ How to apply a fusible interfacing p54   Reducing seam bulk pp102–103   Stitch finishes p103

TECHNIQUES

SHIRT CUFF

1 Apply fusible interfacing to the upper cuff. Place it to the sleeve end, right side to right side, with a seam allowance extending at either end. Pin in place.

2 Machine using a 1.5cm (⅝in) seam allowance.

3 Place the right side of the under cuff to the right side of the upper cuff. Machine together around three sides, stitching in line with the sleeve opening.

4 Trim down the under cuff side of the seam.

5 Remove bulk from the corners. Press.

6 Turn the cuff to the right side and press.

7 Turn under the raw edge of the under cuff and place to the end of the sleeve. With this type of cuff, the edge is machined in place.

8 Add buttonholes to the upper cuff and attach buttons to the under cuff.

DOUBLE CUFF

1 Apply interfacing to the whole of the cuff. Attach the cuff to the sleeve end, right side to right side, using a 1.5cm (⅝in) seam allowance.

2 Fold the cuff back on to itself, right side to right side.

3 Machine stitch the two sides in line with the sleeve opening.

4 Trim the bulk from the seams and corners.

5 Press, then turn the cuff through to the right side.

6 Fold the cuff up in half so that it is doubled.

7 Hand stitch inside to finish the other edge of the cuff.

8 Insert a buttonhole through the top two layers of the cuff and sew a button on to the under cuff.

POCKETS

Pockets can be functional or just for show, and are essential on some items of clothing. Making a pocket requires a little patience, but the finished result is well worth it.

POCKETS

Pockets come in lots of shapes and formats. Some, such as patch pockets, paper bag pockets, and jetted pockets with a flap, are external and can be decorative, while others, including front hip pockets, are more discreet and hidden from view. They can be made from the same fabric as the garment or from a contrasting fabric. Whether casual or tailored, all pockets are functional.

TECHNIQUES

Directory of pockets

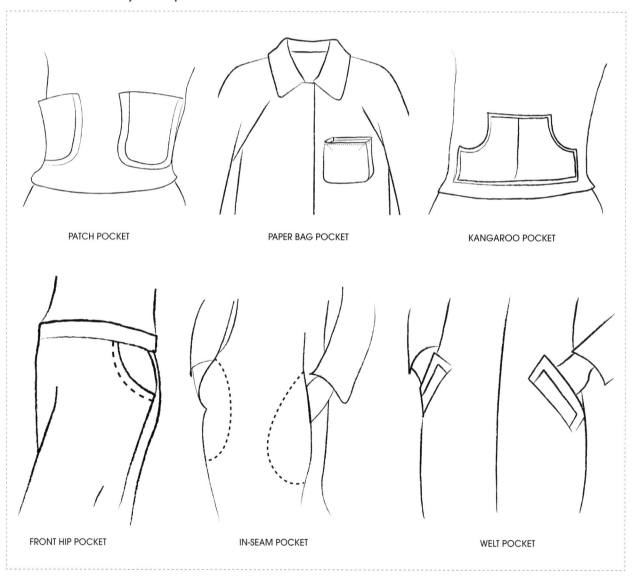

PATCH POCKET

PAPER BAG POCKET

KANGAROO POCKET

FRONT HIP POCKET

IN-SEAM POCKET

WELT POCKET

Unlined patch pocket

LEVEL OF DIFFICULTY **

An unlined patch pocket is one of the most popular types of pocket. It can be found on garments of all kinds and be made from a wide variety of fabrics. On lightweight fabrics, such as used for a shirt pocket, interfacing is not required, but on medium and heavier fabrics it is advisable to apply a fusible interfacing.

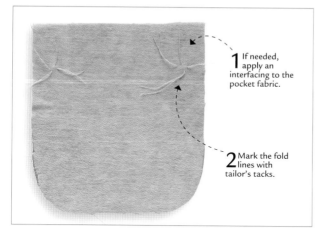

1 If needed, apply an interfacing to the pocket fabric.

2 Mark the fold lines with tailor's tacks.

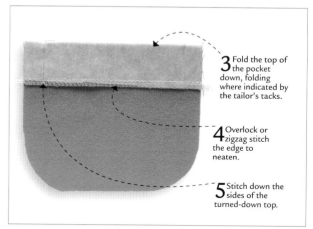

3 Fold the top of the pocket down, folding where indicated by the tailor's tacks.

4 Overlock or zigzag stitch the edge to neaten.

5 Stitch down the sides of the turned-down top.

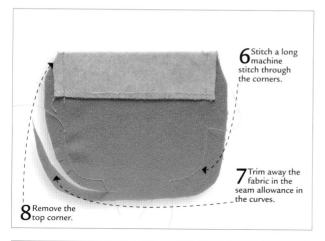

6 Stitch a long machine stitch through the corners.

7 Trim away the fabric in the seam allowance in the curves.

8 Remove the top corner.

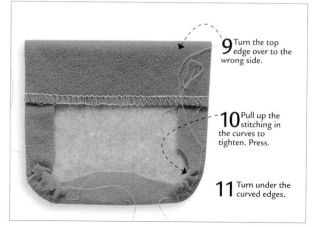

9 Turn the top edge over to the wrong side.

10 Pull up the stitching in the curves to tighten. Press.

11 Turn under the curved edges.

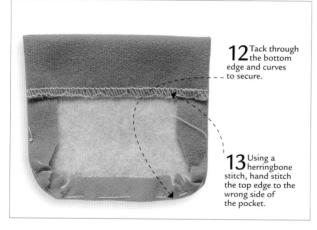

12 Tack through the bottom edge and curves to secure.

13 Using a herringbone stitch, hand stitch the top edge to the wrong side of the pocket.

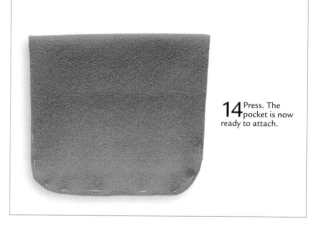

14 Press. The pocket is now ready to attach.

Self-lined patch pocket

LEVEL OF DIFFICULTY **

If a patch pocket is to be self-lined, it needs to be cut with the top edge of the pocket on a fold. Like an unlined pocket, if you are using a lightweight fabric an interfacing may not be required, whereas for medium-weight fabrics a fusible interfacing is advisable. A self-lined patch pocket is not suitable for heavy fabrics.

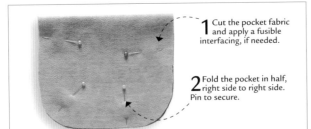

1 Cut the pocket fabric and apply a fusible interfacing, if needed.

2 Fold the pocket in half, right side to right side. Pin to secure.

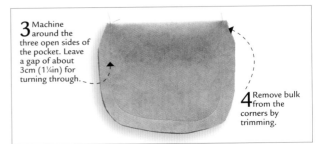

3 Machine around the three open sides of the pocket. Leave a gap of about 3cm (1¼in) for turning through.

4 Remove bulk from the corners by trimming.

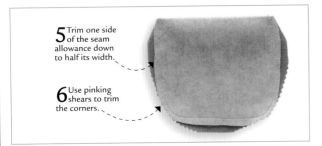

5 Trim one side of the seam allowance down to half its width.

6 Use pinking shears to trim the corners.

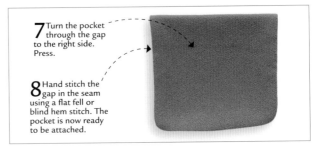

7 Turn the pocket through the gap to the right side. Press.

8 Hand stitch the gap in the seam using a flat fell or blind hem stitch. The pocket is now ready to be attached.

Lined patch pocket

LEVEL OF DIFFICULTY **

If a self-lined patch pocket is likely to be too bulky, then a lined pocket is the answer. It is advisable to interface the pocket fabric.

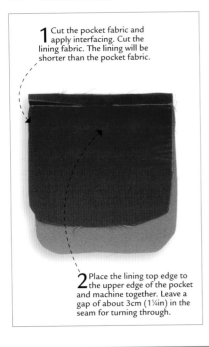

1 Cut the pocket fabric and apply interfacing. Cut the lining fabric. The lining will be shorter than the pocket fabric.

2 Place the lining top edge to the upper edge of the pocket and machine together. Leave a gap of about 3cm (1¼in) in the seam for turning through.

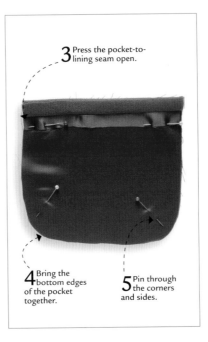

3 Press the pocket-to-lining seam open.

4 Bring the bottom edges of the pocket together.

5 Pin through the corners and sides.

6 Stitch around the other three open sides of the pocket to attach the lining to the pocket fabric.

7 Remove the corners.

8 Use pinking shears to trim the curves.

≪≪≪   How to apply a fusible interfacing p54   Hand stitches pp90–91   Stitches made with a machine pp92–93   Reducing seam bulk pp102–103

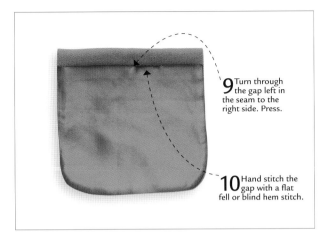

9 Turn through the gap left in the seam to the right side. Press.

10 Hand stitch the gap with a flat fell or blind hem stitch.

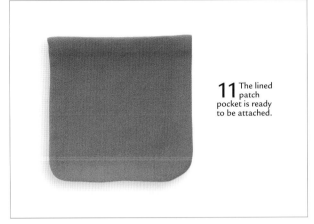

11 The lined patch pocket is ready to be attached.

Square patch pocket

LEVEL OF DIFFICULTY ✹✹

It is possible to have a patch pocket with square corners. This requires mitring the corners to reduce the bulk. Use a fusible interfacing on medium-weight fabrics.

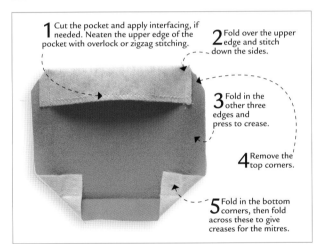

1 Cut the pocket and apply interfacing, if needed. Neaten the upper edge of the pocket with overlock or zigzag stitching.

2 Fold over the upper edge and stitch down the sides.

3 Fold in the other three edges and press to crease.

4 Remove the top corners.

5 Fold in the bottom corners, then fold across these to give creases for the mitres.

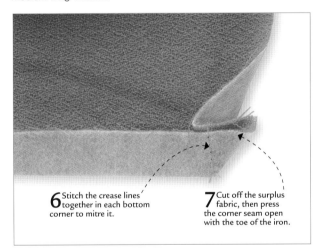

6 Stitch the crease lines together in each bottom corner to mitre it.

7 Cut off the surplus fabric, then press the corner seam open with the toe of the iron.

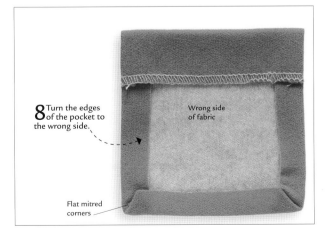

8 Turn the edges of the pocket to the wrong side.

Wrong side of fabric

Flat mitred corners

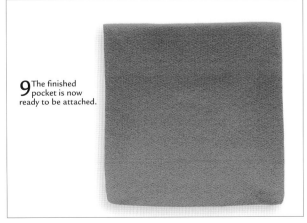

9 The finished pocket is now ready to be attached.

Mitred corners p235 ⟫⟫

Attaching a patch pocket

LEVEL OF DIFFICULTY **

To attach a pocket successfully, accurate pattern marking is essential. It is best to do this by means of tailor's tacks or even trace tacking. If you are using a check or stripe fabric, the pocket fabric must align with the checks or stripes on the garment.

1 Mark the pocket placement lines on the garment with tailor's tacks.

2 Take the completed pocket and place it to the fabric, matching the corners with the tailor's tacks. Pin in position.

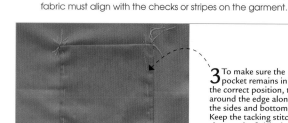

3 To make sure the pocket remains in the correct position, tack around the edge along the sides and bottom. Keep the tacking stitches close to the finished edge of the pocket.

4 Machine stitch about 1mm (¹⁄₂in) from the edge of the pocket.

5 Remove the tacking stitches. Press.

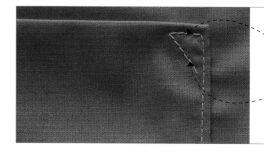

6 Alternatively, the pocket can be hand stitched in place, using a slip hem stitch into the underside of the pocket seam. Do not pull on the thread too tightly or the pocket will wrinkle.

Reinforcing pocket corners

LEVEL OF DIFFICULTY **

On any patch pocket it is essential to reinforce the upper corners as these take all the strain when the pocket is being used. There are several ways to do this, some of which are quite decorative.

REVERSE STITCH

1 Reinforce the corner with a reverse stitch. Make sure the stitches lie on top of one another.

2 Pull the threads to the reverse to tie off.

DIAGONAL STITCH

1 This is a technique used primarily on shirts. When machining the pocket in place, stitch along horizontally for four stitches.

2 Turn and stitch diagonally back to the side, to create a triangular shape in the corner.

ZIGZAG STITCH

1 Using a small zigzag stitch, width 1.0 and length 1.0, stitch diagonally across the corner.

2 Make a feature of this stitch by using a thread in a contrasting colour.

PARALLEL ZIGZAG STITCH

1 Place a patch on the wrong side of the garment, behind the pocket corner, to stitch into for strength.

2 Using a small zigzag stitch, width 1.0 and length 1.0, machine a short vertical line next to the straight stitching.

Paper bag pocket

LEVEL OF DIFFICULTY ★★★

This pocket is so-named because it resembles a paper bag. It is found on men's and women's casual wear. The pocket is attached to the garment with a gusset, which is a straight strip of fabric. A paper bag pocket is best made in a light or medium-weight fabric.

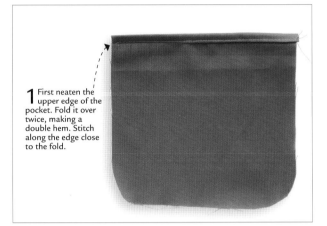

1 First neaten the upper edge of the pocket. Fold it over twice, making a double hem. Stitch along the edge close to the fold.

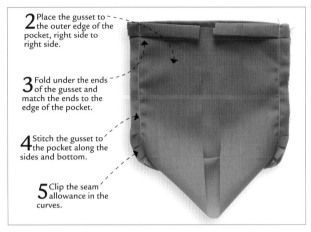

2 Place the gusset to the outer edge of the pocket, right side to right side.

3 Fold under the ends of the gusset and match the ends to the edge of the pocket.

4 Stitch the gusset to the pocket along the sides and bottom.

5 Clip the seam allowance in the curves.

6 Turn under the raw edge of the gusset. Mitre the corners. Tack to secure.

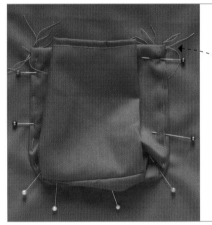

7 Place the tacked edge to the garment. Match the edge to the tailor-tack markings on the garment. Pin.

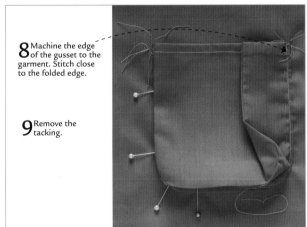

8 Machine the edge of the gusset to the garment. Stitch close to the folded edge.

9 Remove the tacking.

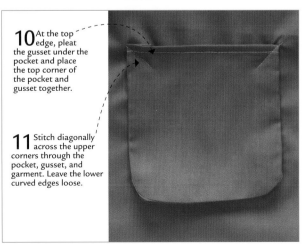

10 At the top edge, pleat the gusset under the pocket and place the top corner of the pocket and gusset together.

11 Stitch diagonally across the upper corners through the pocket, gusset, and garment. Leave the lower curved edges loose.

Making a pocket flap
LEVEL OF DIFFICULTY **

On some styles of garment, there is no pocket, just a flap for decorative purposes. The flap is sewn where the pocket would be, but there is no opening under the flap. This is to reduce the bulk that would arise from having the rest of the pocket.

1 The flap consist of two pieces – a piece of lining and a piece of interfaced fabric. Place the two pieces together, right side to right side.

2 Match the tailor's tacks, then pin to secure.

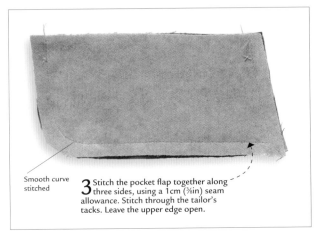

Smooth curve stitched

3 Stitch the pocket flap together along three sides, using a 1cm (⅜in) seam allowance. Stitch through the tailor's tacks. Leave the upper edge open.

4 Layer the seam allowance, trimming away the lining side.

5 Remove the fabric from the point.

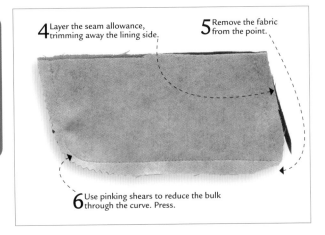

6 Use pinking shears to reduce the bulk through the curve. Press.

7 Turn the flap through to the right side. Push out the point.

8 Press the lining towards the back so that it does not show. Press a smooth curve.

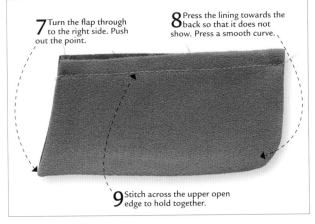

9 Stitch across the upper open edge to hold together.

10 Place the flap to the garment, right side to right side. Match the edges of the flaps to the tailor's tacks on the garment.

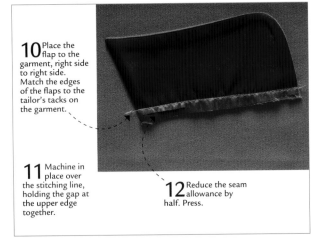

11 Machine in place over the stitching line, holding the gap at the upper edge together.

12 Reduce the seam allowance by half. Press.

13 Press the flap into place. Do not pull too tight.

14 Top-stitch across the upper edge to secure.

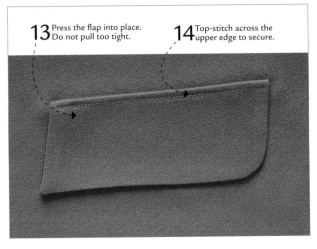

Welt pocket

LEVEL OF DIFFICULTY ★★★

A welt pocket features a small, straight flap that faces upwards on a garment, with the pocket opening behind the flap. This kind of pocket is found on waistcoats and is the usual breast pocket on men's jackets, as well as being used on coats.

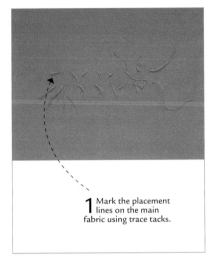

1 Mark the placement lines on the main fabric using trace tacks.

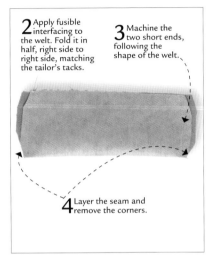

2 Apply fusible interfacing to the welt. Fold it in half, right side to right side, matching the tailor's tacks.

3 Machine the two short ends, following the shape of the welt.

4 Layer the seam and remove the corners.

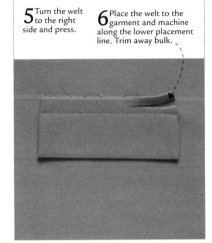

5 Turn the welt to the right side and press.

6 Place the welt to the garment and machine along the lower placement line. Trim away bulk.

7 Place the lining pocket over the welt, right side to right side. Match the pattern markings.

8 Tack the lining in place over the welt.

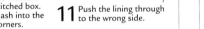

9 Machine the lining over the welt. The upper row of machining will be shorter than the lower row, producing angled sides.

10 Slash through the centre of the machine-stitched box. Slash into the corners.

11 Push the lining through to the wrong side.

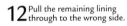

12 Pull the remaining lining through to the wrong side.

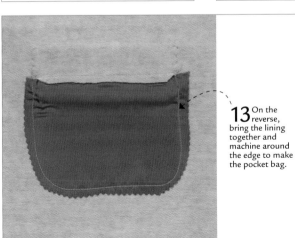

13 On the reverse, bring the lining together and machine around the edge to make the pocket bag.

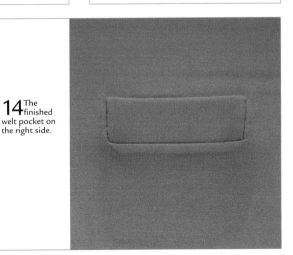

14 The finished welt pocket on the right side.

Jetted pocket with a flap

LEVEL OF DIFFICULTY ★★★★

This type of pocket is found on tailored jackets and coats and men's wear. It is straightforward to make. The main components are the welts (the strips that make the edges of the pocket), the flap, and the lining that makes the pocket bag.

1 First make the upper welt. Apply fusible interfacing to the wrong side.

2 Fold in half lengthways, wrong side to wrong side. Tack down the centre to secure.

3 Next, make the pocket flap. Apply fusible interfacing to the wrong side of the fabric.

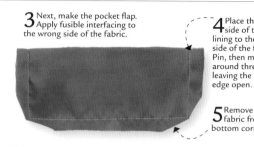

4 Place the right side of the lining to the right side of the flap. Pin, then machine around three sides, leaving the top edge open.

5 Remove the fabric from the bottom corners.

6 Turn the flap through to the right side. Press. Make sure the lining does not show on the right side.

7 If you like, top-stitch the flap around the three sides.

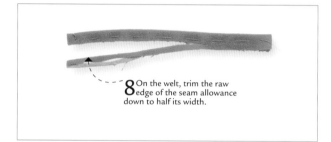

8 On the welt, trim the raw edge of the seam allowance down to half its width.

9 Place the welt to the right side of the pocket. Align the raw edges. Make sure the welt overhangs the flap by equal amounts at each end.

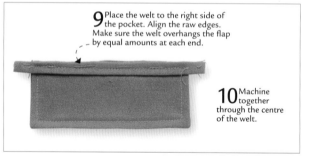

10 Machine together through the centre of the welt.

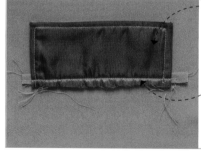

11 Place the right side of the welt and flap to the right side of the garment. Match the ends of the flap to the upper tailor's tacks on the garment. Pin in place.

12 Machine to the garment along the stitching line that is holding the welt and flap together.

13 Make up the lower welt in the same fabric as the upper welt.

14 Place the lower welt to the garment below the upper welt and flap.

15 Machine stitch in place. Make sure the two rows of stitching are exactly the same length. Also make sure the stitching lines are parallel.

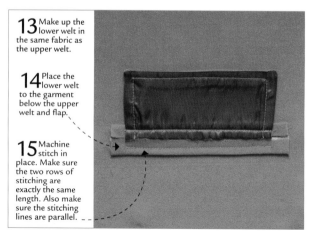

16 Take the lining and press in half, right side to right side, matching the tailor's tacks, to produce a centre crease.

17 Place the right side of the lining over the welt and flaps, matching the tailor's tacks. The crease line should be sitting between the two welts. Pin in place.

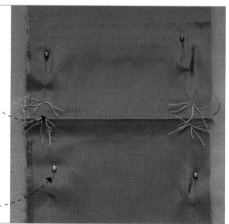

≪≪≪ How to apply a fusible interfacing p54   Pattern marking pp82–83   Tacking stitches p89   Stitches made with a machine pp92–93   Reducing seam bulk pp102–103

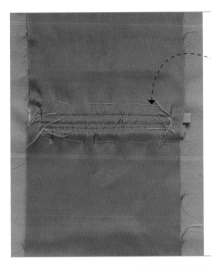

18 Tack the lining in position. Keep the tacking stitches about 1.5cm (⅝in) from the tailor's tacks that mark the welts.

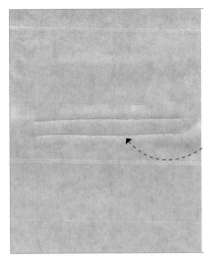

19 Working from the wrong side, machine the lining in place by stitching over the stitching lines that are holding the welts in place. The two rows of stitching should be exactly the same length. Secure at both ends.

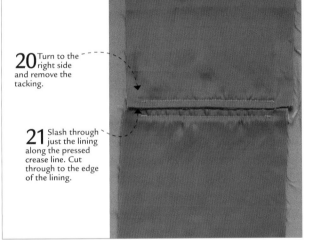

20 Turn to the right side and remove the tacking.

21 Slash through just the lining along the pressed crease line. Cut through to the edge of the lining.

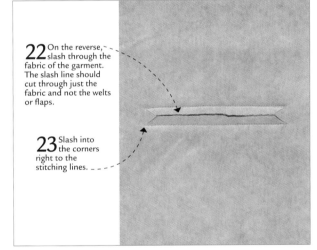

22 On the reverse, slash through the fabric of the garment. The slash line should cut through just the fabric and not the welts or flaps.

23 Slash into the corners right to the stitching lines.

24 Pull the lining through the slash to the wrong side. Push through the ends of the welts. The pocket flap will turn down.

25 To make the pocket, pull the ends of the welts out away from the slash lines. A small triangle of fabric should be on top of these welts.

26 Stitch across the welts and the triangle and around the pocket. Use pinking shears to neaten the seams on the lining.

27 Press everything in place, using a pressing cloth if necessary.

In-seam pocket

LEVEL OF DIFFICULTY **

In trousers and skirts, the pocket is sometimes disguised in the seam line. There are two ways of making an in-seam pocket, either by adding a separate pocket shape or by the pocket shape being cut as part of the main fabric.

SEPARATE IN-SEAM POCKET

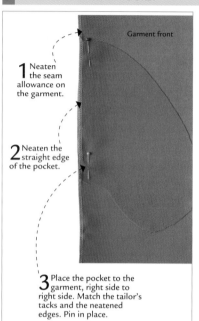

Garment front

1 Neaten the seam allowance on the garment.

2 Neaten the straight edge of the pocket.

3 Place the pocket to the garment, right side to right side. Match the tailor's tacks and the neatened edges. Pin in place.

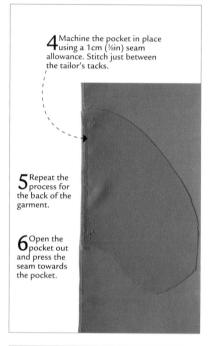

4 Machine the pocket in place using a 1cm (⅜in) seam allowance. Stitch just between the tailor's tacks.

5 Repeat the process for the back of the garment.

6 Open the pocket out and press the seam towards the pocket.

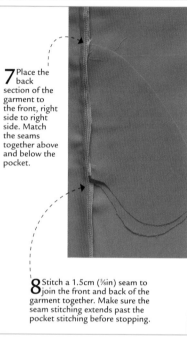

7 Place the back section of the garment to the front, right side to right side. Match the seams together above and below the pocket.

8 Stitch a 1.5cm (⅝in) seam to join the front and back of the garment together. Make sure the seam stitching extends past the pocket stitching before stopping.

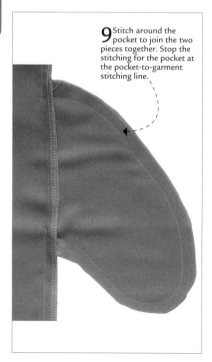

9 Stitch around the pocket to join the two pieces together. Stop the stitching for the pocket at the pocket-to-garment stitching line.

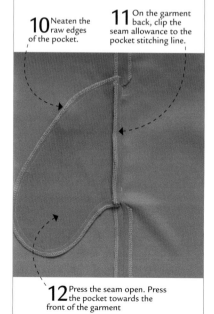

10 Neaten the raw edges of the pocket.

11 On the garment back, clip the seam allowance to the pocket stitching line.

12 Press the seam open. Press the pocket towards the front of the garment

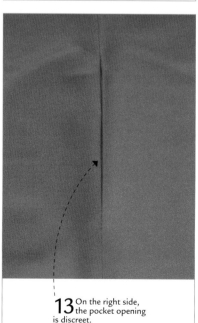

13 On the right side, the pocket opening is discreet.

≪≪≪ How to apply a fusible interfacing p54   Pattern marking pp82–83   Tacking stitches p89

ALL-IN-ONE IN-SEAM POCKET

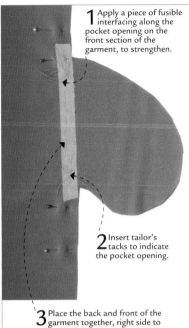

1 Apply a piece of fusible interfacing along the pocket opening on the front section of the garment, to strengthen.

2 Insert tailor's tacks to indicate the pocket opening.

3 Place the back and front of the garment together, right side to right side. Tack the pocket opening closed over the interfacing, stitching between the tailor's tacks.

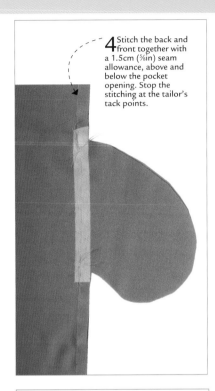

4 Stitch the back and front together with a 1.5cm (⅝in) seam allowance, above and below the pocket opening. Stop the stitching at the tailor's tack points.

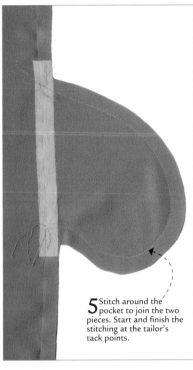

5 Stitch around the pocket to join the two pieces. Start and finish the stitching at the tailor's tack points.

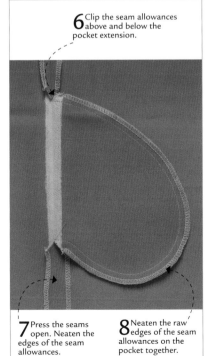

6 Clip the seam allowances above and below the pocket extension.

7 Press the seams open. Neaten the edges of the seam allowances.

8 Neaten the raw edges of the seam allowances on the pocket together.

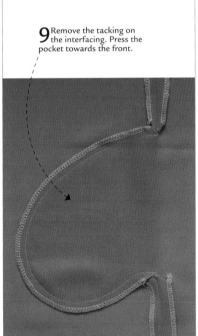

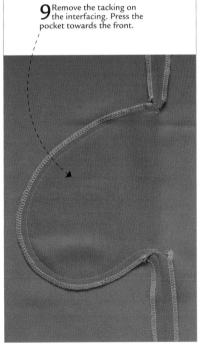

9 Remove the tacking on the interfacing. Press the pocket towards the front.

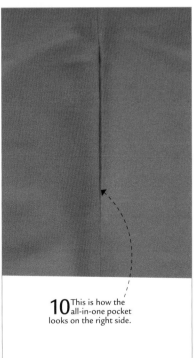

10 This is how the all-in-one pocket looks on the right side.

TECHNIQUES

Front hip pocket

LEVEL OF DIFFICULTY ******

On many trousers and casual skirts, the pocket is placed on the hipline. It can be low on the hipline or cut quite high as on jeans. The construction is the same for all types of hip pockets. When inserted at an angle, hip pockets can slim the figure.

1 Apply a piece of fusible tape on the garment along the line of the pocket.

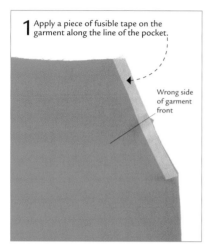

Wrong side of garment front

2 Place the pocket lining to the front of the garment, right side to right side. Match any notches that are on the seam. Pin in place.

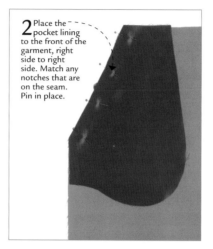

3 Machine the lining in place taking a 1.5cm (⅝in) seam allowance.

4 Trim the lining side of the seam allowance down to half its width.

5 Open out the pocket and press the seam towards the lining.

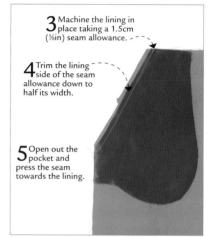

6 Turn the lining to the inside. Press so that the lining is not visible on the outside.

7 Top-stitch 5mm (³⁄₁₆in) from the edge.

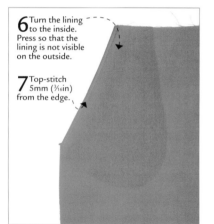

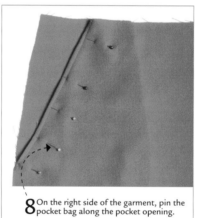

8 On the right side of the garment, pin the pocket bag along the pocket opening.

9 Take the side front section that incorporates the pocket bag and place to the lining pocket section, right side to right side. Match any seams and tailor's tacks. Pin in place.

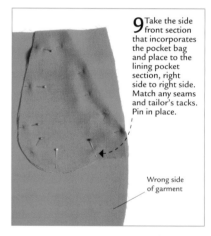

Wrong side of garment

10 Machine the pocket bag together using a 1.5cm (⅝in) seam allowance. Press.

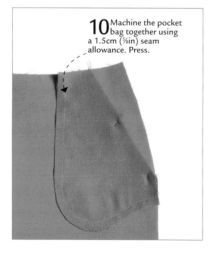

11 Neaten the raw edges of the seam allowance around the pocket.

12 Neaten the side seam allowance, stitching from the top down. Make sure that the fabric lies flat where it joins on to the side seam.

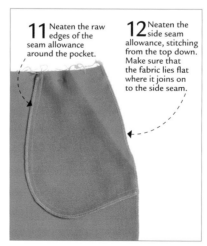

13 The angled front hip pocket from the right side.

⫷⫷   How to apply a fusible interfacing p54   Stitches made with a machine pp92–93   How to make a plain seam p94

Kangaroo pocket

LEVEL OF DIFFICULTY **

This is a variation on a patch pocket. It is a large pocket that is often found on aprons and the front of children's pinafore dresses. A half version of this pocket also features on casual jackets.

1 Neaten all the edges of the pocket.

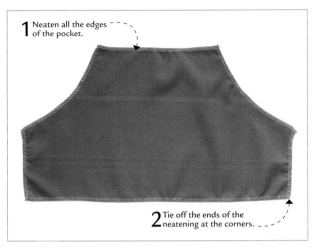

2 Tie off the ends of the neatening at the corners.

3 Turn under the curved edges of the pocket to the wrong side. These will be the two pocket openings.

4 Press the curve and machine to secure.

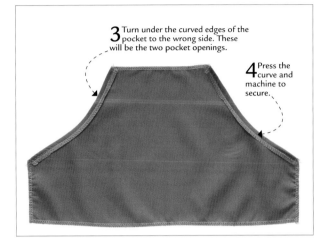

5 Turn under all the remaining edges of the pocket to the wrong side. If the fabric is bulky, mitre the corners. Press in place.

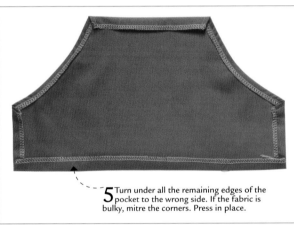

6 Place the pocket to the garment, wrong side of the pocket to right side of the garment. Make sure the pocket is sitting flat and straight. Pin in place.

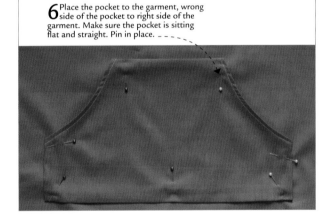

7 Stitch the pocket along the upper edge.

8 Stitch the short straight sides and lower edge of the pocket. Press.

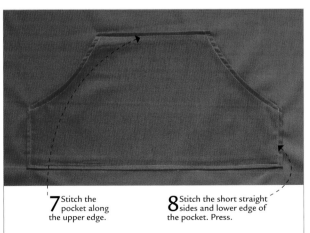

9 Reinforce the corners of the pocket with a diagonal zigzag stitch (see page 216).

10 If required, stitch one or two vertical lines down the centre of the pocket, to divide into two pockets. Press.

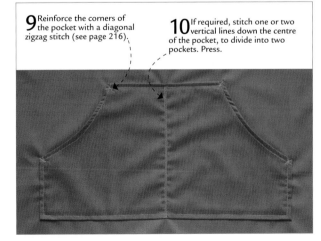

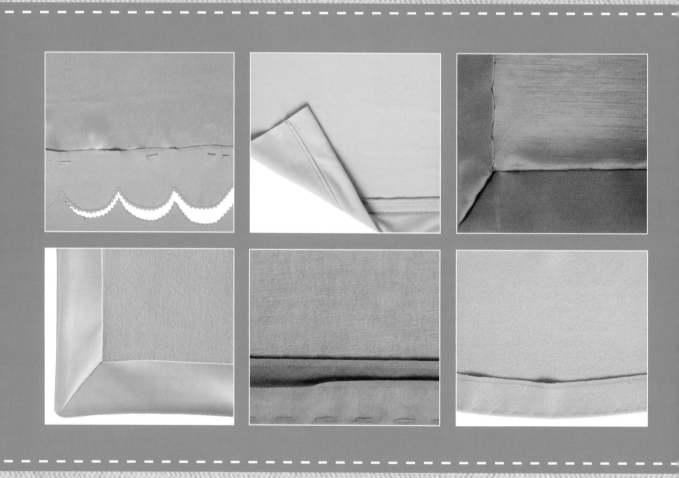

HEMS AND EDGES

The lower edge of a garment or of a curtain or other soft furnishing is normally finished with a hem. This is to give not only a neat finish but also to provide weight at the lower edge so that the garment or curtain hangs properly.

HEMS AND EDGES

The edge of a piece of fabric can be finished with a hem – which is normally used on garments – or with a decorative edge, which is used for crafts and soft furnishings as well as garments. Sometimes the style of what is being constructed dictates the finish that is used, and sometimes it is the fabric.

Directory of hems

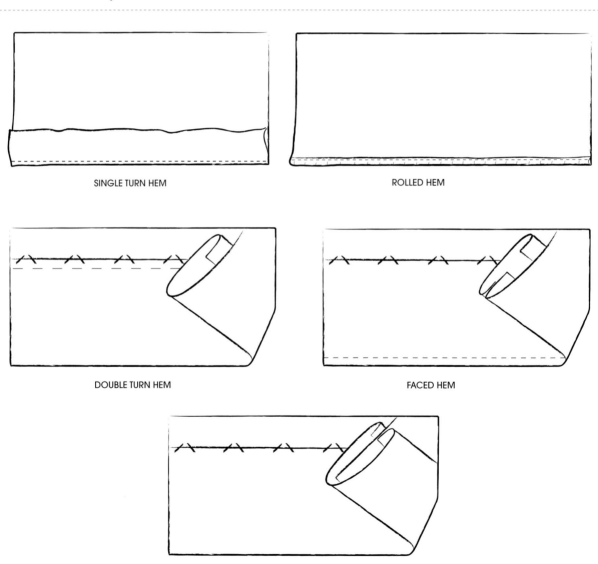

SINGLE TURN HEM

ROLLED HEM

DOUBLE TURN HEM

FACED HEM

BIAS-BOUND HEM

«« Useful extras p21   Tacking stitches p89

Marking a hemline

On a garment such as a skirt or a dress it is important that the hemline is level all around. Even if the fabric has been cut straight, some styles of skirt – such as A-line or circular – will "drop", which means that the hem edge is longer in some places. This is due to the fabric stretching where it is not on the straight of the grain. Poor posture will also cause a hem to hang unevenly.

USING A RULER

1 You'll need a helper for this method. Put on the skirt or dress (without shoes). With the end of the ruler on the floor, measure straight up on to the skirt.

2 Use pins to mark where the crease line of the hem should be. Mark the hemline all the way around to the same point on the ruler.

USING A DRESSMAKER'S DUMMY

1 Adjust the dummy to your height and measurements. Place the skirt or dress on the dummy.

2 Using the hem marker on the stand, mark the crease line of the hem. The hem marker will hold the fabric either side of the hemline.

3 Slide a pin through the slot in the marker, then gently release the marker.

Turning up a straight hem
LEVEL OF DIFFICULTY *

Once the crease line for the hem has been marked by the pins, you need to trim the hem allowance to a reasonable amount. Most straight hems are about 4cm (1½in) deep.

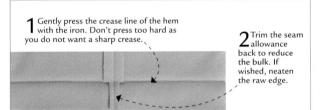

1 Gently press the crease line of the hem with the iron. Don't press too hard as you do not want a sharp crease.

2 Trim the seam allowance back to reduce the bulk. If wished, neaten the raw edge.

3 Turn up the hem at the crease. Match the seams together.

4 Tack the hem into position close to the crease line. The hem is now ready to be stitched in place by hand or machine.

Turning up a curved hem
LEVEL OF DIFFICULTY **

When the hem on a shaped skirt is turned up, it will be fuller at the upper edge. This fullness will need to be eased out before the hem is stitched.

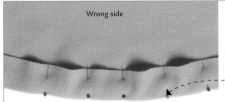
Wrong side

1 Mark the hemline, placing the pins vertically to avoid squashing the fullness out of the upper raw edge.

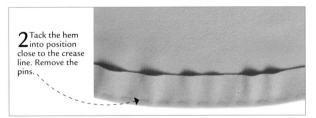

2 Tack the hem into position close to the crease line. Remove the pins.

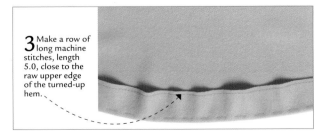

3 Make a row of long machine stitches, length 5.0, close to the raw upper edge of the turned-up hem.

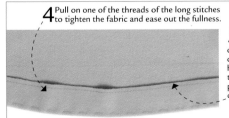

4 Pull on one of the threads of the long stitches to tighten the fabric and ease out the fullness.

5 Use the steam iron to shrink out the remainder of the fullness. The hem is now ready to be stitched in place by hand or machine.

Hand-stitched hems p230–231 Machined hems p232 》》》》

Hand-stitched hems

LEVEL OF DIFFICULTY *

One of the most popular ways to secure a hem edge is by hand. Hand stitching is discreet and, if a fine hand sewing needle is used, the stitching should not show on the right side of the work.

TIPS FOR SEWING HEMS BY HAND

1 Always use a single thread in the needle – a polyester all-purpose thread is ideal for hemming.

2 Once the raw edge of the hem allowance has been neatened by one of the methods below, secure it using a slip hem stitch. For this, take half of the stitch into the neatened edge and the other half into the wrong side of the garment fabric.

3 Start and finish the hand stitching with a double stitch, not a knot, because knots will catch and pull the hem down.

4 It is a good idea to take a small back stitch every 10cm (4in) or so to make sure that if the hem does come loose in one place it will not all unravel.

CLEAN FINISH

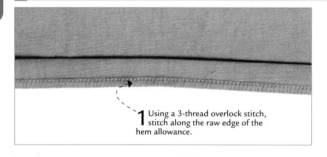

1 This is suitable for fine and lightweight fabrics. Turn the raw edge of the hem allowance to itself, wrong side to wrong side. Tack the edge and then machine.

2 Lightly press the hem into position.

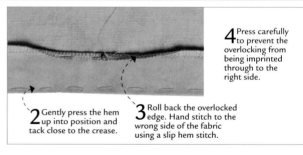

3 Tack the hem in place.

4 Roll the edge stitching back and stitch underneath it.

5 Using a small slip hem stitch, secure the edge of the hem to the wrong side of the fabric. Roll the edge back into place.

6 Remove the tacking and press lightly.

OVERLOCKED FINISH

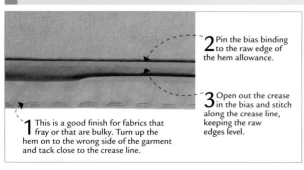

1 Using a 3-thread overlock stitch, stitch along the raw edge of the hem allowance.

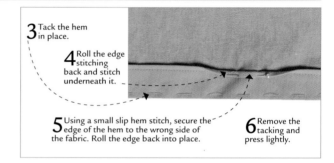

2 Gently press the hem up into position and tack close to the crease.

3 Roll back the overlocked edge. Hand stitch to the wrong side of the fabric using a slip hem stitch.

4 Press carefully to prevent the overlocking from being imprinted through to the right side.

BIAS-BOUND FINISH

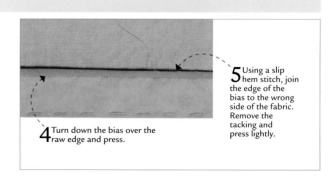

2 Pin the bias binding to the raw edge of the hem allowance.

3 Open out the crease in the bias and stitch along the crease line, keeping the raw edges level.

1 This is a good finish for fabrics that fray or that are bulky. Turn up the hem on to the wrong side of the garment and tack close to the crease line.

4 Turn down the bias over the raw edge and press.

5 Using a slip hem stitch, join the edge of the bias to the wrong side of the fabric. Remove the tacking and press lightly.

《《《 Securing the thread p88   Tacking stitches p89   Hand stitches pp90–91

TECHNIQUES

ZIGZAG FINISH

1 Use this to neaten the edge of the hem on fabrics that do not fray too badly. Set the sewing machine to a zigzag stitch, width 4.0 and length 3.0. Machine along the raw edge. Trim the fabric edge back to the zigzag stitch.

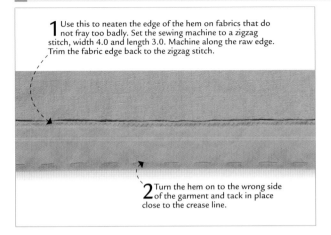

2 Turn the hem on to the wrong side of the garment and tack in place close to the crease line.

3 Fold back the zigzag-stitched edge. Using a slip hem stitch, stitch the hem into place.

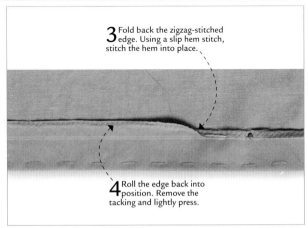

4 Roll the edge back into position. Remove the tacking and lightly press.

PINKED FINISH

1 Pinking shears can give an excellent hem finish on difficult fabrics. Machine a row of straight stitching along the raw edge, 1cm (⅜in) from the edge. Pink the raw edge.

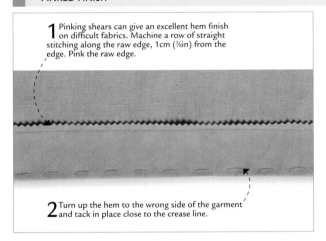

2 Turn up the hem to the wrong side of the garment and tack in place close to the crease line.

3 Fold back the edge along the machine stitching line and hand stitch the hem in place with a slip hem stitch.

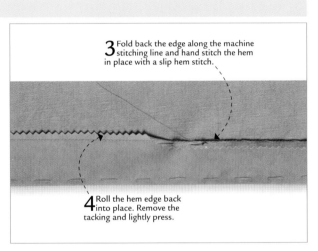

4 Roll the hem edge back into place. Remove the tacking and lightly press.

CURVED HEM FINISH

1 With a curved hem on a cotton or firm fabric, it is important that any fullness does not bulge on to the right side. Prior to turning up the hem into position, zigzag the raw edge, using stitch width 4.0 and stitch length 3.0.

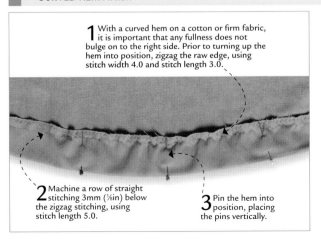

2 Machine a row of straight stitching 3mm (⅛in) below the zigzag stitching, using stitch length 5.0.

3 Pin the hem into position, placing the pins vertically.

4 Tack the hem into position close to the crease line.

5 Pull on the straight stitching to tighten the fabric.

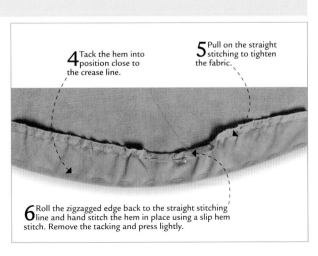

6 Roll the zigzagged edge back to the straight stitching line and hand stitch the hem in place using a slip hem stitch. Remove the tacking and press lightly.

Stitches made with a machine pp92–93 Turning up a curved hem p229 «««

Machined hems

LEVEL OF DIFFICULTY *

On many occasions , the hem or edge of a garment or other item is turned up and secured using the sewing machine. It can be stitched with a straight stitch, a zigzag stitch, or a blind hem stitch. Hems can also be made on the overlocker.

SINGLE TURN HEM

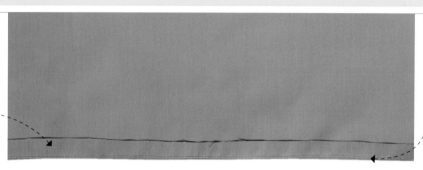

1 This is a popular technique. Turn up the hem to the wrong side of the work. Press in place.

2 Machine with a straight stitch close to the hem edge.

BLIND HEM STITCH

1 This is a single turn hem that is secured using the blind hem stitch on the machine. Neaten the raw edge of the fabric (here an overlock finish has been used).

2 Fold the fabric as indicated for your machine (consult your instruction book). Pin, but not too close to the fold.

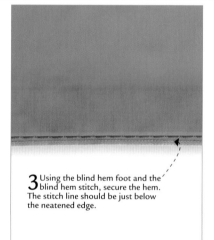

3 Using the blind hem foot and the blind hem stitch, secure the hem. The stitch line should be just below the neatened edge.

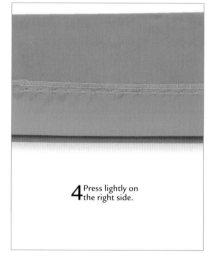

4 Press lightly on the right side.

DOUBLE TURN HEM

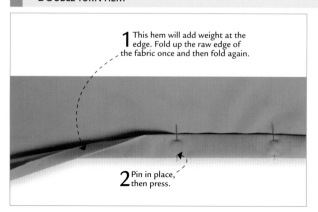

1 This hem will add weight at the edge. Fold up the raw edge of the fabric once and then fold again.

2 Pin in place, then press.

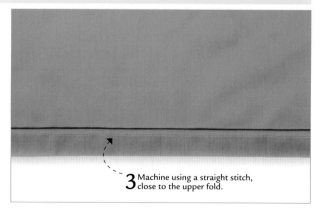

3 Machine using a straight stitch, close to the upper fold.

Hems on difficult fabrics

LEVEL OF DIFFICULTY ✱✱

Some very fine fabrics or fabrics that fray badly require more thought when a hem is to be made. This technique works very well on delicate fabrics.

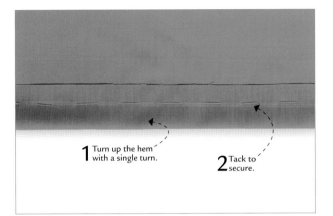

1 Turn up the hem with a single turn.

2 Tack to secure.

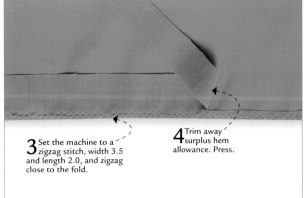

3 Set the machine to a zigzag stitch, width 3.5 and length 2.0, and zigzag close to the fold.

4 Trim away surplus hem allowance. Press.

Rolled hems

LEVEL OF DIFFICULTY ✱✱

A rolled hem is used on lightweight fabrics. It is often found on soft furnishings as well as garments. To make it, the fabric is rolled to the wrong side by using the rolled hem foot on the sewing machine.

STRAIGHT-STITCHED ROLLED HEM

Use the rolled hem foot on the sewing machine and a straight stitch.

ZIGZAG-STITCHED ROLLED HEM

Use the rolled hem foot on the sewing machine and a zigzag stitch.

OVERLOCKER ROLLED HEM

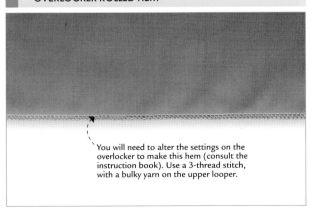

You will need to alter the settings on the overlocker to make this hem (consult the instruction book). Use a 3-thread stitch, with a bulky yarn on the upper looper.

MANUAL ROLLED HEM

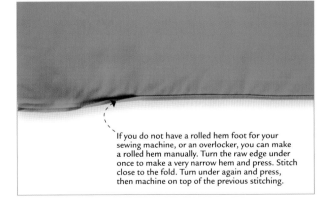

If you do not have a rolled hem foot for your sewing machine, or an overlocker, you can make a rolled hem manually. Turn the raw edge under once to make a very narrow hem and press. Stitch close to the fold. Turn under again and press, then machine on top of the previous stitching.

Machined curtain hems
LEVEL OF DIFFICULTY ∗

Curtains have hems at the bottom edge as well as at the sides. The hem at the bottom is treated differently from the side hems, using different techniques, although both types of hems are folded twice. The hems can be stitched using either machine or hand methods.

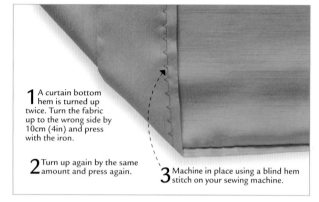

1 A curtain bottom hem is turned up twice. Turn the fabric up to the wrong side by 10cm (4in) and press with the iron.

2 Turn up again by the same amount and press again.

3 Machine in place using a blind hem stitch on your sewing machine.

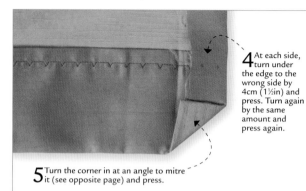

4 At each side, turn under the edge to the wrong side by 4cm (1½in) and press. Turn again by the same amount and press again.

5 Turn the corner in at an angle to mitre it (see opposite page) and press.

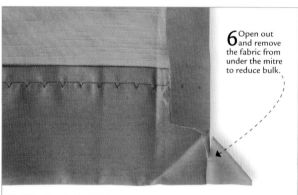

6 Open out and remove the fabric from under the mitre to reduce bulk.

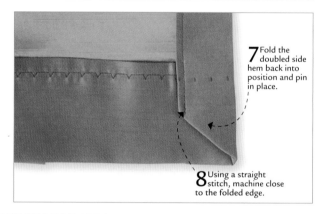

7 Fold the doubled side hem back into position and pin in place.

8 Using a straight stitch, machine close to the folded edge.

Hand-stitched curtain hems
LEVEL OF DIFFICULTY ∗

Hand stitching is used on heavier curtain fabrics or where you do not want a machine stitch to show on the right side. Everything is pressed in place first.

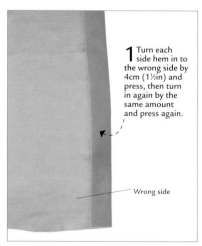

1 Turn each side hem in to the wrong side by 4cm (1½in) and press, then turn in again by the same amount and press again.

Wrong side

2 Turn up the bottom hem to the wrong side by 10cm (4in) and press, then turn up again by the same amount and press.

3 Where the bottom hem and side hem meet, press under the hem at an angle to mitre it (see opposite page).

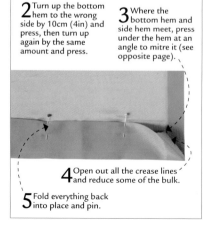

4 Open out all the crease lines and reduce some of the bulk.

5 Fold everything back into place and pin.

6 Use a herringbone stitch to stitch the bottom hem in place. Take shallow stitches that run along the folded edge.

7 Repeat the process down the side hems.

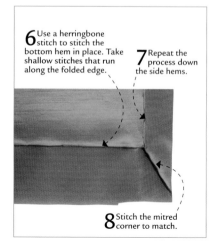

8 Stitch the mitred corner to match.

⟪⟪ Hand stitches pp90–91 Stitches made with a machine pp92–93

Mitred corners
LEVEL OF DIFFICULTY **

At the bottom corners of curtains, where the bottom and side hems meet, the fabric is folded at an angle. This is called a mitre. By pressing the mitre with the iron and then unfolding it, you can use the crease lines that have been formed as a guide for removing surplus fabric to reduce bulk. For lined curtains, where the lining is constructed separately, the side and bottom hems are machined in place. The same mitring technique is used for both curtains and linings.

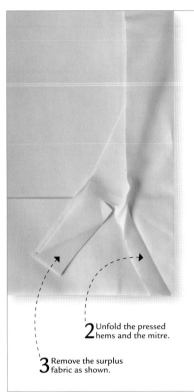

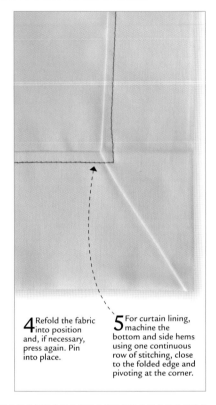

1 After the bottom and side hems have been turned and pressed, fold back the corner at an angle. The angle runs between the outer corner of the curtain and the point where the hems meet, at the inner corner.

2 Unfold the pressed hems and the mitre.

3 Remove the surplus fabric as shown.

4 Refold the fabric into position and, if necessary, press again. Pin into place.

5 For curtain lining, machine the bottom and side hems using one continuous row of stitching, close to the folded edge and pivoting at the corner.

Weighting curtains
LEVEL OF DIFFICULTY *

A weight is often inserted into the bottom hem of a curtain at the corners, to hold the curtain in place and make it hang properly. Specialist weights can be purchased, although a heavy coin can work just as well.

1 Measure the diameter of the weight. Cut a strip of curtain lining that is three times as long and twice as wide.

2 Press under the short edges of the lining to the wrong side and press. Fold the strip in half, matching the turned-under edges, to make a rectangle large enough to enclose the weight.

3 Using a zigzag stitch, machine the two long sides. Insert a coin or weight into the pouch.

4 Zigzag stitch across the open side.

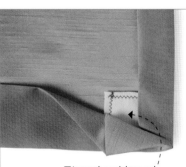

5 Insert the weight pouch into the bottom corner of the curtain.

6 When stitching the hems for the side and bottom, place stitches through into the weight pouch to hold it in place.

Stitching corners and curves pp100–101 ≪≪≪

Hems on stretch knits

LEVEL OF DIFFICULTY ✱✱

When making a garment with a stretch knit, the hem will need to stretch as well. There are two methods for stitching the hem on stretch knits, and the one you use depends on whether the fabric will ladder or not when it is cut.

FABRIC THAT LADDERS

1 Neaten the raw edge using a 3-thread overlock stitch. If no overlocker is available, use a zigzag stitch on the sewing machine.

2 Turn up the hem to the wrong side.

3 Tack the hem close to the crease line.

4 Insert a twin needle into the sewing machine and thread the machine with two threads.

5 Working from the right side of the garment, machine the hem in place.

FABRIC THAT DOES NOT LADDER

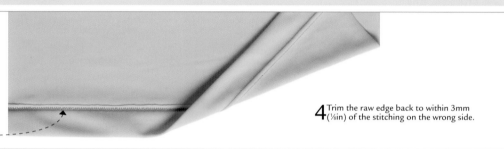

1 Insert the twin needle into the machine and thread the machine with two threads.

2 Turn up the hem to the wrong side and tack to hold in place.

3 Machine the hem in position.

4 Trim the raw edge back to within 3mm (⅛in) of the stitching on the wrong side.

Faced hem

LEVEL OF DIFFICULTY ✱✱

A faced hem is used on garments made from fabrics that may be too bulky to turn up without the hem showing, or on napped fabrics that may catch or ride up when they are worn. A faced hem is also used if there is not enough fabric to turn up to make a hem.

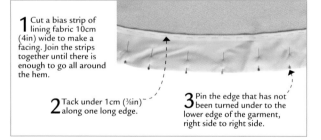

1 Cut a bias strip of lining fabric 10cm (4in) wide to make a facing. Join the strips together until there is enough to go all around the hem.

2 Tack under 1cm (⅜in) along one long edge.

3 Pin the edge that has not been turned under to the lower edge of the garment, right side to right side.

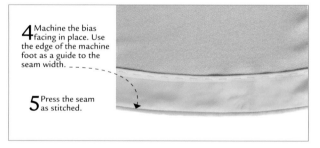

4 Machine the bias facing in place. Use the edge of the machine foot as a guide to the seam width.

5 Press the seam as stitched.

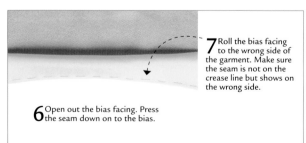

6 Open out the bias facing. Press the seam down on to the bias.

7 Roll the bias facing to the wrong side of the garment. Make sure the seam is not on the crease line but shows on the wrong side.

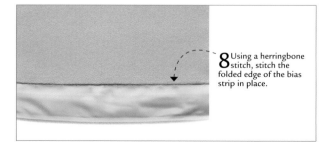

8 Using a herringbone stitch, stitch the folded edge of the bias strip in place.

⟪⟪⟪ Hand stitches pp 90–91   Stitches made with a machine pp92–93   Stitching corners and curves pp100–101   How to cut bias strips p147

TECHNIQUES

Decorative faced hem

LEVEL OF DIFFICULTY ***

If the edge of a garment, blind, cushion, or other item is to have a decorative effect, such as points or scallops (as shown in the photographs here), a faced hem is used.

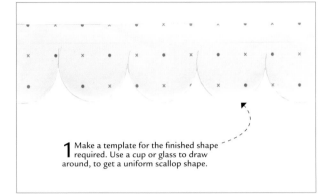

1 Make a template for the finished shape required. Use a cup or glass to draw around, to get a uniform scallop shape.

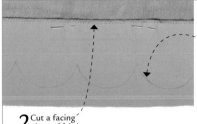

2 Cut a facing piece of fabric 10cm (4in) wide. Neaten one long edge with the overlocker or a zigzag stitch.

3 Pin the facing to the hem edge, right side to right side.

4 Place the template on the facing and use a marking pen or chalk pencil to draw the shaped hem. A seam allowance of 1.5cm (⅝in) is required between the lower edge of the template and the raw edge.

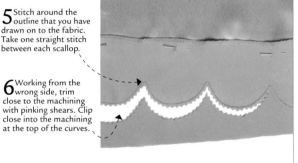

5 Stitch around the outline that you have drawn on to the fabric. Take one straight stitch between each scallop.

6 Working from the wrong side, trim close to the machining with pinking shears. Clip close into the machining at the top of the curves.

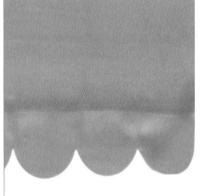

7 Turn through to the right side. Press the fabric as it is being turned, because you can work warm fabric into the required shape.

8 If required, secure the facing on each seam.

Fused hem

LEVEL OF DIFFICULTY *

A fused hem is useful for a fabric that is difficult to hand stitch, as well as for an emergency hem repair. It uses a hemming tape that has a fusible adhesive on both sides.

1 Turn up the hem to the wrong side of the fabric. Press. Tack the hem in place close to the crease line.

2 Neaten the raw edge with an overlock or zigzag stitch.

3 Insert the fusible hemming tape between the hem and the wrong side of the garment. Make sure the tape sits just below the overlock or zigzag stitch. Pin the tape in place.

4 Cover the hem allowance with a pressing cloth and, using a steam iron, press the edge of the hem to fuse the tape to the fabric. Once cool the hem will be stuck in place. Remove the tacking stitches.

Fusible tapes p277 》》》

Bias-bound hems

LEVEL OF DIFFICULTY ✱✱

A bias-bound hem will give a narrow decorative edge to a garment or an item of home furnishing. It is particularly useful for curved shapes, to finish them neatly and securely. On a bulky or chunky fabric a double bias is used so that it will be more substantial and hold its shape better. A double bias is also used on sheer fabrics as there will be no visible raw edges. The bias strip can be made from purchased bias binding or cut from a matching or contrasting fabric.

SINGLE BIAS-BOUND HEM

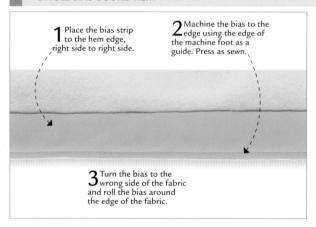

1 Place the bias strip to the hem edge, right side to right side.

2 Machine the bias to the edge using the edge of the machine foot as a guide. Press as sewn.

3 Turn the bias to the wrong side of the fabric and roll the bias around the edge of the fabric.

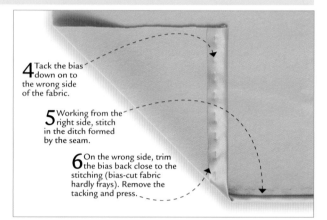

4 Tack the bias down on to the wrong side of the fabric.

5 Working from the right side, stitch in the ditch formed by the seam.

6 On the wrong side, trim the bias back close to the stitching (bias-cut fabric hardly frays). Remove the tacking and press.

DOUBLE BIAS-BOUND HEM

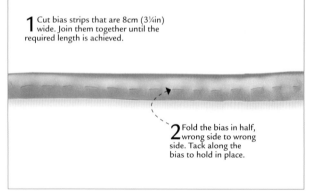

1 Cut bias strips that are 8cm (3¼in) wide. Join them together until the required length is achieved.

2 Fold the bias in half, wrong side to wrong side. Tack along the bias to hold in place.

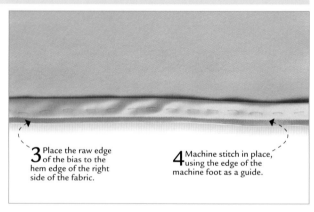

3 Place the raw edge of the bias to the hem edge of the right side of the fabric.

4 Machine stitch in place, using the edge of the machine foot as a guide.

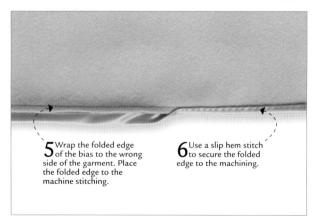

5 Wrap the folded edge of the bias to the wrong side of the garment. Place the folded edge to the machine stitching.

6 Use a slip hem stitch to secure the folded edge to the machining.

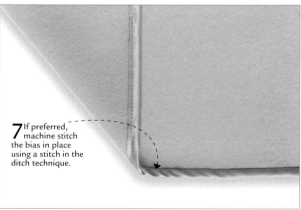

7 If preferred, machine stitch the bias in place using a stitch in the ditch technique.

Interfaced hems
LEVEL OF DIFFICULTY **

On tailored garments, such as jackets and winter skirts, an interfaced hem can be used. It is only suitable for straight hems as it produces a heavy structured edge. A sew-in woven interfacing cut on the bias grain is used for this technique.

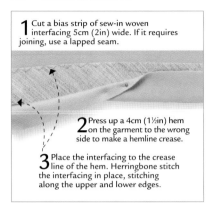

1 Cut a bias strip of sew-in woven interfacing 5cm (2in) wide. If it requires joining, use a lapped seam.

2 Press up a 4cm (1½in) hem on the garment to the wrong side to make a hemline crease.

3 Place the interfacing to the crease line of the hem. Herringbone stitch the interfacing in place, stitching along the upper and lower edges.

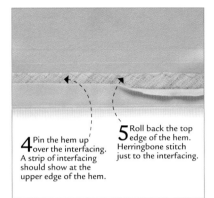

4 Pin the hem up over the interfacing. A strip of interfacing should show at the upper edge of the hem.

5 Roll back the top edge of the hem. Herringbone stitch just to the interfacing.

6 Roll back the hem into position. Press. On the right side, no stitching will be visible.

Horsehair braid hems
LEVEL OF DIFFICULTY ***

On special-occasion wear, a horsehair braid is used in the hem edge as it will hold the edge out and give a look of fullness. Although once made from horsehair, the braid is now made from nylon. It is available in various widths. The braid is stretchy so try not to stretch it when applying.

USING A NARROW HORSEHAIR BRAID

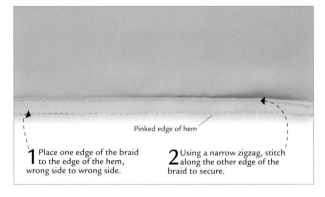

Pinked edge of hem

1 Place one edge of the braid to the edge of the hem, wrong side to wrong side.

2 Using a narrow zigzag, stitch along the other edge of the braid to secure.

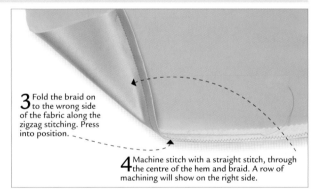

3 Fold the braid on to the wrong side of the fabric along the zigzag stitching. Press into position.

4 Machine stitch with a straight stitch, through the centre of the hem and braid. A row of machining will show on the right side.

USING A WIDE HORSEHAIR BRAID

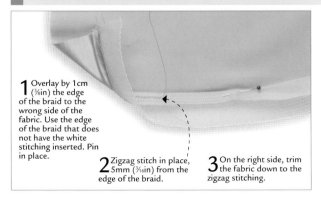

1 Overlay by 1cm (⅜in) the edge of the braid to the wrong side of the fabric. Use the edge of the braid that does not have the white stitching inserted. Pin in place.

2 Zigzag stitch in place, 5mm (³⁄₁₆in) from the edge of the braid.

3 On the right side, trim the fabric down to the zigzag stitching.

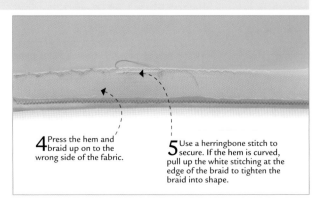

4 Press the hem and braid up on to the wrong side of the fabric.

5 Use a herringbone stitch to secure. If the hem is curved, pull up the white stitching at the edge of the braid to tighten the braid into shape.

Hems with banding

LEVEL OF DIFFICULTY ***

Banding is a term applied to a much wider bias strip. Some banding is visible by the same amount at the hem or edge on both sides of the work, while other bandings are surface-mounted to the edge of a fabric, such as for a decorative effect on a blind or a table runner. Dealing with the corners on banding needs accurate marking and stitching. Most of the following techniques are used primarily on craft and home furnishing items.

BANDING AT INNER CORNERS

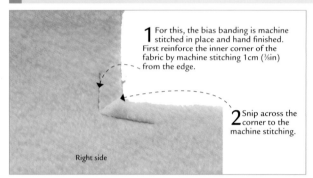

1 For this, the bias banding is machine stitched in place and hand finished. First reinforce the inner corner of the fabric by machine stitching 1cm (⅜in) from the edge.

Right side

2 Snip across the corner to the machine stitching.

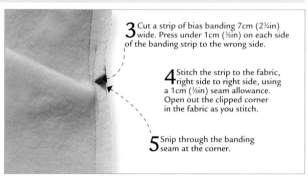

3 Cut a strip of bias banding 7cm (2¾in) wide. Press under 1cm (⅜in) on each side of the banding strip to the wrong side.

4 Stitch the strip to the fabric, right side to right side, using a 1cm (⅜in) seam allowance. Open out the clipped corner in the fabric as you stitch.

5 Snip through the banding seam at the corner.

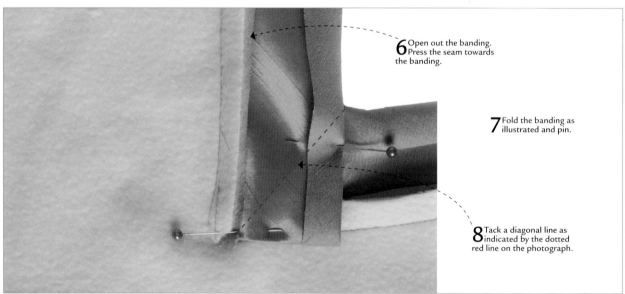

6 Open out the banding. Press the seam towards the banding.

7 Fold the banding as illustrated and pin.

8 Tack a diagonal line as indicated by the dotted red line on the photograph.

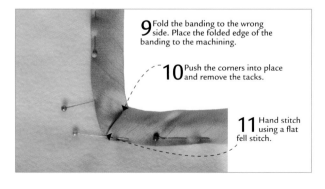

9 Fold the banding to the wrong side. Place the folded edge of the banding to the machining.

10 Push the corners into place and remove the tacks.

11 Hand stitch using a flat fell stitch.

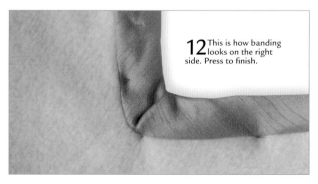

12 This is how banding looks on the right side. Press to finish.

TECHNIQUES

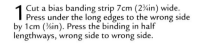

BANDING AT OUTER CORNERS

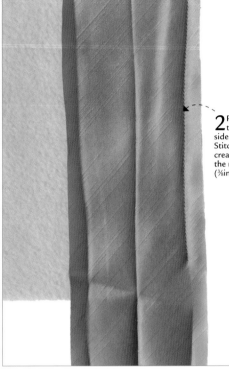

1 Cut a bias banding strip 7cm (2¾in) wide. Press under the long edges to the wrong side by 1cm (⅜in). Press the binding in half lengthways, wrong side to wrong side.

2 Place the banding to the fabric, right side to right side. Stitch along the crease line, stopping the machining 1cm (⅜in) from the corner.

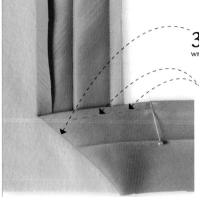

3 Fold the banding on to itself diagonally, wrong side to wrong side.

4 Using a pin or tailor's tack, mark on the banding the centre foldline to the stitching. Then mark the same distance from the stitching line (indicated by the dotted red lines). Mark this point with a vertical pin.

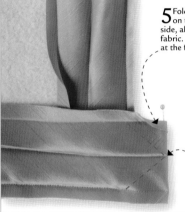

5 Fold the banding at right angles on to itself, right side to right side, aligning edge to edge with the fabric. Make sure the vertical pin is at the fold.

6 Machine along the lower crease in the banding. Extend the machining through the folded part of the banding as well.

7 Stitch in the point for the banding corner as indicated by the dotted red lines. Trim to remove surplus fabric around the point.

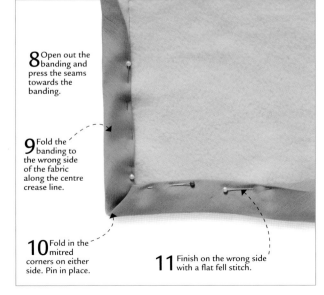

8 Open out the banding and press the seams towards the banding.

9 Fold the banding to the wrong side of the fabric along the centre crease line.

10 Fold in the mitred corners on either side. Pin in place.

11 Finish on the wrong side with a flat fell stitch.

12 Turn to the right side and press.

SURFACE-MOUNTED BANDING AT OUTER CORNERS

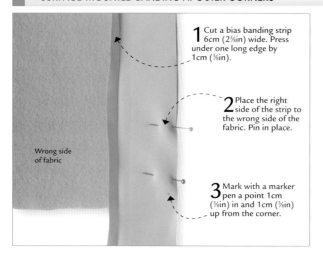

1 Cut a bias banding strip 6cm (2⅜in) wide. Press under one long edge by 1cm (⅜in).

2 Place the right side of the strip to the wrong side of the fabric. Pin in place.

Wrong side of fabric

3 Mark with a marker pen a point 1cm (⅜in) in and 1cm (⅜in) up from the corner.

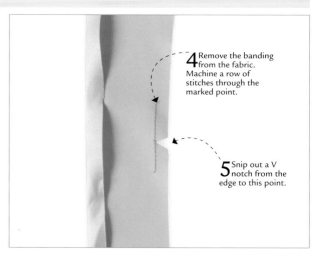

4 Remove the banding from the fabric. Machine a row of stitches through the marked point.

5 Snip out a V notch from the edge to this point.

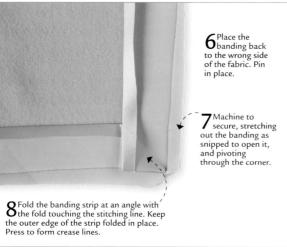

6 Place the banding back to the wrong side of the fabric. Pin in place.

7 Machine to secure, stretching out the banding as snipped to open it, and pivoting through the corner.

8 Fold the banding strip at an angle with the fold touching the stitching line. Keep the outer edge of the strip folded in place. Press to form crease lines.

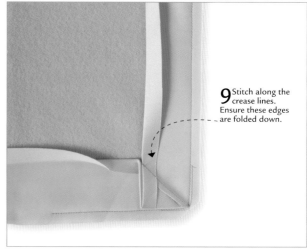

9 Stitch along the crease lines. Ensure these edges are folded down.

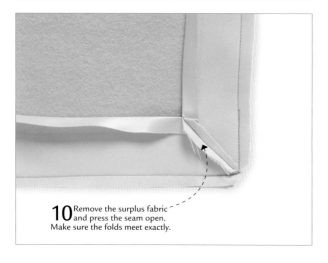

10 Remove the surplus fabric and press the seam open. Make sure the folds meet exactly.

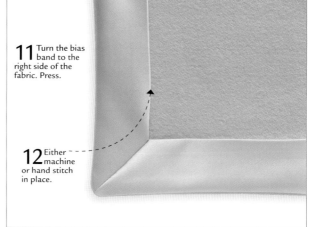

11 Turn the bias band to the right side of the fabric. Press.

12 Either machine or hand stitch in place.

SURFACE-MOUNTED BANDING AT INNER CORNERS

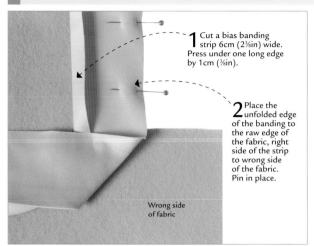

1 Cut a bias banding strip 6cm (2⅜in) wide. Press under one long edge by 1cm (⅜in).

2 Place the unfolded edge of the banding to the raw edge of the fabric, right side of the strip to wrong side of the fabric. Pin in place.

Wrong side of fabric

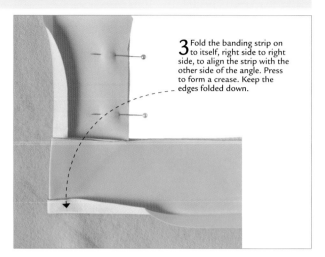

3 Fold the banding strip on to itself, right side to right side, to align the strip with the other side of the angle. Press to form a crease. Keep the edges folded down.

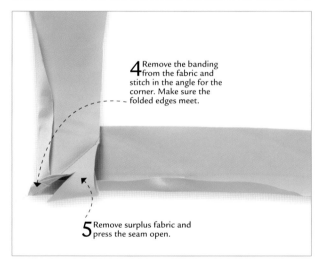

4 Remove the banding from the fabric and stitch in the angle for the corner. Make sure the folded edges meet.

5 Remove surplus fabric and press the seam open.

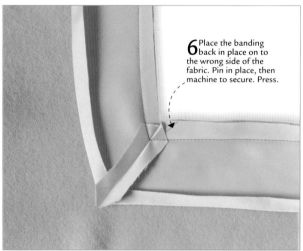

6 Place the banding back in place on to the wrong side of the fabric. Pin in place, then machine to secure. Press.

7 This is how it should look on the right side of the fabric through the corner.

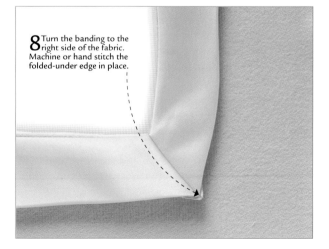

8 Turn the banding to the right side of the fabric. Machine or hand stitch the folded-under edge in place.

How to cut bias strips p147   Mitred corners p235 ◀◀◀

Applying a flat trim
LEVEL OF DIFFICULTY *

On some items a flat trim braid or ribbon is added for a decorative effect. This may be right on the hem or edge, or placed just above it. To achieve a neat finish, any corners should be mitred.

1 Pin the trim to the fabric, wrong side of the trim to right side of the fabric.

2 At the corner point where the trim is to be mitred, fold the trim back on itself and secure with a pin.

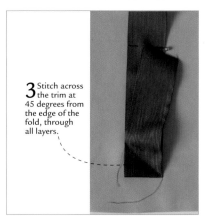

3 Stitch across the trim at 45 degrees from the edge of the fold, through all layers.

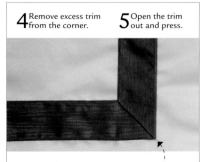

4 Remove excess trim from the corner.

5 Open the trim out and press.

6 Machine stitch the inner and outer sides of the trim to the fabric, close to the edge. Be sure the stitching at the corners is sharp.

Piped edges
LEVEL OF DIFFICULTY ***

A piped edge can look very effective on a garment, especially if it is made in a contrasting colour or fabric. Piping is also an excellent way of finishing special-occasion wear as well as soft furnishings. The piping may be single, double, or gathered.

SINGLE PIPING

1 Just one piece of piping is used. Cut a bias strip 4cm (1½in) wide.

2 Wrap the binding, wrong side to wrong side, around the piping cord. Pin in place.

3 Machine along the binding close to the cord, using the zip foot.

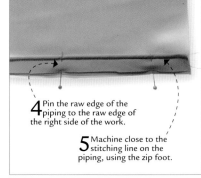

4 Pin the raw edge of the piping to the raw edge of the right side of the work.

5 Machine close to the stitching line on the piping, using the zip foot.

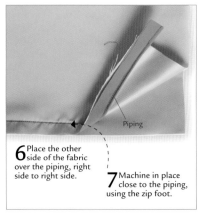

Piping

6 Place the other side of the fabric over the piping, right side to right side.

7 Machine in place close to the piping, using the zip foot.

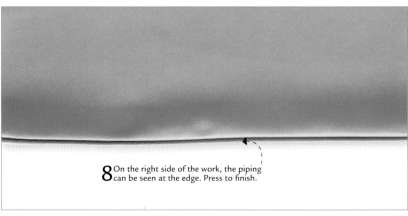

8 On the right side of the work, the piping can be seen at the edge. Press to finish.

«« Stitches made with a machine pp92–93

DOUBLE PIPING

1 Different thicknesses of piping cord can be used for this. Make up single piping (see steps 1–3, opposite page).

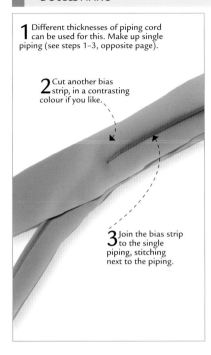

2 Cut another bias strip, in a contrasting colour if you like.

3 Join the bias strip to the single piping, stitching next to the piping.

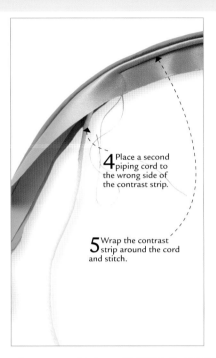

4 Place a second piping cord to the wrong side of the contrast strip.

5 Wrap the contrast strip around the cord and stitch.

6 Attach to the edge of the work as for single piping (see steps 4–7 on the opposite page). On the right side, there is a double row of piping at the edge.

GATHERED PIPING

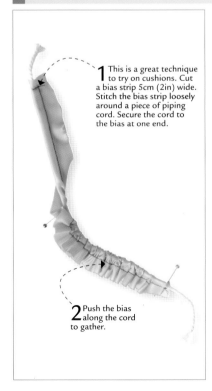

1 This is a great technique to try on cushions. Cut a bias strip 5cm (2in) wide. Stitch the bias strip loosely around a piece of piping cord. Secure the cord to the bias at one end.

2 Push the bias along the cord to gather.

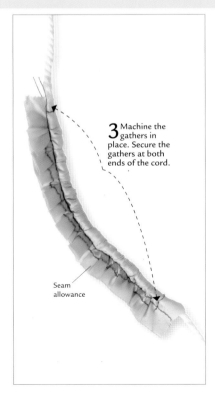

3 Machine the gathers in place. Secure the gathers at both ends of the cord.

Seam allowance

Gathered piping

4 Attach to the edge of the work as for single piping (see steps 4–7, opposite page).

How to cut bias strips p147 Mitred corners p235 «««

Attaching a lace trim

LEVEL OF DIFFICULTY **

A lace edge can give a look of luxury to any garment. There are many ways of applying lace, depending on how the lace has been made. A heavy lace trim has a definite edge to be sewn on to the fabric. Lace edging has a decorative edge and an unfinished edge, whereas a galloon lace is decorative on both edges.

HEAVY LACE TRIM

1 Pin the lace to the right side of the fabric.

2 Using a small zigzag stitch, machine along the edge of the lace. All of the stitching should be on the lace.

3 Trim away surplus fabric behind.

LACE EDGING

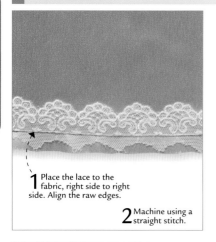

1 Place the lace to the fabric, right side to right side. Align the raw edges.

2 Machine using a straight stitch.

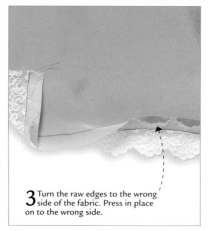

3 Turn the raw edges to the wrong side of the fabric. Press in place on to the wrong side.

4 Working from the right side of the fabric, zigzag stitch close to the fabric edge.

5 Trim away surplus fabric on the reverse side.

GALLOON LACE

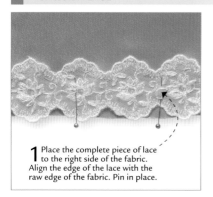

1 Place the complete piece of lace to the right side of the fabric. Align the edge of the lace with the raw edge of the fabric. Pin in place.

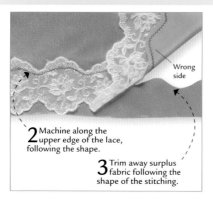

Wrong side

2 Machine along the upper edge of the lace, following the shape.

3 Trim away surplus fabric following the shape of the stitching.

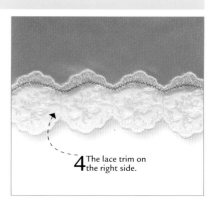

4 The lace trim on the right side.

Applying other trimmings

LEVEL OF DIFFICULTY ★★★

There are many kinds of trimmings – ribbons, braids, beads, feathers, sequins, fringes, and so on – that can be applied to a fabric edge. If a trim is made on a narrow ribbon or braid it can often be inserted into a seam during construction. Other trims are attached after the garment or item has been completed.

INSERTING A TRIM IN A SEAM

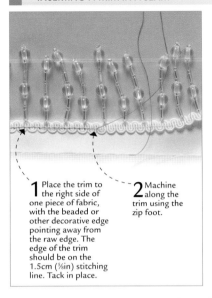

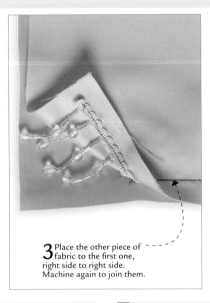

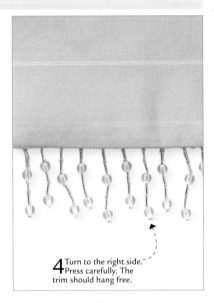

1 Place the trim to the right side of one piece of fabric, with the beaded or other decorative edge pointing away from the raw edge. The edge of the trim should be on the 1.5cm (⅝in) stitching line. Tack in place.

2 Machine along the trim using the zip foot.

3 Place the other piece of fabric to the first one, right side to right side. Machine again to join them.

4 Turn to the right side. Press carefully. The trim should hang free.

ATTACHING A TRIM TO AN EDGE

1 Pin the trim in position along the finished edge of the work. Be sure the trim is aligned to the edge. Tack in place.

2 Using the zip foot, machine in place close to the upper edge, leaving the lower edge of the trim free.

HAND STITCHING A TRIM

Delicate trims are best hand stitched in place because machining the trim may damage it. Place the trim in position and carefully stitch down with a flat fell stitch.

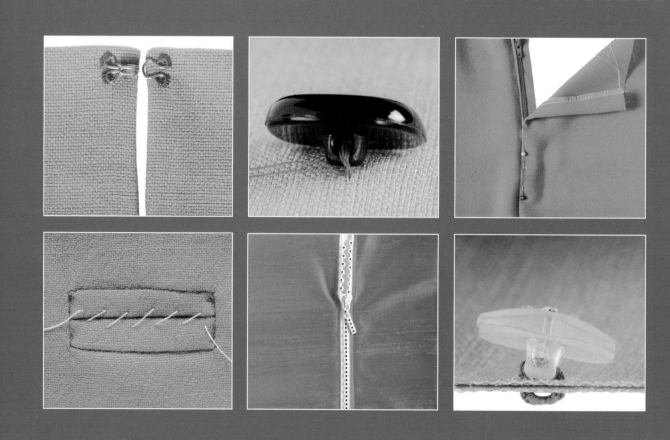

FASTENERS

There are many types of fastening available. Some of them are purely functional while others are more decorative as well as practical. A great many fastenings are hand stitched in place.

ZIPS

The zip is probably the most used of all fastenings. There are a great many types available, in a variety of lengths, colours, and materials, but they all fall into one of five categories: skirt or trouser zips, metal or jeans zips, concealed zips, open-ended zips, and decorative zips.

Directory of zips

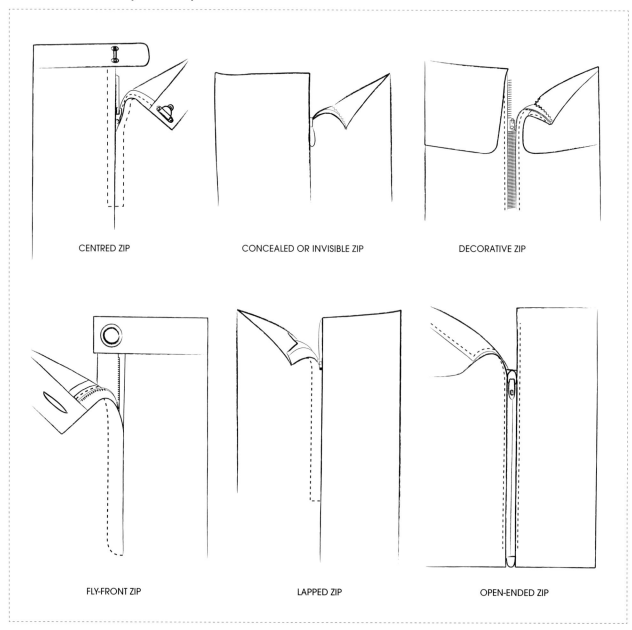

CENTRED ZIP

CONCEALED OR INVISIBLE ZIP

DECORATIVE ZIP

FLY-FRONT ZIP

LAPPED ZIP

OPEN-ENDED ZIP

≪≪ Measuring tools and marking aids pp18–19 Tacking stitches p89 Stitches made with a machine pp92–93 How to make a plain seam p94

How to shorten a zip

LEVEL OF DIFFICULTY ✱

Zips do not always come in the length that you need, but it is easy to shorten them. Skirt or trouser zips and concealed zips are all shortened by stitching across the teeth or coils, whereas an open-ended zip is shortened at the top and not at the bottom.

SHORTENING A SKIRT/TROUSER OR CONCEALED ZIP

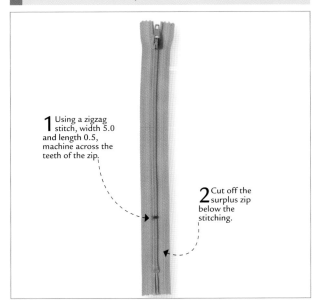

1 Using a zigzag stitch, width 5.0 and length 0.5, machine across the teeth of the zip.

2 Cut off the surplus zip below the stitching.

SHORTENING AN OPEN-ENDED ZIP

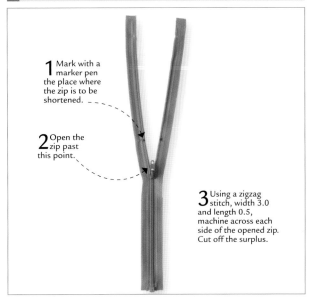

1 Mark with a marker pen the place where the zip is to be shortened.

2 Open the zip past this point.

3 Using a zigzag stitch, width 3.0 and length 0.5, machine across each side of the opened zip. Cut off the surplus.

Marking for zip placement

LEVEL OF DIFFICULTY ✱

For a zip to sit accurately in the seam, the seam allowances where the zip will be inserted need to be marked. The upper seam allowance at the top of the zip also needs marking to ensure the zip pull sits just fractionally below the stitching line.

1 Stitch the seam, leaving a gap for the zip.

2 Secure the end of the stitching.

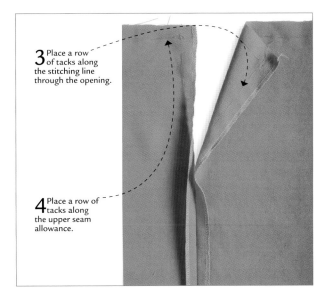

3 Place a row of tacks along the stitching line through the opening.

4 Place a row of tacks along the upper seam allowance.

Repairing a broken zip p303 ≫

Lapped zip

LEVEL OF DIFFICULTY **

A skirt zip in a skirt or a dress is usually put in by means of a lapped technique or a centred zip technique (see opposite page). For both of these techniques you will require the zip foot on the sewing machine. A lapped zip features one side of the seam – the left-hand side – covering the teeth of the zip to conceal them.

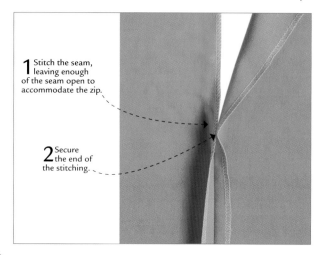

1 Stitch the seam, leaving enough of the seam open to accommodate the zip.

2 Secure the end of the stitching.

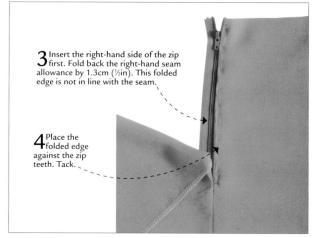

3 Insert the right-hand side of the zip first. Fold back the right-hand seam allowance by 1.3cm (½in). This folded edge is not in line with the seam.

4 Place the folded edge against the zip teeth. Tack.

5 Using the zip foot, stitch along the tack line to secure the zip tape to the fabric. Stitch from the bottom of the zip to the top.

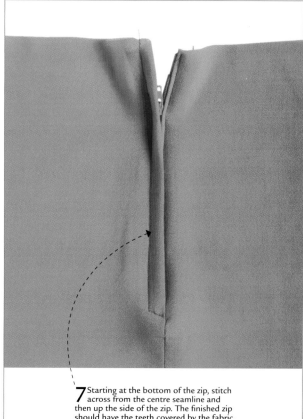

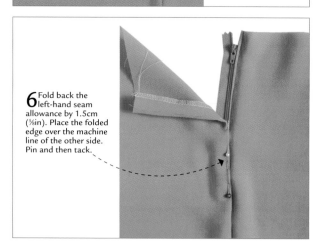

6 Fold back the left-hand seam allowance by 1.5cm (⅝in). Place the folded edge over the machine line of the other side. Pin and then tack.

7 Starting at the bottom of the zip, stitch across from the centre seamline and then up the side of the zip. The finished zip should have the teeth covered by the fabric.

Centred zip

LEVEL OF DIFFICULTY **

With a centred zip, the two folded edges of the seam allowances meet over the centre of the teeth, to conceal the zip completely.

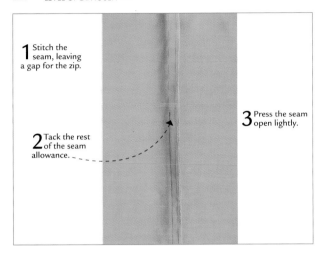

1 Stitch the seam, leaving a gap for the zip.

2 Tack the rest of the seam allowance.

3 Press the seam open lightly.

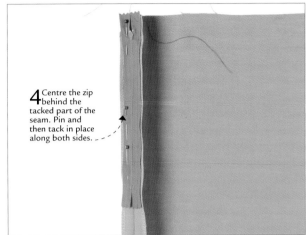

4 Centre the zip behind the tacked part of the seam. Pin and then tack in place along both sides.

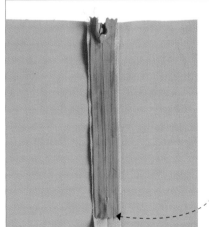

5 On the wrong side, lift the seam allowance and the zip tape away from the main fabric. Pin.

6 Machine the zip tape to the seam allowance. Make sure both sides of the zip tape are secured to the seam allowances. Stitch through to the end of the zip tape.

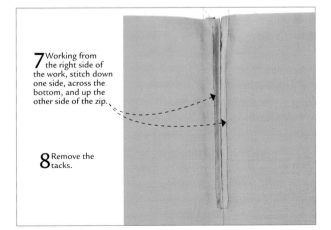

7 Working from the right side of the work, stitch down one side, across the bottom, and up the other side of the zip.

8 Remove the tacks.

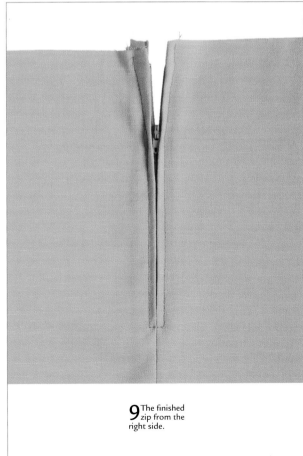

9 The finished zip from the right side.

Faced fly-front zip

LEVEL OF DIFFICULTY ★★★

Whether it be for a classic pair of trousers or a pair of jeans, a fly front is the most common technique for inserting a trouser zip. The zip usually has a facing behind it to prevent the zip teeth from catching.

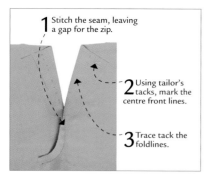

1 Stitch the seam, leaving a gap for the zip.

2 Using tailor's tacks, mark the centre front lines.

3 Trace tack the foldlines.

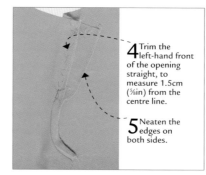

4 Trim the left-hand front of the opening straight, to measure 1.5cm (⅝in) from the centre line.

5 Neaten the edges on both sides.

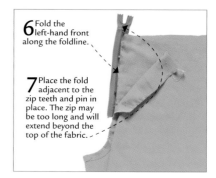

6 Fold the left-hand front along the foldline.

7 Place the fold adjacent to the zip teeth and pin in place. The zip may be too long and will extend beyond the top of the fabric.

8 Machine along the foldline using the zip foot. Extend the machining past the seam stitching line.

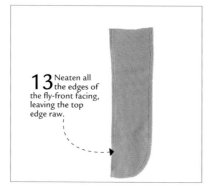

9 Fold the right front along the foldline. Place the foldline over the zip and pin the foldline to the machine stitching on the left-hand side.

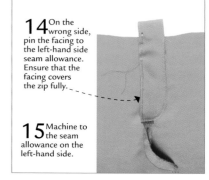

10 On the inside, pin the zip tape to the fabric extension.

11 Machine the zip tape to the fabric along the centre of the tape.

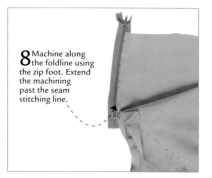

12 On the right side, top-stitch around the zip. Start stitching at the centre front. Stitch a smooth curve.

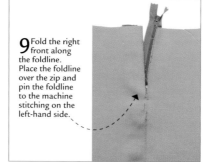

13 Neaten all the edges of the fly-front facing, leaving the top edge raw.

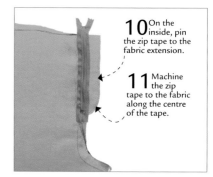

14 On the wrong side, pin the facing to the left-hand side seam allowance. Ensure that the facing covers the zip fully.

15 Machine to the seam allowance on the left-hand side.

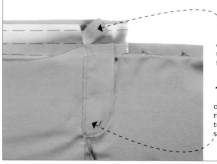

16 Attach the waistband over the zip and the facings. Trim facing and zip.

17 Secure the lower edge of the facing on the right-hand side to the right-hand seam allowance.

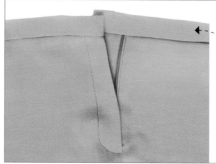

18 The waistband goes over the zip and acts as the zip stop. Attach a trouser hook and eye.

Concealed or invisible zip

LEVEL OF DIFFICULTY **

This type of zip looks different from other zips because the teeth are on the reverse and nothing except the pull is seen on the front. The zip is inserted before the seam is stitched. A special concealed zip foot is required.

1 Mark the seam allowance with tacking stitches.

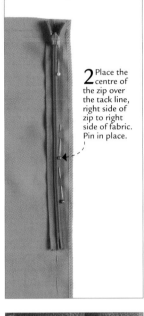

2 Place the centre of the zip over the tack line, right side of zip to right side of fabric. Pin in place.

3 Undo the zip. Using the concealed zip foot, stitch from the top of the zip down as far as possible. Stitch under the teeth. The machine will stop when the foot hits the zip pull.

4 Do the zip up. Place the other piece of fabric to the zip. Match along the upper edge. Pin the other side of the zip tape in place.

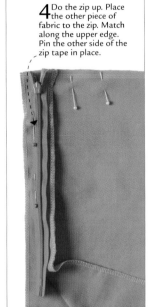

5 Open the zip again. Using the concealed zip foot, stitch down the other side of the zip to attach to the second piece of fabric. Remove any tacking stitches.

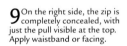

6 Close the zip. On the wrong side at the bottom of the zip, the two rows of stitching that hold in the zip should be finishing at the same place.

Free end of zip tape

7 Stitch the seam below the zip. Use the normal machine foot for this. There will be a small gap of about 3mm (⅛in) between the stitching line for the zip and that for the seam.

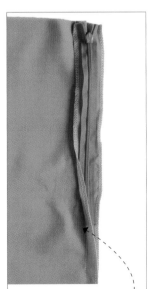

8 Stitch the last 3cm (1¼in) of the zip tape to just the seam allowances. This will stop the zip pulling loose.

9 On the right side, the zip is completely concealed, with just the pull visible at the top. Apply waistband or facing.

Hooks and eyes p271 »»»

Open-ended zip

LEVEL OF DIFFICULTY ✱✱

The open-ended zip is used on garments where the two halves need to be fully opened in order to put the garment on – for example, on a jacket or cardigan.

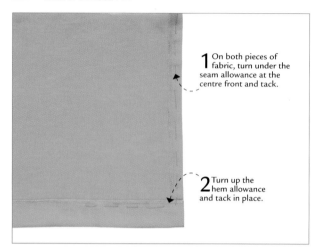

1 On both pieces of fabric, turn under the seam allowance at the centre front and tack.

2 Turn up the hem allowance and tack in place.

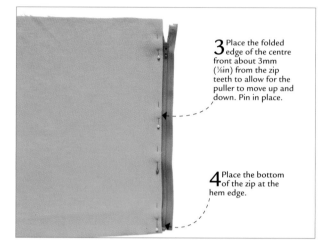

3 Place the folded edge of the centre front about 3mm (⅛in) from the zip teeth to allow for the puller to move up and down. Pin in place.

4 Place the bottom of the zip at the hem edge.

5 Using the zip foot, machine the zip in place. Start with the zip open. Stitch 5cm (2in), then place the machine needle in the work, raise the zip foot, and close the zip.

6 Stitch to the end of the zip tape and secure.

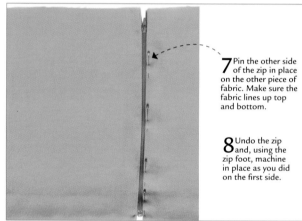

7 Pin the other side of the zip in place on the other piece of fabric. Make sure the fabric lines up top and bottom.

8 Undo the zip and, using the zip foot, machine in place as you did on the first side.

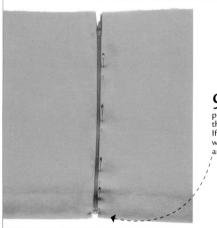

9 Once the zip is machined in place, check that the hems line up. If they do not, you will have to unpick and start again.

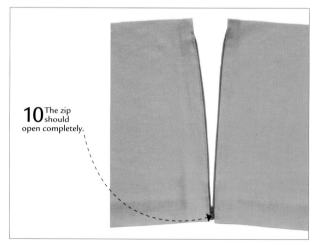

10 The zip should open completely.

A decorative zip

LEVEL OF DIFFICULTY ★★★

Some zips are meant to be seen – they may have crystals in the teeth, or they may have decorative coloured teeth.

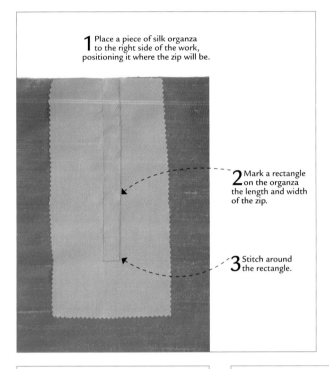

1 Place a piece of silk organza to the right side of the work, positioning it where the zip will be.

2 Mark a rectangle on the organza the length and width of the zip.

3 Stitch around the rectangle.

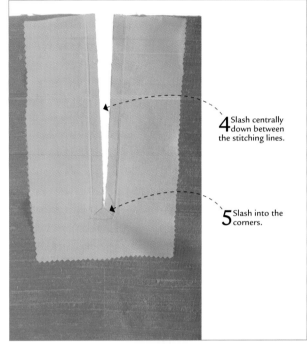

4 Slash centrally down between the stitching lines.

5 Slash into the corners.

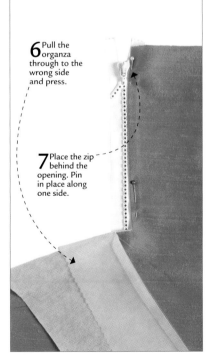

6 Pull the organza through to the wrong side and press.

7 Place the zip behind the opening. Pin in place along one side.

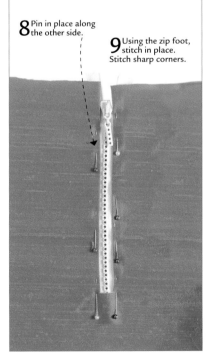

8 Pin in place along the other side.

9 Using the zip foot, stitch in place. Stitch sharp corners.

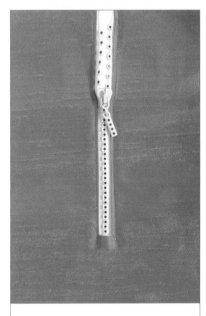

10 On the right side, the zip is exposed.

BUTTONS

Buttons are one of the oldest forms of fastening. They come in many shapes and sizes, and can be made from a variety of materials including shell, bone, plastic, nylon, and metal. Buttons are sewn to the fabric either through holes on their face, or through a hole in a stalk called a shank, which is on the back. Buttons are normally sewn on by hand, although a two-hole button can be sewn on by machine.

Directory of buttons

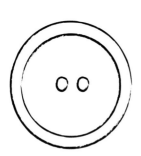

TWO-HOLE BUTTON

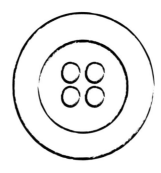

FOUR-HOLE BUTTON

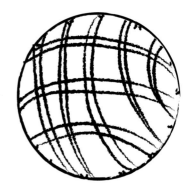

COVERED BUTTON

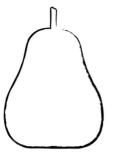

NOVELTY BUTTON

RIVET BUTTON

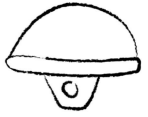

SHANKED BUTTON

⋘ Buttons p26 Securing the thread p88 Hand stitches pp90–91

Sewing on a 2-hole button

LEVEL OF DIFFICULTY ✱✱

This is the most popular type of button and requires a thread shank to be made when sewing in place. A cocktail stick will help you to sew on this type of button.

1 Position the button on the fabric. Start with a double stitch and double thread in the needle.

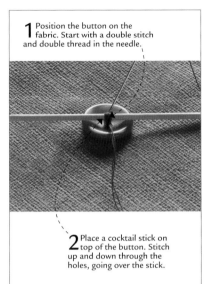

2 Place a cocktail stick on top of the button. Stitch up and down through the holes, going over the stick.

3 Remove the cocktail stick.

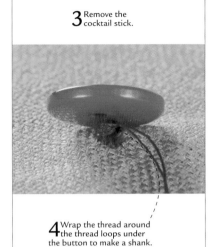

4 Wrap the thread around the thread loops under the button to make a shank.

5 Take the thread through to the back of the fabric.

6 Buttonhole stitch over the loop of threads on the back of the work.

Sewing on a 4-hole button

LEVEL OF DIFFICULTY ✱✱

This is stitched in the same way as for a two-hole button except that the threads make an X over the button on the front.

1 Position the button on the fabric. Place a cocktail stick on the button.

2 Using double thread, stitch up and down through alternate sets of holes, over the cocktail stick. Make an X shape as you stitch.

3 Remove the cocktail stick.

4 Wrap the thread around the thread loops under the button to make the shank.

5 On the reverse of the fabric, buttonhole stitch over the thread loops in an X shape.

Sewing on a shanked button
LEVEL OF DIFFICULTY ✱✱

When sewing this type of button in place, use a cocktail stick under the button to enable you to make a thread shank on the underside of the fabric.

1 Position the button on the fabric. Hold a cocktail stick on the other side of the fabric, behind the button.

2 Using double thread, stitch the button to the fabric, through the shank.

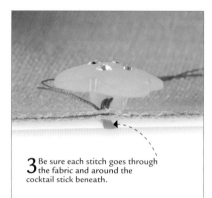

3 Be sure each stitch goes through the fabric and around the cocktail stick beneath.

4 Remove the cocktail stick. Work buttonhole stitching over the looped thread shank.

Sewing on a reinforced button
LEVEL OF DIFFICULTY ✱✱✱

A large, heavy button often features a second button sewn to it on the wrong side and stitched on with the same threads that secure the larger button. The smaller button helps support the weight of the larger button.

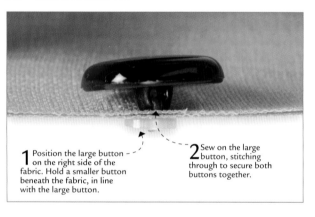

1 Position the large button on the right side of the fabric. Hold a smaller button beneath the fabric, in line with the large button.

2 Sew on the large button, stitching through to secure both buttons together.

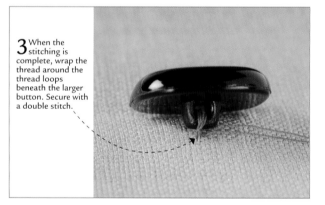

3 When the stitching is complete, wrap the thread around the thread loops beneath the larger button. Secure with a double stitch.

Oversized and layered buttons
LEVEL OF DIFFICULTY ✱✱

There are some huge buttons available, many of which are really more decorative than functional. By layering buttons of varying sizes together, you can make an unusual feature on a garment or item of soft furnishing.

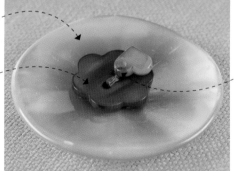

1 First position the oversized button on the fabric.

2 Top with a smaller button and stitch the two together to the fabric.

3 Place a small one-hole button on the layered buttons and attach to the thread using a buttonhole stitch.

Covered buttons

LEVEL OF DIFFICULTY **

Covered buttons are often found on expensive clothes and will add a professional finish to any jacket or other garment that you make. A purchased button-making gadget will enable you to create covered buttons very easily.

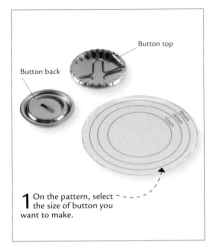

1 On the pattern, select the size of button you want to make.

Button top

Button back

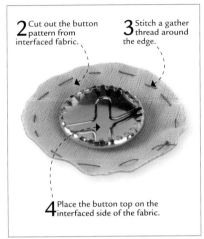

2 Cut out the button pattern from interfaced fabric.

3 Stitch a gather thread around the edge.

4 Place the button top on the interfaced side of the fabric.

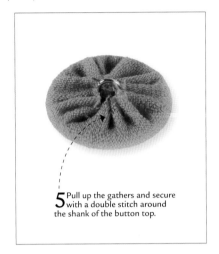

5 Pull up the gathers and secure with a double stitch around the shank of the button top.

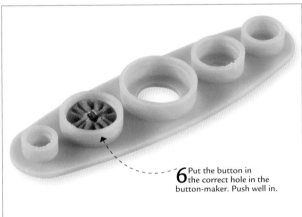

6 Put the button in the correct hole in the button-maker. Push well in.

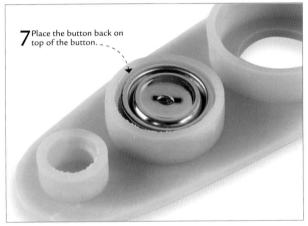

7 Place the button back on top of the button.

8 Take the other side of the button-maker and press down on the button back until it clicks into position.

9 Remove the button from the button-maker and check to be sure the back is firmly in place.

10 The finished covered button.

BUTTONHOLES

A buttonhole is essential if a button is to be truly functional, although for many oversized buttons a snap fastener on the reverse is a better option, because the buttonhole would be just too big and could cause the garment to stretch.

Directory of buttonholes and button loops

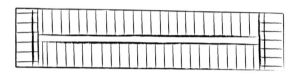

BASIC BUTTONHOLE

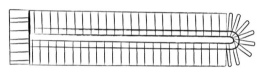

ROUND-END BUTTONHOLE

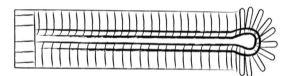

KEYHOLE BUTTONHOLE

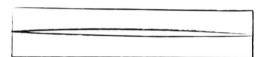

BOUND BUTTONHOLE

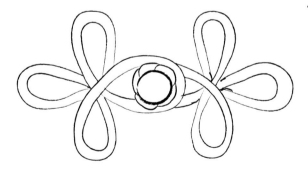

FROG FASTENER WITH
CHINESE BALL BUTTON

ROULEAU LOOPS

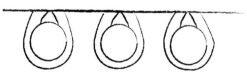

SPACED ROULEAU LOOPS

Stages of a buttonhole

A sewing machine stitches a buttonhole in three stages. The stitch can be slightly varied in width and length to suit the fabric or item, but the stitches need to be tight and close together.

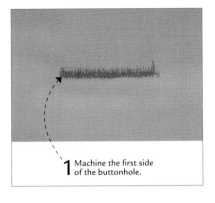

1 Machine the first side of the buttonhole.

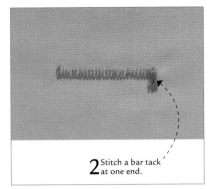

2 Stitch a bar tack at one end.

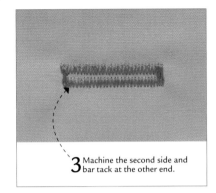

3 Machine the second side and bar tack at the other end.

Positioning buttonholes

LEVEL OF DIFFICULTY *

Whether the buttonholes are to be stitched by machine or another type of buttonhole is to be made, the size of the button will need to be established in order to work out the position of the button on the fabric.

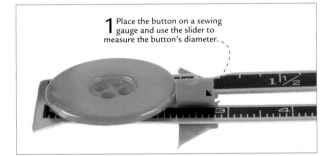

1 Place the button on a sewing gauge and use the slider to measure the button's diameter.

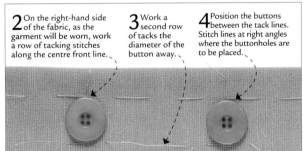

2 On the right-hand side of the fabric, as the garment will be worn, work a row of tacking stitches along the centre front line.

3 Work a second row of tacks the diameter of the button away.

4 Position the buttons between the tack lines. Stitch lines at right angles where the buttonholes are to be placed.

Vertical or horizontal?

As a general rule, buttonholes are only vertical on a garment when there is a placket or a strip into which the buttonhole fits. All other buttonholes should be horizontal. Any strain on the buttonhole will then pull to the end stop and prevent the button from coming undone.

HORIZONTAL BUTTONHOLES

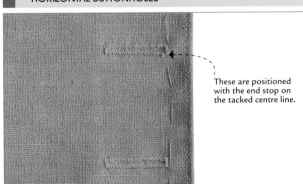

These are positioned with the end stop on the tacked centre line.

VERTICAL BUTTONHOLES

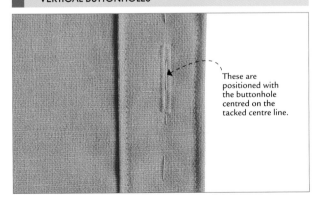

These are positioned with the buttonhole centred on the tacked centre line.

Repairing a damaged buttonhole p299 »»»

Machine-made buttonholes

LEVEL OF DIFFICULTY *

Modern sewing machines can stitch various types of buttonhole, suitable for all kinds of garments. On many machines the button fits into a special foot, and a sensor on the machine determines the correct size of buttonhole. The width and length of the stitch can be altered to suit the fabric. Once the buttonhole has been stitched, always slash through with a buttonhole chisel, to ensure that the cut is clean.

BASIC BUTTONHOLE

The most popular shape for a buttonhole is square on both ends.

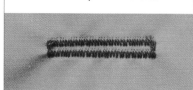

ROUND-END BUTTONHOLE

A buttonhole featuring one rounded end and one square end is used on lightweight jackets.

KEYHOLE BUTTONHOLE

This is also called a tailor's buttonhole. It has a square end and a keyhole end, and is used on jackets and coats.

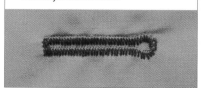

Machine-corded buttonhole

LEVEL OF DIFFICULTY **

This buttonhole has a cord of heavier sewing thread running through it. You may have to consult your sewing machine manual for the positioning of the cord.

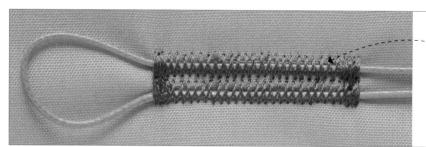

1 Place the cord into the buttonhole foot as directed by your machine manual.

2 Work the buttonhole on the machine – the machine will stitch the buttonhole over the cord.

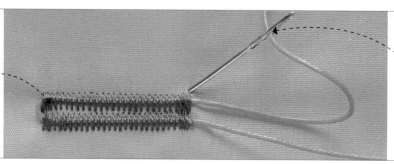

3 Gently pull on the ends of the cord to eliminate the loop.

4 Thread the ends of the cord into a large needle.

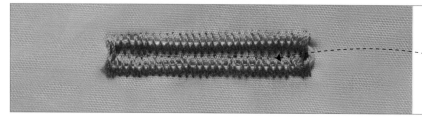

5 Take the cord to the back of the fabric. Secure with a hand stitch.

TECHNIQUES

Piped buttonhole

LEVEL OF DIFFICULTY ★★★

A buttonhole can also be made using piping cord. This is a type of buttonhole that is worked early in the construction of the garment. Very narrow piping cord needs to be used, otherwise the buttonhole will be too bulky.

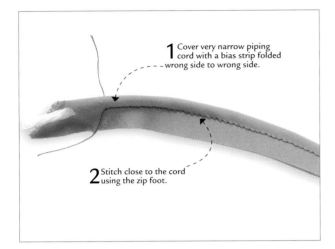

1 Cover very narrow piping cord with a bias strip folded wrong side to wrong side.

2 Stitch close to the cord using the zip foot.

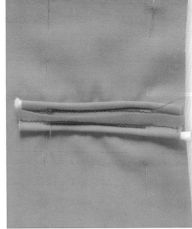

3 Place the cord against the buttonhole markings on the right side of the fabric, the raw edges of the cord to the centre of the buttonhole markings.

4 Use the zip foot to machine close to the cord. Stop stitching at the markings on the garment.

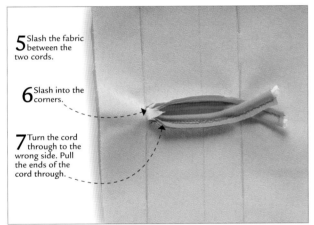

5 Slash the fabric between the two cords.

6 Slash into the corners.

7 Turn the cord through to the wrong side. Pull the ends of the cord through.

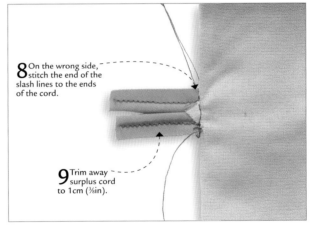

8 On the wrong side, stitch the end of the slash lines to the ends of the cord.

9 Trim away surplus cord to 1cm (⅜in).

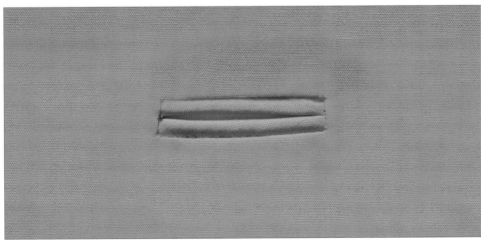

10 The finished piped buttonhole on the right side.

Stitches made with a machine pp92–93 How to cut bias strips p147 ⫷

Patch method bound buttonhole

LEVEL OF DIFFICULTY ✳✳✳

Another method of creating a buttonhole is to use a patch of fabric stitched on to the main fabric. The technique is ideal for jackets and coats. A contrast fabric can be used for an attractive detail. This is known as a bound buttonhole.

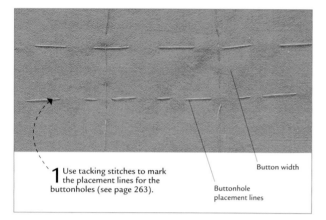

1 Use tacking stitches to mark the placement lines for the buttonholes (see page 263).

Button width

Buttonhole placement lines

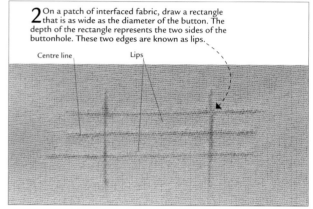

2 On a patch of interfaced fabric, draw a rectangle that is as wide as the diameter of the button. The depth of the rectangle represents the two sides of the buttonhole. These two edges are known as lips.

Centre line   Lips

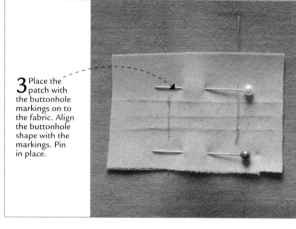

3 Place the patch with the buttonhole markings on to the fabric. Align the buttonhole shape with the markings. Pin in place.

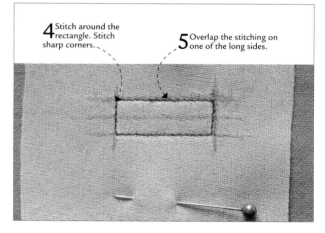

4 Stitch around the rectangle. Stitch sharp corners.

5 Overlap the stitching on one of the long sides.

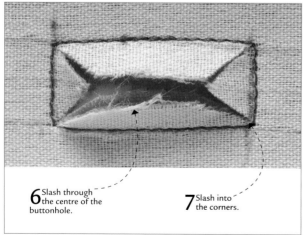

6 Slash through the centre of the buttonhole.

7 Slash into the corners.

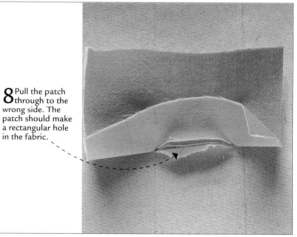

8 Pull the patch through to the wrong side. The patch should make a rectangular hole in the fabric.

≪≪ How to apply a fusible interfacing p54   Hand stitches pp90–91   Stitches made with a machine pp92–93   Stitching corners and curves pp100–101

TECHNIQUES

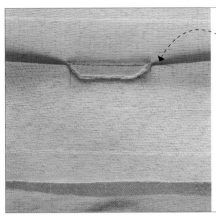

9 Press down the lip on one side of the buttonhole, then press the patch back over the lip.

10 Repeat on the other side of the buttonhole. The patch will fold over the lips to meet in the centre.

11 Turn to the right side and press.

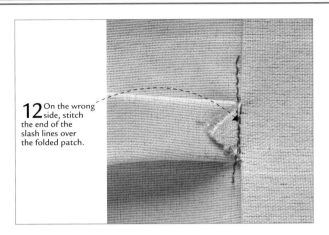

12 On the wrong side, stitch the end of the slash lines over the folded patch.

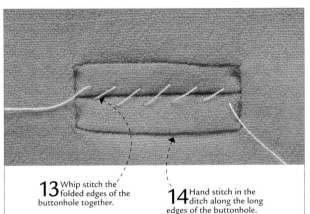

13 Whip stitch the folded edges of the buttonhole together.

14 Hand stitch in the ditch along the long edges of the buttonhole.

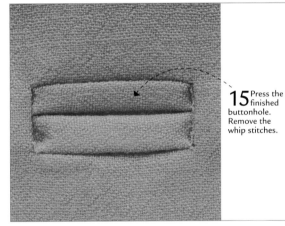

15 Press the finished buttonhole. Remove the whip stitches.

In-seam buttonhole
LEVEL OF DIFFICULTY *

This is a buttonhole formed in a seam allowance. It is found down decorative centre fronts that feature seam detailing. It is a very discreet buttonhole.

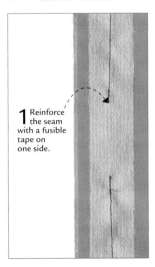

1 Reinforce the seam with a fusible tape on one side.

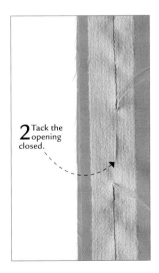

2 Tack the opening closed.

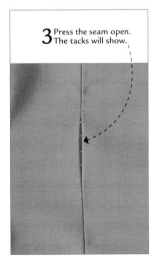

3 Press the seam open. The tacks will show.

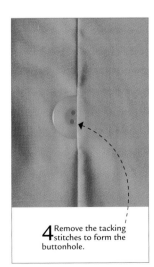

4 Remove the tacking stitches to form the buttonhole.

Interfacings pp276–277 »»»

BUTTON LOOPS

A buttonhole is not the only way of using buttons. Buttons can also be fastened by means of a fabric loop, which is usually attached at the edge of a garment. Fabric loops are often found on the back of special-occasion wear, where multiple loops secure rows of small, often covered buttons. Loops called frog fasteners can also be made from decorative cord.

Rouleau loop
LEVEL OF DIFFICULTY ✱✱✱

This button loop is formed from a bias strip. Choose a smooth fabric for the strip as it will be easier to turn through. A rouleau loop is used with a round ball-type button.

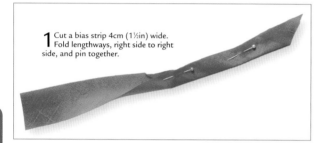

1 Cut a bias strip 4cm (1½in) wide. Fold lengthways, right side to right side, and pin together.

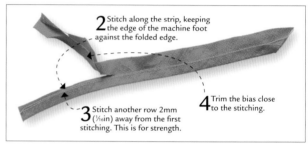

2 Stitch along the strip, keeping the edge of the machine foot against the folded edge.

3 Stitch another row 2mm (⅟₁₆in) away from the first stitching. This is for strength.

4 Trim the bias close to the stitching.

5 Turn the bias strip to the right side, using a loop turner.

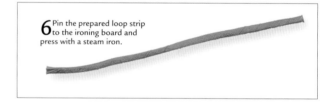

6 Pin the prepared loop strip to the ironing board and press with a steam iron.

Corded loop
LEVEL OF DIFFICULTY ✱✱✱

It is possible to make a very fine button loop that has a cord running through it. This type of loop is suitable for lightweight fabrics. Use a shanked button with a corded loop.

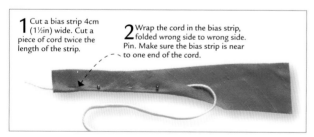

1 Cut a bias strip 4cm (1½in) wide. Cut a piece of cord twice the length of the strip.

2 Wrap the cord in the bias strip, folded wrong side to wrong side. Pin. Make sure the bias strip is near to one end of the cord.

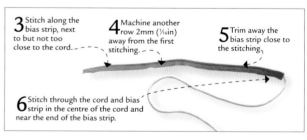

3 Stitch along the bias strip, next to but not too close to the cord.

4 Machine another row 2mm (⅟₁₆in) away from the first stitching.

5 Trim away the bias strip close to the stitching.

6 Stitch through the cord and bias strip in the centre of the cord and near the end of the bias strip.

7 At the centre point, ease the fabric over the cord to turn it to the right side.

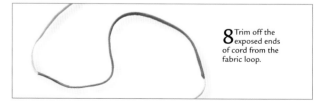

8 Trim off the exposed ends of cord from the fabric loop.

Spacing the loops
LEVEL OF DIFFICULTY ✱✱

Once the loops have been made, the next step is to attach them to the garment. It is important that all the loops are the same size and positioned the same distance apart. To achieve this you will need to tack your fabric to mark the placement lines. The loops go on the right-hand front or the left-hand back of the garment or item you are making.

1 Mark the placement lines on the fabric using tacking stitches. Be sure the horizontal lines are equally spaced.

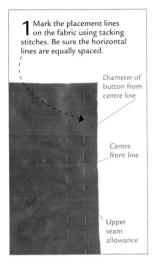

Diameter of button from centre line

Centre front line

Upper seam allowance

2 Place the loop to the fabric. The folded end of the loop should be on the inner tacking line and the cut ends to the raw edge. Centre the loop over the tack line.

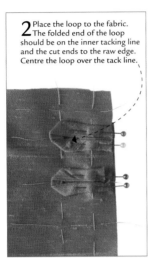

3 Machine the loops just inside the seam allowance at the centre line.

4 Stitch another row to ensure the loops are secure.

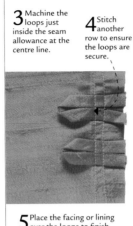

5 Place the facing or lining over the loops to finish.

6 The completed loop will extend from the edge of the fabric.

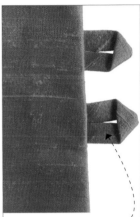

Frog fastenings
LEVEL OF DIFFICULTY ✱✱✱✱

A loop made from a decorative cord is often found on garments with an oriental influence. These so-called frog fastenings can be purchased, although they are straightforward to make. A matching ball button can be made from cord as well, by twisting the cord over and under itself.

MAKING A FROG FASTENER

1 Using a fabric glue to secure the cord, twist the cord into the shape seen in the photograph and stick it on to the edge of the fabric. Hide the ends of the cord under the centre.

Loop to go over the button

2 Secure the cord by stitching along each edge with a small hand stitch. Use a matching thread.

TYING A BALL BUTTON

1 Start by making a loop in the cord.

2 Twist the cord to make another loop over the first loop. The end of the cord goes under the first side.

3 Take the cord over, under, over, and under all the other loops.

4 Pull the two ends to tighten into a ball button.

5 Stitch the ends into a decorative pattern to match the frog fastener.

OTHER FASTENINGS

There are many alternative ways to fasten garments, craft projects, and other items, some of which can be used instead of or in conjunction with other fasteners. These include hooks and eyes, snaps, tape fasteners, and laced eyelets.

Directory of other fastenings

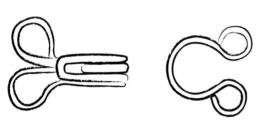

HOOK AND LOOPED EYE

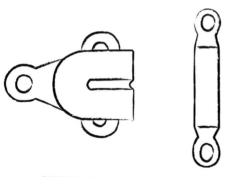

SKIRT/TROUSER HOOK AND EYE

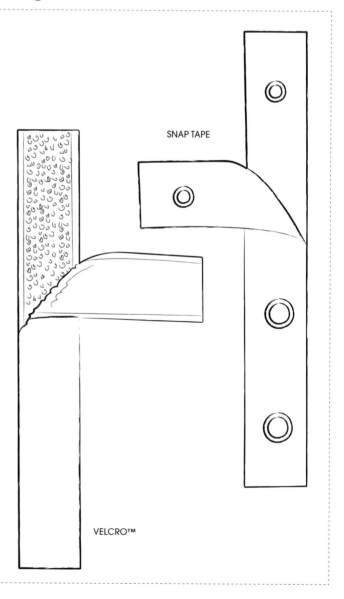

SNAP TAPE

VELCRO™

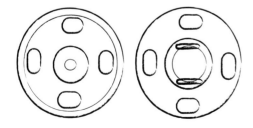

SNAP FASTENER

≪≪ Other fasteners p26   Tacking stitches p89   Hand stitches pp90–91

Hooks and eyes

LEVEL OF DIFFICULTY ∗∗

There are a multitude of different types of hook and eye fasteners. Purchased hooks and eyes are made from metal and are normally silver or black in colour. Different shaped hooks and eyes are used on different garments – large, broad hooks and eyes can be decorative and stitched to show on the outside, while the tiny fasteners are meant to be discreet. A hook that goes into a hand-worked eye produces a neat, close fastening.

ATTACHING HOOKS AND EYES

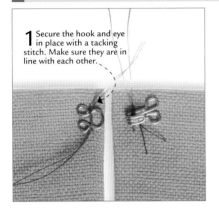

1 Secure the hook and eye in place with a tacking stitch. Make sure they are in line with each other.

2 Stitch around each circular end with a buttonhole stitch.

3 Place a few over-stitches under the hook to stop it moving.

HAND-WORKED EYE

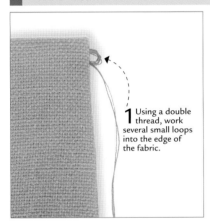

1 Using a double thread, work several small loops into the edge of the fabric.

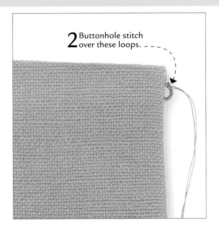

2 Buttonhole stitch over these loops.

3 The completed loop will have a neat row of tight buttonhole stitches.

TROUSER HOOK AND EYE

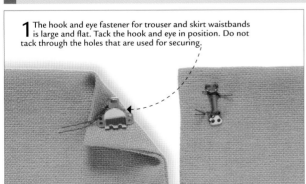

1 The hook and eye fastener for trouser and skirt waistbands is large and flat. Tack the hook and eye in position. Do not tack through the holes that are used for securing.

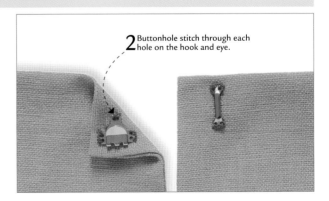

2 Buttonhole stitch through each hole on the hook and eye.

Hook and eye tape p273 ≫

TECHNIQUES

Snaps
LEVEL OF DIFFICULTY **

A snap is a ball and socket fastener that is used to hold two overlapping edges closed. The ball side goes on top and the socket side underneath. Snaps can be round or square and can be made from metal or plastic.

1 Tack the ball and socket halves of the snap in place.

2 Secure permanently using a buttonhole stitch through each hole in the outer edge of the snap half.

3 Remove the tacks.

PLASTIC SNAPS

A plastic snap may be white or clear plastic and is usually square in shape. Stitch in place as for a metal snap (see left).

Tape fasteners
LEVEL OF DIFFICULTY **

In addition to individual small fasteners, there are fastenings in the form of tapes that can be sewn on or stuck on. Velcro™, a hook and loop tape, is available in many colours and types. Sewn-on Velcro™ is ideal for both clothing and soft furnishings, while the stick-on variety can be used to fix curtain pelmets and blinds to battens on windows. Plain cotton tape with snap fasteners is used primarily in soft furnishings. Hook and eye tape is found in underwear or down the front of a shirt or jacket, where it can be very decorative.

VELCRO™

1 Pin the Velcro™ in place. The loop side should be underneath and the hook side on top.

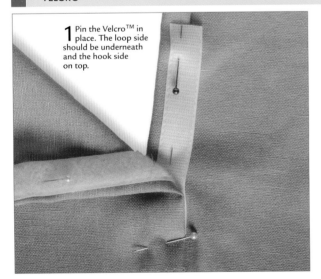

2 Stitch around all the edges.

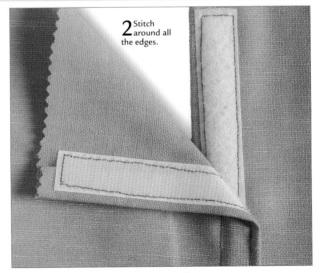

«« Useful extras p21 Boning p27 Tacking stitches p89

SNAP TAPE

1 Pin the tape in position. Make sure that the snaps align.

2 Use the zip foot to stitch around all sides of the tape.

HOOK AND EYE TAPE

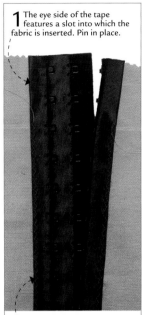

1 The eye side of the tape features a slot into which the fabric is inserted. Pin in place.

2 Stitch along the edge using either a stretch stitch or a narrow 3-step zigzag stitch.

3 Wrap the hook side of the tape over the raw edge of the fabric.

4 Stitch to match up with the eye side.

Eyelets

LEVEL OF DIFFICULTY **✱✱**

An eyelet fastening can be very decorative and is often found on bridal wear and prom dresses. A piece of boning needs to be inserted into the fabric between the edge and the eyelets, to give strength. You will require eyelet pliers to punch the holes and then insert the eyelets.

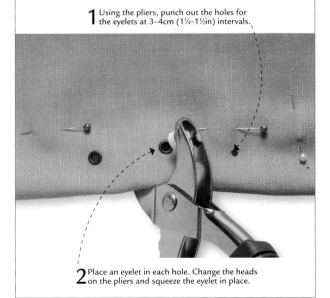

1 Using the pliers, punch out the holes for the eyelets at 3–4cm (1¼–1½in) intervals.

2 Place an eyelet in each hole. Change the heads on the pliers and squeeze the eyelet in place.

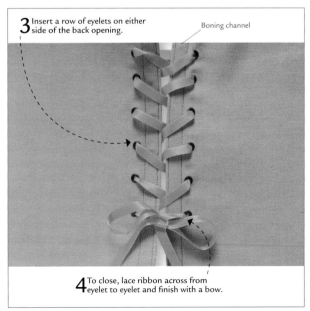

3 Insert a row of eyelets on either side of the back opening.

Boning channel

4 To close, lace ribbon across from eyelet to eyelet and finish with a bow.

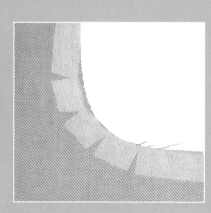

LININGS AND INTERFACINGS

Linings and interfacings are very important in sewing. Interfacings provide shape and structure in a garment or in soft furnishing, while a lining will make any garment more comfortable to wear as well as hiding the inside seams and stitching from view.

INTERLININGS AND INTERFACINGS

Interlinings are similar to interfacings, the difference being that an interfacing is an extra layer of fabric attached in a small area, while an interlining is attached to a whole garment or item. Interlinings and interfacings may be woven, knitted, or non-woven and can be applied with heat (fusible) or sewn-in. Always try to buy products recommended for domestic use. Be sure to cut all these fabrics on the straight of the grain even if they are non-woven.

Interlinings

These are fabrics that cover the inside of an entire garment. They are cut to the same pattern pieces and joined to the main fabric by means of tacking stitches around the edges. The two layers are treated as one during construction.

MUSLIN

This is a cotton muslin. Use it to interline wools and cottons, for jackets, skirts, and dresses.

SILK ORGANZA

An interlining of silk organza will give shape and structure. Use on special-occasion wear and silk fabrics as well as wool in tailored skirts.

DRESS NET

Net is used for bounce and rustle! Use in all special-occasion wear for effect and to prevent creasing.

Interfacings
LEVEL OF DIFFICULTY **

An interfacing may be fusible or non-fusible (sew-in) and is only attached to part of a garment or item. Sections of a garment normally interfaced include the collar and cuffs and the facings. In addition to fusible interfacings, there are also fusible tapes available, which are used to prevent a fabric from stretching and will support edges, and fusible webs that provide stiffening.

NON-FUSIBLE INTERFACINGS
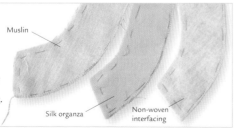
All of these interfacings need to be tacked to the main fabric around the edges prior to construction of the work or seam neatening.

Muslin · Silk organza · Non-woven interfacing

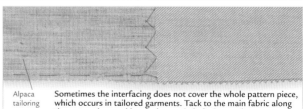
Alpaca tailoring canvas
Sometimes the interfacing does not cover the whole pattern piece, which occurs in tailored garments. Tack to the main fabric along the outer edges and herringbone stitch the inner edges.

« Interfacings pp54–55 Tacking stitches p89 Hand stitches pp90–91 Applying interfacing to a facing p145

FUSIBLE INTERFACINGS

A fusible interfacing is used in the same areas as a sew-in interfacing. To prevent the fusible interfacing from showing on the right side of the work, use pinking shears on the edge of the interfacing.

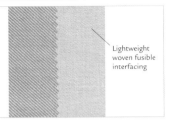

Lightweight woven fusible interfacing

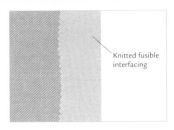

Knitted fusible interfacing

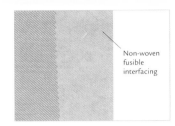

Non-woven fusible interfacing

INTERFACINGS AND INTERLININGS COMBINED

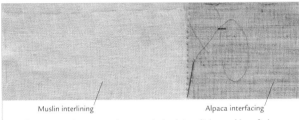

Muslin interlining

Alpaca interfacing

On structured garments there may be both interlining and interfacing. The interlining is applied first and the interfacing is attached on top. Tack around the outside edge and herringbone stitch the inner edges.

FRAME FUSING

Sew-in interfacing, seams removed

Fusible interfacing

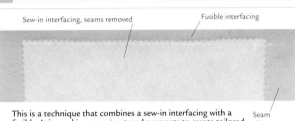

Seam allowance

This is a technique that combines a sew-in interfacing with a fusible. It is used in more structured garments to create tailored collars and cuffs. The fusible interfacing is placed on top to seal the sew-in interfacing in place in the seam allowances.

STRAIGHT FUSIBLE TAPE

Straight grain tape is about 2cm (¾in) wide and has little give in it. Use it to stabilize edges. On some seams it may replace stay stitching. To fuse around curves, snip through the tape at 90 degrees.

BIAS FUSIBLE TAPE

Bias tape has a machined straight stitch through it. As the tape is cut on the bias, it will bend around curves. When fusing the tape in position, the stitching line in the tape should be on the fabric stitching line.

SLOTTED FUSIBLE TAPE

Slotted fusible is wider than other fusible tapes, and has a slotted edge. The tape is used to shape pocket tops and hems on jackets. Fuse in position so that the slots correspond to the foldline in the fabric.

Interfacings, facings, and linings

LEVEL OF DIFFICULTY **

On tailored and more structured garments, the facing will be interfaced and this is then attached to the lining.

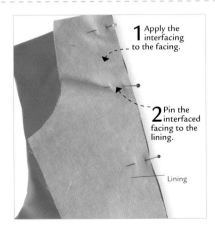

1 Apply the interfacing to the facing.

2 Pin the interfaced facing to the lining.

Lining

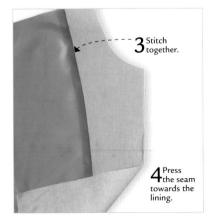

3 Stitch together.

4 Press the seam towards the lining.

Flat collar p161   Reinforced straight belt pp182–183   Cuffs and openings pp202–209 «««

LININGS

A lining is placed inside a garment primarily to make the garment more comfortable to wear – it will prevent the garment from sticking to you. It will also make the garment last longer. Choose a good-quality lining made from rayon or acetate as these fabrics will breathe with your body. Polyester linings can be sticky to wear.

TECHNIQUES

Lining a skirt
LEVEL OF DIFFICULTY ✳✳✳

Cut the lining out the same as the skirt, using the same pattern pieces, and join together, leaving a gap for the zip. Do not stitch in the darts.

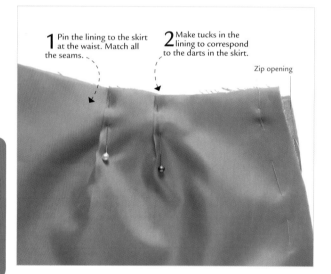

1 Pin the lining to the skirt at the waist. Match all the seams.

2 Make tucks in the lining to correspond to the darts in the skirt.

Zip opening

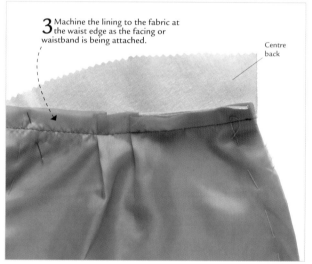

3 Machine the lining to the fabric at the waist edge as the facing or waistband is being attached.

Centre back

Hemming a lining
LEVEL OF DIFFICULTY ✳✳

The lining on a skirt or dress should be slightly shorter – about 4cm (1½in) – than the finished garment, so that the lining does not show when you are walking or sitting.

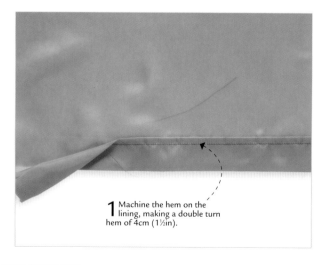

1 Machine the hem on the lining, making a double turn hem of 4cm (1½in).

2 Turn up the hem on the garment and stitch in place. The lining hem should sit about 4cm (1½in) from the hem fold.

《《《 Tacking stitches p89 Hand stitches pp90–91 Stitches made with a machine pp92–93

Lining around a split

LEVEL OF DIFFICULTY ★★★

If there is a split in a hemline, the lining will need to be stitched around it securely. First construct the skirt, with its split finished, corners mitred, and hemmed. Finish the lining hem in the same way.

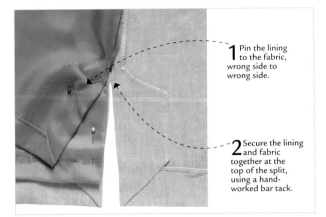

1 Pin the lining to the fabric, wrong side to wrong side.

2 Secure the lining and fabric together at the top of the split, using a hand-worked bar tack.

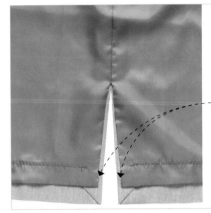

3 Hand stitch the lining to the fabric around both sides of the split. The lining should be level at the hem edge.

Lining a bodice

LEVEL OF DIFFICULTY ★★★

On dresses and fitted tops, a lined bodice is so comfortable and it reduces bulk. The insertion of a lining is done prior to the centre back seam being joined and the side seams being joined.

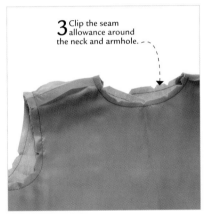

1 Place the lining bodice to the fabric bodice, right side to right side. Match the shoulder seams and the neck and armhole edges.

2 Stitch together around the neck edge and the armhole edge using a 1.5cm (⅝in) seam allowance.

3 Clip the seam allowance around the neck and armhole.

4 To turn through to the right side, pull the back bodice through the shoulder.

5 Repeat for the other shoulder. Press.

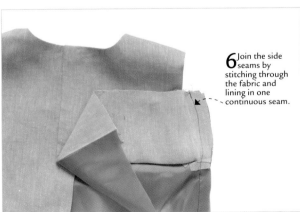

6 Join the side seams by stitching through the fabric and lining in one continuous seam.

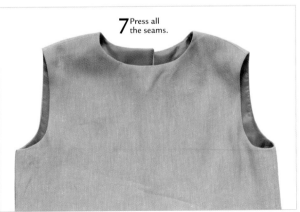

7 Press all the seams.

Reducing seam bulk pp102–103   Attaching a straight waistband p178   Machined hems p232 ««

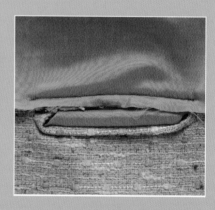

PROFESSIONAL TECHNIQUES

Once you have mastered the basics of sewing it is time to try some more advanced techniques, such as those involved in modern tailoring or boning a bodice for special-occasion wear. None of these techniques is difficult, but they take a little more time and care to execute.

SPEED TAILORING

Speed tailoring is the term given to modern tailoring techniques that use fusible interfacings to give shape and structure to a jacket or coat. Choose woven fusible interfacings and cut on the same grain as the jacket fabric pieces. If possible, use two different interfacings – one a medium weight and one a light weight – in conjunction with fusible tapes to stabilize the edges of the jacket. If interfacings of different weights are not available, choose a lightweight product and use two layers if required in the front of the jacket.

Components of a jacket

LEVEL OF DIFFICULTY ★★★

These photographs show where to place the fusible interfacing on a jacket or coat. Your pattern may be cut differently to this – the front and back may be one piece, not two as shown here, and you may have a two-piece sleeve – but the same principle will apply, of a heavier interfacing at the front and a lighter one at the back, with reinforcement through the shoulder.

FRONT

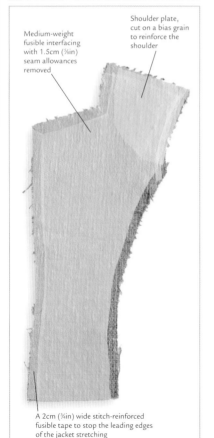

Medium-weight fusible interfacing with 1.5cm (⅜in) seam allowances removed

Shoulder plate, cut on a bias grain to reinforce the shoulder

A 2cm (¾in) wide stitch-reinforced fusible tape to stop the leading edges of the jacket stretching

SIDE FRONT

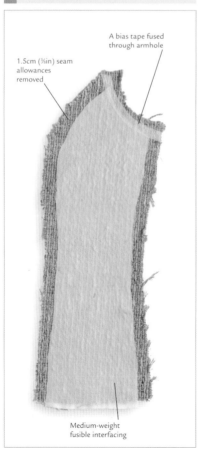

1.5cm (⅜in) seam allowances removed

A bias tape fused through armhole

Medium-weight fusible interfacing

SIDE BACK

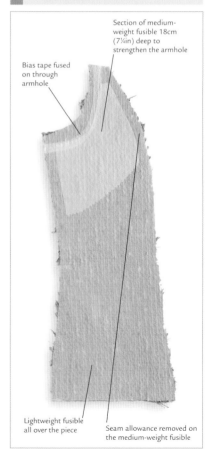

Bias tape fused on through armhole

Section of medium-weight fusible 18cm (7¼in) deep to strengthen the armhole

Lightweight fusible all over the piece

Seam allowance removed on the medium-weight fusible

TECHNIQUES

BACK

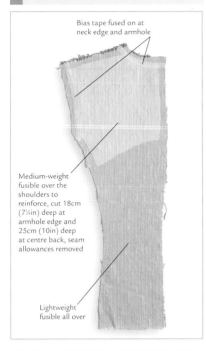

Bias tape fused on at neck edge and armhole

Medium-weight fusible over the shoulders to reinforce, cut 18cm (7¼in) deep at armhole edge and 25cm (10in) deep at centre back, seam allowances removed

Lightweight fusible all over

SLEEVE

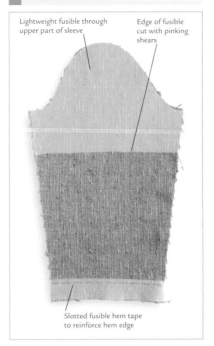

Lightweight fusible through upper part of sleeve

Edge of fusible cut with pinking shears

Slotted fusible hem tape to reinforce hem edge

FRONT FACING

Lightweight fusible all over

UPPER COLLAR

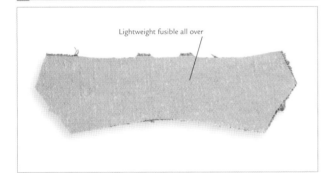

Lightweight fusible all over

UNDER COLLAR

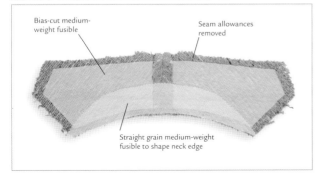

Bias-cut medium-weight fusible

Seam allowances removed

Straight grain medium-weight fusible to shape neck edge

FINISHED JACKET

Jetted pocket
LEVEL OF DIFFICULTY ✴✴✴✴

This is a professional pocket found on many suit jackets. Great care has to be taken when making this pocket because there is no flap for it to hide behind!

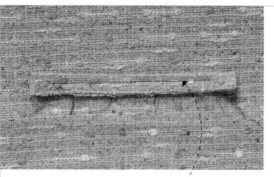

1 Cut out the welts (the strips that make the edges of the pocket). Apply lightweight fusible interfacing to them on the wrong side.

2 Transfer the marks from the pattern using tailor's tacks.

3 Press in half, wrong side to wrong side.

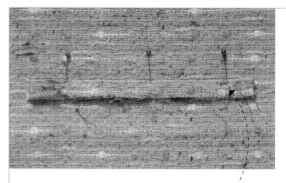

4 Start with the upper welt. Place it to the right side of the jacket front. The raw edge of the welt is towards the hem. Match the tailor's tacks. Pin in place.

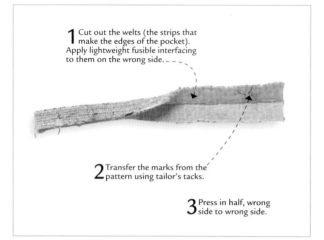

5 Machine along the centre of the welt. Stitch between the tailor's tacks only.

6 Position the lower welt on the jacket, placing the raw edges together.

7 Stitch through the centre of the lower welt. Ensure both rows of stitching are exactly the same length.

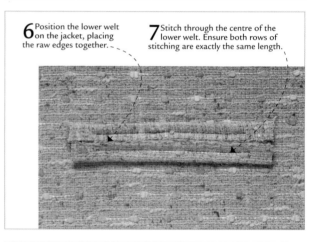

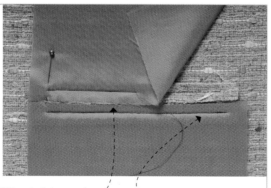

8 Place the lining over the welts, raw edges to the centre. Pin to secure.

9 Stitch the lining in place over the stitching line of the welts – you can feel the indentation of welt stitching.

10 Slash through the jacket fabric between the welts (see Jetted pocket with flap, pages 220–221).

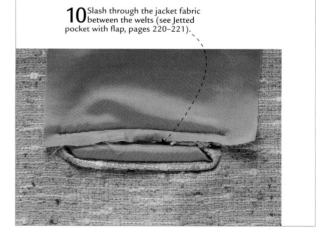

11 Push the lining and the ends of the welts through to the back.

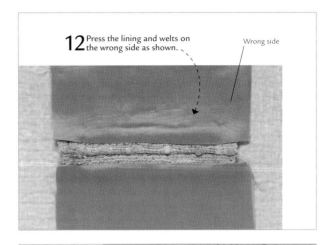

12 Press the lining and welts on the wrong side as shown.

Wrong side

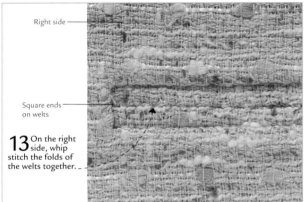

Right side

Square ends on welts

13 On the right side, whip stitch the folds of the welts together.

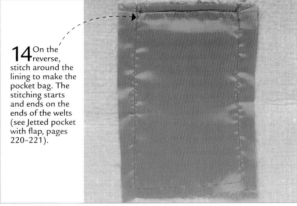

14 On the reverse, stitch around the lining to make the pocket bag. The stitching starts and ends on the ends of the welts (see Jetted pocket with flap, pages 220–221).

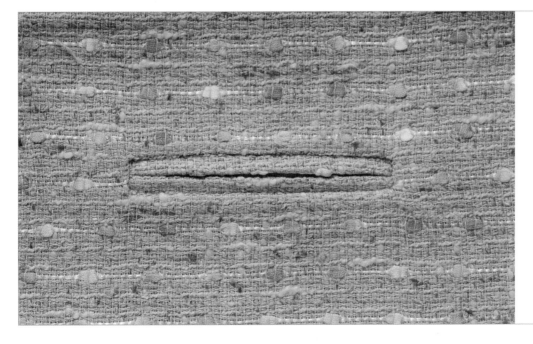

15 Remove the whip stitches from across the pocket opening.

TECHNIQUES

Collar application

LEVEL OF DIFFICULTY ★★★★

A notched collar is a sign of a tailored jacket. This type of collar consists of an upper and under collar, and a facing that folds back to form the rever on either side. Careful stitching and accurate marking are required.

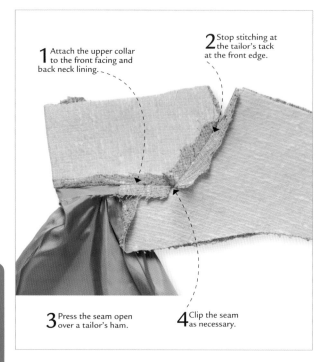

1 Attach the upper collar to the front facing and back neck lining.

2 Stop stitching at the tailor's tack at the front edge.

3 Press the seam open over a tailor's ham.

4 Clip the seam as necessary.

5 Join the under collar to the jacket front and back.

6 Stop stitching at the tailor's tack at the front edge.

7 Press the seam open. Clip as necessary.

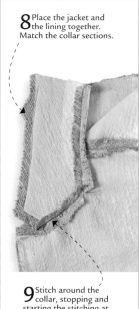

8 Place the jacket and the lining together. Match the collar sections.

9 Stitch around the collar, stopping and starting the stitching at the tailor's tacks at the front edge.

10 Stitch the front facing to the jacket front. Start stitching at the tailor's tack at the front edge. The stitching line from the collar and the stitching line from the facing should line up but not cross each other.

11 Layer the seam.

12 On the inside, herringbone stitch the neck seams together.

13 Turn the collar and rever to the right side.

14 Press using a steam iron and cloth. Roll the seam towards the back of the garment so that it does not show on the right side.

⟪⟪ Pressing aids pp28–29 Fusible interfacings p54 Pattern marking pp82–83 Hand stitches pp90–91

Set-in sleeve

LEVEL OF DIFFICULTY ★★★

On a tailored jacket, the sleeve needs to be set in to have a rounded sleeve head, which is created with polyester wadding. The sleeve head will ensure that the sleeve hangs perfectly.

1 Make up the sleeve.

2 Cut a piece of polyester wadding to fit the sleeve head. The wadding should be approx 5cm (2in) deep at the centre. Pin in place.

3 Insert two rows of gather (ease) stitches to attach the wadding to the sleeve.

4 Insert the sleeve into the armhole, right side to right side. Pin in place.

5 Pull up the ease stitches to fit. The sleeve head will absorb the fullness.

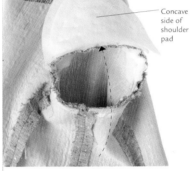

6 Machine in place. Make a second row of machining close to the first stitching.

7 The shoulder pad can now be inserted. The back slope of the shoulder pad is longer than the front slope. The concave side will face the jacket lining.

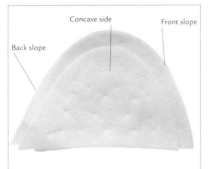

Back slope
Concave side
Front slope

8 Attach the shoulder pad at the edge of the sleeve seam using a firm running stitch.

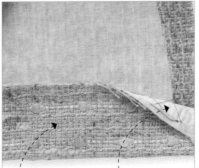

Concave side of shoulder pad

9 On the right side, the finished sleeve has a rounded sleeve head.

Hem and lining

LEVEL OF DIFFICULTY ★★★

When making a jacket, the jacket hem is turned up first and then the lining is hemmed. The jacket hem needs to be reinforced first with a slotted fusible hem tape. Make sure that the hem edge is parallel to the ground.

3 Bring the lining down over the jacket hem. Turn up the hem of the lining so that it is level to the jacket hem, then push up to 2cm (¾in) from the hem edge. At the facing edge, the lining is level with the hem edge. Pin.

1 Turn up the hem on the jacket by about 4cm (1½in). Pin to secure.

2 Roll back the edge of the hem and herringbone stitch in place.

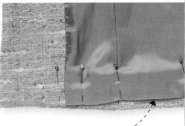

4 Use a slip hem stitch to secure the lining in place.

Reducing seam bulk pp102–103 How to make and fit gathers p127 Inserting a set-in sleeve p191 Interfacings pp276–277 ◀◀◀

BONED BODICES

A strapless bodice will require boning inserted to prevent the bodice from falling down. The boning will also give extra structure to the bodice and prevent wrinkles. Boning can be a simple process, or more complex using interfacings for additional structure and shape.

Couture boned bodice

LEVEL OF DIFFICULTY ★★★★

A couture boned bodice is the more complicated of the two methods of bodice construction, but it is well worth the extra work involved as the finished result is wrinkle-free and self-supporting. This technique can be used for bridal bodices and special-occasion wear.

COMPONENTS OF THE BODICE

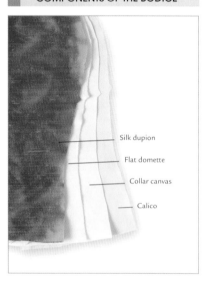

- Silk dupion
- Flat domette
- Collar canvas
- Calico

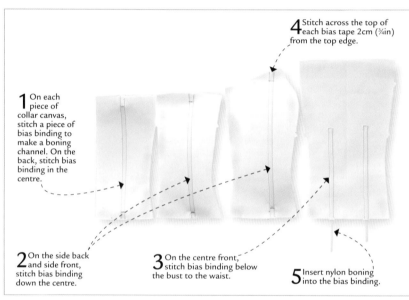

1 On each piece of collar canvas, stitch a piece of bias binding to make a boning channel. On the back, stitch bias binding in the centre.

2 On the side back and side front, stitch bias binding down the centre.

3 On the centre front, stitch bias binding below the bust to the waist.

4 Stitch across the top of each bias tape 2cm (¾in) from the top edge.

5 Insert nylon boning into the bias binding.

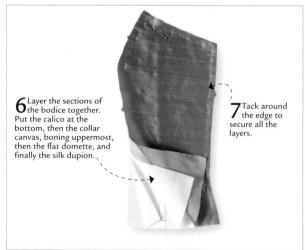

6 Layer the sections of the bodice together. Put the calico at the bottom, then the collar canvas, boning uppermost, then the flat domette, and finally the silk dupion.

7 Tack around the edge to secure all the layers.

8 Place the bodice sections together, right side to right side. Stitch using a 1.5cm (⅝in) seam allowance.

9 Trim the collar canvas from the seam allowance.

TECHNIQUES

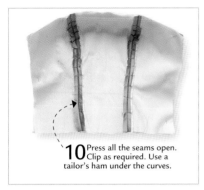

10 Press all the seams open. Clip as required. Use a tailor's ham under the curves.

11 After pressing, the princess seams at the front will be smoothly tapered to the waist.

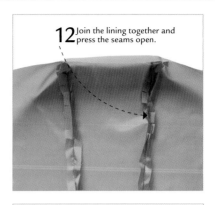

12 Join the lining together and press the seams open.

13 Pin the lining to the bodice around the top edge and down the centre back. Match all vertical seam allowances.

14 Clip and layer the seam, then turn to the right side. Press.

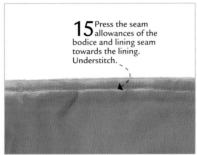

15 Press the seam allowances of the bodice and lining seam towards the lining. Understitch.

18 The completed bodice will stand on its own!

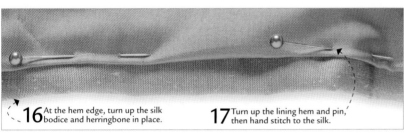

16 At the hem edge, turn up the silk bodice and herringbone in place.

17 Turn up the lining hem and pin, then hand stitch to the silk.

A basic boning technique

LEVEL OF DIFFICULTY ★★★

For a simpler bodice on a dress or as a bodice on its own, this is a lightweight, quick technique.

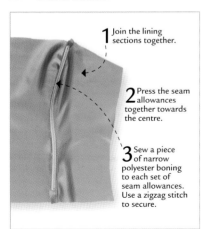

1 Join the lining sections together.

2 Press the seam allowances together towards the centre.

3 Sew a piece of narrow polyester boning to each set of seam allowances. Use a zigzag stitch to secure.

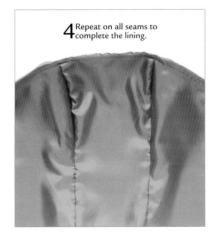

4 Repeat on all seams to complete the lining.

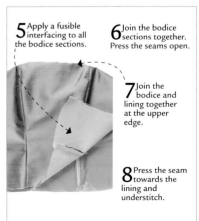

5 Apply a fusible interfacing to all the bodice sections.

6 Join the bodice sections together. Press the seams open.

7 Join the bodice and lining together at the upper edge.

8 Press the seam towards the lining and understitch.

Stitches made with a machine pp92–93   Reducing seam bulk pp102–103   Stitch finishes p103   Lining a bodice p279 ≪≪

APPLIQUÉ AND QUILTING

Simple finishing touches can be used to good effect on many items. The term appliqué applies to one fabric being stitched to another in a decorative manner. The fabric to be appliquéd must be interfaced to support the fabric that is to be attached. Appliqué can be drawn by hand, then cut and stitched down, or it can be created by a computer pattern on the embroidery machine. The embroidery machine can also be used to create quilting, or this can be done by hand or with a sewing machine.

Hand-drawn appliqué
LEVEL OF DIFFICULTY ★★★

This technique involves drawing the chosen design on to a piece of double-sided fusible web, after which the design is fused in place on fabric prior to being stitched.

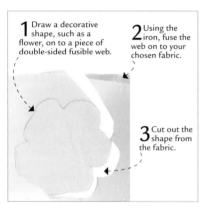

1 Draw a decorative shape, such as a flower, on to a piece of double-sided fusible web.

2 Using the iron, fuse the web on to your chosen fabric.

3 Cut out the shape from the fabric.

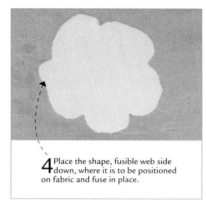

4 Place the shape, fusible web side down, where it is to be positioned on fabric and fuse in place.

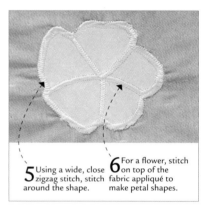

5 Using a wide, close zigzag stitch, stitch around the shape.

6 For a flower, stitch on top of the fabric appliqué to make petal shapes.

Machine appliqué
LEVEL OF DIFFICULTY ★★

There are designs available for appliqué if you have an embroidery machine. You will need to use a special fusible embroidery backer on both the fabric for the appliqué and the base fabric.

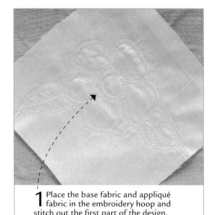

1 Place the base fabric and appliqué fabric in the embroidery hoop and stitch out the first part of the design.

2 Trim the appliqué fabric back to the stitching lines.

3 Complete the computerized embroidery.

Quilting

LEVEL OF DIFFICULTY **

This is a technique that involves stitching through two layers of fabric, one of which is a wadding. The stitching sinks into the wadding, creating a padded effect. Quilting can be done by hand, with a sewing machine, or using computerized embroidery.

COMPONENTS OF QUILTING

Top fabric

Wadding

HORIZONTAL QUILTING

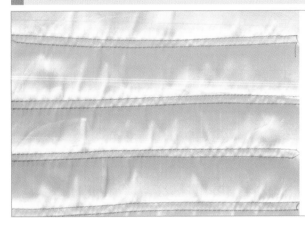

Tack the wadding and top fabric together. Stitch double lines with spaces between. Use a stitch length of 4.0 on your machine.

DIAMOND QUILTING

1 Diagonally tack the wadding and top fabric together.

2 Set the machine to a stitch length of 4.0, with the needle on the one side of the foot. Stitch rows of machining diagonally across. Use the width of the machine foot as a guide to keep the rows parallel.

3 Stitch parallel rows in the opposite diagonal directions, to create diamond shapes.

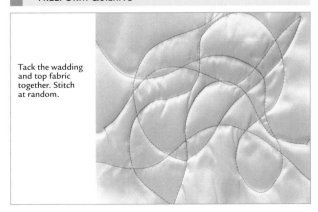

FREEFORM QUILTING

Tack the wadding and top fabric together. Stitch at random.

COMPUTERIZED QUILTING

Tack the wadding and top fabric together, then stitch on a quilted pattern with the embroidery machine.

Stitches made with a machine pp92–93   Interfacings pp276–277 «««

Roses and bows

LEVEL OF DIFFICULTY **

On special-occasion wear a rose can add a superb finishing touch. When the raw edges of a rose are exposed, as in version 2 below, it also looks great made in tweed and suiting fabrics, to add a decorative finish to a tailored jacket. A bow that is permanently fixed in place is a beautiful embellishment on bridal wear.

ROSE VERSION 1

1 Cut a bias strip 10cm (4in) wide. Fold in half lengthways, wrong side to wrong side.

Angled end

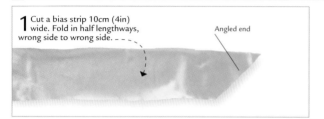

2 Pin the raw edges together.

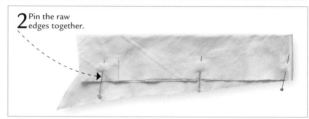

3 Insert two rows of gather stitches at the raw edge – one row at 1cm (⅜in) from the edge and the other row at 1.3cm (½in).

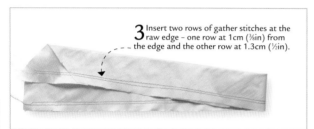

4 Pull up the gathers, grouping them together and leaving spaces between the groups. The groups and spaces will give the impression of petals.

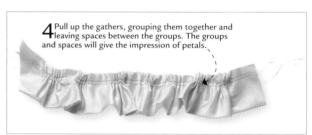

5 Hold the lower edge of one end in your left hand and loosely wrap the strip around.

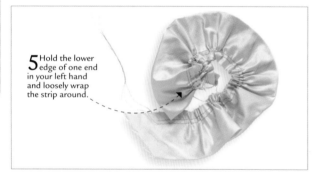

6 When you have a rose shape, tuck any raw edges that show into the base.

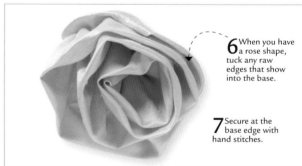

7 Secure at the base edge with hand stitches.

ROSE VERSION 2

1 Cut a bias strip 10cm (4in) wide.

2 Insert two rows of gather stitches along the centre of the strip. Leave a gap of 3mm (⅛in) between the rows of stitching.

3 Pull up the gathers into groups and spaces (see step 4 above).

4 The groups and spaces will pull up to give a diagonal effect. Fold in half along the stitching lines.

5 Hold the end of the gathers in your left hand and wrap the strip around loosely.

6 Secure at the base with hand stitches. Although the edge is raw, fraying is minimal as the strip has been bias-cut.

BOW

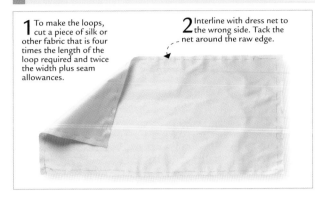

1 To make the loops, cut a piece of silk or other fabric that is four times the length of the loop required and twice the width plus seam allowances.

2 Interline with dress net to the wrong side. Tack the net around the raw edge.

3 Fold in half, right side to right side. Stitch along the raw edge leaving a 1.5cm (⅝in) seam allowance.

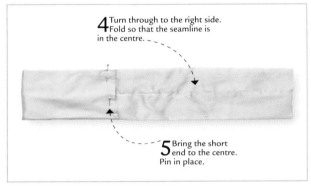

4 Turn through to the right side. Fold so that the seamline is in the centre.

5 Bring the short end to the centre. Pin in place.

6 Tack through the centre, using double thread.

7 Pull along the tacking stitches to gather the centre.

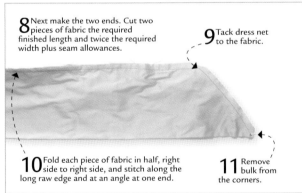

8 Next make the two ends. Cut two pieces of fabric the required finished length and twice the required width plus seam allowances.

9 Tack dress net to the fabric.

10 Fold each piece of fabric in half, right side to right side, and stitch along the long raw edge and at an angle at one end.

11 Remove bulk from the corners.

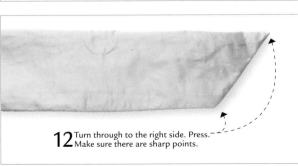

12 Turn through to the right side. Press. Make sure there are sharp points.

13 To assemble the bow, wrap a piece of fabric around the gathered centre of the loops and stitch in place by hand.

14 Scrunch the raw ends of the ends together and hand stitch behind the loop.

INTERLINING CURTAINS

A lined curtain that is also interlined will not only hang beautifully but will also be warm and keep out any draughts. This technique is for hand-sewn curtains and requires a large, flat table to work on. There are different weights of interlining available.

Lined and interlined curtains

LEVEL OF DIFFICULTY ★★★

Preparation and accurate measuring of the window and the curtain fabric will ensure that this technique works every time. Choose a thicker quality curtain lining for interlined curtains because it will hang better.

Curtain fabric   Interlining   Lining

1 Cut out the fabric, lining, and interlining.

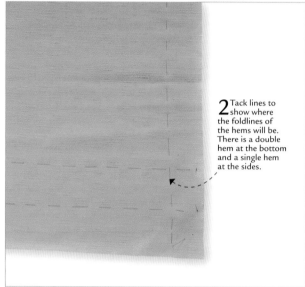

2 Tack lines to show where the foldlines of the hems will be. There is a double hem at the bottom and a single hem at the sides.

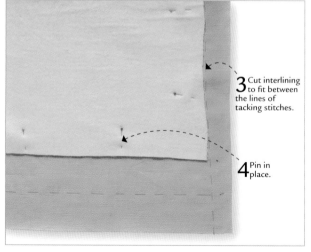

3 Cut interlining to fit between the lines of tacking stitches.

4 Pin in place.

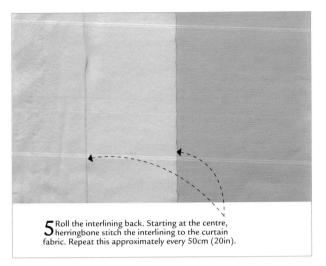

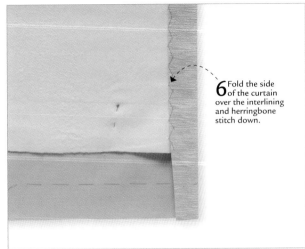

5 Roll the interlining back. Starting at the centre, herringbone stitch the interlining to the curtain fabric. Repeat this approximately every 50cm (20in).

6 Fold the side of the curtain over the interlining and herringbone stitch down.

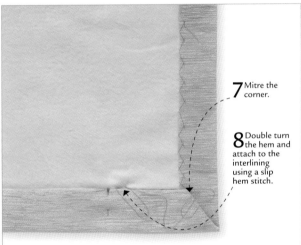

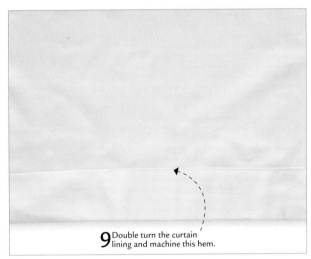

7 Mitre the corner.

8 Double turn the hem and attach to the interlining using a slip hem stitch.

9 Double turn the curtain lining and machine this hem.

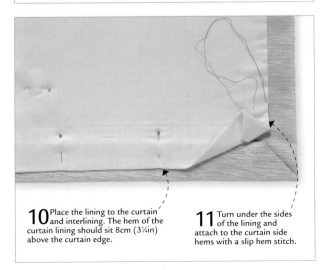

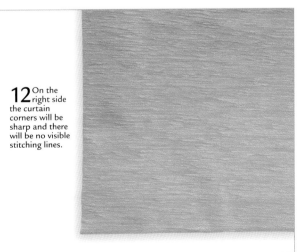

10 Place the lining to the curtain and interlining. The hem of the curtain lining should sit 8cm (3¼in) above the curtain edge.

11 Turn under the sides of the lining and attach to the curtain side hems with a slip hem stitch.

12 On the right side the curtain corners will be sharp and there will be no visible stitching lines.

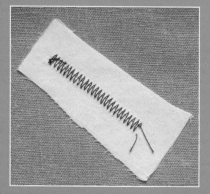

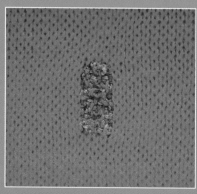

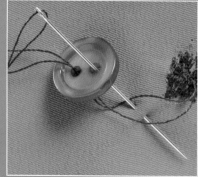

MENDING

Mending can preserve the life of your favourite clothes or furnishings. As a golden rule, always try to fix lost buttons or dropped hems as soon as possible. Here you will find more complex mending techniques for split seams, holes, tears, and broken zips.

TECHNIQUES

MENDING

Repairing a tear in fabric, patching a worn area, or fixing a zip or a buttonhole can add extra life to a garment or an item of soft furnishing. Repairs like these may seem tedious, but they are very easy to do and well worthwhile. For some of the mending techniques shown here, a contrast colour thread has been used so that the stitching can be seen clearly. However, when making a repair, be sure to use a matching thread.

Unpicking stitches

LEVEL OF DIFFICULTY **

All repairs involve unpicking stitches. This must be done carefully to avoid damaging the fabric because the fabric will have to be restitched. There are three ways you can unpick stitches.

SMALL SCISSORS

Pull the fabric apart and, using very small, sharply pointed scissors, snip through the stitches that have been exposed.

SEAM RIPPER

Slide a seam ripper carefully under a stitch and cut it. Cut through every fourth or fifth stitch, and the seam will unravel easily.

PIN AND SCISSORS

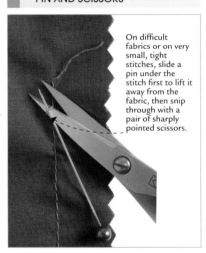

On difficult fabrics or on very small, tight stitches, slide a pin under the stitch first to lift it away from the fabric, then snip through with a pair of sharply pointed scissors.

Darning a hole

LEVEL OF DIFFICULTY **

If you accidentally catch a piece of jewellery in a sweater or other knitted garment, it may make a small hole. Or a moth could cause this. It is worth darning the hole, especially if the sweater was expensive or is a favourite. Holes can also occur in the heels of socks and these can be darned in the same way.

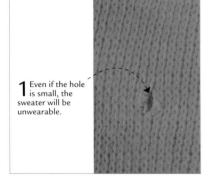

1 Even if the hole is small, the sweater will be unwearable.

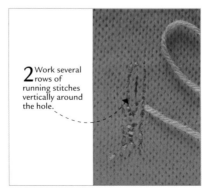

2 Work several rows of running stitches vertically around the hole.

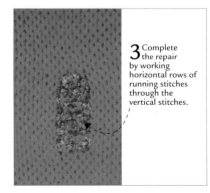

3 Complete the repair by working horizontal rows of running stitches through the vertical stitches.

TECHNIQUES

Repairing fabric under a button

LEVEL OF DIFFICULTY **

A button under strain can sometimes pull off a garment. If this happens, a hole will be made in the fabric, which needs fixing before a new button can be stitched on.

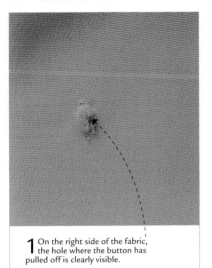

1 On the right side of the fabric, the hole where the button has pulled off is clearly visible.

2 Turn to the wrong side and apply a patch of fusible interfacing over the hole.

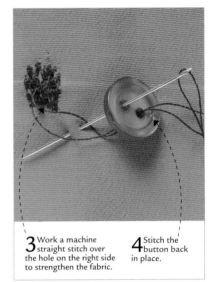

3 Work a machine straight stitch over the hole on the right side to strengthen the fabric.

4 Stitch the button back in place.

Repairing a damaged buttonhole

LEVEL OF DIFFICULTY **

A buttonhole can sometimes rip at the end, or the stitching on the buttonhole can come unravelled. When repairing, use a thread that matches the fabric so the repair will be invisible.

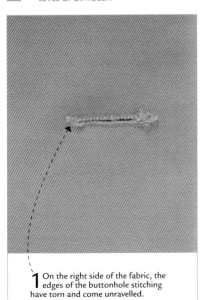

1 On the right side of the fabric, the edges of the buttonhole stitching have torn and come unravelled.

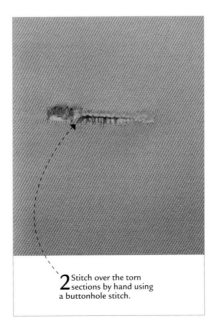

2 Stitch over the torn sections by hand using a buttonhole stitch.

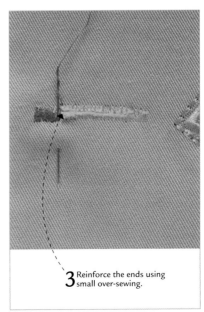

3 Reinforce the ends using small over-sewing.

Mending a split in a seam

LEVEL OF DIFFICULTY **

A split seam can be very quickly remedied with the help of some fusible mending tape and new stitching.

1 Where the split has occurred in the seam, unpick the stitching on either side. Press the fabric back into shape.

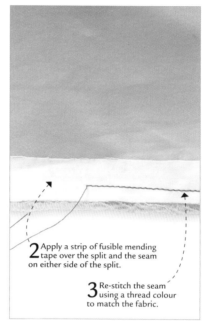

2 Apply a strip of fusible mending tape over the split and the seam on either side of the split.

3 Re-stitch the seam using a thread colour to match the fabric.

4 On the other side, the repair will not be visible.

Mending a tear with a fusible

LEVEL OF DIFFICULTY *

Tears easily happen to clothing, especially children's wear, and they may occur on soft furnishings too. There are several methods for mending a tear. Most use a fusible patch of some kind, which may or may not be seen on the front, but you can also use a patch cut from matching fabric (see page 302).

FUSIBLE APPLIQUÉ PATCH

1 Place a fusible appliqué over the tear and pin in place.

2 Apply heat to fuse the decorative patch in place.

VISIBLE FUSED PATCH

1 Measure the tear in the fabric.

2 Cut a piece of fusible mending fabric that is slightly longer and wider than the tear.

3 Fuse the fabric in place on the right side.

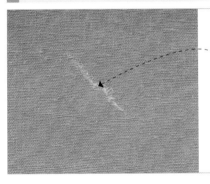

4 Using a zigzag stitch, machine all around the edge of the patch on the right side of the work.

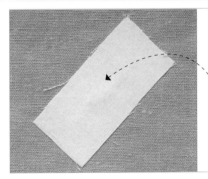

5 On the reverse side of the fabric, the tear will be firmly stuck to the mending patch, which will prevent the tear getting any bigger.

FUSED PATCH ON THE WRONG SIDE

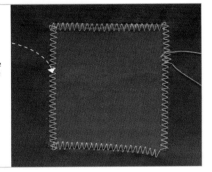

1 Measure the length of the tear. Cut a piece of fusible mending tape to fit.

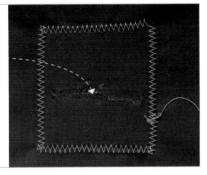

2 On the wrong side of the fabric, fuse the mending tape over the tear.

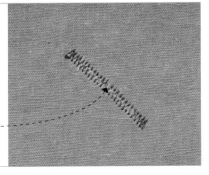

3 Using a zigzag stitch, width 5.0 and length 0.5, stitch over the tear, working from the right side.

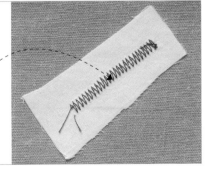

4 On the wrong side, the zigzag stitching will have gone through the fusible tape.

Unpicking stitches p298 Interfacings pp276–277 ◀◀◀

Mending a tear with a matching patch

On a patterned fabric, such as a check or a stripe, it is possible to mend a tear almost invisibly by using a patch that matches the pattern.

LEVEL OF DIFFICULTY **

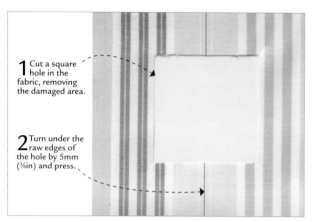

1 Cut a square hole in the fabric, removing the damaged area.

2 Turn under the raw edges of the hole by 5mm (⅜in) and press.

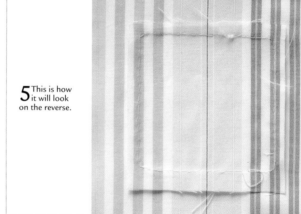

3 Cut a piece of fabric from matching fabric to fill the hole (this fabric could be taken from the hem). Match the stripes or checks. Tack in place.

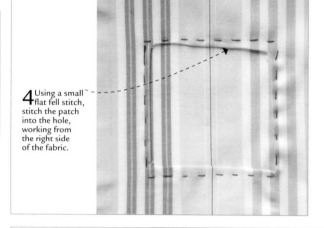

4 Using a small flat fell stitch, stitch the patch into the hole, working from the right side of the fabric.

5 This is how it will look on the reverse.

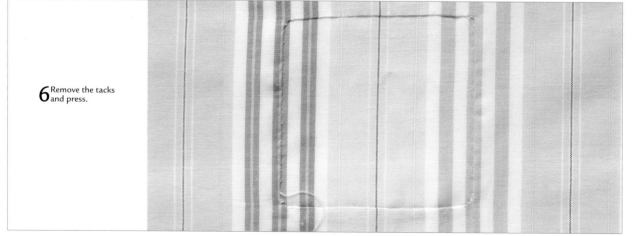

6 Remove the tacks and press.

Repairing or replacing elastic

LEVEL OF DIFFICULTY *

Elastic can frequently come unstitched inside the waistband, or it may lose its stretch and require replacing. Here is the simple way to re-insert elastic or insert new elastic.

1 Carefully unpick a seam in the elastic casing.

Old elastic

2 Pull the old elastic through the gap in the seam and cut through it.

3 Attach new elastic to the old with a safety pin. Use the old elastic to pull the new elastic through inside the casing.

4 Secure the ends on the new elastic.

5 Hand stitch the unpicked seam back together.

Repairing a broken zip

LEVEL OF DIFFICULTY **

Zips can break if they come under too much strain. Sometimes the zip has to be removed completely and a new zip inserted. However, if only a few teeth have been broken far enough down so that the zip can still be opened sufficiently, you can make this repair.

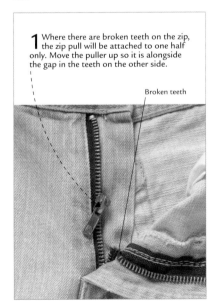

1 Where there are broken teeth on the zip, the zip pull will be attached to one half only. Move the puller up so it is alongside the gap in the teeth on the other side.

Broken teeth

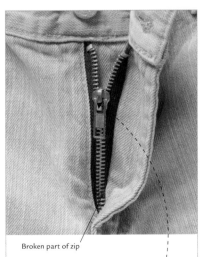

Broken part of zip

2 Carefully feed the teeth on the broken side into the top of the zip.

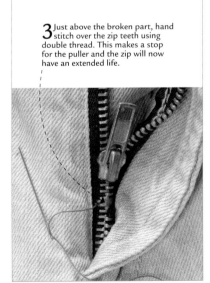

3 Just above the broken part, hand stitch over the zip teeth using double thread. This makes a stop for the puller and the zip will now have an extended life.

Zips pp250–257 Unpicking stitches p298 ⋘

PROJECTS

DRAWSTRING BAG

This pretty drawstring bag is suitable for evening wear and special occasions, especially for a bride or flower girl. Try using silk or satin for this – I have used two slightly different colours as the fabrics will provide lots of contrasting shadows. However, it would look very different if made in a floral cotton. The size of the bag can easily be adjusted by cutting the initial pattern larger or smaller.

TECHNIQUES INVOLVED

PATTERN MARKING See pages 82–83.

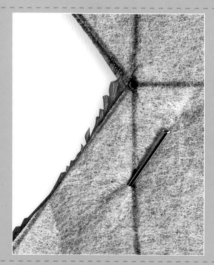

HOW TO APPLY A FUSIBLE INTERFACING
See page 54.

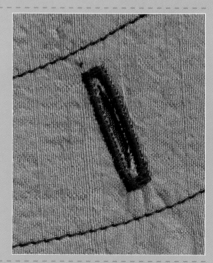

BUTTONHOLES See pages 263–264.

LEVEL OF DIFFICULTY ★★★★★

SHOPPING LIST

1.5m x 60cm (60 x 24in)
  non-woven fusible interfacing
75 x 115cm (30 x 46in) silk dupion
75 x 115cm (30 x 46in) contrast
  silk dupion
1 reel thread
Beads, to decorate
2m (80in) organza or satin
  ribbon, 12–15mm (½–⅝in) wide

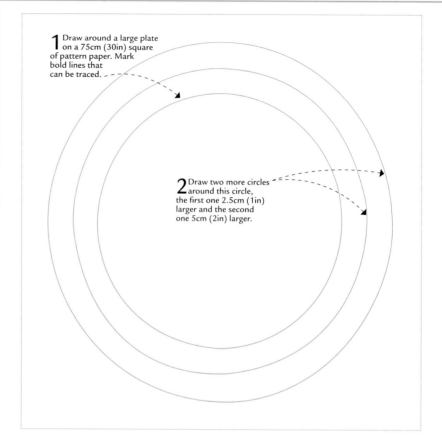

1 Draw around a large plate on a 75cm (30in) square of pattern paper. Mark bold lines that can be traced.

2 Draw two more circles around this circle, the first one 2.5cm (1in) larger and the second one 5cm (2in) larger.

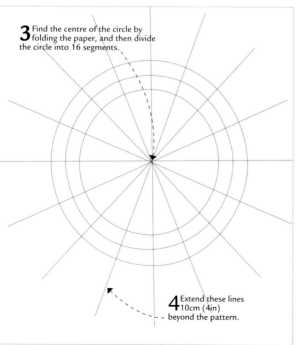

3 Find the centre of the circle by folding the paper, and then divide the circle into 16 segments.

4 Extend these lines 10cm (4in) beyond the pattern.

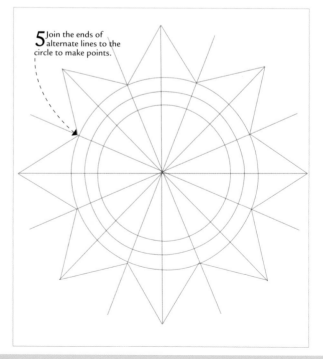

5 Join the ends of alternate lines to the circle to make points.

6 This is your pattern. Cut out carefully.

7 Cut the interfacing in half. Take one piece of interfacing and place it over the paper pattern. Using a soft pencil or water-soluble marker pen, trace the pattern on to the interfacing.

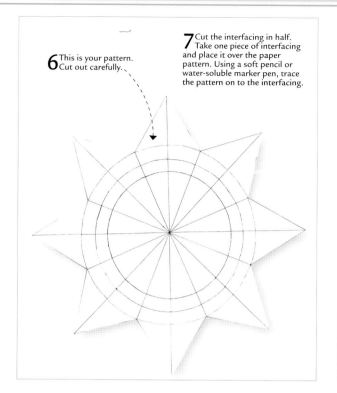

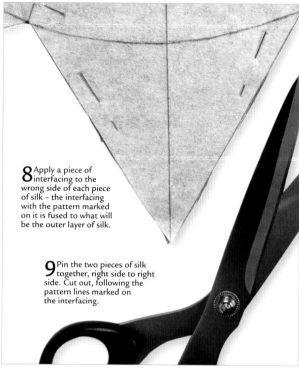

8 Apply a piece of interfacing to the wrong side of each piece of silk – the interfacing with the pattern marked on it is fused to what will be the outer layer of silk.

9 Pin the two pieces of silk together, right side to right side. Cut out, following the pattern lines marked on the interfacing.

10 Trace tack the two inner circles on the pattern. Cut through the thread loops.

11 Carefully separate the two pieces of silk, snipping through the trace tackings.

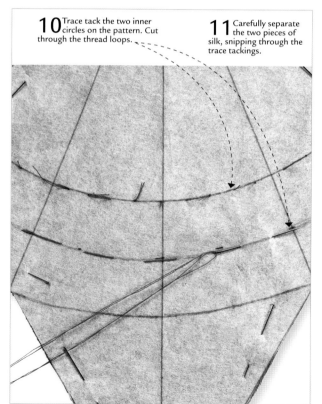

12 On the interfaced side of the outer layer of silk, mark the position of the two buttonholes. They should be on opposite sides of the bag, between the two trace-tacked lines.

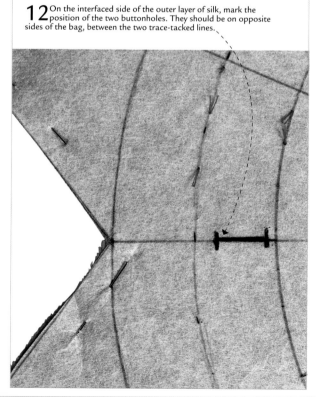

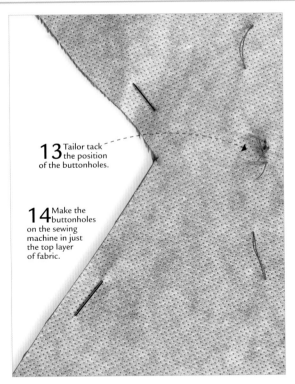

13 Tailor tack the position of the buttonholes.

14 Make the buttonholes on the sewing machine in just the top layer of fabric.

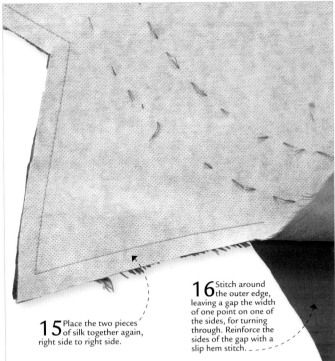

15 Place the two pieces of silk together again, right side to right side.

16 Stitch around the outer edge, leaving a gap the width of one point on one of the sides, for turning through. Reinforce the sides of the gap with a slip hem stitch.

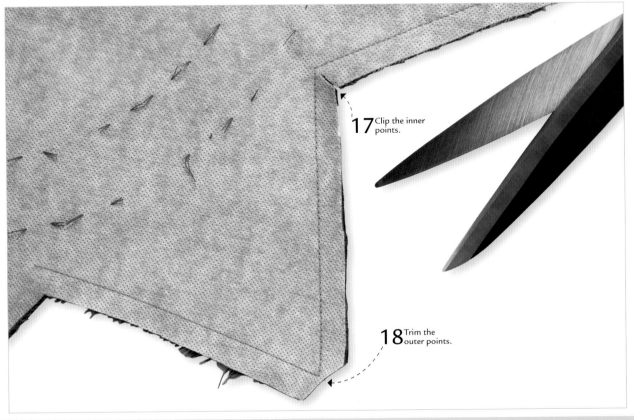

17 Clip the inner points.

18 Trim the outer points.

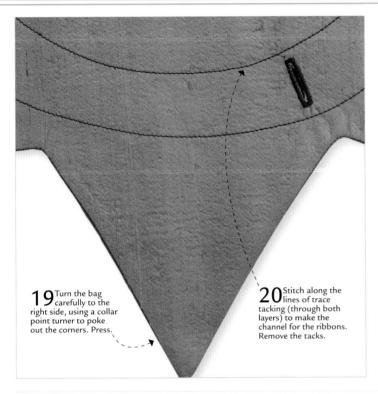

19 Turn the bag carefully to the right side, using a collar point turner to poke out the corners. Press.

20 Stitch along the lines of trace tacking (through both layers) to make the channel for the ribbons. Remove the tacks.

21 Embellish each point by sewing on a few beads.

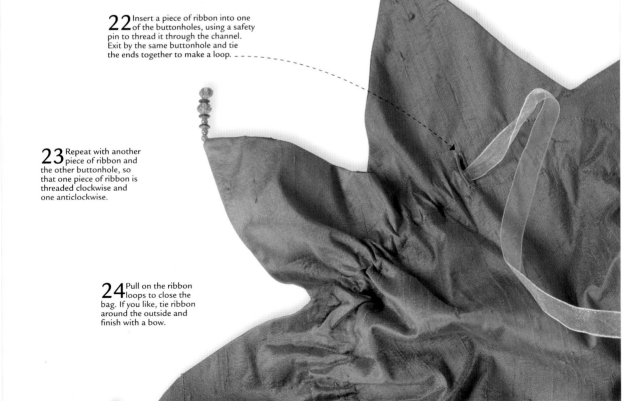

22 Insert a piece of ribbon into one of the buttonholes, using a safety pin to thread it through the channel. Exit by the same buttonhole and tie the ends together to make a loop.

23 Repeat with another piece of ribbon and the other buttonhole, so that one piece of ribbon is threaded clockwise and one anticlockwise.

24 Pull on the ribbon loops to close the bag. If you like, tie ribbon around the outside and finish with a bow.

Stitches made with a machine pp92–93 ≪≪

BOOK COVER

Matching stationery can make office work far more enjoyable, so why not try covering a notebook or diary? A cover will make the book easy to find, as well as protecting the corners. It looks great in a vibrant silk dupion but works just as well with other fabrics, such as cotton. For a finishing touch, decorate the cover with beads or ribbon.

TECHNIQUES INVOLVED

HOW TO APPLY A FUSIBLE INTERFACING See page 54.

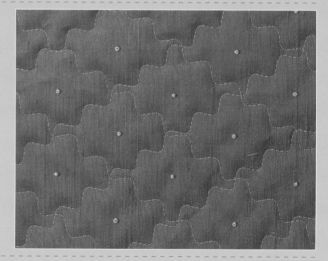

QUILTING See page 291.

LEVEL OF DIFFICULTY ***

SHOPPING LIST For an A4 notebook:

40 x 115cm (16 x 46in) fabric, such as silk dupion or cotton

40 x 90cm (16 x 36in) heavy fusible interfacing

40 x 90cm (16 x 36in) polyester wadding about 6mm (¼in) thick

40 x 115cm (16 x 46in) tear-away embroidery backing

40 x 115cm (16 x 46in) contrast lining

1 reel machine embroidery thread

40 x 115cm (16 x 46in) double-sided fusible web

Seed beads, to decorate

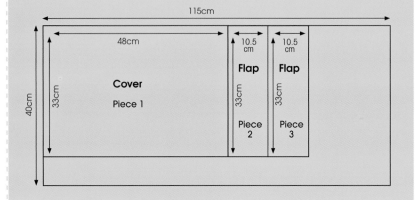

1 Apply a fusible interfacing to the wrong side of the fabric.

2 Cut out fabric and lining according to the cutting diagram. Cut wadding and embroidery backing to fit piece 1.

3 Place the wadding under piece 1, and tear-away embroidery backing under the wadding. Pin all together to secure.

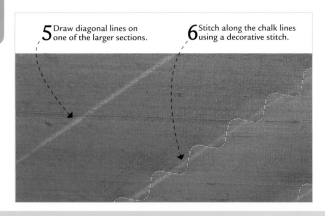

4 Using tailor's chalk, divide this piece into three sections by drawing a 4cm (1½in) wide strip vertically down the centre. Machine a row of decorative stitches down the strip.

5 Draw diagonal lines on one of the larger sections.

6 Stitch along the chalk lines using a decorative stitch.

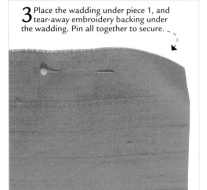

7 Draw lines in the opposite direction and machine decorative stitches.

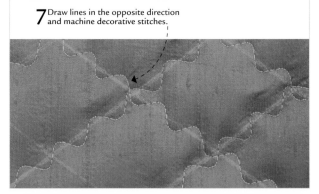

8 On the other large section, stitch lines at random.

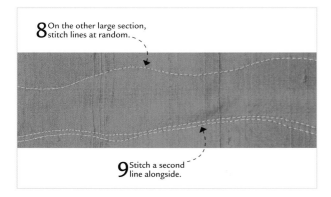

9 Stitch a second line alongside.

10 Repeat in the opposite direction.

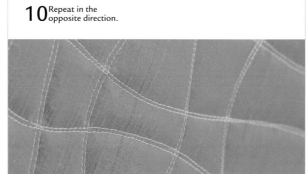

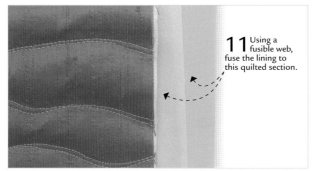

11 Using a fusible web, fuse the lining to this quilted section.

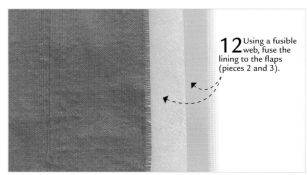

12 Using a fusible web, fuse the lining to the flaps (pieces 2 and 3).

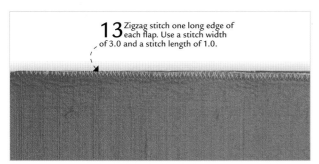

13 Zigzag stitch one long edge of each flap. Use a stitch width of 3.0 and a stitch length of 1.0.

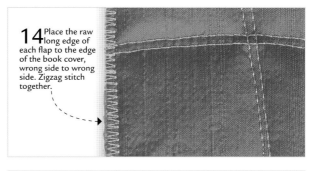

14 Place the raw long edge of each flap to the edge of the book cover, wrong side to wrong side. Zigzag stitch together.

15 Zigzag all around the book cover sides, stitching over the flaps as you do so. Stitch again to reinforce the edges.

16 If you wish, decorate with beads to finish.

CUSHION

A pretty cushion can add a luxurious look to any sofa or bed. This one features a gathered frill and a decorative gathered panel. It is in a plain silk fabric so that the sheen shows off the gathers, but you could try a tartan or stripe for a different look. Make half a dozen of these in co-ordinating colours for a very rich effect.

TECHNIQUES INVOLVED

HOW TO MAKE GATHERS See page 127.

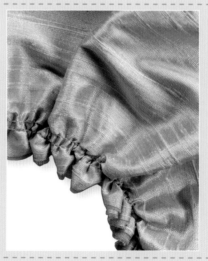

DOUBLE RUFFLE VERSION 3 See page 137.

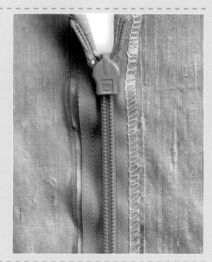

CONCEALED ZIP See page 255.

LEVEL OF DIFFICULTY ★★★★

SHOPPING LIST

145 x 115cm (57 x 46in) silk dupion
1 reel polyester all-purpose thread

40cm (16in) concealed zip
1 cushion pad, 40 x 40cm (16 x 16in)

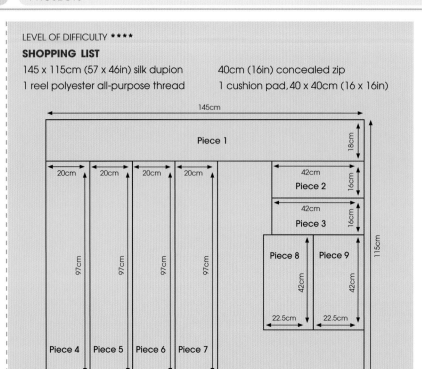

145cm

Piece 1

18cm

20cm | 20cm | 20cm | 20cm

42cm
Piece 2
16cm

42cm
Piece 3
16cm

Piece 8 | Piece 9

42cm

97cm | 97cm | 97cm | 97cm

115cm

22.5cm | 22.5cm

Piece 4 | Piece 5 | Piece 6 | Piece 7

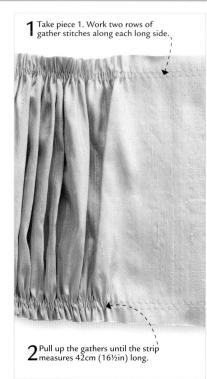

1 Take piece 1. Work two rows of gather stitches along each long side.

2 Pull up the gathers until the strip measures 42cm (16½in) long.

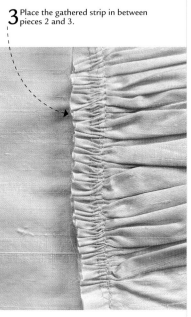

3 Place the gathered strip in between pieces 2 and 3.

4 Join right side to right side, and stitch the strip between the rectangles, using a 1.5cm (⅝in) seam allowance. Press the seam to the non-gathered side. Make sure the piece measures 42 x 42cm (16½ x 16½in). Trim if necessary.

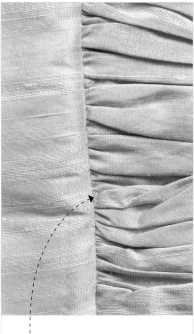

5 On the right side, the central gathered strip meets the side panels neatly.

6 Make a double ruffle. Cut out pieces 4–7 and join together, right side to right side, to make a very long strip. Press the seams open. Fold the strip in half lengthways wrong side to wrong side. Divide into four equal sections and mark with pins. Place two rows of gather stitches between each set of pins.

7 Start to gently pull up the gathers.

8 On the cushion front, mark the centre point of each side with a pin. Place the right side of the ruffle to the right side of the cushion, matching the break in the gathers with the pin markings on the cushion.

9 Pull up the gathers to fit accurately between the pins. Tack through the layers.

10 Machine in place with a long machine stitch – length 4.0.

11 Inset a concealed zip between pieces 8 and 9.

12 Overlock the edge of the zip tape to the seam allowance.

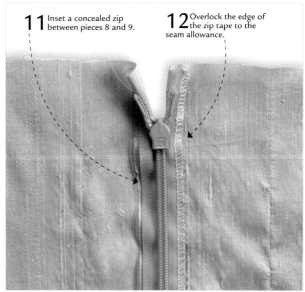

13 Place the cushion back to the cushion front, right side to right side. Make sure the zip is undone.

14 Pin in place, then machine the layers together, keeping the fabric under tension to prevent wrinkles. Use stitch length 3.0.

15 Turn to the right side to check that the seam is not caught anywhere.

16 Turn back to the wrong side and neaten the seam, using your preferred method.

17 Inset the cushion pad through the zip opening to finish.

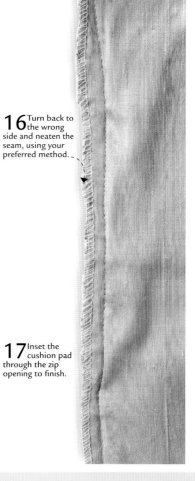

CHILD'S SKIRT

This is a simple skirt, cut from a long strip of fabric. The skirt features tucks at the hem edge that have been top-stitched to produce a decorative effect, and then embroidered with a machine stitch. The waist edge of the skirt has an elasticated finish. This pattern could be adapted for a child of any age – or even an adult.

TECHNIQUES INVOLVED

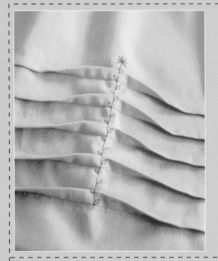

PLAIN TUCKS See page 111.

MAKING A CASING AT THE WAIST EDGE
See page 172.

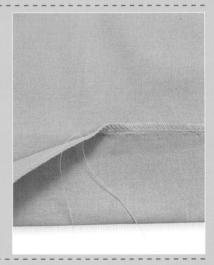

HAND-STITCHED HEMS: OVERLOCKED FINISH
See page 230.

LEVEL OF DIFFICULTY ★★★★

SHOPPING LIST

For a child age six:

55 x 115cm (22 x 46in) cotton
   fabric

1 reel matching thread

Contrast embroidery thread

50cm (20in) non-roll elastic,
   2.5cm (1in) wide

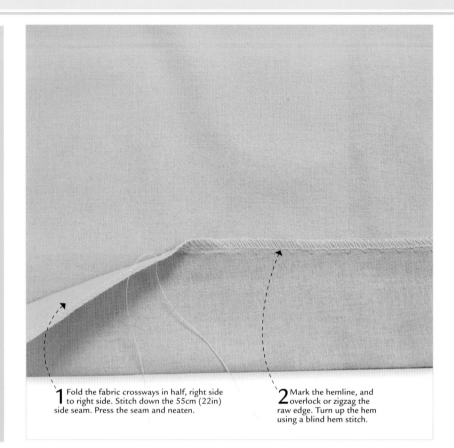

1 Fold the fabric crossways in half, right side to right side. Stitch down the 55cm (22in) side seam. Press the seam and neaten.

2 Mark the hemline, and overlock or zigzag the raw edge. Turn up the hem using a blind hem stitch.

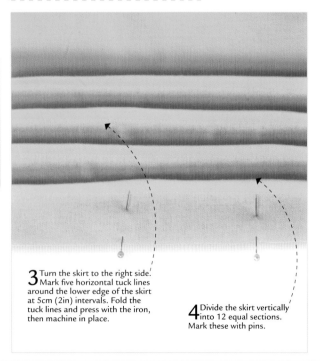

3 Turn the skirt to the right side. Mark five horizontal tuck lines around the lower edge of the skirt at 5cm (2in) intervals. Fold the tuck lines and press with the iron, then machine in place.

4 Divide the skirt vertically into 12 equal sections. Mark these with pins.

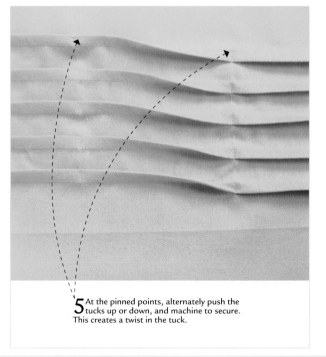

5 At the pinned points, alternately push the tucks up or down, and machine to secure. This creates a twist in the tuck.

6 On all of the tucks pointing towards the waist, stitch over the machining with a decorative stitch, or do this by hand.

7 At the top of the decorative stitching, hand stitch a flower using straight stitches: one stitch; a second stitch across it at right angles; a third stitch at an angle; and finally a fourth stitch at right angles to the third.

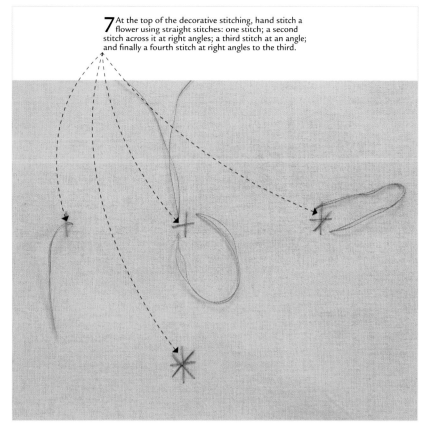

8 To make a casing for the elastic, fold down the waist edge of the skirt twice.

9 Top-stitch along the top folded edge.

10 Stitch along the lower edge of the casing, leaving a gap for inserting the elastic.

11 Insert the elastic into the casing and machine the ends together. Hand stitch across the gap.

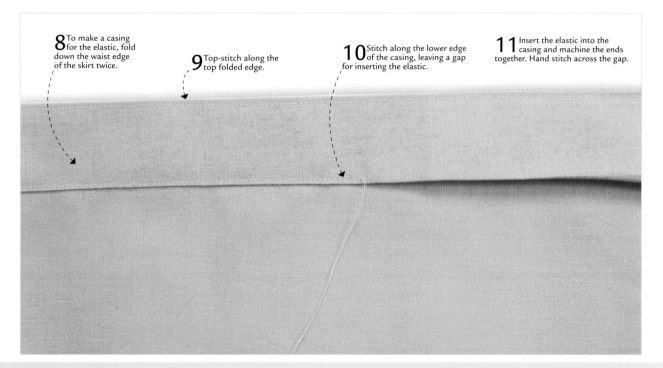

Plain tucks p111   Making a casing at the waist edge p172   Hand-stitched hems: overlocked finish p230   ≪≪≪

APRON

An apron is a simple project, and makes an ideal present. It could co-ordinate with your kitchen or may be worn for work in the garden. You could try making the apron in a print or stripe fabric, using a heavy cotton material that will wash. As not much fabric is required, look in the remnant bin at your local store.

TECHNIQUES INVOLVED

3-THREAD OVERLOCK STITCH See page 93.

HOW TO CUT BIAS STRIPS See page 147.

KANGAROO POCKET See page 225.

LEVEL OF DIFFICULTY **

SHOPPING LIST

1 x 1.5m (40 x 60in) fabric, such as heavy cotton or linen

60 x 115cm (24 x 46in) contrast colour fabric

1 reel matching thread for each fabric

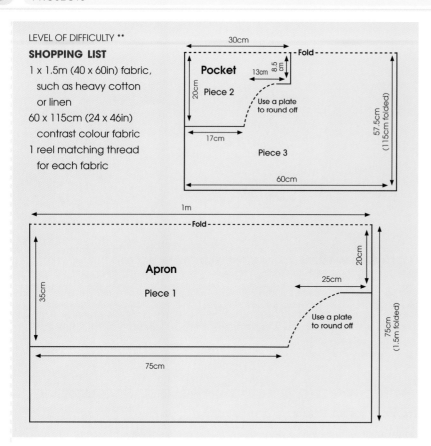

30cm

- - - - - Fold - - - - -

Pocket

Piece 2

13cm | 8.5cm

20cm

Use a plate to round off

17cm

Piece 3

57.5cm (115cm folded)

60cm

1m

- - - - - Fold - - - - -

Apron

Piece 1

35cm

20cm

25cm

Use a plate to round off

75cm

75cm (1.5m folded)

1 Overlock or zigzag the three sides of the apron skirt (piece 1).

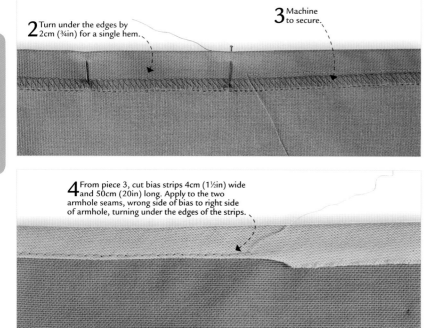

2 Turn under the edges by 2cm (¾in) for a single hem.

3 Machine to secure.

4 From piece 3, cut bias strips 4cm (1½in) wide and 50cm (20in) long. Apply to the two armhole seams, wrong side of bias to right side of armhole, turning under the edges of the strips.

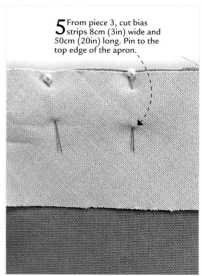

5 From piece 3, cut bias strips 8cm (3in) wide and 50cm (20in) long. Pin to the top edge of the apron.

6 Machine all the bias strips in place. Wrap to the wrong side, turn under the raw edge, and machine to secure.

7 Cut the pocket (piece 2) from the contrast fabric.

8 Mark the centre line with a row of tacking stitches.

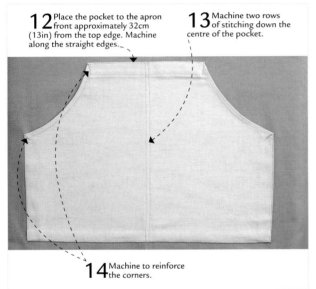

9 Neaten all the pocket edges with overlock or zigzag stitching.

10 Turn under the curved edge by 5mm (³⁄₁₆in) and machine in place.

11 Turn under all the straight edges by 1.5cm (⅝in). Pin, then press.

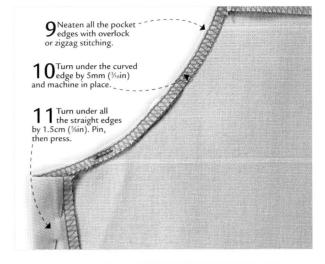

12 Place the pocket to the apron front approximately 32cm (13in) from the top edge. Machine along the straight edges.

13 Machine two rows of stitching down the centre of the pocket.

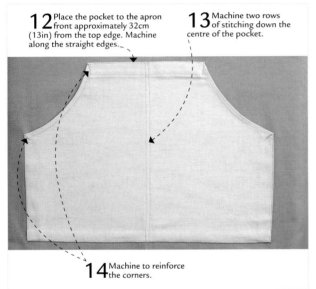

14 Machine to reinforce the corners.

15 To make the tie ends, cut strips measuring approximately 90 x 7cm (36 x 2¾in). Press under the long sides by 1cm (⅜in).

16 Press the strips lengthways in half. Top-stitch both edges to complete.

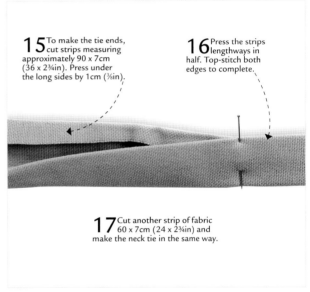

17 Cut another strip of fabric 60 x 7cm (24 x 2¾in) and make the neck tie in the same way.

18 Attach the side tie ends and the neck tie to the apron.

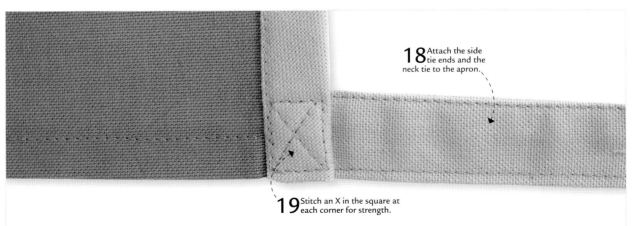

19 Stitch an X in the square at each corner for strength.

Reinforcing pocket corners p216   Kangaroo pocket p225   Bias-bound hems p238   ≪≪

SEWING AIDS

Here's a perfect starting point if you are new to sewing – make yourself some matching sewing aids: a scissor cover, needle case, and pin cushion. This project allows you to practise your machine stitching and experiment with a range of decorative stitches. Cotton fabric and machine embroidery thread will work well, but you could always try silk fabric or variegated embroidery thread.

TECHNIQUES INVOLVED

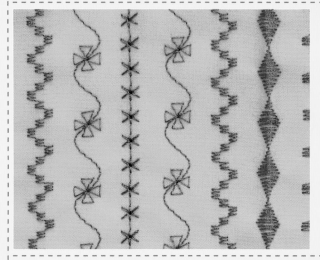

DECORATIVE STITCHES See page 93.

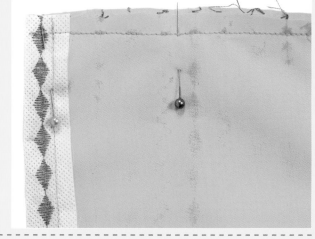

HOW TO MAKE A PLAIN SEAM See page 94.

LEVEL OF DIFFICULTY **

SHOPPING LIST

30 x 115cm (12 x 46in) cotton fabric

30 x 115cm (12 x 46in) heavy fusible interfacing

1 reel machine embroidery thread

30 x 90cm (12 x 36in) polyester wadding

2m (80in) ribbon, about 5mm (³/₁₆in wide)

2 squares felt, about 15 x 12cm (6 x 5in)

Small amount polyester stuffing, about 85g (3oz)

```
        57.5cm (115cm folded)

        25cm          14cm      14cm

   Scissor          Pin       Needle
   holder         cushion      case
                                       16cm
                                     Piece 3
30cm
Fold              20cm
   Piece 1       Piece 2
```

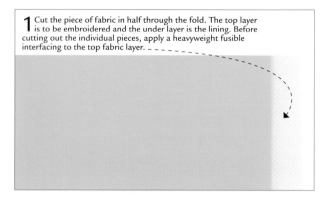

1 Cut the piece of fabric in half through the fold. The top layer is to be embroidered and the under layer is the lining. Before cutting out the individual pieces, apply a heavyweight fusible interfacing to the top fabric layer.

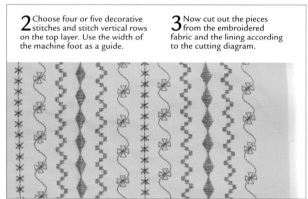

2 Choose four or five decorative stitches and stitch vertical rows on the top layer. Use the width of the machine foot as a guide.

3 Now cut out the pieces from the embroidered fabric and the lining according to the cutting diagram.

Scissor holder

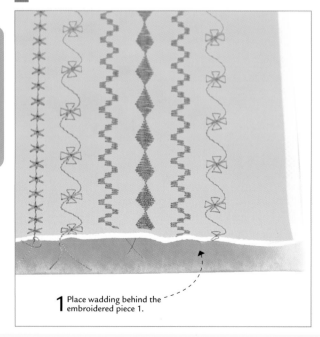

1 Place wadding behind the embroidered piece 1.

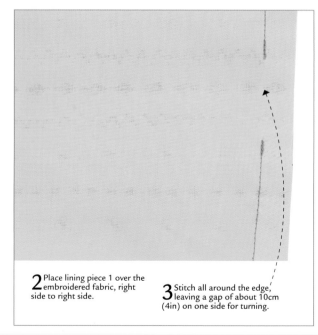

2 Place lining piece 1 over the embroidered fabric, right side to right side.

3 Stitch all around the edge, leaving a gap of about 10cm (4in) on one side for turning.

⋘ How to apply a fusible interfacing p54

4 Trim the seams to reduce bulk. Press, then turn the fabric through to the right side while still warm. Hand stitch the gap.

5 Fold one side of the square down. Make sure that your scissors fit into this folded section. Edge-stitch to secure and press.

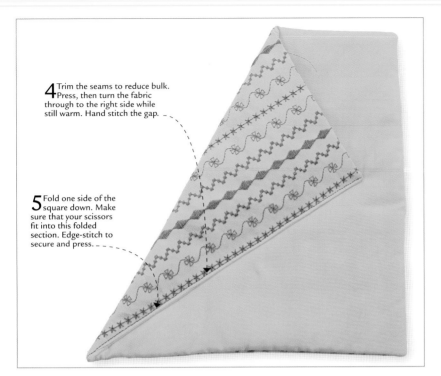

6 Fold the other side across the first side, to the folded edge.

7 Stitch two-thirds of the way up, through all layers.

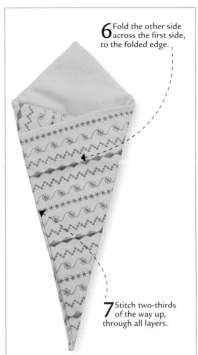

8 Fold down the corner of the upper layer and press.

9 Sew on a ribbon bow to trim the edge.

Needle case

1 Trim 2cm (¾in) off one short side of lining piece 3.

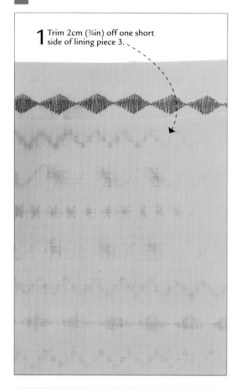

2 Stitch the short edges of the lining and embroidered piece 3 together, right side to right side. (The embroidered fabric will appear too big – just let it bulge out.) Stitch ribbon ties in to the middle of each side as you sew.

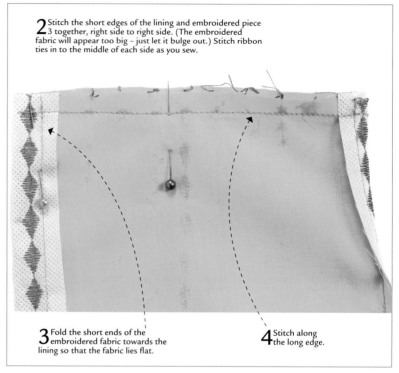

3 Fold the short ends of the embroidered fabric towards the lining so that the fabric lies flat.

4 Stitch along the long edge.

5 Turn through the other long edge. Hand stitch the lower edge with a blind hem or flat fell stitch.

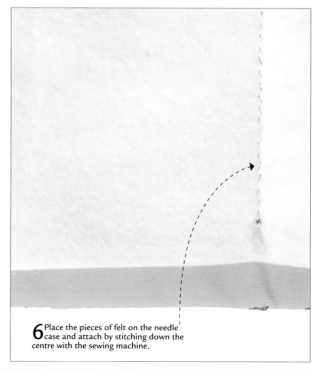

6 Place the pieces of felt on the needle case and attach by stitching down the centre with the sewing machine.

≪≪ Hand stitches pp90–91

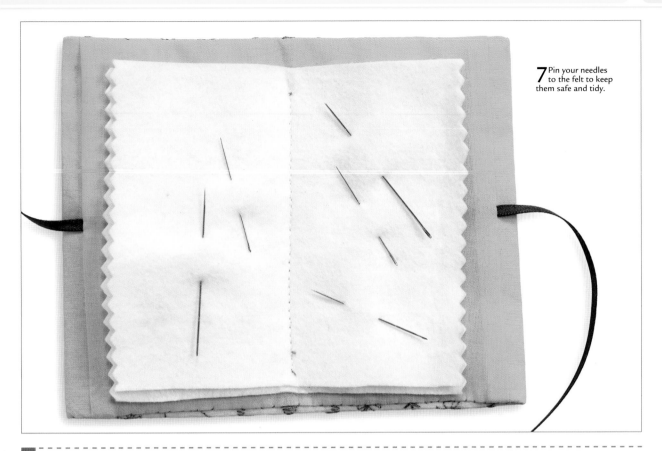

7 Pin your needles to the felt to keep them safe and tidy.

Pin cushion

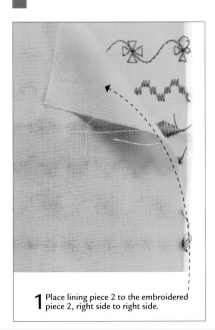

1 Place lining piece 2 to the embroidered piece 2, right side to right side.

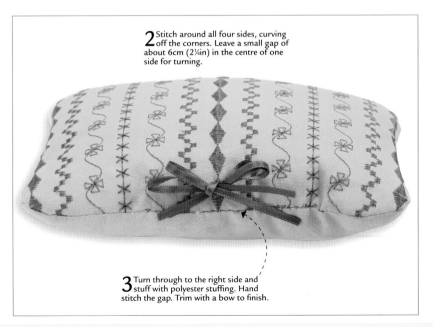

2 Stitch around all four sides, curving off the corners. Leave a small gap of about 6cm (2¼in) in the centre of one side for turning.

3 Turn through to the right side and stuff with polyester stuffing. Hand stitch the gap. Trim with a bow to finish.

Stitches made with a machine pp92–93 «««

HESSIAN BAG

It's easy to make your own stylish bag. There are some amazing handles available to purchase in the shops, and you could replace the hessian used here with denim or heavy cotton. You can make the bag to your own measurements, if you would like it to be longer or deeper – just remember to use the template for the lower corners.

TECHNIQUES INVOLVED

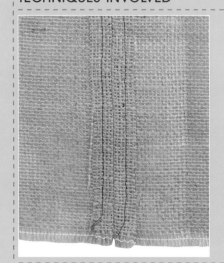

STITCH FINISHES See page 103.

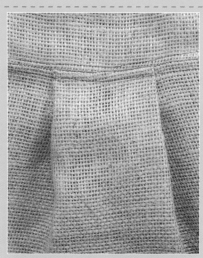

STRAIGHT DARTED TUCKS See page 113.

MACHINE-STITCHED BELT CARRIERS
See page 181.

LEVEL OF DIFFICULTY ✱✱✱

SHOPPING LIST

1m x 115cm (40 x 46in) hessian

1 reel thread

1 pair bag handles

1m x 115cm (40 x 46in) cotton fabric
for lining

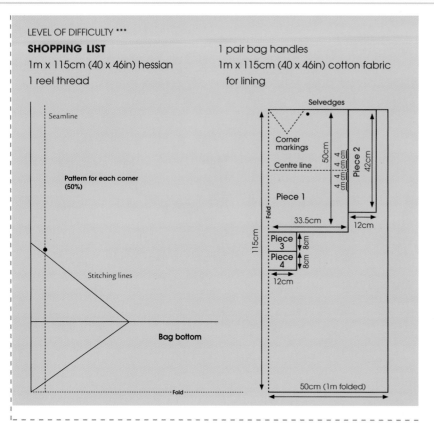

Seamline

**Pattern for each corner
(50%)**

Stitching lines

Bag bottom

Fold

Selvedges

Corner
markings

Centre line

Piece 1

50cm

4 4 4
cm cm cm

4 4 4
cm cm cm

Piece 2

42cm

33.5cm

12cm

115cm

Piece
3

8cm

Piece
4

8cm

12cm

50cm (1m folded)

1 Mark the tucks and corners on to piece 1 with chalk. Pin the tucks in place.

2 On both ends, attach the band (piece 2) to the top edge of piece 1 over the tucks, using a 1.5cm (⅝in) seam allowance.

3 Press the seam open and top-stitch.

4 Join the side seams from the top, stopping at the dot. Press the seam open.

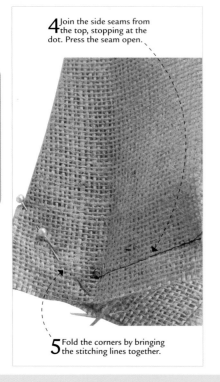

5 Fold the corners by bringing the stitching lines together.

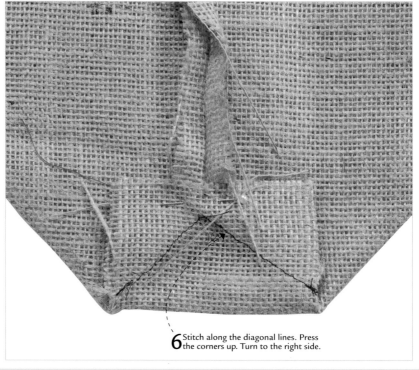

6 Stitch along the diagonal lines. Press the corners up. Turn to the right side.

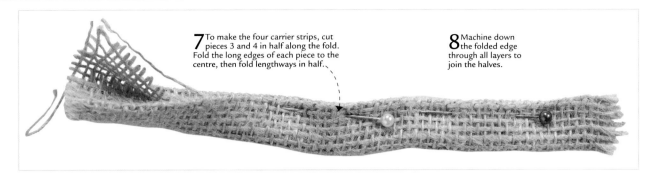

7 To make the four carrier strips, cut pieces 3 and 4 in half along the fold. Fold the long edges of each piece to the centre, then fold lengthways in half.

8 Machine down the folded edge through all layers to join the halves.

9 Wrap the carriers around the handles and pin in place.

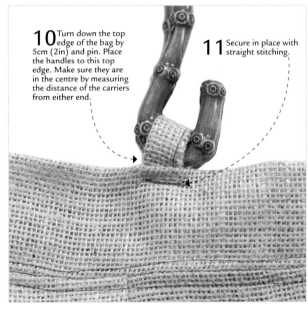

10 Turn down the top edge of the bag by 5cm (2in) and pin. Place the handles to this top edge. Make sure they are in the centre by measuring the distance of the carriers from either end.

11 Secure in place with straight stitching.

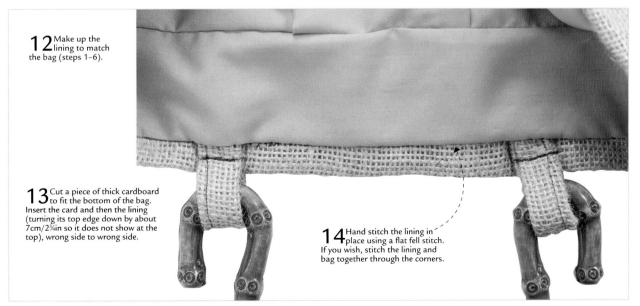

12 Make up the lining to match the bag (steps 1–6).

13 Cut a piece of thick cardboard to fit the bottom of the bag. Insert the card and then the lining (turning its top edge down by about 7cm/2¾in so it does not show at the top), wrong side to wrong side.

14 Hand stitch the lining in place using a flat fell stitch. If you wish, stitch the lining and bag together through the corners.

Plain darted tucks p113   Machine-stitched belt carriers p181   ≪≪

BABY TOWEL

A snuggly towel for a baby or toddler is a must-make project. If you cannot find towelling, you can always buy a large bath sheet and cut it up. Choose a contrast or matching binding and towelling for the edges and the ears. You could even embroider on eyes, a mouth, and whiskers!

TECHNIQUES INVOLVED

HAND STITCHES See pages 90–91.

BIAS-BOUND HEMS See page 238.

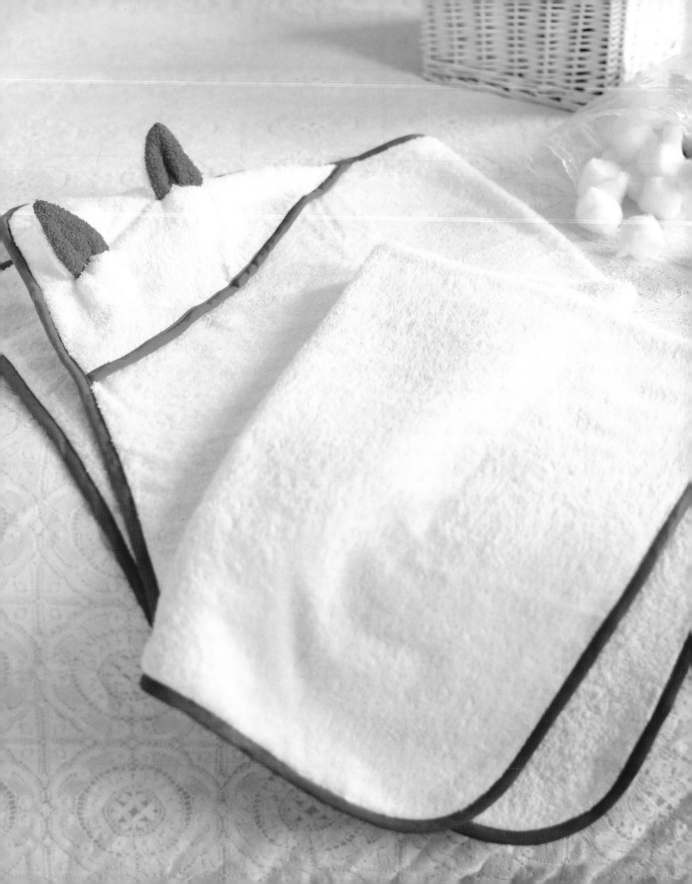

LEVEL OF DIFFICULTY ***

SHOPPING LIST

1.2 x 1.5m (48 x 60in)
   towelling, or one
   large bath sheet
   for the wrap and
   a hand towel for
   the hood

1 contrast colour
   face towel (flannel)
   for the inside of
   the ears

1 reel thread

5m (16ft) bias binding,
   2cm (¾in) wide
   (same colour as
   inside of ears)

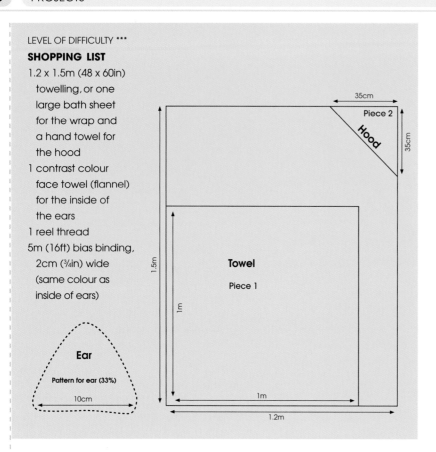

Ear

Pattern for ear (33%)

10cm

Towel

Piece 1

1.5m

1m

1m

1.2m

35cm

Hood

Piece 2

35cm

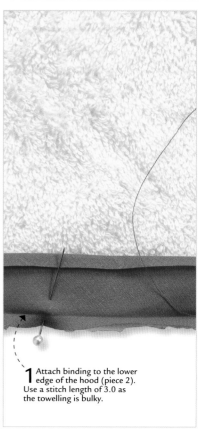

1 Attach binding to the lower edge of the hood (piece 2). Use a stitch length of 3.0 as the towelling is bulky.

2 Wrap the binding to the right side and machine in place.

3 Make the ears. Cut out two from the towelling and two from the face towel. Place one of each colour together, right side to right side. Pin together.

4 Hand stitch around the ear, leaving the bottom edge open.

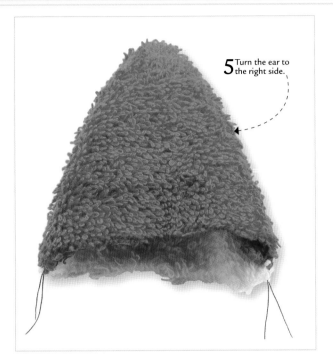

5 Turn the ear to the right side.

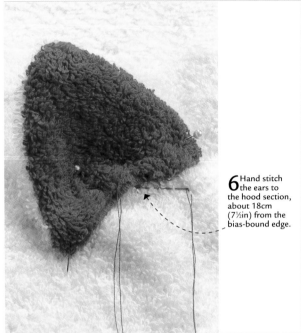

6 Hand stitch the ears to the hood section, about 18cm (7½in) from the bias-bound edge.

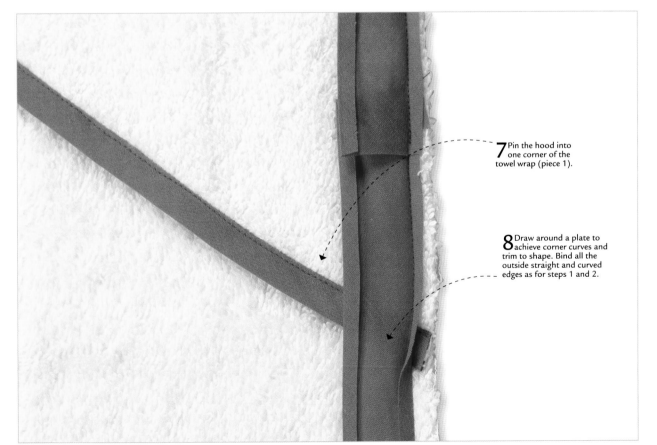

7 Pin the hood into one corner of the towel wrap (piece 1).

8 Draw around a plate to achieve corner curves and trim to shape. Bind all the outside straight and curved edges as for steps 1 and 2.

DOOR HANGING

Just what do you do with all the clutter in a bathroom, bedroom, or child's room? Keep it all in this stylish door hanging. Use a strong cotton fabric, such as curtain material, as it will not require interfacing, and choose colours that will complement your room. The coat hanger needs to be fairly straight in order to hang the fabric effectively – some hangers slope too much.

TECHNIQUES INVOLVED

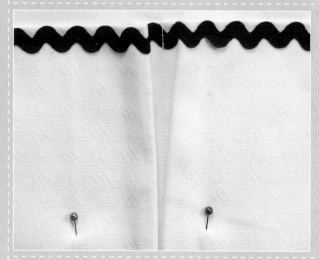

PLEATS ON THE RIGHT SIDE See page 115.

ATTACHING A TRIM TO AN EDGE See page 247.

LEVEL OF DIFFICULTY ★★★★

SHOPPING LIST

1m x 115cm (40 x 46in) fabric, such as heavy
    cotton, linen, drill, or damask

50cm (20in) stretch ribbon, 2cm (¾in) wide

1 reel matching thread

1.2m (48in) ric-rac braid

1 padded coat hanger

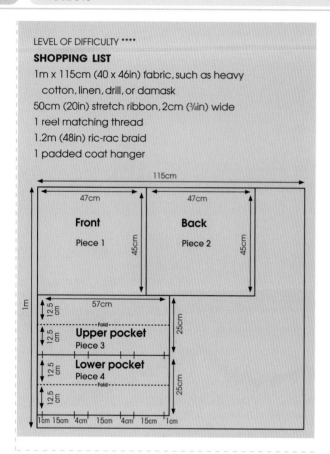

1 Place ribbon (without stretching it) on to the right side of piece 1, 10cm (4in) from the top edge. Secure at the ends with machining.

2 Stitch vertically across the ribbon. This creates sections for small objects, such as pens or brushes.

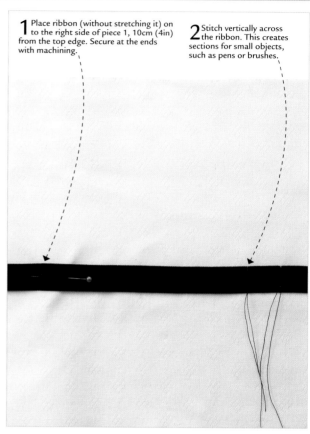

3 Take piece 4 and press lengthways in half, wrong side to wrong side. Apply ric-rac braid along the pressed edge.

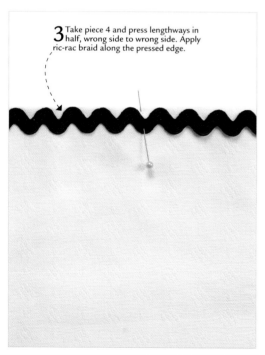

4 Mark with clips the position of the pleats. Fold the fabric to make pleats. Press.

5 Place the raw edge of piece 4 to the lower edge of piece 1 and pin in place. This will make the lower pocket.

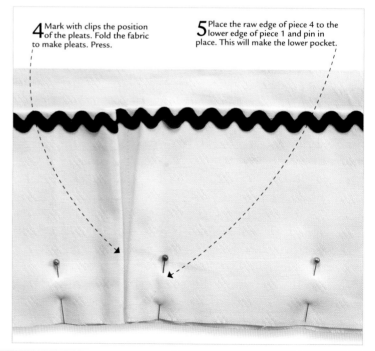

6 Stitch the pocket band at either end to secure, then stitch vertically in the middle of the pleat.

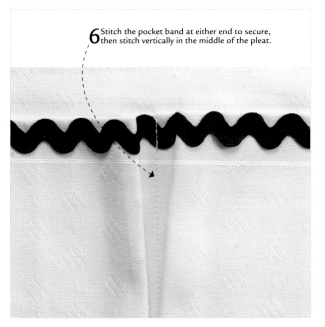

7 Fold and trim piece 3 in the same way as steps 3 and 4 to make the upper pocket. Make and press the pleat.

8 On piece 1, use a row of tacks to mark the placement line for the upper pocket 27cm (11in) from the top edge.

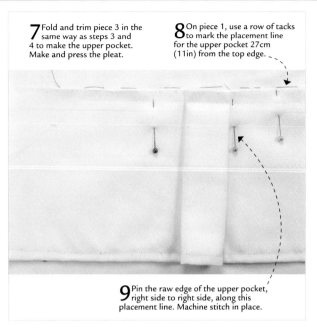

9 Pin the raw edge of the upper pocket, right side to right side, along this placement line. Machine stitch in place.

10 Trim away any bulk. Turn the pocket up into position and carefully press.

11 Stitch either end to secure, and then vertically between the pleat.

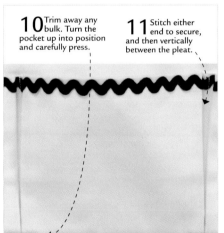

12 On piece 2 draw the shape of the coat hanger on to the wrong side of the fabric, using tailor's chalk.

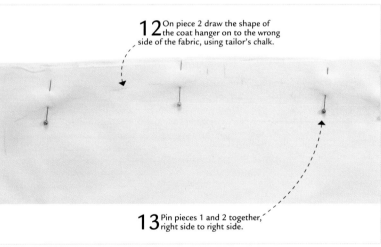

13 Pin pieces 1 and 2 together, right side to right side.

14 Following the shape of the coat hanger, stitch around. Use a 1cm (⅜in) seam allowance, and leave a wide gap at the bottom edge for turning and about 1cm (⅜in) at the centre top for the coat hanger. Clip the seams, then turn and press.

15 Insert the coat hanger. To finish, hand stitch the gap closed at the bottom edge with a blind hem stitch.

Reducing seam bulk pp102–103   Pleats on the right side p115   Attaching a trim to an edge p247   ≪≪≪

ROMAN BLIND

A Roman blind is a great way to provide privacy at a window and a splash of colour in the room. Cotton, linen, damask, and brocade are all suitable fabrics. The blind is quick and straightforward to make and will easily fit behind curtains if you so desire. Careful measuring of the window is essential, and a trip to the wood yard will be required to purchase the dowelling and the slat for the bottom edge. You will need a batten fixed to the top of the window frame from which to hang the blind.

TECHNIQUES INVOLVED

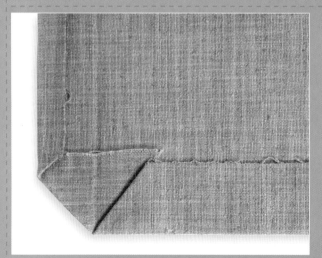

MACHINED CURTAIN HEMS See page 234.

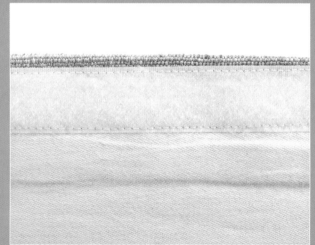

TAPE FASTENERS See page 272.

LEVEL OF DIFFICULTY *****

SHOPPING LIST

Fabric: to calculate the amount you need, measure the window's width (at the widest part where the blind will hang), and also the drop (the finished length of the blind). Add 12cm (5in) to the width and 15cm (6in) to the drop for the hems – 5cm (2in) at the top and 10cm (4in) at the bottom

Curtain lining, of matching size

1 reel matching thread

Decorative trim (optional)

Sew-and-stick Velcro™

2 or more pieces of wooden dowelling to fit

4cm (1½in) x finished width slat of wood

Plastic curtain rings, about 1cm (⅜in) diameter

Blind cord

1 Press under 6cm (2¼in) down either side of the blind fabric (single fold hem).

2 Press up a double hem on the bottom edge to give a finished depth of 5cm (2in). Press in a mitred corner.

3 Trim the lining at the side edges by 4cm (1½in) each side. Press under a side hem of 6cm (2¼in).

4 Place the lining to the blind fabric, wrong side to wrong side, so that the cut edge of the lining sits along the hem crease of the fabric. The folded side hems should be 4cm (1½in) from the folded edge of the blind. Pin in place.

5 Before securing the lining, make the casings for the wooden dowelling. Measure the lining, and form a pleat at regular intervals. The pleats need to be at regular 30–40cm (12–16in) intervals, starting 40cm (16in) from the hem.

6 Re-position the lining to the blind. Machine across the pleat through both blind and lining to secure. Make sure you leave an opening wide enough to fit the dowelling through.

7 Using a flat fell stitch, hand stitch the lining to the blind down the sides. Leave the ends of the pleats open.

PROJECTS

8 Machine the bottom hem in place, over the lining. Leave open at the sides so the wooden slat can be inserted.

9 Place a row of stitching at the lower edge of the hem to keep the hem fold sharp.

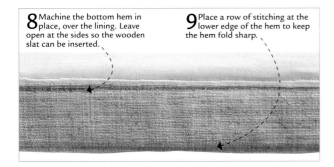

10 If you wish to add a trim, you will need a length equal to the finished width of the blind plus 5cm (2in) for turnings. Machine it in place using the zip foot, over either of these rows of stitching.

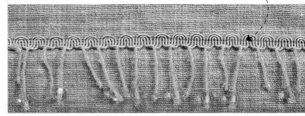

11 Turn down the top edge so that the blind measures the required finished length. Pin in place.

12 Cut a piece of Velcro™ equal to the width of the blind. Sew the soft loop side of the Velcro™ to the blind along the top hem edge.

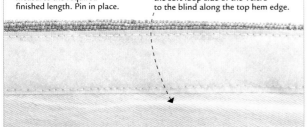

13 Insert wooden dowelling through the pleats, and the slat through the hem. Hand stitch the ends closed with a flat fell stitch.

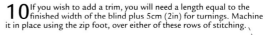

14 Using a buttonhole stitch, sew a curtain ring on to each end of the pleats, and at regular intervals along the dowelling. One, two, or three rings may be required, depending on the width and weight of the blind. Make sure all the rings are in line with each other.

15 Add another row of rings just underneath the Velcro™.

16 For each set of rings you need blind cord equal to twice the drop. Knot blind cord around each ring nearest to the hem.

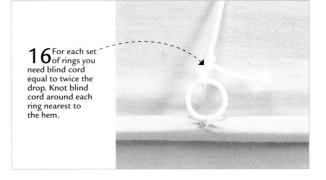

17 Thread the cord up through each line of rings (see illustration, right). Take all of the cords to one side at the top (see top right). Trim the cords to level, and knot to secure.

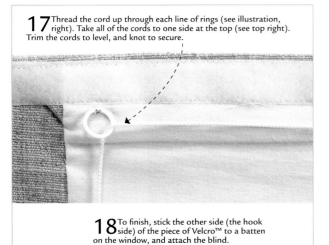

18 To finish, stick the other side (the hook side) of the piece of Velcro™ to a batten on the window, and attach the blind.

HOW TO THREAD A ROMAN BLIND

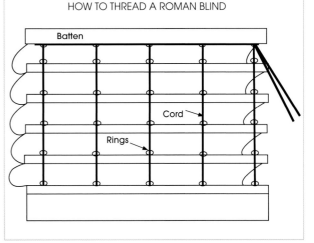

Batten

Cord

Rings

MAN'S TIE

This is not a difficult project, and it is great fun to make your partner a tie from the remnants of your favourite dress, especially if you are invited to a function that requires you to look smart! Or you could try a tie in a fun cartoon print.

TECHNIQUES INVOLVED

HOW TO MAKE A PLAIN SEAM See page 94.

MACHINE STITCHES See pages 92–93.

HOW TO APPLY A NON-FUSIBLE INTERFACING See page 55.

LEVEL OF DIFFICULTY ***

SHOPPING LIST

70 x 115cm (28 x 46in) fabric, such as
   silk or duchesse satin
70 x 115cm (28 x 46in) medium-weight
   woven sew-in interfacing
1 reel matching thread
Remnant of lining, about 30cm (12in)

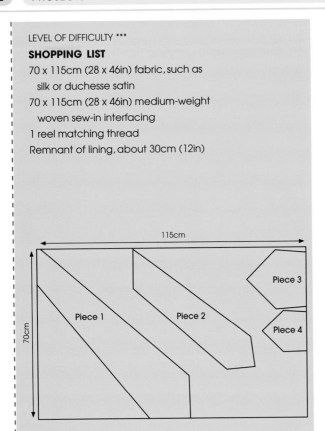

1 Cut pieces 1 and 2 from the tie fabric and interfacing on the bias, and pieces 3 and 4 from lining. Join the interfacing using a lapped seam and zigzag stitch.

2 Join pieces 1 and 2 of the tie fabric together along the short edge using a plain seam, and press it open.

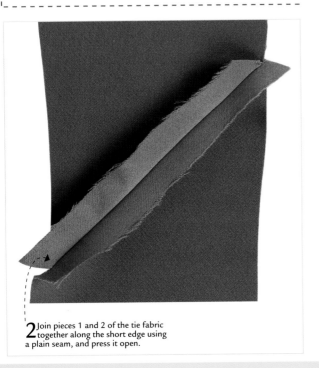

3 Tack the interfacing and fabric together, wrong side to wrong side.

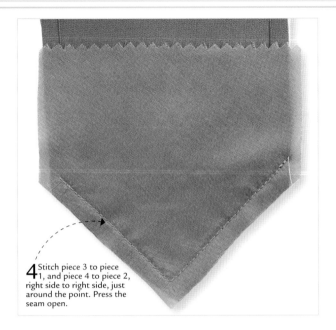

4 Stitch piece 3 to piece 1, and piece 4 to piece 2, right side to right side, just around the point. Press the seam open.

5 Turn the tie right side to right side lengthways.

6 Stitch along the raw edges.

7 Pivot to stitch through the lining.

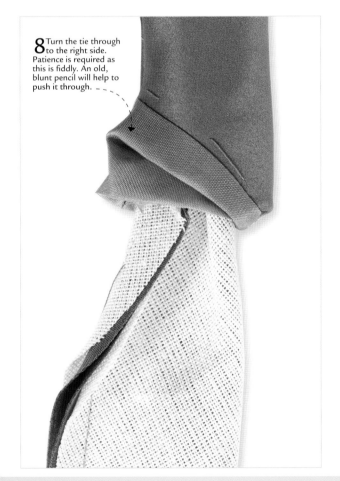

8 Turn the tie through to the right side. Patience is required as this is fiddly. An old, blunt pencil will help to push it through.

9 Press carefully to finish.

PLACE MAT

Quilted place mats will be an asset to any table. Not only are they functional, they also protect the table from excessive heat. The mats feature a slot for a serviette and a pocket to hold your cutlery. Use a cotton fabric to make these as then they can be laundered regularly. Choose a toning colour for the serviette and bound edges.

TECHNIQUES INVOLVED

SELF-LINED PATCH POCKET See page 214.

BIAS-BOUND HEMS See page 238.

QUILTING See page 291.

LEVEL OF DIFFICULTY **

SHOPPING LIST

For each place mat:

40 x 1.5m (16 x 60in) fabric, such as cotton or linen

40 x 90cm (16 x 36in) polyester wadding about 6mm (¼in) thick

1 reel matching thread

1.5m (60in) cotton bias binding, 2cm (¾in) wide

For one serviette:

40 x 60cm (16 x 24in) toning colour fabric, such as cotton or polyester cotton

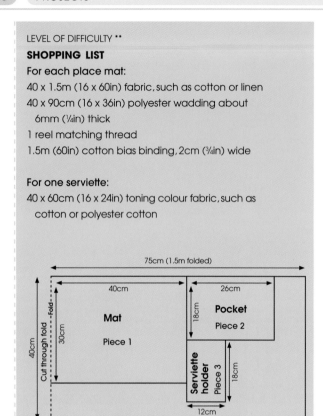

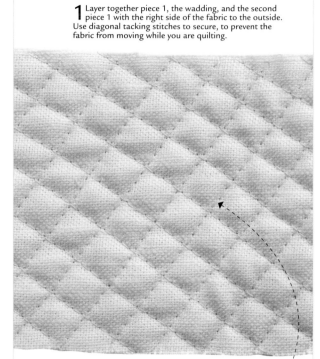

1 Layer together piece 1, the wadding, and the second piece 1 with the right side of the fabric to the outside. Use diagonal tacking stitches to secure, to prevent the fabric from moving while you are quilting.

2 Using a stitch length of 3.5, quilt the fabric, using the width of the machine foot as a guide to spacing the stitching lines. Start in the centre and work to either side. Trim the edges to neaten, if necessary.

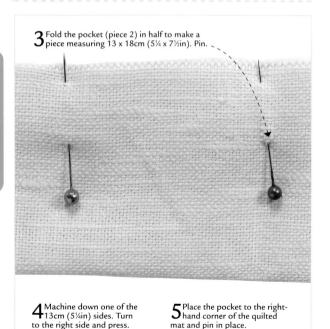

3 Fold the pocket (piece 2) in half to make a piece measuring 13 x 18cm (5¼ x 7½in). Pin.

4 Machine down one of the 13cm (5¼in) sides. Turn to the right side and press.

5 Place the pocket to the right-hand corner of the quilted mat and pin in place.

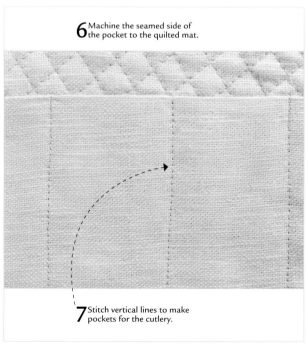

6 Machine the seamed side of the pocket to the quilted mat.

7 Stitch vertical lines to make pockets for the cutlery.

⟪⟪⟪ Tacking stitches p89   Stitches made with a machine pp92–93   Stitching corners and curves pp100–101

8 Fold the serviette holder (piece 3) in half lengthways and stitch. Turn to the right side and press. Secure to the mat.

9 Next bind the edges. Place the binding to the mat, right side binding to wrong side mat, aligning the raw edges. Machine together, turning under the edges as you begin.

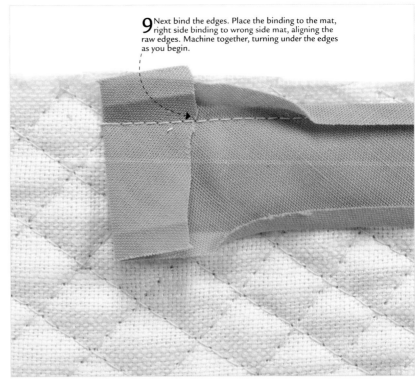

10 Bring the binding to the right side and machine in place.

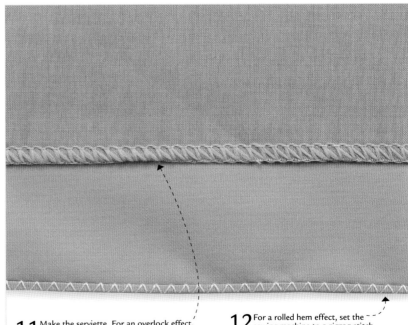

11 Make the serviette. For an overlock effect, use a 3-thread overlock stitch and an embroidery thread on the upper looper to stitch around the square of fabric, pivoting at the corners. Thread the ends of the overlock stitch back into the work.

12 For a rolled hem effect, set the sewing machine to a zigzag stitch and use a rolled hem foot to stitch around the serviette.

Self-lined patch pocket p214   Rolled hems p233   Quilting p291   ◀◀◀

KIMONO

A kimono-style dressing gown always looks stylish. You can use any fabric – this kimono is made from a heavy polyester satin but a cotton would look pretty too. A shorter version could also be made. The obi sash holds the kimono tightly around the waist.

TECHNIQUES INVOLVED

KIMONO SLEEVE See page 194.

MACHINED HEMS See page 232.

OBI SASH See pages 184–185.

LEVEL OF DIFFICULTY *****

SHOPPING LIST

2.2 x 1.5m (88 x 60in) fabric for kimono, such as polyester satin, cotton print, brocade, or "Chinese-type" satin brocade

75cm x 1.5m (30 x 60in) contrast colour fabric for obi sash

1 reel matching thread for each fabric

75 x 115cm (30 x 46in) very firm fusible interfacing

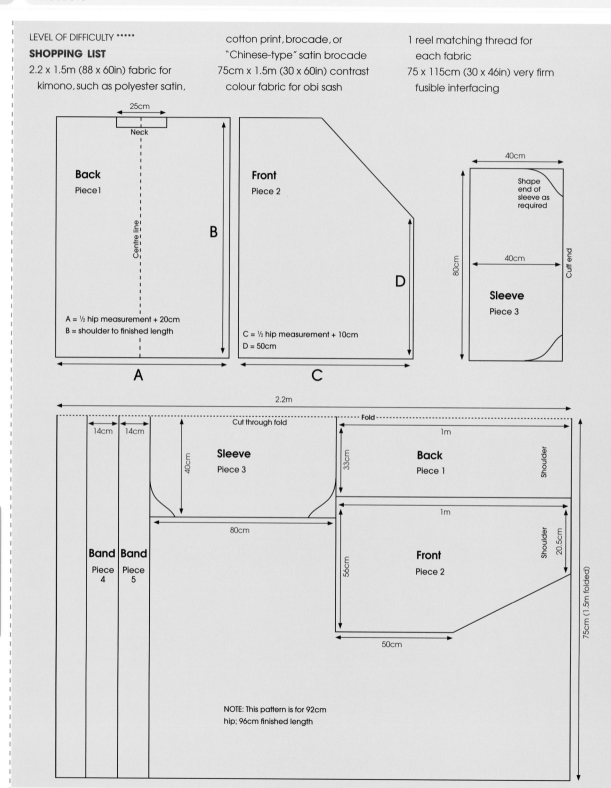

25cm

Neck

Back
Piece 1

Centre line

B

A = ½ hip measurement + 20cm
B = shoulder to finished length

A

Front
Piece 2

D

C = ½ hip measurement + 10cm
D = 50cm

C

40cm

Shape end of sleeve as required

40cm

80cm

Cuff end

Sleeve
Piece 3

2.2m

Cut through fold

Fold

14cm   14cm

40cm

Sleeve
Piece 3

80cm

1m

33cm

Back
Piece 1

Shoulder

1m

Band
Piece 4

Band
Piece 5

56cm

Front
Piece 2

Shoulder

20.5cm

75cm (1.5m folded)

50cm

NOTE: This pattern is for 92cm hip; 96cm finished length

1 Overlock all the edges of the kimono pieces, except for the hems and front edges.

2 Join the back (piece 1) to the two front pieces (double piece 2) at the shoulder seams, using a 1.5cm (⅝in) seam allowance. Press open.

3 Attach the two sleeves (double piece 3), from the centre point on the sleeve to the shoulder seam. Machine at 1.5cm (⅝in). Press open.

4 Join the side seams of the kimono, stopping at the sleeves. Join the sleeves.

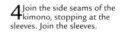

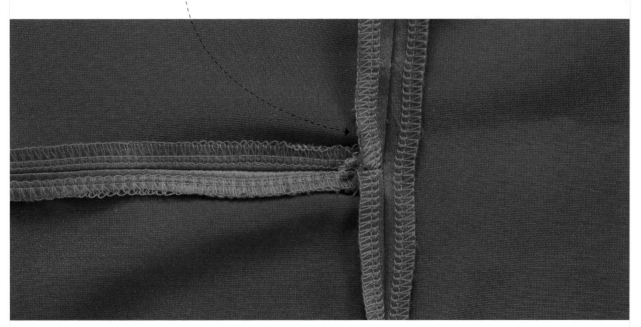

5 Join piece 4 to piece 5 to make one long band and press the seam open. Press the band in half lengthways, wrong side to wrong side.

6 Centre the join in the band at the back of the neck. Pin to the kimono, right side to right side. Machine in place, stopping 20cm (8in) above the hem on each front edge.

How to make a plain seam p94 ⟪⟪⟪

7 Neaten the hem of the kimono (not the band) with an overlock or zigzag stitch. Turn up by 4cm (1½in).

8 Use a blind hem stitch on the machine to secure.

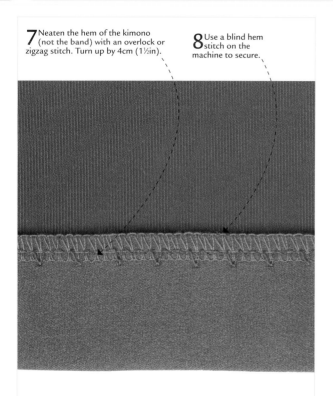

9 Turn up the hem on the band to match the finished kimono hem. Top-stitch to hold in place.

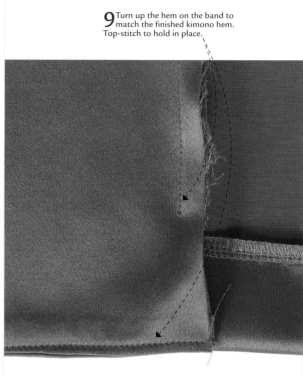

10 Overlock the band-to-kimono seam and press. Top-stitch to hold in place.

11 Turn up the hem on each sleeve once.

12 Machine in place.

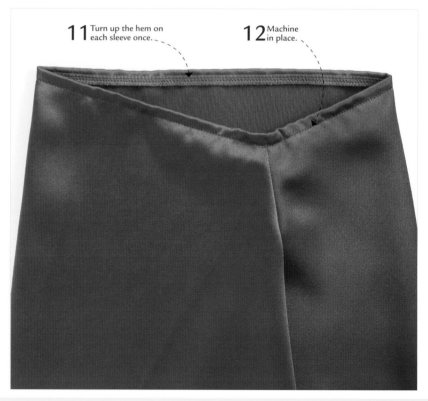

⟪⟪ How to apply a fusible interfacing p54   Hand stitches pp90–91   Stitches made with a machine pp92–93

To make the obi sash

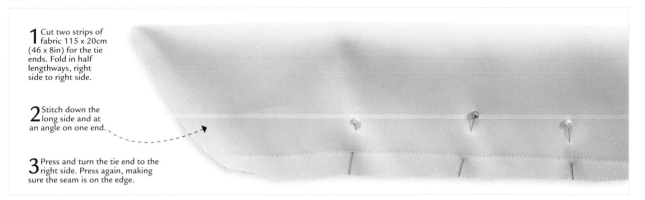

1 Cut two strips of fabric 115 x 20cm (46 x 8in) for the tie ends. Fold in half lengthways, right side to right side.

2 Stitch down the long side and at an angle on one end.

3 Press and turn the tie end to the right side. Press again, making sure the seam is on the edge.

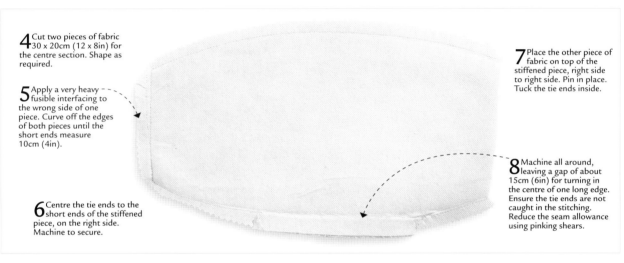

4 Cut two pieces of fabric 30 x 20cm (12 x 8in) for the centre section. Shape as required.

5 Apply a very heavy fusible interfacing to the wrong side of one piece. Curve off the edges of both pieces until the short ends measure 10cm (4in).

6 Centre the tie ends to the short ends of the stiffened piece, on the right side. Machine to secure.

7 Place the other piece of fabric on top of the stiffened piece, right side to right side. Pin in place. Tuck the tie ends inside.

8 Machine all around, leaving a gap of about 15cm (6in) for turning in the centre of one long edge. Ensure the tie ends are not caught in the stitching. Reduce the seam allowance using pinking shears.

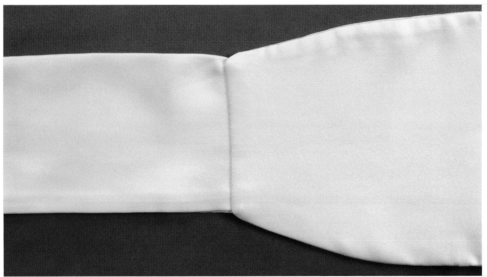

9 Pull the tie ends through the gap. Turn the centre section through to the right side and press. Hand stitch the gap with a blind hem stitch.

10 Tie the sash around the kimono to finish.

Stitch finishes p103   Obi sash pp184–185   Kimono sleeve p194   《《《

BABY BLANKET

This fleece baby blanket can be cut to any size – it could fit into a crib or even make a cosy wrap in the pushchair. A soft washable wool or acrylic would also be ideal. The edges of the blanket have been bound with a soft satin polyester to make a contrasting tactile edge for the baby, but they could be bound in cotton if you prefer.

TECHNIQUES INVOLVED

EMBROIDERY See page 36.

HEMS WITH BANDING See pages 240–243.

APPLIQUÉ See page 290.

LEVEL OF DIFFICULTY •••

SHOPPING LIST

1m x 1.5m (40 x 60in) fleece

Machine embroidery threads
   or fusible appliqué

1 reel matching thread

About 30 x 115cm (12 x 46in)
   satin polyester or cotton

1 Cut out two pieces of fleece large enough to fit your baby's cot. If you are going to machine embroider the fleece, this is the time to do so, following your machine's instruction manual.

2 Place the two pieces of fleece together, wrong side to wrong side, and lay them on a flat surface so you can avoid wrinkles. Tack around the outside edge.

3 Cut bias banding strips 12cm (5in) wide from the satin and join them together to make a strip that is long enough to go all around the blanket (measure around the edge of the blanket and add about 9cm/3¾in for each corner). Apply the banding to the edge of the blanket.

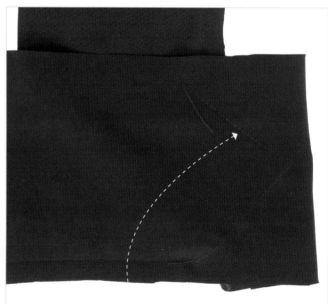

4 As all four corners of the banding need to match, it is a good idea to make a triangular-shaped template from card or paper to give the angle of the point. Machine one point first and make sure it is correct, then trace off the stitching lines to make your template.

◀◀◀   How to apply a fusible interfacing p54   Tacking stitches p89   Hand stitches pp90–91

5 Remove surplus fabric from the corners by trimming. Turn the banding to the other side.

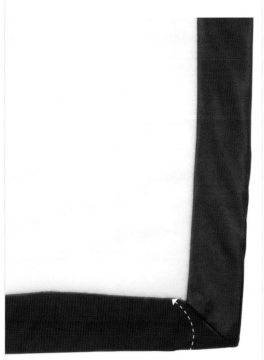

6 Turn under the edge of the banding and hand stitch in place with a flat fell stitch.

7 If you are using a fusible appliqué, apply the appliqué using the iron and a pressing cloth.

8 Fold up your completed teddy blanket ready to present to the lucky baby of your choice!

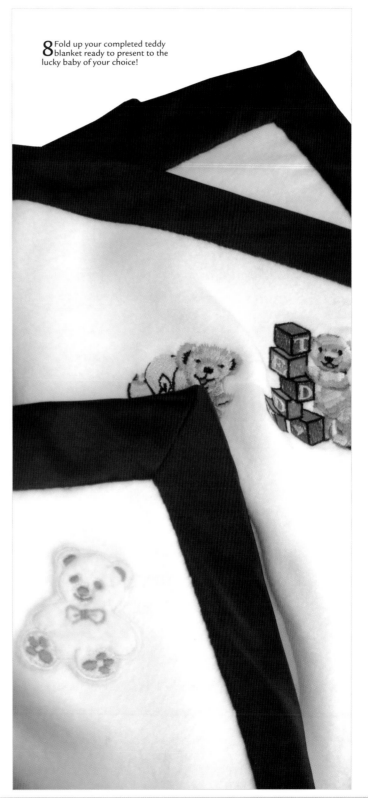

BOLSTER PILLOW

This is such an easy project to make, even though it looks quite complicated. Make at least two of these – they look great on a bed or nestling along the sides of a sofa. Experiment with contrast piping and look in the shops for decorative tassels that can be sewn on to the ends. The instructions can be adapted to suit any size of bolster.

TECHNIQUES INVOLVED

HOW TO MAKE GATHERS See page 127.

PIPED EDGES See pages 244–245.

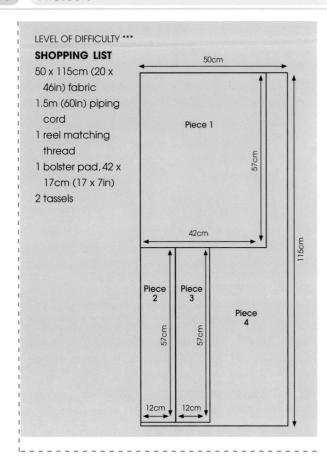

LEVEL OF DIFFICULTY ***

SHOPPING LIST

50 x 115cm (20 x 46in) fabric

1.5m (60in) piping cord

1 reel matching thread

1 bolster pad, 42 x 17cm (17 x 7in)

2 tassels

50cm

Piece 1

57cm

42cm

115cm

Piece 2

Piece 3

Piece 4

57cm

57cm

12cm

12cm

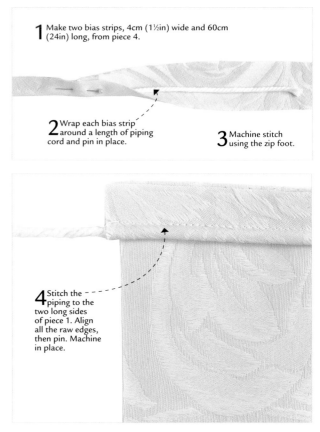

1 Make two bias strips, 4cm (1½in) wide and 60cm (24in) long, from piece 4.

2 Wrap each bias strip around a length of piping cord and pin in place.

3 Machine stitch using the zip foot.

4 Stitch the piping to the two long sides of piece 1. Align all the raw edges, then pin. Machine in place.

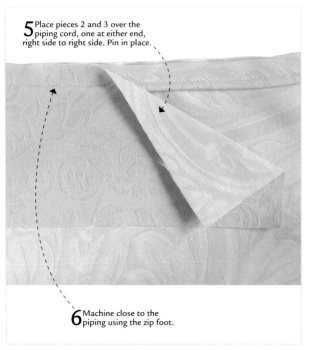

5 Place pieces 2 and 3 over the piping cord, one at either end, right side to right side. Pin in place.

6 Machine close to the piping using the zip foot.

7 Turn under the unattached edges of pieces 2 and 3 to the wrong side by 1.5cm (⅝in) and press. Using a long stitch on your sewing machine, insert two rows of gather stitches.

PROJECTS

8 Fold the cushion fabric in half lengthways, right side to right side, matching the piping with the ends.

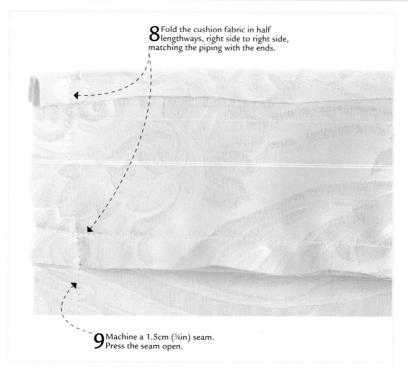

9 Machine a 1.5cm (⅝in) seam. Press the seam open.

10 Turn to the right side.

11 Pull the fabric over the bolster pad, so that the pad is between the piping.

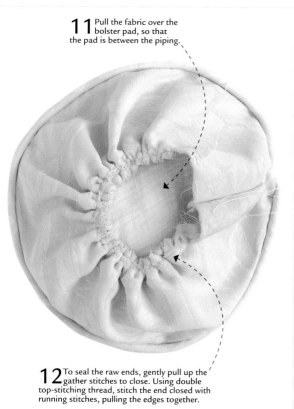

12 To seal the raw ends, gently pull up the gather stitches to close. Using double top-stitching thread, stitch the end closed with running stitches, pulling the edges together.

13 To finish, sew a tassel on to each end.

JEWELLERY ROLL

Going away? Where do you put your jewellery? This handy wrap will fit any handbag or weekend holdall, and keep not only earrings but also your rings and chains. It could easily be adjusted to have more than one ring holder and could also have a larger zip pocket or two.

TECHNIQUES INVOLVED

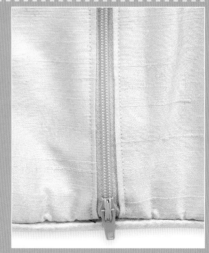

UNLINED PATCH POCKET See page 213.

PIPED EDGES See pages 244–245.

CENTRED ZIP See page 253.

LEVEL OF DIFFICULTY ***

SHOPPING LIST

60 x 115cm (24 x 46in) silk dupion

60 x 115cm (24 x 46in) non-woven fusible interfacing

25 x 90cm (10 x 36in) polyester wadding about 6mm (¼in) thick

18cm (7in) skirt zip

1 reel matching thread

1 snap fastener

1m (40in) no 3 piping cord

1m (40in) ribbon, 5mm (³⁄₁₆in) wide

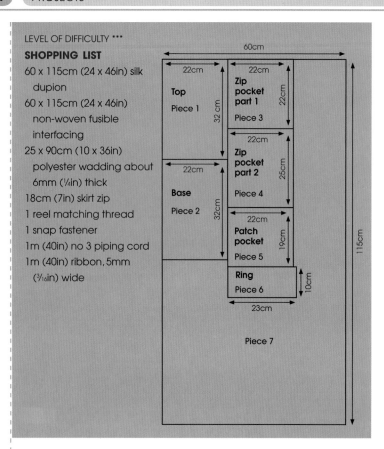

1 Prior to cutting out, apply the fusible interfacing to the wrong side of the silk. Pin wadding securely to the top layer of piece 1 (the top of the jewellery roll) and tack across diagonally to secure.

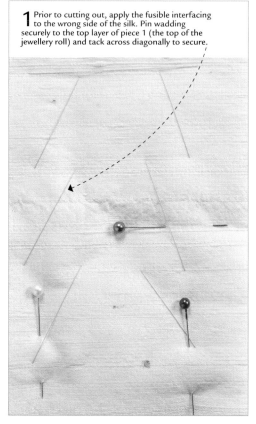

2 Make a pocket with the zip. Take piece 3 and press in half, wrong side to wrong side. Place the folded pressed edge to the side of the zip and stitch in place with the zip foot.

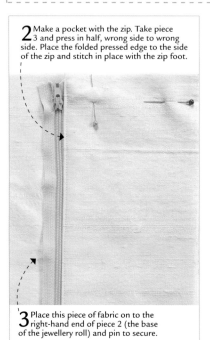

3 Place this piece of fabric on to the right-hand end of piece 2 (the base of the jewellery roll) and pin to secure.

4 Take piece 4 and press under 1.5cm (⅝in) along one short edge. Place the pressed edge along the other side of the zip, and pin in place.

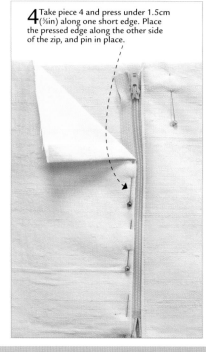

5 Using the zip foot, stitch along the side of the zip through all layers. This makes a pocket on just the right-hand side.

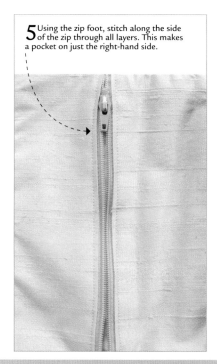

6 To make a pocket at the other end, take piece 5 and press in half, wrong side to wrong side. Edge-stitch along the folded side.

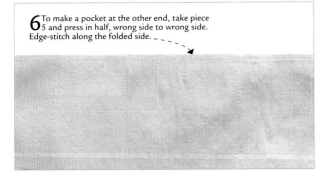

7 Place this piece to the left-hand side of the base and pin around the edges to secure. Stitch along the centre of the piece to make two pockets.

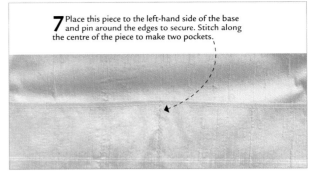

8 To make the ring holder, take piece 6 and a piece of wadding 6 x 22cm (2¼ x 9in). Wrap the silk around the wadding to make a fat tube shape, turning in the raw edge by 1.5cm (⅝in) on one long side and one end. Press if required.

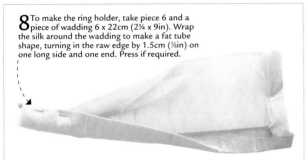

9 Secure by hand with a flat fell stitch.

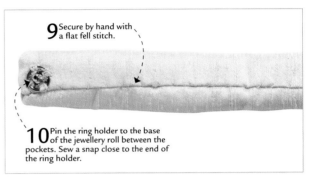

10 Pin the ring holder to the base of the jewellery roll between the pockets. Sew a snap close to the end of the ring holder.

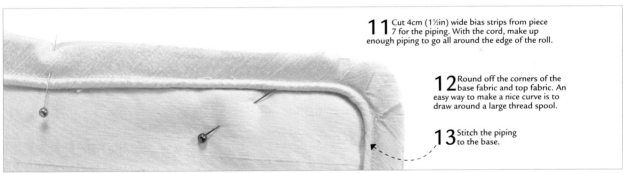

11 Cut 4cm (1½in) wide bias strips from piece 7 for the piping. With the cord, make up enough piping to go all around the edge of the roll.

12 Round off the corners of the base fabric and top fabric. An easy way to make a nice curve is to draw around a large thread spool.

13 Stitch the piping to the base.

14 Before attaching the top layer, stitch on the ribbon ties. Attach one piece of ribbon at the centre point on the left-hand side and another piece about 15cm (6in) to the right of this piece.

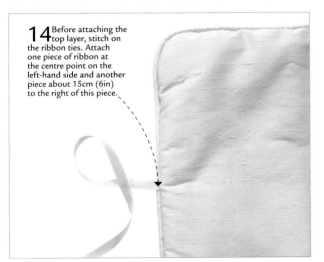

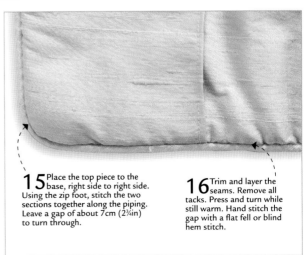

15 Place the top piece to the base, right side to right side. Using the zip foot, stitch the two sections together along the piping. Leave a gap of about 7cm (2¾in) to turn through.

16 Trim and layer the seams. Remove all tacks. Press and turn while still warm. Hand stitch the gap with a flat fell or blind hem stitch.

POLAR FLEECE HAT & SCARF

This must be the easiest project ever! Suitable for both children and adults, this matching hat-and-scarf set keeps you so warm in the winter months. As polar fleece fabric is available in a wide variety of colours and prints, you can make yourself a whole wardrobe of hats and scarves. These also make perfect Christmas presents.

TECHNIQUES INVOLVED

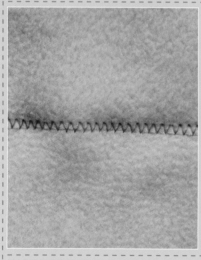

MACHINE STITCHES See pages 92–93.

HOW TO MAKE A PLAIN SEAM See page 94.

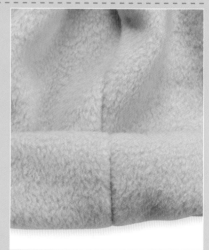

HEMS See pages 231–232.

LEVEL OF DIFFICULTY *

SHOPPING LIST

90cm x 1.5m (36 x 60in) polar
    fleece – this will make
    approximately two hats and
    one scarf

1 reel matching thread

1m (40in) ribbon

Hat

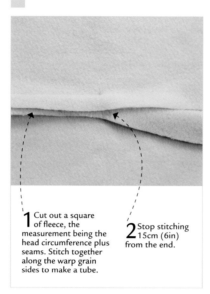

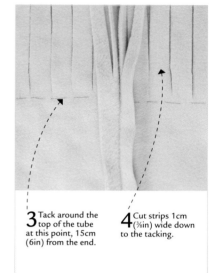

1 Cut out a square of fleece, the measurement being the head circumference plus seams. Stitch together along the warp grain sides to make a tube.

2 Stop stitching 15cm (6in) from the end.

3 Tack around the top of the tube at this point, 15cm (6in) from the end.

4 Cut strips 1cm (⅜in) wide down to the tacking.

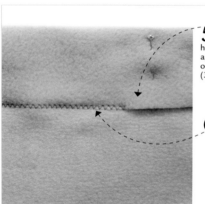

5 On the non-fringed end, turn up the hem to the wrong side – approximately 10cm (4in) on an adult hat and 8cm (3in) on a child's hat.

6 Zigzag stitch the hem in place.

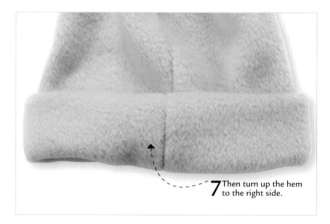

7 Then turn up the hem to the right side.

8 Cut a strip of fleece 1cm (⅜in) wide. Tie it tightly around the base of the fringing (over the tacking stitches), to make a tassel.

9 Decorate the hem with a bow.

⟪⟪ Tacking stitches p89

Scarf

1 Cut a piece of fleece 30cm x 1.5m (12 x 60in). Cut strips of fringing, 1cm (⅜in) wide and 15cm (6in) deep, at each short end.

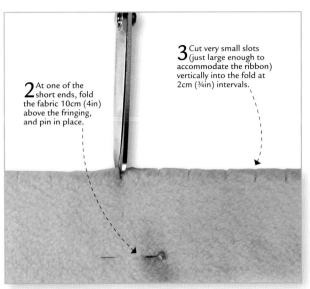

2 At one of the short ends, fold the fabric 10cm (4in) above the fringing, and pin in place.

3 Cut very small slots (just large enough to accommodate the ribbon) vertically into the fold at 2cm (¾in) intervals.

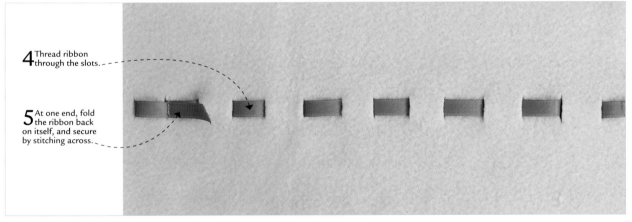

4 Thread ribbon through the slots.

5 At one end, fold the ribbon back on itself, and secure by stitching across.

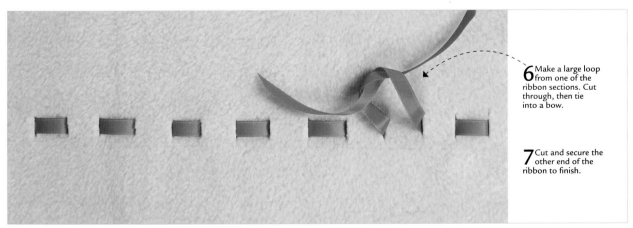

6 Make a large loop from one of the ribbon sections. Cut through, then tie into a bow.

7 Cut and secure the other end of the ribbon to finish.

CAFÉ CURTAIN

A café curtain is a half curtain that fits the lower part of a window for privacy but allows the light in at the top. A café curtain can be made from a curtaining fabric or you could use a semi-sheer voile. It hangs from a simple rod that fits across the window.

TECHNIQUES INVOLVED

ATTACHING A FACING See page 176.

HEMS ON CURTAINS See pages 234–235.

COVERED BUTTONS See page 261.

LEVEL OF DIFFICULTY ★★★★

SHOPPING LIST

Fabric: to calculate the amount
you need, measure the window's
width, where the track for the
curtain will be, and also the
drop (the finished length of
the curtain). Multiply the width
measurement by 2.5 in order to
give fullness (you may have to
join fabric to obtain this width).
Add 20cm (8in) on to the width
and 40cm (16cm) on to the drop
for the hems. You'll also need
30cm (12in) fabric for the facing
and tabs

Materials to make large covered
buttons (i.e. buttons and scraps
of fabric)

1 reel matching thread

1 On all sides of the curtain fabric, press 5cm (2in) under to the wrong side once. Fold under 5cm (2in) again and press. Machine in place, close to the upper folded edge.

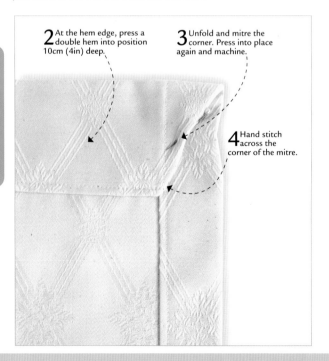

2 At the hem edge, press a double hem into position 10cm (4in) deep.

3 Unfold and mitre the corner. Press into place again and machine.

4 Hand stitch across the corner of the mitre.

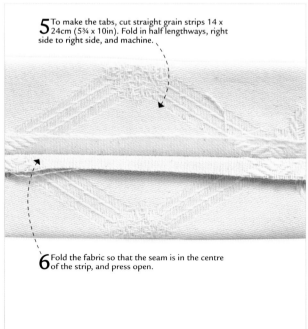

5 To make the tabs, cut straight grain strips 14 x 24cm (5¾ x 10in). Fold in half lengthways, right side to right side, and machine.

6 Fold the fabric so that the seam is in the centre of the strip, and press open.

PROJECTS

7 Using a template, stitch one end of each tab into a point. Draw around the template with tailor's chalk to make sure all the tabs are the same.

8 Clip, turn through to the right side, and press.

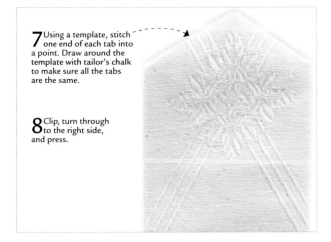

9 Place the tabs to the upper edge of the curtain, seam-side down to the curtain and matching at the raw edge. Place a tab at each side and the rest at equal distances, approximately every 30cm (12in).

10 Pin the tabs into position.

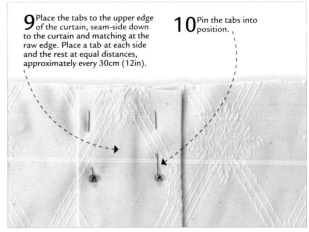

11 For the facing, cut a strip of fabric 10cm (4in) wide and as long as the curtain width.

12 Place the facing over the tabs, right side to right side, and machine in place along the top edge.

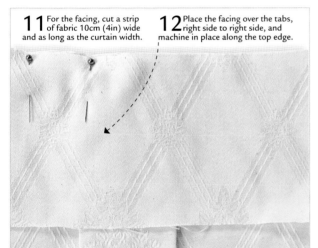

13 Press the seam and turn the facing to the wrong side. Top-stitch.

14 Fold under the lower edge of the facing and machine in place.

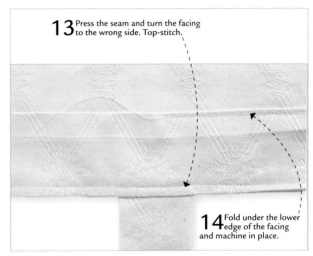

15 Cover a large button for each tab. Fold the tab over to the front of the curtain, to create a loop for the curtain rod. Sew a button on to each tab to secure it to the curtain.

DIRECTORY OF FASHION AND SOFT FURNISHINGS

Shirts

LADIES' SHIRT   MEN'S SHIRT   MEN'S FITTED SHIRT   LADIES' DRESS SHIRT   CHILDREN'S DRESS SHIRT

WING-COLLAR DRESS SHIRT   DENIM SHIRT   SHORT-SLEEVED SHIRT   WESTERN-STYLE SHIRT 1   WESTERN-STYLE SHIRT 2

Tops

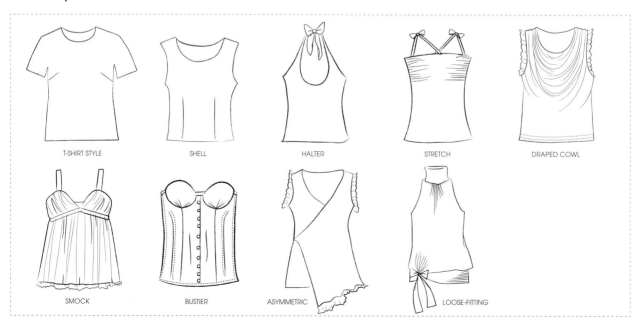

T-SHIRT STYLE   SHELL   HALTER   STRETCH   DRAPED COWL

SMOCK   BUSTIER   ASYMMETRIC   LOOSE-FITTING

Blouses

TIE NECK

ROLL NECK

SLEEVELESS

WRAP

BLOUSE WITH YOKE

KAFTAN

GYPSY

VICTORIAN

CHINESE-STYLE

Cardigans, sweaters, and vests

ROUND-NECK CLASSIC CARDIGAN

SCOOP-NECK CARDIGAN

TIE-FRONT

LONG SWEATER-STYLE

CASUAL KNITTED JACKET

SHORT KIMONO-STYLE

POLO-NECK

KNITTED V-NECK

SLEEVELESS V-NECK

Skirts

STRAIGHT TAILORED

SKIRT WITH GODETS

BUTTON-THROUGH

GORED

CIRCULAR

PLEATED

KILT

PUFFBALL

GYPSY

Dresses

TAILORED

WRAP

EMPIRE

1960S-STYLE

SHIRT WAISTER

CHINESE-STYLE

COAT DRESS

HALTER NECK

BALLGOWN

Trousers and shorts

CLASSIC TROUSERS   TAPERED TROUSERS   TIGHT JEANS   JODHPURS   COMBAT TROUSERS

DRAWSTRING TROUSERS   OXFORD BAGS   SHORTS   WALKING SHORTS

Jackets

CLASSIC-TAILORED   DOUBLE-BREASTED   TUXEDO   MILITARY-STYLE BLOUSON   BOLERO

PARKA   ANORAK   BOMBER   SAFARI

Coats

CLASSIC

CLASSIC DOUBLE-BREASTED

TRENCH

FLY FRONT

NEHRU-STYLE

DUFFLE

REEFER JACKET

PEACOAT/COCOON-STYLE

CAPE

Cushions

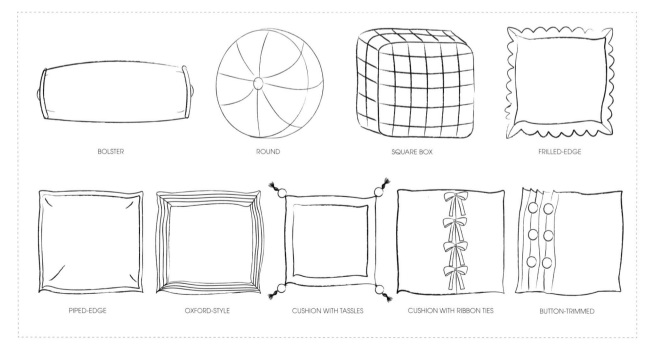

BOLSTER

ROUND

SQUARE BOX

FRILLED-EDGE

PIPED-EDGE

OXFORD-STYLE

CUSHION WITH TASSLES

CUSHION WITH RIBBON TIES

BUTTON-TRIMMED

Blinds

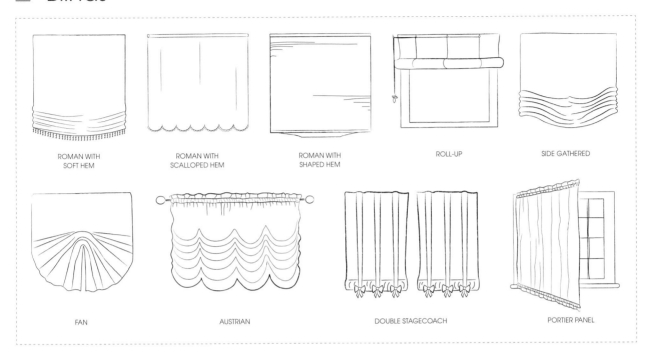

ROMAN WITH
SOFT HEM

ROMAN WITH
SCALLOPED HEM

ROMAN WITH
SHAPED HEM

ROLL-UP

SIDE GATHERED

FAN

AUSTRIAN

DOUBLE STAGECOACH

PORTIER PANEL

Curtains

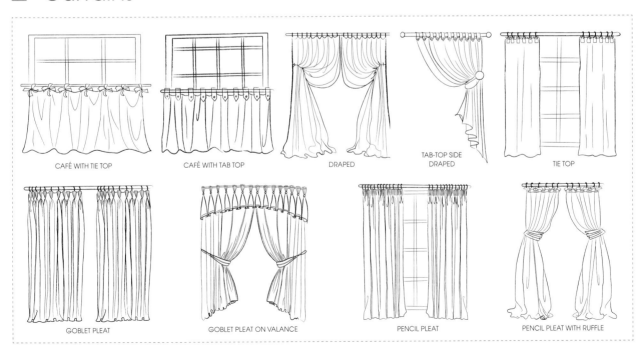

CAFÉ WITH TIE TOP

CAFÉ WITH TAB TOP

DRAPED

TAB-TOP SIDE
DRAPED

TIE TOP

GOBLET PLEAT

GOBLET PLEAT ON VALANCE

PENCIL PLEAT

PENCIL PLEAT WITH RUFFLE

GLOSSARY

Acetate Man-made fabric widely used for linings.

Acrylic Man-made fabric resembling wool.

Alpaca Canvas made from wool and alpaca. This fabric can be used as a non-fusible interfacing.

Appliqué One piece of fabric being stitched to another in a decorative manner.

Armhole Opening in a garment for the sleeve and arm.

Arrowhead Small, triangular set of straight stitches worked either by hand or by machine across a seam to add strength at a point of possible strain (for example, at the top of a split).

Back stitch A strong hand stitch with a double stitch on the wrong side, used for outlining and seaming.

Banding Method of finishing a raw edge by applying a wide strip of fabric over it. The strip can also be used to add length to a garment.

Bar tack A hand-worked bar of buttonhole stitches used to loosely attach two layers of fabric.

Belt carrier Loop made from a strip of fabric, which is used to support a belt at the waist edge of a garment.

Bias 45-degree line on fabric that falls between the lengthways and the crossways grain. Fabric cut on the bias drapes well. *See also* **Grain**.

Bias binding Narrow strips of fabric cut on the bias. Used to give a neat finish to hems and seam allowances.

Binding Method of finishing a raw edge by wrapping it in a strip of bias-cut fabric.

Blanket stitch Hand stitch worked along the raw or finished edge of fabric to neaten, and for decorative purposes.

Blind hem stitch Tiny hand stitch used to attach one piece of fabric to another, mainly to secure hems. Also a machine stitch consisting of two or three straight stitches and one wide zigzag stitch.

Blind tuck A tuck that is stitched so that it touches the adjacent tuck without machine stitches showing. *See also* **Tuck**.

Bobbin Round holder beneath the needle plate of a sewing machine on which the thread is wound.

Bodice Upper body section of a garment.

Bodkin Blunt-headed needle used for threading elastic or cord through a casing or heading.

Boning Narrow nylon, plastic, or metal strip, available in various widths, that is used for stiffening and shaping close-fitting garments, such as bodices.

Box pleat Pleat formed on the wrong side of the fabric, and fuller than a knife pleat. *See also* **Pleat**.

Broderie anglaise A fine plain-weave cotton embroidered to make small decorative holes.

Buttonhole Opening through which a button is inserted to form a fastening. Buttonholes are usually machine stitched but may also be worked by hand or piped for reinforcement or decorative effect.

Buttonhole chisel Very sharp, small chisel that cuts cleanly through a machine-stitched buttonhole.

Buttonhole stitch Hand stitch that wraps over the raw edges of a buttonhole to neaten and strengthen them. Machine-stitched buttonholes are worked with a close zigzag stitch.

Button shank Stem of a button that allows room for the buttonhole to fit under the button when joined.

Calico A plain weave, usually unbleached fabric.

Cashmere The most luxurious of all wools.

Casing Tunnel of fabric created by parallel rows of stitching, through which elastic or a drawstring cord is threaded. Often used at a waist edge. Sometimes extra fabric is required to make a casing; this can be applied to the inside or outside of the garment.

Catch stitch *See also* **Slip hem stitch**.

Challis Fine woollen fabric with uneven surface texture.

Chambray A light cotton with a coloured warp thread.

Chiffon Strong, fine, transparent silk.

Chintz Floral print or plain cotton fabric with a glazed finish.

Clapper Wooden aid that is used to pound creases into heavy fabric after steaming.

Contour dart Also known as double-pointed dart, this is used to give shape at the waist of a garment. It is like two darts joined together. *See also* **Dart**.

Corded gathers Gathers that are pulled up over a narrow cord or thick thread, used for thicker fabrics. *See also* **Gathers**.

Corded seam A seam with piping in it, often used to join together two different fabrics.

Corded shirring A method of shirring where a piece of piping cord is stitched into a fold in the fabric. *See also* **Shirring**.

Corded tuck Substantial fold of fabric that has a cord running through it. *See also* **Tuck**.

Corduroy A soft pile fabric with distinctive stripes.

Cotton Soft, durable, and inexpensive fabric widely used in dressmaking. Made from the fibrous hairs covering the seed pods of the cotton plant.

Crease Line formed in fabric by pressing a fold.

Crepe Soft fabric made from twisted yarn.

Crepe de chine Medium-weight fabric with uneven surface, often made from silk.

Crinkle cotton Cotton fabric with creases added by a heat process.

Cross stitch A temporary hand stitch used to hold pleats in place and to secure linings. It can also be used for decoration.

Cross tuck Tuck that crosses over another by being stitched in opposite directions. *See also* **Tuck**.

Curtain weight Weight inserted into the bottom hem of a curtain to hold the curtain in place and make it hang properly.

Cutting line Solid line on a pattern piece used as a guide for cutting out fabric.

Cutting mat Self-healing mat used in conjunction with a rotary cutter to protect the blade and the cutting surface.

Damask Woven cotton with a floral pattern.

Darning Mending holes or worn areas in a knitted garment by weaving threads in rows along the grain of the fabric.

Dart Tapered stitched fold of fabric used on a garment to give it shape so that it can fit around the contours of the body. There are different types of dart, but all are used mainly on women's clothing.

Darted tuck A tuck that can be used to give fullness of fabric at the bust or hip. *See also* **Tuck**.

Denim Hard-wearing twill weave fabric with coloured warp and white weft.

Double-pointed dart *See* **Contour dart**

Double ruffle Decorative trim made from two plain ruffles where one side is longer than the other. Also a ruffle made from doubled fabric.

Drape The way a fabric falls into graceful folds; drape varies with each fabric.

Dressmaker's carbon paper Used together with a tracing wheel to transfer pattern markings to fabric. Available in a variety of colours.

Drill Hard-wearing twill or plain-weave fabric with the same colour warp and weft.

Drop The length of fabric required to make a curtain, the 'drop' being the measurement from top to bottom of the window.

Duchesse satin Heavy, expensive satin fabric.

Dupion Fabric with a distinctive weft yarn with many nubbly bits; made from 100 per cent silk.

Ease Distributing fullness in fabric when joining two seams together of slightly different lengths, for example a sleeve to an armhole.

Ease stitch Long machine stitch, used to ease in fullness where the distance between notches is greater on one seam edge than on the other.

Embroidery machine A machine that is capable of embellishing fabric with embroidery designs.

Enclosed edge Raw fabric edge that is concealed within a seam or binding.

Facing Layer of fabric placed on the inside of a garment and used to finish off raw edges of an armhole or neck of a garment. Usually a separate piece of fabric, the facing can sometimes be an extension of the garment itself.

Felt A natural wool fabric can felt when it is stimulated by friction and lubricated by moisture and the fibres bond together to form a cloth. Felting can also be done in a washing machine in a hot cycle.

Filament fibres Very fine synthetic thread, manufactured using plant materials and minerals.

Flannel Wool or cotton with a lightly brushed surface.

Flat fell seam See Run and fell seam.

Flat fell stitch A strong, secure stitch used to hold two layers together permanently. Often used to secure linings and bias bindings.

French dart Curved dart used on the front of a garment. See also Dart.

French seam A seam traditionally used on sheer and silk fabrics. It is stitched twice, first on the right side of the work and then on the wrong side, enclosing the first seam. See also Mock French seam.

Frog fastener Decorative fastener made from cord arranged into four overlapping loops stitched at the centre. Used with a Chinese ball button.

Fusible tape Straight grain tape used to stabilize edges and also replace stay stitching. The heat of the iron fuses it into position.

Gabardine Hard-wearing fabric with a distinctive weave.

Galloon lace Decorative lace trim shaped on both sides, used to edge a hem.

Gathers Bunches of fabric created by sewing two parallel rows of loose stitching, then pulling the threads up so that the fabric gathers and reduces in size to fit the required space.

Georgette Soft, filmy silk fabric.

Gingham Two-colour, checked cotton fabric.

Goblet pleat Decorative curtain heading in which the fabric is stitched into narrow tubes that are then stuffed with wadding. See also Pleat.

Godet A section that is inserted into a garment to give fullness at the hem edge. It is usually triangular in shape but it can also be a semi-circle. See also Pleat.

Grain Lengthways and crossways direction of threads in a fabric. Fabric grain affects how a fabric hangs and drapes.

Grosgrain Synthetic, ribbed fabric often used to make ribbons.

Gusset Small piece of fabric shaped to fit into a slash or seam for added ease of movement.

Haberdashery Term that covers all the bits and pieces needed to complete a pattern, such as fasteners, elastics, ribbons, and trimmings.

Habutai Smooth, fine silk originally from Japan.

Heading tape Wide fabric tape containing loops that is stitched to the top of a curtain. Hooks are inserted into the loops and then attached to a rail. The heading tape is drawn up to make pleats.

Hem The edge of a piece of fabric neatened and stitched to prevent unravelling. There are several methods of doing this, both by hand and by machine.

Hem allowance Amount of fabric allowed for turning under to make the hem.

Hemline Crease or foldline along which a hem is marked.

Hemming tape Fusible tape with adhesive on both sides. Iron in place to fuse and secure hems that are difficult to hand stitch.

Herringbone stitch Hand stitch used to secure hems and interlinings. This stitch is worked from left to right.

Herringbone weave A zigzag weave where the weft yarn goes under and over warp yarns in a staggered pattern.

Hong Kong finish A method of neatening raw edges particularly on wool and linen. Bias-cut strips are wrapped around the raw edge.

Hook and eye fastening Two-part metal fastening used to fasten overlapping edges of fabric where a neat join is required. Available in a wide variety of styles.

Horsehair braid A braid that is woven from strands of nylon thread and sewn into the hemlines of dressy garments to stiffen the lower edge.

Interfacing A fabric placed between garment and facing to give structure and support. Available in different thicknesses, interfacing can be fusible (bonds to the fabric by applying heat) or non-fusible (needs to be sewn to the fabric).

Interlining Layer of fabric attached to the main fabric prior to construction, to cover the inside of an entire garment to provide extra warmth or bulk. The two layers are then treated as one. Often used in jackets and coats.

Jacquard loom Device used in weaving to control individual yarns. This allows looms to produce intricately patterned fabric such as tapestry, brocade, and damask.

Jersey Cotton or wool yarn that has been knitted to give stretch.

Jetted pocket A type of pocket found on tailored jackets and coats. It consists of strips of fabric that form the edges of the pocket (welts) and the lining.

Keyhole buttonhole stitch A machine buttonhole stitch characterized by having one square end while the other end is shaped like a loop to accommodate the button's shank without distorting the fabric. Often used on jackets.

Kick pleat Inverted pleat extending upwards from the hemline of a narrow skirt to allow freedom when walking. See also Pleat.

Knife pleat Pleat formed on the right side of the fabric where all the pleats face the same direction. See also Pleat.

Lapped seam Used on fabrics that do not fray, such as suede and leather, the seam allowance of one edge is placed over the edge to be joined, then topstitched close to the overlapping edge. Also called an overlaid seam.

Lightening stitch See Stretch stitch.

Linen Natural fibre derived from the stem of the flax plant, linen is available in a variety of qualities and weights.

Lining Underlying fabric layer used to give a neat finish to an item, as well as concealing the stitching and seams of a garment.

Locking stitch A machine stitch where the upper and lower threads in the machine "lock" together at the start or end of a row of stitching.

Madras Brightly coloured, unevenly checked cotton fabric from India.

Matka A silk suiting fabric with uneven yarn.

Mitre The diagonal line made where two edges of a piece of fabric meet at a corner, produced by folding. See also Mitred corner.

Mitred corner Diagonal seam formed when fabric

is joined at a corner. After stitching, excess fabric is cut away.

Mock casing Where there is an effect of a casing, but in fact elastic is attached to the waist, or is used only at the back in a partial casing.

Mock French seam Similar to a French seam, but best used on cotton or firmer fine fabrics. It is constructed on the wrong side of the work. *See also* **French seam.**

Mohair Fluffy wool yarn cloth used for sweaters, jackets, and soft furnishings.

Multi-size pattern Paper pattern printed with cutting lines for a range of sizes on each pattern piece.

Muslin Fine, plain open-weave cotton.

Nap The raised pile on a fabric made during the weaving process, or a print pointing one way. When cutting out pattern pieces, ensure the nap runs in the same direction.

Needle threader Gadget that pulls thread through the eye of a needle. Useful for needles with small eyes.

Notch V-shaped marking on a pattern piece used for aligning one piece with another. Also V-shaped cut taken to reduce seam bulk.

Notion An item of haberdashery, other than fabric, needed to complete a project, such as a button, zip, or elastic. Notions are normally listed on the pattern envelope.

Nylon Hard-wearing, man-made fabric.

Organza Thin, sheer fabric made from silk or polyester.

Overedge stitch Machine stitch worked over the edge of a seam allowance and used for neatening the edges of fabric.

Overlaid seam *See* **Lapped seam.**

Overlocker Machine used for quick stitching, trimming, and edging of fabric in a single action; it gives a professional finish to a garment. There are a variety of accessories that can be attached to an overlocker, which enable it to perform a greater range of functions.

Overlock stitch A machine stitch that neatens edges and prevents fraying. It can be used on all types of fabric.

Over-stitch *See* **Buttonhole stitch.**

Pattern markings Symbols printed on a paper pattern to indicate the fabric grain, foldline, and construction details, such as darts, notches, and tucks. These should be transferred to the fabric using tailor's chalk or tailor's tacks.

Pencil pleat The most common curtain heading where the fabric forms a row of parallel vertical pleats. *See also* **Pleat.**

Petersham Stiff, ridged tape that is 2.5cm (1in) wide and curved. It can be used as an alternative finish to facing.

Pile Raised loops on the surface of a fabric, for example velvet.

Pill A small, fuzzy ball formed from tangled fibres which is formed on the surface of a fabric, making it look old and worn; it is often caused by friction. To remove fabric pills, stretch the fabric over a curved surface and carefully cut or shave off the pills.

Pinking A method of neatening raw edges of fray-resistant fabric using pinking shears. This will leave a zigzag edge.

Pinking shears Cutting tool with serrated blades, used to trim raw edges of fray-resistant fabrics to neaten seam edges.

Pin tuck Narrow, regularly spaced fold or gather. *See also* **Tuck.**

Piped tuck *See* **Corded tuck.**

Piping Trim made from bias-cut strips of fabric, usually containing a cord. Used to edge garments or soft furnishings.

Pivoting Technique used to machine stitch a corner. The machine is stopped at the corner with the needle in the fabric, then the foot is raised, the fabric turned following the direction of the corner, and the foot lowered for stitching to continue.

Placket An opening in a garment that provides support for fasteners, such as buttons, snaps, or zips.

Plain weave The simplest of all the weaves; the weft yarn passes under one warp yarn, then over another one.

Pleat An even fold or series of folds in fabric, often partially stitched down. Commonly found in skirts to shape the waistline, but also in soft furnishings for decoration.

Pocket flap A piece of fabric that folds down to cover the opening of a pocket.

Polyester Man-made fibre that does not crease.

Presser foot The part of a sewing machine that is lowered on to the fabric to hold it in place over the needle plate while stitching. There are different feet available.

Pressing cloth Muslin or organza cloth placed over fabric to prevent marking or scorching when pressing.

Prick stitch Small spaced hand stitch with large spaces between each stitch. Often used to highlight the edge of a completed garment.

Raw edge Cut edge of fabric that requires finishing, for example using zigzag stitch, to prevent fraying.

Rayon Also known as viscose, rayon is often blended with other fibres.

Rever The turned-back front edge of a jacket or blouse to which the collar is attached.

Reverse stitch Machine stitch that simply stitches back over a row of stitches to secure the threads.

Right side The outer side of a fabric, or the visible part of a garment.

Rotary cutter Tool for cutting fabric neatly and easily, and useful for cutting multiple straight edges. It has different sizes of retractable blade.

Rouleau loop Button loop made from a strip of bias binding. It is used with a round ball-type button.

Round-end buttonhole stitch Machine stitch characterized by one end of the buttonhole being square and the other being round, to allow for the button shank.

Ruching Several lines of stitching worked to form a gathered area.

Ruffle Decorative gathered trim made from one or two layers of fabric.

Run and fell seam Also known as a flat fell seam, this seam is made on the right side of a garment and is very strong. It uses two lines of stitching and conceals all the raw edges, reducing fraying.

Running stitch A simple, evenly spaced straight stitch separated by equal-sized spaces, used for seaming and gathering.

Satin A fabric with a satin weave.

Satin weave A weave with a sheen, where the weft goes under four warp yarns, then over one.

Seam Stitched line where two edges of fabric are joined together.

Seam allowance The amount of fabric allowed for on a pattern where sections are to be joined together by a seam; usually this is 1.5cm (⅝in).

Seam edge The cut edge of a seam allowance.

Seamline Line on paper pattern designated for stitching a seam; usually this is 1.5cm (⅝in) from the seam edge.

Seam ripper A small, hooked tool used for undoing seams and unpicking stitches.

Seam roll Tubular pressing aid for pressing seams open on fabrics that mark.

Seersucker Woven cotton with a bubbly appearance due to stripes of puckers.

Self-bound seam Similar to the run and fell seam, except that it is stitched on the wrong side of the fabric.

Self-healing mat *See* **Cutting mat.**

Selvedge Finished edge on a woven fabric. This runs parallel to the warp (lengthways) threads.

Sewing gauge Measuring tool with adjustable slider for checking small measurements, such as hem depths and seam allowances.

Sharps General purpose needle used for hand sewing.

Shell tuck Decorative fold of fabric stitched in place with a scalloped edge. *See also* **Tuck**.

Shirring Multiple rows of gathers sewn by machine. Often worked with shirring elastic in the bobbin to allow for stretch.

Shirting Closely woven, fine cotton with coloured warp and weft yarns.

Silk Threads spun by the silkworm and used to create cool, luxurious fabrics.

Slip hem stitch Similar to herringbone stitch but is worked from right to left. It is used mainly for securing hems.

Slotted seam A decorative seam where the edges of the seam open to reveal an under layer, which can be in a contrasting fabric.

Smocking Traditional way of gathering fabric using multiple rows of parallel gathers, stitched by hand, to produce fine tubes in the fabric.

Smocking dots Heat-transfer dots that can be transferred to fabric to be used as a guide for hand gathers.

Snaps Also known as press studs, these fasteners are used as a lightweight hidden fastener.

Snips Spring-loaded cutting tool used for cutting off thread ends.

Spandex Lightweight, soft, stretchable fibre.

Staple fibres These include both natural and manufactured fibres such as cotton, wool, flax, and polyester. They are short in length, and relatively narrow in thickness.

Stay stitch Straight machine stitch worked just inside a seam allowance to strengthen it and prevent it from stretching or breaking.

Stay tape Tape sewn to a specific area of an item for reinforcement, for example to help strengthen a seam.

Stem stitch An embroidery stitch frequently used to outline other stitched decoration.

Stitch in the ditch A line of straight stitches sewn on the right side of the work, in the ditch created by a seam. Used to secure waistbands and facings.

Stitch ripper *See* **Seam ripper**.

Straight stitch Plain machine stitch, used for most applications. The length of the stitch can be altered to suit the fabric.

Stretch stitch Machine stitch used for stretch knits and to help control difficult fabrics. It is worked with two stitches forwards and one backwards so that each stitch is worked three times.

Tacking stitch A temporary running stitch used to hold pieces of fabric together or for transferring pattern markings to fabric.

Taffeta Smooth plain-weave fabric with a crisp appearance.

Tailor's buttonhole A buttonhole with one square end and one keyhole-shaped end, used on jackets and coats.

Tailor's chalk Square or triangular shaped piece of chalk used to mark fabric. Available in a variety of colours, tailor's chalk can be removed easily by brushing.

Tailor's ham A ham-shaped pressing cushion that is used to press shaped areas of garments.

Tailor's tacks Loose thread markings used to transfer symbols from a pattern to fabric.

Tape maker Tool for evenly folding the edges of a fabric strip, which can then be pressed to make binding.

Tape measure Flexible form of ruler made from plastic or fabric.

Tartan Fabric made using a twill weave from worsted yarns. Traditionally used for kilts.

Thimble Metal or plastic cap that fits over the top of a finger to protect it when hand sewing.

Toile A test or dry run of a paper pattern using calico. The toile helps you analyse the fit of the garment.

Top-stitch Machine straight stitching worked on the right side of an item, close to the finished edge, for decorative effect. Sometimes stitched in a contrasting colour.

Top-stitched seam A seam finished with a row of top-stitching for decorative effect. This seam is often used on crafts and soft furnishings as well as garments.

Towelling Cotton fabric with loops on the surface.

Trace tacking A method of marking fold and placement lines on fabric. Loose stitches are sewn along the lines on the pattern to the fabric beneath, then the thread loops are cut and the pattern removed.

Tracing wheel Tool used together with dressmaker's carbon paper to transfer pattern markings to fabric.

Tuck Fold or pleat in fabric that is sewn in place, normally on the straight grain of the fabric. Often used to provide a decorative addition to a garment.

Tweed Traditional tweed is a rough fabric with a distinctive warp and weft. Modern tweed is a mix of chunky and bobbly wool yarns, often in bright colours.

Twill weave Diagonal patterned weave.

Underlay Strip of fabric placed under the main fabric to strengthen it, for example under a pleat or buttonhole.

Understitch Machine straight stitching through facing and seam allowances that is invisible from the right side; this helps the facing to lie flat.

Velcro™ Two-part fabric fastening consisting of two layers, a "hook" side and a "loop" side; when pressed together the two pieces stick to each other.

Velvet Luxurious pile-weave fabric.

Venetian Luxurious wool with a satin weave.

Waistband Band of fabric attached to the waist edge of a garment to provide a neat finish.

Warp Lengthways threads or yarns of a woven fabric.

Warp knit Made on a knitting machine, this knit is formed in a vertical and diagonal direction.

Weft Threads or yarns that cross the warp of a woven fabric.

Weft knit Made in the same way as hand knitting, this uses one yarn that runs horizontally.

Welt Strip of fabric used to make the edges of a pocket. *See also* **Jetted pocket**.

Whip stitch Diagonal hand stitch sewn along a raw edge to prevent fraying.

Wool A natural animal fibre, available in a range of weights, weaves, and textures. It is comfortable to wear, crease-resistant, and ideal for tailoring.

Wool worsted A light, strong cloth made from good quality fibres.

Wrong side Reverse side of a fabric, the inside of a garment or other item.

Yoke The top section of a dress or skirt from which the rest of the garment hangs.

Zigzag stitch Machine stitch used to neaten and secure seam edges and for decorative purposes. The width and length of the zigzag can be altered.

Zip Fastening widely used on garments consisting of two strips of fabric tape, carrying specially shaped metal or plastic teeth that lock together by means of a pull or slider. Zips are available in different colours and weights.

Zip foot Narrow machine foot with a single toe that can be positioned on either side of the needle.

INDEX

About the Author

Alison Smith trained as an Art and Fashion Textile teacher, before becoming Head of Textiles at one of the largest schools in Birmingham, where she was able to pursue one of her key interests: the importance of teaching needlecrafts to boys, as well as girls. After successful spells as textiles tutor at the Liberty Sewing School, London, and the Janome Sewing School, Cheshire, Alison set up her own shop, Fabulous Fabric, and sewing school, Alison Victoria School of Sewing, in Ashby de la Zouch,

Leicestershire. Her school is the largest independent sewing school in England and offers courses and workshops on all aspects of dressmaking, tailoring, and corsetry.

Alison regularly lectures at specialist sewing shows, is a regular contributor to *Sewing World* magazine, and has appeared on the ITV television series *Ladette to Lady* teaching dressmaking skills. She lives with her husband in Leicestershire, and has two grown-up children.

Acknowledgements

Author's acknowledgements

No book could ever be written without a little help. I would like to thank the following people for their help with the techniques and projects: Jackie Boddy, Nicola Corten, Ruth Cox, Helen Culver, Yvette Emmett, Averil Wing, and especially my husband, Nigel, for his continued encouragement and support, as well as my mother, Doreen Robbins, who is responsible for my learning to sew. The following companies have also provided invaluable help, by supplying the sewing machines, haberdashery, and fabrics: Janome UK Ltd, EQS, Linton, Adjustoform, Guttermann threads, The Button Company, YKK zips, Graham Smith Fabrics, Fabulous Fabric, Simplicity patterns, and Freudenberg Nonwovens LP.

Dorling Kindersley would like to thank:

Heather Haynes and Katie Hardwicke for editorial assistance; Elaine Hewson and Victoria Charles for design assistance; Susan Van Ha for photographic assistance; Hilary Bird for indexing; Elma Aquino; Alice Chadwick-Jones; and Beki Lamb. Special thanks from all at DK to Norma MacMillan for her exceptional professionalism and patience.
Picture Credits: Additional photography Laura Knox p76 tl, tr, 78 t, 80 t/2 and 4, 81b; Alamy images: D. Hurst, front jacket c. **Illustrator** Debajyoti Datta. **Patterns** John Hutchinson, pp 58-9, 62 b row, 63 t and c row, 65, 66, 67 t row, br, 68, 69 t row, bl, 70 tr, bc, br, 71, 72 tl, b row, 73, 81. **Additional artworks** Karen Cochrane p59 r.

Useful Websites

www.janome.co.uk
Sewing machines, overlockers, embroidery machines, software, and accessories.

www.schoolofsewing.co.uk
Alison Smith's sewing school and fabric shop. Offers courses and workshops on tailoring, dressmaking, and corsetry.

www.burdastyle.com
Sewing patterns, tutorials, and projects.

www.isew.co.uk
www.sewingworldmagazine.com
Event listings, networks, projects, and advice for people who love sewing.

www.tauntonpress.com
Threads magazine: sewing patterns, advice, and features.

www.sewing.org
Educational articles and projects.

www.startsewing.co.uk
Expert advice on all aspects of sewing.

www.simplicitynewlook.com
www.johnkaldor.co.uk
www.sewdirect.com
www.sewessential.co.uk
www.kwiksew.com
www.sewingpatterns.com
www.thesewingplace.com
Sewing patterns and supplies.